Third Edition

The Principalship

A Reflective Practice Perspective

Thomas J. Sergiovanni
Trinity University
San Antonio, Texas

Allyn and Bacon
Boston • London • Toronto • Sydney • Tokyo • Singapore

Series Editor: Ray Short
Editorial Assistant: Christine Shaw
Editorial-Production Service: Spectrum Publisher Services
Cover Administrator: Suzanne Harbison
Manufacturing Buyer: Louise Richardson
Composition and Prepress Buyer: Linda Cox

Copyright © 1995 by Allyn and Bacon
A Simon & Schuster Company
Needham Heights, MA 02194

Library of Congress Cataloging-in-Publication Data

Sergiovanni, Thomas J.
    The principalship: a reflective practice perspective / Thomas J. Sergiovanni. — 3rd ed.
        p.   cm.
    Includes bibliographical references and index.
    ISBN 0-205-15585-5
    1. School principals—United States.   2. Leadership.   3. School management and organization—United States.   4. School supervision—United States.   5. School improvement programs—United States.
I. Title.
LB2831.92.S47 1995
371.2′012′0973—dc20   94-26379
                                                                            CIP

 This book is printed on
acid-free, recycled paper.

Printed in the United States of America

10 9 8 7 6 5 4 3 2 1   99 98 97 96 95 94

Contents

Preface

Everywhere one looks there is someone with an easy solution for improving schools. "Research says" if you put these correlates in place; if you teach, manage, or supervise using this list of behaviors all will be well. Careers are built, journals are filled, and, for some with entrepreneurial bents, fortunes are amassed as the "solutions" are proposed.

The engine that drives this grand solutions machine is our search for simple answers. This searching, I fear, drives us to think in the rationalistic tradition about our work, to make unwarranted assumptions about the linearity and predictability that exist in the world, and to overestimate the tightness of links between research and practice. The result is the adoption of management theories and leadership practices that look great on paper, sound compelling when heard, and maybe even make us feel good, but which don't fit the actual world of schooling very well.

The term *rationalistic* is chosen over *rational* or *irrational* deliberately, for what is often thought to be irrational is actually rational, and vice versa. Winograd and Flores (1986) sort the differences as follows:

> *In calling it [traditional theory] "rationalistic" we are not equating it with "rational." We are not interested in a defense of irrationality or a mystic appeal to nonrational intuition. The rationalistic tradition is distinguished by its narrow focus on certain aspects of rationality which often lead to attitudes and activities that are not rational when viewed in a broader perspective. Our commitment is to develop a new ground for rationality—one that is as rigorous as the rationalistic tradition in its aspirations but that does not share the presuppositions behind it. (8)*

In a similar vein, Alex Kozlov (1988) uses the categories "Neats" and "Scruffies" to sort researchers in the field of artificial intelligence as follows: "For a Neat, if an idea about thinking can't be represented in terms of mathematical logic, it isn't worth thinking about. For a Scruffy, on the other hand, ideas that can't be proved are the most interesting ones" (77–78).

It isn't easy for anyone to be a Scruffy. After all, it's very comfortable to be a Neat. You have all the answers and you fit nicely into our bureaucratic, technical, and rational culture. Fitting nicely reaps many career rewards. But still, many of us feel uncomfortable with the position of the Neats. A frequent first response to this uncomfortableness is to try to change the world to fit our theories and to damn those aspects of the world that will not cooperate. A better alternative, I propose, is for us to change our theories to fit the world. A scruffy world needs scruffy theories. Reflective practice, as I will argue in Chapter 2, is key to making scruffy theories work. John Stuart Mill wrote, "No great improvements in the lot of mankind are possible, until a great change takes place in the fundamental constitution of their modes of thought." His prophetic statement describes the situations we face today. If we want better schools, we are going to have to learn how to manage and lead differently. This book doesn't provide the answers, but it can help you find them.

The key to accepting the challenges of leadership in a scruffy world is for principals to understand leadership differently. When writing articles and books for principals, it is common to point out how important a principal is to the successful functioning of the school. Part of this ritual is to portray the principal as some sort of superhero who combines the best qualities of strong "instructional leadership" with a messianic ability to inspire people to great heights. It turns out that principals are indeed important, and their leadership is indeed indispensable, but in different ways than commonly thought.

From the perspective of the Neats, principals practice leadership directly by calculating what levers to pull to get the school structured differently and what buttons to push to get people motivated to do what is needed. Mystic principals rely less on rational calculation and more on their charismatic qualities to transform people. Both types of principals are highly visible players in the drama of leadership. Everything revolves around them. Should either of these types of principals fail to provide the needed leadership, things go awry.

Scruffy principals view the problem of leadership differently. Their leadership is much more subtle and aimed at building into the school substitutes for leadership. Substitutes, they argue, are the keys needed to encourage teachers and students to become self-managing. The sources of authority for leadership, as scruffy principals see it, need to be idea-based and anchored to moral commitments. Their job is to create new connections among people and to connect them to an idea structure. They do this by practicing leadership by bonding and binding. Their aim is to build a followership in the school. For the secret to leadership, they argue, is to have something worth following—something to which followers become morally committed.

A key theme in this book is that what we believe to be true about management and leadership depends on the metaphor we use to understand the school. Schools, for example, have traditionally been understood as *organizations* of one kind or another, and this metaphor encourages us to think about school organization structure, teacher motivation, power and authority, curriculum development, and supervision and evaluation in certain ways. If the metaphor were changed to *community,* these ways of viewing the world of school management and leadership would no longer make sense. Instead, a new management and leadership would need to be invented that would be more congruent with what communities are and how they function.

Throughout the book, readers will find a number of inventories and questionnaires. Their purpose is to help raise and clarify issues, stimulate thought, encourage reflection, and provide a basis for discussion of concepts and ideas. They are not presented as fine-tuned measurement devices suitable for "research purposes," although faculties and groups may benefit from collecting school data and using results as a basis for discussion and reflection.

Readers are encouraged to read the last chapter (Chapter 15, "Administering as a Moral Craft") before examining the book's contents more systematically. Enhancing the principalship is the road on which this book journeys, and Chapter 15 lets readers know how the journey ends. Knowing the book's ending first may be helpful in providing an integrating perspective for the concepts, ideas, values, principles, and practices discussed in other chapters.

Thomas J. Sergiovanni

About the Author

Thomas J. Sergiovanni is Lillian Radford Professor of Education at Trinity University, San Antonio, Texas, where he teaches in the school leadership program and in the 5-year teacher education program. He is senior fellow at the Center for Educational Leadership and the founding Director of the Trinity Principals' Center. Prior to joining the faculty at Trinity, he was on the faculty of education administration at The University of Illinois, Urbana-Champaign, for 19 years, where he chaired the department for 7 years. A former associate editor of *Educational Administration Quarterly,* he is consulting editor to the *Journal of Personnel Evaluation in Education* and *Teaching Education.* He has served on the editorial boards of the *Journal of Educational Research,* the *Journal of Curriculum and Supervision,* the *Journal of Research and Development in Education,* and the *Journal of Educational Equity and Leadership.* Among his recent books are *Value-Added Leadership* (1990), *Moral Leadership* (1992), *Supervision: A Re-Definition* (1993), and *Building Community in Schools* (1994).

The Principalship

Part *I*

Toward a New Theory

Chapter *1*

Views of the Principal's Job

Let's begin our examination of the principal's job with your perceptions of the tasks and functions that should make up this role and of their relative importance.

Imagine yourself as a candidate for the principalship of an 800-student junior high school in a community close to Philadelphia. You have taught for several years in a school and community much like this one; however, beyond temporary administrative assignments (e.g., chairing committees and project teams), you have had no full-time administrative experience. Your overall credentials and your background as a teacher are, nonetheless, sufficiently impressive that the search committee considers you one of its top three candidates. You have been invited to visit the school and to be interviewed by the committee and the superintendent for this job. To help you prepare for your visit, the committee informs you of a number of areas that they wish to explore and a number of issues that they wish to discuss. Among these are:

What do you consider to be the major tasks of a principal?

Which of these tasks do you believe to be most important?

As you plan your daily and weekly schedule, what proportion of time would you allocate to each of these tasks?

You want to be as prepared as possible for your visit and interview. Therefore, consider these questions and write down some of your ideas. Start by writing a brief general description of your perception of the role of the principal and her or his prime reasons for existing as part of the structure of schooling. Follow this general description with a listing of roles and task areas that you believe should define the principal's responsibilities. Curriculum and program development, supervision and evaluation, and student discipline are examples of task areas that might come to mind. As you examine your list, rank the tasks in order of their importance to you. Then, using 100 percent of the time available to you in an average work week, allocate percentages of time that you would try to spend in each area if you were to obtain this principalship.

In your deliberations about principalship responsibilities, roles, and tasks, you have probably been thinking in terms of the school in the ideal. You have been describing your perceptions of what is important and what you think the principal *ought* to do.

Ideal Conceptions of the Principalship

Definitions of the principal's roles and responsibilities have changed over time. Traditional definitions focused on the administrative processes and functions that must be emphasized for schools to work well. Effective principals, for example, are responsible for planning, organizing, leading, and controlling. *Planning* means setting goals and objectives for the school and developing blueprints and strategies for implementing them. *Organizing* means bringing together the necessary human, financial, and physical resources to accomplish goals efficiently. *Leading* has to do with guiding and supervising subordinates. *Controlling* refers to the principal's evaluation responsibilities and includes reviewing and regulating performance, providing feedback, and otherwise tending to standards of goal attainment.

The acronym POSDCoRB is another example of how administrative processes have been defined. Proposed in 1937 by Luther Gulick, POSDCoRB stands for planning, organizing, staffing, directing, coordinating, reporting, and budgeting. Lists such as these are continuously being revised. In 1955, for example, the American Association of School Administrators added such processes as stimulating staff and evaluating staff to the POSDCoRB list.

Gradually, lists of tasks and roles have given way to lists of competencies and proficiencies as the favored way to map out the territory of educational administration. For example, in 1986, the National Association of Elementary School Principals (NAESP) issued the document "Elementary and Middle School Proficiencies for Principals," which contained a list of 74 proficiencies grouped into 10 categories that define *expertness* in the principalship. The categories and the first three proficiencies listed for each category follow.

Leadership Behavior

Inspire all concerned to join in accomplishing the school's mission . . .

Apply effective human relations skills . . .

Encourage the leadership of others . . .

Communication Skills

Persuasively articulate their beliefs and effectively defend their decisions . . .

Write clearly and concisely so that the message is understood by the intended audience . . .

Apply facts and data to determine priorities . . .

Group Processes

Involve others in setting short- and long-term goals . . .

Apply validated principles of group dynamics and facilitation skills . . .

Understand how to resolve difficult situations by use of conflict-resolution methods . . .

Curriculum

Understand the community's values and goals and what it wants the curriculum to achieve . . .

Set forth, as a continuum, the skills and concepts the curriculum is designed to provide . . .

Monitor the curriculum to ensure that the appropriate content and sequence are followed . . .

Instruction

Understand and apply the principles of growth and development . . .

Regularly assess the teaching methods and strategies being used at the school to ensure that they are appropriate and varied . . .

Understand and apply validated principles of teaching and learning . . .

Performance

Set high expectations for students, staff, parents, and self . . .

Appropriately match particular learning styles with particular teaching styles . . .

Enhance student and staff strengths and remediate weaknesses . . .

Evaluation

Use a variety of techniques and strategies to assess—

    Student performance
    Individual teacher and staff performance
    The achievement of curriculum goals
    The effectiveness of the total instructional program . . .

Assess progress toward achieving goals established for students, teachers, the principalship, and the involvement of parents and the community at large . . .

Seek and encourage input from a variety of sources to improve the school's program . . .

Organization

Comprehend and employ validated principles of effective time management . . .

Capitalize on the findings of research and making program decisions . . .

Develop and implement equitable and effective schedules . . .

Fiscal

Understand the school district budget and its specific implications for the school . . .

Plan, prepare, justify, and defend the school budget . . .

Manage the school within the allocated resources . . .

Political

Understand the dynamics of local, state, and national politics . . .

Develop plans and strategies for helping to achieve appropriate financial support of education . . .

Involve the community's movers and shakers in the development and support of the school's program . . .

(National Association of Elementary School Principals, 1986)

For parochial school principals, the religious dimension must be added to any array of roles and responsibilities that define the principalship. In his analysis of the socialization of Catholic school principals, Augenstein (Augenstein, 1989; Augenstein and Konnert, 1991) defines the role requirements of the religious dimension as knowing about and making available church documents and other religious resources, providing for spiritual development, being a leader of prayer, creating an environment for religious education, integrating gospel values and other religious principles into the curriculum, and service to parish and civic community. Modern lists of proficiencies provide a rendering of tasks and roles that are much more descriptive than the generic lists of the past and that emphasize much more the specific context of schooling, teaching, and learning.

In recent years, more emphasis is being given to what principals in schools are supposed to accomplish as a way of defining the job. The idea behind this trend is to determine the outcomes that schools should pursue and students should achieve. Much less attention is given to pointing out the processes that must be used. Presumably, principals in schools are expected to do whatever is necessary to achieve the outcomes. Defining the job this way has the advantage of freeing principals and others with whom they work from bureaucratic restrictions and constraints. Few scripts for the principal to follow are provided. Lists of things principals must do are kept to a minimum.

Defining the role of the principal in terms of outcomes, however, increases the likelihood that means will be separated from ends. Separating the two is risky business in any setting but can be particularly troublesome in schools. There are several reasons for this; for example, it is hard to specify all the important outcomes in advance. A tendency exists to specify outcomes that are easy to understand and easy to evaluate. As a result, many other outcomes that may be more important are overlooked. Furthermore, a difference exists between effective practices and good practices. What principals and teachers may do, for example, may work but may not be right. The outcomes approach tends to define effectiveness more in terms of what works than what is right, and this tendency raises important moral questions.

One way to capitalize on the advantages of an outcomes-based approach to defining the role of the principal, while avoiding some of the disadvantages, is to adopt a values-based approach. When using this approach, assumptions and beliefs presumed to be important are specified and used as a basis for deciding what it is that principals and others should do. The specification of assumptions and beliefs provides a standard for determining what is good and bad, effective and ineffective, and acceptable and unacceptable. Using a values-based approach for defining the role of the principal not only ensures that what principals decide to do meets acceptable standards, but also provides the school with a set of indicators that defines its educational and moral health. A values-based approach is used in this book to define the job of the principal.

The Complex Nature of Managerial Work

The 1973 publication of Henry Mintzberg's book *The Nature of Managerial Work* sparked a great deal of interest in descriptive studies of administration in education. Descriptive studies attempt to map out the actual roles and tasks of principals by focusing on what administrators actually do.

Mintzberg studied five executives, including a school superintendent. He relied on continued, detailed, and systematic observations of what these administrators actually did, almost moment by moment, over an extended period of time. His research has become a model for others who have studied the specific context of educational administration. In one such study, Sproul (1976) found that such words as *local, verbal, choppy,* and *varied* were most often used to describe the typical administrative work day. Choppiness, for example, was evidenced by the presence of many activities of brief duration. A composite administrator in Sproul's study engaged in 56 activities daily, each averaging about nine minutes; and participated in 65 events, each averaging six minutes. Events were described as periods of time one minute or longer during which administrators used one medium of communication such as the phone, a conversation, or a memo.

Similarly, Mintzberg found that the work of administrators was characterized by brevity, variety, and fragmentation, and that the majority of administrative activities were of brief duration, often taking only minutes. Activities were not only varied but also patternless, disconnected, and interspersed with trivia; as a result, the administrator often shifted moods and intellectual frames. These findings suggest a high level of *superficiality* in the work of administration. Mintzberg noted further that, because of the open-ended nature of administrative work, the administrator is compelled to perform a great number of tasks at an unrelenting pace. This contributes further to superficiality. Free time is only rarely available, and job responsibilities seem inescapable.

The administrators in Mintzberg's study demonstrated a preference for live action and for oral means of handling this action. They favored the job's current and active elements over abstract, technical, and routine elements. They preferred to visit with others personally, to talk on the telephone, and to conduct formal and informal conferences, rather than to rely on written means of communication. Because of this propensity for oral action, most of the business of the organization remained unrecorded and was stored in the administrator's memory. This, in turn, made delegation and shared decision making difficult. Mintzberg found that administrators are overloaded with *exclusive* knowledge about the organization and overburdened, as well, with incursions on their time as others seek this information. He observed further that administrators had difficulty in keeping on top of events and that no mechanisms existed to relieve them of minor responsibilities. Faced with the apparent requirement that one be involved in almost everything, the recourse was to treat work activities in a distinctly superficial manner.

School principals, too, often must deal with aspects of work superficially. The reasons for this can be understood as one examines the full range of responsibilities that principals have. Roland Barth (1980) describes the extent of such responsibilities as follows:

> *The principal is ultimately responsible for almost everything that happens in school and out. We are responsible for personnel—making sure that employees are physically present and working to the best of their ability. We are in charge of program—making sure that teachers are teaching what they are supposed to and that children are learning it. We are accountable to parents—making sure that each is given an opportunity to express problems and that those problems are addressed and resolved. We are expected to protect the physical safety of children—making sure that the several hundred lively organisms who leave each morning return, equally lively, in the afternoon.*
>
> *Over the years principals have assumed one small additional responsibility after another—responsibility for the safe passage of children from school to home, responsibility for the safe passage of children from home to school, responsibility for making sure the sidewalks are plowed of snow in winter, responsibility for health education, sex education, moral education, responsibility for teaching children to evacuate school buses and to ride their bikes safely. We have taken on lunch programs, then breakfast programs; responsibility for the physical condition of the furnace, the wiring, the playground equipment. We are now accountable for children's achievement of minimum standards at each grade level, for the growth of children with special needs, of the gifted, and of those who are neither. The principal has become a provider of social services, food services, health care, recreation programs and transportation—with a solid skills education worked in somehow. (4–6)*

How is the challenge of superficiality in administrative work met by those who prescribe how administrators should behave? The well-known management consultant and theorist Peter Drucker recommended that principals set and stick to priorities. This is good advice, when it can be followed. Another well-known theorist, Chester Barnard (1938), suggested that administrators be more selective in the questions they address. In his words: "The fine art of executive decision-making consists of not deciding questions that are not pertinent, in not deciding prematurely, in not making decisions that cannot be made effectively, and in not making decisions that others should make" (194). How realistic are these prescriptions? When is it not possible to follow them? What gets in the way of following them? How might practicing principals react to them?

Following the Mintzberg research approach, Van Cleve Morris and his colleagues (1984) studied elementary and secondary school principals in Chicago. They concluded:

> *The principalship is a moving, dynamic occupation in almost a literal sense; the rhythm of the job, from arrival at the parking lot to the close of the business day, is typified by pace and movement, by frequent and abrupt shifts from one concern to another, and by the excitement pervading any institution dealing with young people. . . , the principal's job is different from other managerial positions because it is essentially an oral occupation, a job of talking. The principal governs the school mostly by talking with other people, usually one at a time, throughout the day. (209)*

They noted that principals spend about 50 percent of their time outside the main office and in face-to-face contact with teachers and students. In their words:

> *A busy principal covers a great deal of ground. In making these rounds, from office to corridor to classroom to gymnasium to boilerroom to playground and back, the principal is managing the school. But it is management in a form unusual for most organizations because it is, in large part, administration at the work stations of other persons. This means that the principal carries the office around with him or her through at least 50% of the work day. . . . It is the principal who gets around, who visits teachers in their offices, who investigates areas of potential trouble, who smooths the flow of messages from one area of the building to another, who is on call and easily summoned by those needing assistance. (211)*

Morris and his colleagues noted that the job of building principal is open-ended; that is, the job becomes largely what each principal wishes to make of it. Despite a tightly structured paper hierarchy, principals have a great deal of autonomy that allows their own values and preferences to influence the job (220). This open-endedness is not to suggest that principals are free to do whatever they wish, for they still must cope with constraints they face. It does suggest, however, that options do exist, that principals are not necessarily hopeless victims, and that principals do have some control over their priorities and the extent to which they pursue priorities.

Studies of principals at work indicate that the real world of school administration is often quite different from the world described in the theoretical literature and in principals' preferences. At the end of this chapter, two appendices appear. Appendix 1–1 is a detailed portrait, in the form of a time log, of a day in the life of a high school principal. The 98 entries begin at 7:35 A.M. with arrival at the school and end at 3:50 P.M. with the principal leaving school for a personal appointment. Appendix 1–2 is a portrait, in the form of a case study, of one day in the life of an urban elementary school principal. How do these descriptions of actual administrative work contrast with the views you had of the principal's job at the beginning of this chapter?

Demands, Constraints, and Choices

Rosemary Stewart (1982) describes managerial jobs "as consisting of an inner core of *demands,* an outer boundary of *constraints,* an in-between area of *choices*" (14). Demands are the things that principals must do. If they fail to do these things, sanctions are invoked, and often these sanctions are serious enough to endanger one's job. Demands are determined by school outcome specifications, legal requirements, bureaucratic rules and regulations, and the array of role expectations of important others such as superintendents, school board members, teachers, and parents. Constraints are determined by norms and values that exist in the community or school, availability of human and material resources, union contracts, space limitations, and the capability limitations of teachers and others with whom the principal must work. As with demands, principals who ignore constraints face the likelihood of threatened job security.

Although two principals may be subjected to the same demands and constraints, their leadership practices nonetheless typically vary. Within any demand-and-constraint set there are always choices in the form of opportunities to do the same things differently and to do other things that are not required or prohibited. It is in this area of choices that the opportunities for excellence exist. Whether these opportunities flourish depends on the latitude that principals are able to make for themselves. One hallmark of a successful principal is her or his ability to expand the area of choices and thus reduce demands and constraints. This extra margin of latitude makes an important difference in enhancing the overall effectiveness of the school.

In a recent National Association of Secondary School Principals (NASSP) study (Pellicer et al., 1988), respondents were asked to select from each of three pairs of statements the one that best characterized the role of the principal. Seventy-five percent chose "take initiative in developing and implementing school policy according to his or her professional judgment." This is compared to 25 percent who chose "primarily represent the interests of parents, leaders, and patrons of the school." Sixty-five percent chose "lead the school in new educational directions according to his or her best professional judgment." This is compared to 35 percent who chose "effectively and efficiently manage the day-to-day affairs of the school." Eighty-two percent chose "share decision making with the faculty on important issues." This is compared to 18 percent who chose "play the major role in establishing the agenda and deciding the important issues in the school" (p. 15). This study suggests that principals have clear and quite progressive views as to what they should be doing. Are highly successful principals more likely to come closer to the ideal than ordinary ones? How close do they come to this ideal in their everyday practice? A 1978 NASSP study, for example, found that successful school principals use time differently than do their more ordinary counterparts. Two of the NASSP researchers, Richard A. Gorton and Kenneth E. McIntyre (1978), studied time use by successful high school principals and found that real and ideal allocations of time corresponded fairly well. In a parallel study conducted by Lloyd E. McCleary and Scott D. Thomson (1979), the actual and ideal time allocations of a random sample of principals were surveyed. Table 1–1 summarizes the data from these studies, showing that although "successful" and "random" principals agree on how time should be spent, successful principals came closer to this ideal. The sum of differences between actual and ideal rankings for successful principals was 8, while that for randomly selected principals was 18.

TABLE 1–1 Comparing Rankings of Ideal and Actual Allocation of Time for Successful and Randomly Selected High School Principals

Task Areas	SUCCESSFUL PRINCIPALS*			RANDOM PRINCIPALS**		
	Ideal Time Planned *(Ranked biweekly)*	Actual Time Spent *(Ranked biweekly)*	DIFFERENCE	Ideal Time Planned *(Ranked biweekly)*	Actual Time Spent *(Ranked biweekly)*	DIFFERENCE
Program development (curriculum, instructional leadership)	1	3	2	1	5	4
Personnel (evaluation, advising, conferencing, recruiting)	2	1	1	2	2	0
School management (weekly calendar, office, budget, correspondence, memos, etc.)	3	2	1	3	1	2
Student activities (meetings, supervision, planning)	4	4	0	4	3	1
District office (meetings, task forces, reports, etc.)	5	5	0	9	6	3
Community (PTA, advisory groups, parent conferences)	6	6	0	8	8	0
Planning (annual, long range)	7	9	2	5	7	2
Professional development (reading, conferences, etc.)	8	8	0	6	9	3
Student behavior (discipline, attendance, meetings)	9	7	2	7	4	3
			Sum = 8			Sum = 18

*Data are from Richard A. Gorton and Kenneth E. McIntyre, *The Senior High School Principalship. Vol. II: The Effective Principal,* Reston VA: National Association of Secondary School Principals, 1978.
**Data are from Lloyd E. McCleary and Scott D. Thomson, *The Senior High School Principalship. Vol. III: The Summary Report,* Reston VA: National Association of Secondary School Principals, 1979.

The randomly selected principals, according to McCleary and Thomson (1979:16), appear to fall short of devoting the time they would like in two areas of responsibility: (1) program development and (2) professional development. They report spending considerably more time than they would like dealing with problems of student behavior. According to these researchers, principals who are able to spend time as they intend credit this fact to their ability to delegate, to having capable assistant principals, to having faith in the competence of others, and to concentrating on priority goals. It appears that successful principals are able to devote more time and effort to a few critical areas; perhaps, as a result, they neglect other areas of comparatively less importance. Furthermore, they bring to their practice a high regard for those with whom they work and a commitment to the concept of empowerment.

A recent update of the 1978 study noted little change in the way principals spend time and would like to spend time. "In general, the ways principals spend time and believe they should . . . have changed very little during the past decade" (Pellicer et al., 1988:17).

Principals report spending less time on program development and planning than they would like and more time on student problems and working with the central office than they think they should.

In a study contrasting problem-solving strategies of moderately and highly effective principals, Leithwood and Stager (1986) concluded that highly effective principals are more task-focused and reflective. They bring to their leadership practice a concern for substance that overrides management processes and human relationships. When concerned with people, highly effective principals view them as human resources that are key to the work of the school. Some of their findings are summarized in Exhibit 1–1.

In their monumental study of how principals make a difference in promoting quality schooling, Wilma F. Smith and Richard L. Andrews (1989) concluded that strong

EXHIBIT 1–1   Principals' Problem Classification and Management, Problem-Solving Strategies, and Influences

	Highly Effective Principals	*Moderately Effective Principals*
Specific Strategies	Use a more deliberate model for problem solving	Tend to use more imprecise "rules of thumb"
	Agree that any strategy must include certain elements (i.e., communications, participation by stakeholders, extensive information collection)	
	Clarify many facets of problem-solving situation (e.g., type of problem, own position, own and others' roles)	May use strategies (e.g., not delaying) that prevent much clarification
	Have organizational structures in place for group problem solving	
	Have as reasons for involving others those cited by moderately effective principals, and, in addition: to help with school-wide problem management, to produce better solutions, to help other staff develop as problem solvers	Have as reasons for involving others: to gather information, to increase ownership, to (less often) "bounce solutions"
Knowledge	List more crucial knowledge (e.g., of resources outside school, of self) and skills (of problem solving, of communication, of leadership)	Regard knowledge of staff, staff strengths and weaknesses, and "people skills" as crucial
	List more specific sources of knowledge (especially other principals' experiences and networks outside of school and system)	Rely on smaller number of sources, often only staff in own school
Experience as an Administrator	Report, as main changes, more reflection on problem solving and a more refined, considered process	Report, as main changes, more involvement of others in problem solving and more skill in accomplishing this

EXHIBIT 1–1   *(Continued)*

	Highly Effective Principals	*Moderately Effective Principals*
Personal Values and Beliefs	Are better able to articulate values Focus more on their own staff and "responsibilities"	Are less able to articulate visions Do not appear to be aware of making decisions with reference to principles or values
Determination of Priorities	Give emphasis to programs, overall school directions, building staff morale, and excitement about programs Provide arguments in support of priorities Work harder to manage their time to free themselves for their "proper" work (i.e., program development, planning, initiating change) Mention more specific strategies to control paperwork	Give emphasis to building or maintaining interpersonal relationships Provide little rationale for priorities Are marginally more satisfied with how they spend their time, but express desire to spend more time in classrooms with students and staff
Problem Difficulty	Tend to label as easy problems those encountered before, for which they have clear procedures Find hardest problems are those outside their control, those impacting widely, and those concerned with staff morale Insist that there are some entirely new problems facing principals and see clearly the ways in which problems are related to former similar ones	Find hardest problems are those involving teacher firings or other less critical personnel problems Tend to view most problems as familiar or "old" and display a greater tendency to be bored by them
Overall Style	Refer more often to solving problems with others (e.g., "collaborative" or "shared") Are "front-end" risk-takers, but careful information collectors Are more reflective about their own style and process	Are "tail-end" risk-takers, and less careful to collect comprehensive information
Attitude Toward Problem Solving	Are definitely aware of problem solving as an activity Enjoy new problems and see problems as opportunities Are confident, but realistic about inevitability of making some mistakes	Little sense of problem solving as an activity, and may even reject idea of "designed" problem-solving strategies

Excerpted from K. J. Leithwood and M. Stager, "Differences in Problem-Solving Processes Used by Moderately and Highly Effective Principals," paper presented to the annual meeting of the American Educational Research Association, San Francisco, 1986.

principals functioned as forceful and dynamic leaders who brought to their practice high energy, initiative, tolerance for ambiguity, a sense of humor, analytical ability, and a practical stance toward life (8). They identified four broad areas of strategic role interaction between principal and teachers: (1) the principal as resource provider, (2) instructional resource, (3) communicator, and (4) visible presence. Their research reveals important differences in the ways teachers viewed strong, average, and weak principals across these four role dimensions. In every case, strong principals received more positive ratings than average and weak, and average principals more positive ratings than weak. Their findings are summarized in Exhibit 1–2. The Smith and Andrews research demonstrates the importance of principals giving prime attention to the schools' *core technology,* teaching and learning: a finding now well established in the literature (Teddlie, Kirby, and Stringfield, 1989).

Other studies of successful principals are examined in later chapters. These studies suggest that the ability to rely on symbolic and cultural leadership as enhancements of the more traditional technical, human, and educational leadership may provide an additional margin of latitude that expands choices in a world of demands and constraints. Furthermore, successful principals are able to expand their practice beyond the limits of traditional management theory, and this too may help account for their success in expanding choices.

Certain personal qualities of principals seem also to make a difference. For example, a pioneering study of the characteristics of principals of successful elementary schools, conducted by Keith Goldhammer, Gerald Becker, and their colleagues in 1971, found that successful principals frequently tested the limits of bureaucracy and were driven by a commitment to schooling that resembled missionary zeal.

Less successful schools in the Goldhammer study were characterized by weak leadership, poor teacher and student morale, control by fear, traditional and ritualistic instructional programs, a general lack of enthusiasm, and principals who were "serving out their time." More successful schools, by contrast, were characterized by high morale, enthusiasm, and adaptability. They were uplifting places to visit and inhabit. The principals of those schools were able not only to recognize problems but also to face up to them with inspiring leadership and hard work. They displayed leadership supported by a belief system that included an overriding commitment to children, teaching, and teachers. They seemed to follow Peter Drucker's (1967) advice to concentrate "efforts and energies in a few major areas where superior performance produces outstanding results" (24). They established priorities and stayed with priority decisions. They seemed to feel that they had no alternative but to do first things first. The characteristics shared by these principals of successful schools are described in Exhibit 1–3.

The studies of principals of successful schools reviewed in this chapter reveal a hopeful portrait. The work of successful principals corresponds more closely to what principals themselves say they should emphasize. Furthermore, in the face of the same demands and constraints, successful principals are able to find the necessary latitude that provides them with expanded choices and, thus, the extra margin needed for better performance. They do this, in part, because their view of how schools as organizations work and their conceptions of management theory and leadership practice are able to expand the concepts and practices of traditional management theory, and this is the theme of the next chapter.

EXHIBIT 1–2   How Teachers Rate Their Principals: A Comparison of Strong, Average, and Weak Leaders

	Percentage of Positive Ratings		
	Strong Leader (n = 800)	*Average Leader (n = 2,146)*	*Weak Leader (n = 300)*
Principal as Resource Provider			
1. My principal promotes staff development activities for teachers.	95	68	41
2. My principal is knowledgeable about instructional resources.	90	54	33
3. My principal mobilizes resources and district support to help achieve academic achievement goals.	90	52	33
4. My principal is considered an important instructional resource person in this school.	79	35	8
Principal as Instructional Resource			
1. My principal encourages the use of different instructional strategies.	89	78	75
2. My principal is sought out by teachers who have instructional concerns or problems.	72	47	25
3. My principal's evaluation of my performance helps improve my teaching.	78	46	17
4. My principal helps faculty interpret test results.	54	35	9
Principal as Communicator			
1. Improved instructional practice results from interactions with my principal.	80	49	25
2. My principal leads formal discussions concerning instruction and student achievement.	85	41	17
3. My principal uses clearly communicated criteria for judging staff performance.	90	63	17
4. My principal provides a clear vision of what our school is all about.	90	49	17
5. My principal communicates clearly to the staff regarding instructional matters.	92	50	17
6. My principal provides frequent feedback to teachers regarding classroom performance.	68	29	18
Principal as Visible Presence			
1. My principal makes frequent classroom observations.	72	31	17
2. My principal is accessible to discuss matters dealing with instruction.	94	68	66
3. My principal is a "visible presence" in the building to both staff and students.	93	75	46
4. My principal is an active participant in staff development activities.	97	64	50

Source: Wilma F. Smith and Richard L. Andrews, *Instructional Leadership: How Principals Make a Difference,* Alexandria, VA: Association for Supervision and Curriculum Development, 1989. This exhibit combines data from figures 2.4, 2.5, 2.6 and 2.7 in the original, pp. 32–37.

EXHIBIT 1–3   Characteristics of Successful Principals

1. Most did not intend to become principals. Most indicated that they had intended to teach, but were encouraged to become principals by their superiors.
2. Most expressed a sincere faith in children. Children were not criticized for failing to learn or for having behavioral difficulties. The principals felt that these were problems that the school was established to correct; thus the administrators emphasized their responsibilities toward the solution of children's problems.
3. They had an ability to work effectively with people and to secure their cooperation. They were proud of their teachers and accepted them as professionally dedicated and competent people. They inspired confidence and developed enthusiasm. The principals used group processes effectively; listened well to parents, teachers, and pupils; and appeared to have intuitive skill and empathy for their associates.
4. They were aggressive in securing recognition of the needs of their schools. They frequently were critical of the restraints imposed by the central office and of the inadequate resources. They found it difficult to live within the constraints of the bureaucracy; they frequently violated the chain of command, seeking relief for their problems from whatever sources that were potentially useful.
5. They were enthusiastic as principals and accepted their responsibilities as a mission rather than as a job. They recognized their role in current social problems. The ambiguities that surrounded them and their work were of less significance than the goals they felt were important to achieve. As a result, they found it possible to live with the ambiguities of their position.
6. They were committed to education and could distinguish between long-term and short-term educational goals. Consequently, they had established fairly well philosophies of the role of education and their relationship within it.
7. They were adaptable. If they discovered something was not working, they could make the necessary shifts and embark with some security on new paths.
8. They were able strategists. They could identify their objectives and plan means to achieve them. They expressed concern for the identification of the most appropriate procedures through which change could be secured.

Source: Keith Goldhammer et al., *Elementary School Principals and Their Schools,* Eugene, OR: Center for the Advanced Study of Educational Administration, 2–3.

References

Augenstein, John J., and W. William Konnert. 1991. "Implications of Informal Socialization Process of Beginning Elementary School Principals for Role Preparation and Initiation," *Journal of Educational Administration* 29(1), 39–50.

Augenstein, John J. 1989. "Socialization Differences Among Principals in Catholic Schools," *The Living Light* 25(3), 226–231.

Barnard, Chester. 1938. *The Functions of an Executive.* Cambridge, MA: Harvard University Press.

Barth, Roland S. 1980. "Reflections on the Principalship," *Thrust for Educational Leadership* 9(5).

Drucker, Peter. 1967. *The Effective Executive.* New York: Harper & Row.

Goldhammer, Keith, Gerald Becker, Richard Withycombe, Frank Doyel, Edgar Miller, Claude Morgan, Louis DeLoretto, and Bill Aldridge. 1971. *Elementary School Principals and Their Schools.* Eugene: University of Oregon, Center for the Advanced Study of Educational Administration.

Gorton, Richard A., and Kenneth E. McIntyre. 1978. *The Senior High School Principalship. Vol. II: The Effective Principal.* Reston, VA: National Association of Secondary School Principals.

Gulick, Luther, and L. Urwick, Eds. 1937. *Papers on the Science of Administration.* New York: Institute for Public Administration.

Leithwood, K. I., and M. Stager. 1986. "Differences in Problem-Solving Processes Used by Moderately and Highly Effective Principals." American Educational Research Association, San Francisco.

McCleary, Lloyd E., and Scott D. Thomson. 1979. *The Senior High School Principalship. Vol. III: The Summary Report.* Reston, VA: National Association of Secondary School Principals.

Mintzberg, Henry. 1973. *The Nature of Managerial Work.* New York: Harper & Row.

Morris, Van Cleve, Robert L. Crowson, Cynthia Porter-Gehrie, and Emmanuel Hurwitz, Jr. 1984. *Principals in Action: The Reality of Managing Schools.* Columbus, OH: Merrill.

National Association of Elementary School Principals, 1986. *Elementary and Middle Schools: Proficiencies for Principals Kindergarten through Eighth Grade.* Alexandria, VA: The Association.

Pellicer, Leonard O., Lorin W. Anderson, James W. Keefe, Edgar A. Kelley, and Lloyd E. McCleary. 1988. *High School Leaders and Their Schools. Vol. I: A National Profile.* Reston, VA: National Association of Secondary School Principals.

Smith, Wilma A., and Richard L. Andrews. 1989. *Instructional Leadership: How Principals Make a Difference.* Alexandria, VA: Association for Supervision and Curriculum Development.

Sproul, Lee S. 1976. "Managerial Attention in New Educational Systems." Seminar on Organizations as Loosely Couple Systems, University of Illinois, Urbana, Nov. 13–14.

Stewart, Rosemary, 1982. "The Relevance of Some Studies of Managerial Work and Behavior to Leadership Research," in James G. Hunt, Uma Sekaran, and Chester A. Schriesheim, Eds., *Leadership Beyond Establishment Views.* Carbondale: Southern Illinois University.

Taylor, Paul W. 1961. *Normative Discourse.* Englewood Cliffs, NJ: Prentice Hall.

Teddlie, Charles, Peggy D. Kirby, and Sam Stringfield. 1989. "Effective versus Ineffective Schools: Observable Differences in the Classroom," *American Journal of Education* 97(3).

Zeleznik, Abraham. 1977. "Managers and Leaders: Are They Different?" *Harvard Business Review* 55(3).

Appendix 1–1   Time Log of a High School Principal

7:35 A.M.	Arrived at school. Picked up mail and communications. Unlocked desk.
7:36 A.M.	Looked for dean who wasn't in yet. Left word for him to see me.
7:38 A.M.	Looked at mail—Heart Association wanting to promote a "Heart Day." Worked at desk, proofread two teacher evaluations.
7:47 A.M.	Secretary came in. Gave her evaluations of teachers for retyping.
7:49 A.M.	Checked with substitute clerk for absentees and late-comers (exceptionally foggy morning).
7:50 A.M.	Spoke briefly with arriving English teacher about his spelling bee and award certificates I had signed.
7:52 A.M.	Called five administrative offices, suggesting they check classrooms for possible late teachers.
7:54 A.M.	Gave secretary instructions on duplicating and distribution of material on change in graduation requirement.
7:55 A.M.	Saw dean about student who had called after school yesterday—threatened and beaten up by other students getting off bus.
7:58 A.M.	On way to staffing, stopped at attendance office to visit with parent who was in about son not doing well in school.
8:00 A.M.	Joined staffing with social worker, psychologist, counselor, therapist, parent, and student who had been removed from all classes for truancy.
9:10 A.M.	Left staffing to look for student who had been told to wait in outer office but had wandered off.
9:15 A.M.	Found student in hall, returned to staffing.
9:30 A.M.	Left staffing to keep appointment with candidate for maintenance job.
9:31 A.M.	While waiting for building and grounds director to arrive, gave secretary instructions for cover and illustrations for the open house printed program.
9:33 A.M.	While waiting read:
	Note from student needing early release.
	Bulletin from National Federation of Athletic Associations on college recruiting of high school athletes.
	Note from teacher upset over misbehavior in previous day's homeroom program.
	Staff absentee report for the day.
9:36 A.M.	Went to outer office to greet candidate and explain why we were waiting.
9:37 A.M.	Called building and grounds director and learned he wasn't coming over.
9:39 A.M.	Interviewed maintenance supervisor candidate.
10:00 A.M.	Took call from registrar—to be returned.
10:07 A.M.	Completed interview.
10:08 A.M.	Saw teacher who had pictures from German exchange program.
10:09 A.M.	Called for building and grounds director—busy.

From Gilbert R. Weldy, *Principals: What They Do and Who They Are*, Reston, VA: National Association of Secondary School Principals, 1979, 65–71.

Appendix 1–1 *(Continued)*

10:10 A.M.	Returned call to registrar about purging of records of a dropout.
10:11 A.M.	Called building and grounds director to discuss maintenance candidate.
10:14 A.M.	Returned call to personnel director about administrator's inservice program next week. Agreed to make a presentation.
10:22 A.M.	Read:
	Two suspension notices.
	Plans of special programs coming up.
10:25 A.M.	Saw special programs coordinator in outer office. Approved her plans and discussed possible appearance of Navy Band in February.
10:27 A.M.	Saw dean to learn what he had done about yesterday's incident.
10:30 A.M.	Left for cafeteria—talked with counselor in hall about Guidance Information Service (computer service for college selection).
10:31 A.M.	Stopped by to see psychologist to hear outcome of staffing meeting.
10:36 A.M.	Stopped by health center to give nurses information from Heart Association about "Heart Day."
	Talked with nurse about her program at a PTSA meeting the previous day.
10:37 A.M.	Stopped in Audiovisual Center to ask director to prepare transparencies I had given him for inservice program.
10:40 A.M.	Stopped by athletic director's office to relate comments by parents about physical education that had come up at the PTSA meeting.
10:45 A.M.	Checked on the room where I was to have lunch with two students. Visited with a student congress representative who was there.
10:46 A.M.	Looked in on yearbook photographer who was waiting for students to come in for underclass pictures.
	Visited with student who had performed with choir previous day when students had misbehaved.
10:49 A.M.	Walked down to maintenance office to tell men about holes broken in wall of the student council office.
10:52 A.M.	Stayed around student cafeteria. Spoke with teacher who was in school exchange.
10:54 A.M.	Stopped in faculty lounge to visit with three soccer coaches who were concerned about new play-off rules that eliminated our team.
10:57 A.M.	Picked up lunch and went to council office to meet students.
11:00 A.M.	Lunched with two students.
11:30 A.M.	Stopped and visited with a few students in the cafeteria.
11:35 A.M.	Returned to the office. On the way, stopped to visit with CVE teacher about cosmetology program and a student in the program.
11:38 A.M.	Visited with workmen installing new air conditioning units in office area.
11:40 A.M.	Made four telephone calls. No answer on two of them.
11:47 A.M.	Returned call from fellow principal, discussed graduation requirement proposal.
11:48 A.M.	Answered note from teacher.

Appendix 1–1 *(Continued)*

11:50 A.M.	Reviewed minutes of previous day's principal's advisory committee meeting (principal is chairman and secretary).
11:51 A.M.	Read note from teacher about a student's early release.
11:52 A.M.	Looked up material needed for next day's athletic conference meeting.
11:58 A.M.	Read communications:
	Memo regarding special education student.
	Note from teacher about conduct in homeroom.
	Memo from special program coordinator about upcoming program.
	Board of Education summary.
	November homeroom calendar.
12:07 P.M.	Called in building manager to discuss his problems that students had brought up in advisory meeting.
12:22 P.M.	Saw student who was upset with dean's handling of his absence.
12:28 P.M.	Took call from a mother who didn't want her daughter to drop out of school.
12.30 P.M.	Met with two teachers to make plans for disseminating information to faculty, parent, and student groups on graduation requirement change.
1:08 P.M.	Completed conference.
	Instructed secretary to prepare materials.
1:09 P.M.	The day's mail—read, routed, and filed.
1:12 P.M.	Made two calls. No answer for either.
1:13 P.M.	Called PTSA president. No answer.
1:15 P.M.	Wrote note to superintendent to accompany graduation requirement proposals.
1:20 P.M.	Saw student council representative about floor hockey marathon project.
1:23 P.M.	Gave dictation to secretary:
	Memo to administrators and faculty inservice committee about faculty meeting date.
	Petition form for faculty for graduation requirement proposal.
	Letter to parents for principal's coffee next month.
	Welcome letter to parents for the open house program.
	Faculty bulletin for next day.
1:46 P.M.	Took call from district administrator's secretary.
1:48 P.M.	Received note from teacher on a student's early release.
	Gave secretary several instructions
1:54 P.M.	Called PTSA president. No answer.
1:55 P.M.	Called assistant administrator about our school hosting a student congress (forensic event).
1:56 P.M.	Went to student services office to review memo to teachers responsible for the previous day's homeroom.
2:02 P.M.	Walked out to smoking area. Admonished a student athlete for being there.

Appendix 1–1 (*Continued*)

2:11 P.M.	Called both fellow principals, neither in, left word to call.
2:14 P.M.	Called administrator at sister school who was on graduation requirements committee.
2:15 P.M.	Conferred with secretary about dictation.
2:15 P.M.	Called personnel office about tuition scholarships from college whose student teachers we help train.
2:18 P.M.	Read more communications:
	Five suspension notices.
	Note from teacher on the early release of student.
	Daily bulletin.
2:20 P.M.	Wrote note to student services director about homeroom programs for November.
2:21 P.M.	Read bulletin from National Federation of Activities Associations.
2:27 P.M.	Studied six-week grade distributions—computer printout.
2:33 P.M.	Answered question for student reporter about early dismissal on open house day.
2:34 P.M.	Continued study of grade distributions. Made summary table of withdraw-passing and withdraw-failing grades.
2:42 P.M.	Read confirmation of an order to change telephone service.
2:44 P.M.	Read principals' association newsletter.
2:48 P.M.	Took return call from fellow principal. Discussed institute day program.
	Arrangements for next day's league meeting.
	Graduation requirements proposal strategy.
2:50 P.M.	Received material from superintendent to be distributed to faculty—read material and gave secretary instructions for distribution.
3:00 P.M.	Saw newspaper adviser about a story on graduation requirement proposal.
3:02 P.M.	Returned to reading principals' newsletter.
3:05 P.M.	Called fellow principal about ride to league meeting next day.
3:07 P.M.	Called PTSA president. No answer.
3:08 P.M.	Reviewed agenda for league meeting—got material together.
3:10 P.M.	Took call from athletic director about cuts in capital equipment budget.
3:12 P.M.	Read a teacher evaluation.
3:15 P.M.	School is out.
3:18 P.M.	Went into hall—watched students and teachers leave.
3:22 P.M.	Helped a student look for a lost jacket.
3:25 P.M.	Back in office, went over open house program with secretary.
3:30 P.M.	Called assistant administrator. No answer.
	Left word to call.
3:33 P.M.	Called PTSA president. Busy this time.
3:37 P.M.	Studied curriculum council's grade weighting system.
3:45 P.M.	Called PTSA president—discussed agenda for next week's board meeting.
3:50 P.M.	Left school for a personal appointment.

Appendix 1–2   A Day in the Life of an Urban Elementary Principal

When Mary Stewart arrived at Blaire Elementary School at 8:15 A.M., the teachers were stopping by the office to sign in on their way to their classrooms. Stewart removed her coat and boots, hanging them in the closet outside her office. She put on a pair of medium heeled shoes, explaining to the researcher, " . . . the children like to see the principal a little dressed up." Joining her clerk in the outer office, the two of them reviewed the list of teachers who would be absent and the steps to be taken to secure substitutes. One substitute, sent by the central office "Sub Center," had already arrived, and Stewart asked the clerk to give her the regular teachers file containing a class seating chart and lesson plans.

Returning to her desk, Stewart's eyes drifted to the Continuous Progress Program packet and accompanying memorandum from district offices which had arrived the previous afternoon. It was a reminder that the next reporting period was imminent and that all forms must be filed this coming Friday before the close of business. This meant that Stewart would be spending part of each of the next three days buttonholing the teachers to get their reports to her on each child, and then summarizing these figures in an all-school report. Stewart anticipated that she would have to divert some time from other managerial duties to get this paperwork finished on time.

As she reviewed her calendar, Stewart mentally prepared for a meeting with faculty representatives of the Professional Problems Committee. The Union contract provided that this group, elected by the teachers, must meet regularly with the principal. At 8:30, Stewart left her office for the short walk to the school library, where the committee members were gathering. Stewart called the meeting to order about 8:35. High on her list of items was the matter of selecting textbooks for next year. But before this discussion got underway, the teachers wanted to relay questions to Stewart that individual teachers had raised with them: a problem in supervising the third floor washrooms, a question about how next year's faculty advisor to the eighth grade graduating class was to be selected, and a problem in getting supplies during a particular free period when the office clerk was often not available. After promising to work on these problems, Stewart spent most of the remaining time discussing plans with the teachers to host upcoming meetings with publisher representatives. Together they also reviewed plans to form faculty text-book review committees, and procedures for selecting a common textbook for each grade level.

After the meeting, Stewart was approached by two teachers with individual questions. Miss La Pointe wanted to know whether Stewart would be available during eighth period. Stewart nodded and invited her to stop by the office at that time. Mr. Fields, the gym teacher, informed her that the basketball team did well at yesterday's game. They came close to beating Doyle, which is one of the best teams in the district. Stewart congratulated him, and took the opportunity to ask how Marvin Goth was behaving in class lately. Fields said that Marvin still got "edgy," but in general was "doing a lot better."

From Van Cleve Morris, Robert L. Crowson, Emanuel Hurwitz, Jr., and Cynthia Porter-Gehrie. "The Urban Principal: Discretionary Decision-Making in a Large Educational Organization," Washington, DC. National Institute for Education, NIE-G-79-0019, 1981, 40–47.

Appendix 1–2   (Continued)

As Stewart walked through the hallway back to her office, Mrs. Noyes motioned to her from inside the classroom. The students were already in their classrooms or moving quickly through the halls in the last moments before the class bell rang. Noyes told Stewart that she was scheduled to take the students on a field trip this morning, but that one of the parents had called at the last moment to say that she would not be able to come. This left Noyes one parent volunteer short. Should she cancel the trip? Stewart remembered that Mrs. Case would be volunteering in the reading center this morning. She offered to ask her if she would fill in.

On the way to the reading center, Stewart peeked into several classrooms. As she passed the student washrooms she quickly looked into each, checking to see that no students were present and that the rooms were in order. As one student hurried past her, she asked him why he was not in class. He said that he had arrived late. She checked to see that he had a late admittance slip, and then urged him to get to school on time in the future.

When she entered the reading center, she nodded in the direction of the reading teacher and motioned that she wanted to speak with Mrs. Case. Mrs. Case quickly joined her and agreed to help with the field trip. On her way out the door, Stewart complimented the reading teacher on a bulletin board entitled "Read for Experience."

Instead of returning to her office, Stewart continued to walk the halls on the second and third floors. On the third floor, she spent a few minutes studying the washroom situation. Then, stopping briefly at each classroom, she asked the teachers to be sure that only one student at a time was excused to use them. On her way back down the stairs, she detoured for a moment on the second floor to swing by a classroom with a substitute teacher, "just to see how he's doing." Finding the students somewhat unruly, she stopped into the classroom, fixing the well-known principal's stare on the children. As expected, her presence quieted the room. She greeted the substitute and inquired whether the regular teacher's substitute file was in order. He said that everything seemed fine, "they're just testing a little bit."

When Stewart returned to the office, she spoke briefly with the clerk, reviewing the arrival and assignment of substitute teachers. Stewart asked the clerk to inform the librarian that she would have to cover one of the classes during second period, if the substitute teacher did not arrive by then. Then Stewart picked up the mail that had arrived via the school system's delivery service. She asked the clerk to inform Mrs. Noyes that Mrs. Case would come on the field trip. She also asked the clerk to be sure that a teacher aide was available during seventh period to give out teaching supplies. As they talked, the clerk handed her two telephone messages.

Stewart entered her office, leaving the door to the outer office open. (A second door connecting directly to the hallway was kept closed. In this way, anyone who wanted to see Stewart had to go through the clerk. Stewart, herself, usually passed through the outer office in order to exchange information with the clerk on the way in or out of her own private office.) She quickly wrote a note to Mrs. Reynolds, on the second floor, informing her that the teacher aide would be available during seventh period to give out supplies. She also wrote a bulletin to all teachers in longhand: "Teachers: It appears that students from different classes are meeting at pre-arranged times in the third floor washrooms again. When excusing students to the washrooms, please be sure they use the nearest washroom, only. Thank you." She got up, walked to the outer office and taped the bulletin on the counter by the sign-in book. She also placed the note to Mrs. Reynolds in her mailbox.

Stewart returned to her office and placed a call to another principal who had left a message. The principal told her that he was calling a meeting of the district's science fair committee and would appreciate knowing when a convenient time would be for Stewart. They agreed to meet at 10:00 A.M. the following day at Blaire School. After the phone conversation, Stewart wrote a note to the cafeteria director, asking that coffee and some rolls be available the next morning in the conference room adjoining her office. She consulted the teachers' schedule and then also wrote a note to Mrs. St. Antoine, asking her to come to her office during seventh period. She got up, walked to the outer office and placed the notes in St. Antoine's and the cafeteria director's mailboxes.

Returning to her office, Stewart once again picked up the telephone and dialed the number of a representative from a photography company that took students' yearly pictures. No answer, so Stewart left a message that she called. She set the phone message at the corner of her desk, so that she "would remember his name when he calls again."

She then began to look at the morning mail and some items the clerk had placed in her "in" box:

- A personnel bulletin listing several openings in the system for teachers and administrators
- An announcement of a conference for reading teachers
- A set of rating cards to be completed for each teacher; these teacher rating cards were filled out each year by the principal and placed in the teachers' personal files.

Stewart placed the rating cards to one side on her desk, then got up, taking the other items to the outer office with her. She placed the conference announcement in the reading teacher's mailbox and tacked the personnel bulletin to the teacher's bulletin board. As she did so, the clerk informed her of an incoming telephone call.

Returning to her desk, she picked up the phone and heard the voice of the photographer's representative, glancing in recognition at the name on the earlier phone message. After some preliminary pleasantries, this: "Mr. Haskins, every year we make a selection from among several school photographers to take school pictures. You say you'd like to be considered this year? Fine, I'll be glad to include you in the group. Could you send me some materials—a list of the size and kind of photo to be included in each student's packet . . . maybe a sample packet, O.K.? Also the cost to the student, and the amount the school keeps for each packet sold. Also any other items that you make available, such as class pictures and teacher photographs."

Stewart went on to explain to the photographer that the eighth grade faculty sponsor participated in the selection. However, the sponsor for the following year had not yet been picked out. "I'll make sure that you get the information on the selection process and the

Appendix 1–2   *(Continued)*

date and time of the meeting when we ask all photographers to come to the school to demonstrate their work. However, I'd appreciate it if you would not meet directly with the faculty sponsor, except of course at the demonstration session. I look forward to seeing your materials, and thanks for your interest in the school."

Stewart put down the phone and turned to the researcher: "You know, its a pleasure dealing with these photographers. They really enjoy coming to the school, and I must say, the kids get a kick out of these sessions too." Then, turning to another subject, Stewart explained to the researcher that she had gotten a hurry-up phone call from downtown headquarters a day or so ago calling her to a special meeting on the Access to Excellence program. "It's scheduled for Friday at eleven, and that's just when I'll be putting the finishing touches on the Continuous Progress materials. I hope I can get them done in time. But, you know, these meetings . . . they're having more and more of them. They want to turn this school into an "academy," whatever that is. And we've got to go downtown and sit around for a couple hours to be told what it is. Then, no doubt, there'll be more meetings at district (headquarters) setting it up. Seems as if I spend more and more of my time away from here, going to meetings, meetings. Hard to keep on top of things here when I'm not around."

The researcher listened intently, and the two of them discussed the possibility of "academy" status and what that would mean for the school and for the community.

After a discussion of 15 minutes, Stewart looked at her watch and saw that it was nearly time for the primary grades recess. Breaking off the conversation with the researcher, she got up, walked through the outer office, and went to stand by the exit doors to the primary play area. When the bell sounded, the children were escorted through the building toward the exit. In the ensuing commotion, Stewart spoke sharply to a few boisterous children, telling them to "walk, don't run," and to "move slowly down the stairs."

She explained in an aside to the researcher that her customary practice was to accompany the youngsters out onto the playground where she and the teachers could supervise their play. However, today, she had to get back to the office to prepare a schedule for teacher rating conferences with each teacher. Returning to her desk, she assembled the teacher evaluation materials and got from her drawer the teachers' daily schedules. Allowing 20 minutes for each teacher, she began making up a conference schedule. In the middle of this activity, she was interrupted by three boys entering the outer office, with a teacher aide following close behind. One of the boys was crying and holding the back of his head. The aide explained that the injured boy had fallen and hit his head on a patch of ice near the rim of the play area. The other two boys, she reported, had been chasing the injured boy.

Stewart moved to the outer office and told the two chasers to sit down on a bench inside the hallway door. She inspected the head injury and found that it was beginning to swell at the point of impact. Sending a student helper to the cafeteria to fetch some ice, she asked the injured boy for his name, his home telephone number, and his mother's name. She then dialed the number and spoke with the mother. After hearing what had happened, the mother said that she would come pick him up as soon as she could get a neighbor to drive her to the school. The helper soon arrived back with the ice, and Stewart wrapped it in a paper towel and gave it to the boy to place on the bump. She told him to sit down on the bench and wait for his mother, whereupon she invited the two chasers into the inner office and closed the door. "Now look, you know you're not supposed to run where there is ice . . . it's too dangerous. Now that someone's hurt, the matter is serious. I want your parents to know about this." She filled out a form that requested a parent to come to school with the boys the following morning. With the boys still at her desk, she telephoned their homes and orally requested that a parent come to see her the next morning. She explained to the boy's mothers "There's been an injury and your son was involved. Something must be done about their wild behavior during recess." She then sent the boys back to their classrooms, explaining that she would see them again in the morning.

As she gave them their hall passes, the injured boy's mother arrived. Stewart explained to her that two other boys had been involved and that she would be meeting with their parents in the morning. The mother asked her son, "Who did it?" and he replied it was "Jeff and Michael." "Those boys," the mother said, "why do they pick on him so much? Last week they pushed him in the bushes on the way home from school. Now they've gone too far." Stewart asked the mother to "Let me see if I can't work something out." She promised to call her back in the morning, after she met with the other parents.

As the boy and his mother left, Stewart looked up and saw that it was beginning to snow heavily. She went to the public address system and announced that students eating lunch at school would remain inside the building during the lunchtime recess.

Stewart returned to her desk and worked on the conference schedule, but was shortly interrupted by two phone calls. One concerned the placement of a student teacher in the school. The other was from her husband, asking if she would like to meet him downtown for dinner. As Stewart was finishing the schedule, the clerk brought in a master copy of the parents' bulletin for her to approve before it was duplicated. She set aside the schedule and read through the bulletin as the clerk waited to one side. She pointed out two typos and then placed her signature on the copy master. The clerk took it and left. A moment later she returned with the U.S. mail. Stewart took a quick glance at the envelopes before setting them to one side and continuing to finish the schedule. Stewart neatly copied the final schedule by hand and then asked the clerk to place a copy of the schedule in each teacher's mailbox.

Stewart then headed toward the cafeteria, speaking with students in the hall on the way, telling them to "slow down" and "go to your recess areas." She took a tray and moved through the lunch line. Instead of going to the faculty room, she returned to her office to eat. There, she was available for teachers who might want to stop by. As she ate, she looked through the U.S. mail: promotional material for textbooks, school administration booklets, and instructional supplies. Also an announcement of a tea at a local Catholic High School for the eighth graders. Stewart set this aside and threw out the rest.

A student asked to see Stewart. As student council president, she wanted to know when the next student council meeting would be (the last meeting had been cancelled

Appendix 1–2 *(Continued)*

because of snow). They picked a date and the student said that she would inform the council members. Stewart chatted for a few minutes with the girl about her plans for high school.

Getting up from her desk, Stewart carried her tray and the tea announcement to the outer office. She left the announcement in the eighth grade class sponsor's mailbox and returned her tray to the cafeteria. Then she began her tour of the hallways, inspecting the building as the students returned to their classes to settle down for the afternoon's course work.

When she returned to her office, the clerk handed her a phone message. Stewart dialed the phone for an in-house call and reached the building engineer. He told her that a small window at the back of the building had been broken during the lunch hour by some loitering high school students. He said he had covered it with some heavy cardboard, "but I thought you should know about it. Also, you know the art room . . . the shades in there have been damaged. The (art) teacher just lets the kids go wild in there during seventh and eighth periods. I think you should talk to him." Stewart agreed to check on it.

Miss La Pointe arrived. She had agreed to start a dramatic program in the school and wanted to report to Stewart the plans she was making for a Spring production. They discussed use of the auditorium, rehearsal schedules, the play La Pointe had selected, and the tryout announcement La Pointe had prepared. Toward the end of the seventh period, the conference was concluded and La Pointe left to return to her classroom. Stewart got up and, checking to make sure that the teacher's aide was on station in the outer office to give out supplies, headed for the art room to see the damaged shades and to make sure the students were under control.

When she returned to the office, Stewart found Mrs. St. Antoine waiting for her in the outer office. Stewart invited her into her own office and asked for an update about the plans for the eighth grade tea, dinner, and other graduation festivities. St. Antoine discussed with her the results of faculty and student committee meetings to that point. Then Stewart asked St. Antoine whether she was thinking about remaining eighth grade sponsor next year. St. Antoine seemed a bit embarrassed. She said that she enjoyed working with the students very much, but that there was some jealousy from some of the other eighth grade teachers who felt excluded. They discussed how some of the other eighth grade teachers might be brought more closely into the planning, and St. Antoine left agreeing that she would try to mend some of the fences that had been neglected.

Seeing that it was near the end of the day, Stewart checked her desk to see what remained to be done. Noting the stack of material in the "in" box, she looked through it. It contained several forms that required signing; they pertained to the ordering of supplies, teacher absences, and a field trip permission. Stewart signed all of the forms but one. It was a request to order a film. Stewart was unfamiliar with the film and wanted to discuss its nature and use with the teacher before signing.

Stewart put on her hat and coat and walked to the main exit doors just as the students were beginning to leave. Stationed just outside the exit, she called to the students inside the hallway and out on the playground to "slow down," and "watch out, its slippery." When the students were gone she returned to her office to find a tiny kindergartner sitting with tear-filled eyes next to the teacher aide. The aide explained that the girl's father was supposed to pick her up from school, but had not arrived. They tried to make some phone calls to find out who was coming for the girl, but could not get an answer. The girl suggested that they call her aunt, which they did. The aunt agreed to take the girl, but said no one could come and get her right now. Stewart agreed to bring the girl by the aunt's house. "There now," the aide told the girl, "the principal will take you to your aunt's house." Stewart placed a few items in a small brief case and was ready to leave. She waited as the aide and clerk prepared to leave also. As they put on their coats, she checked the teachers' sign-in sheets to be sure that they were all out of the building. Then she locked the office as they left together. Stewart reached for the small girl's hand and helped her down the slippery steps. Before going to her car, she muttered to the researcher, "I suppose I shouldn't be doing this . . . liability and all. But someone has to."

Chapter 2

The Nature of Reflective Practice in the Principalship

It is not by chance that some principals are more effective than others, even when all are faced with the same demands and constraints. Effective principals have a better understanding of how the world of schooling and school leadership works. They base their practice on a different theory, and this enables them to create a more effective practice.

Principals are faced with an important choice. On the one hand, they can base their practice on the assumption that predetermined solutions exist for most of the problems they face in the form of research-based theories and techniques. On the other hand, they can base their practice on the assumption that few of the problems they face lend themselves to predetermined solutions. They can resign themselves to the difficult task of having to create knowledge in use as they practice. Principals who make the second choice realize that despite the attractiveness of the first, predetermined solutions can only be trusted to work for the few problems that are fixed and located in stable environments. They realize that the majority of problems and situations faced are characterized by ambiguity and confusion. These are problems located in a turbulent environment where practice is largely indeterminate. They would argue, as does Donald Schön, that the most important problems principals face are beyond the reach of technical, rational solutions. In Schön's words: "The practitioner must choose. Shall he remain on the high ground where he can solve relatively unimportant problems according to prevailing standards of rigor, or shall he descend to the swamp of important problems and nonrigorous inquiry?" (Schön, 1987:3).

The choice that a principal makes is largely dependent on her or his theory or "mindscape" of practice. Mindscapes influence what we see, believe, and do. Recall, for example, the picture of the vase formed by two profiles in your college psychology textbook chapter on perception. If that picture were shown to a novice, she or he would probably see only one of the two images. A conversation with someone who saw the other image would be difficult. The image each sees functions as a mindscape that creates a different reality. Similarly, our mindscapes of leadership, how schools work, and the nature of human rationality shape the way we think about theoretical knowledge and the link between this knowledge and how we practice.

Mindscapes of Practice

In many respects, mindscapes are our intellectual security blankets and road maps through an uncertain world. As road maps, they provide the rules, assumptions, images, and principles that define what the principalship is and how its practice should unfold. These road maps make us feel safe, certain, and secure. Mindscapes are so dominant that their assumptions and related practices are not thought about much; they are just assumed to be true. Thus, when a mindscape does not fit the world of practice, the problem is thought to lie with that world. Rarely is the world accepted for what it is and the prevailing mindscape changed.

An important question is: To what extent do mindscapes of the principalship fit the actual landscapes of teaching, administering, and schooling? Unfortunately, they often don't fit very well. They do not provide us with a realistic view of the world of practice.

Although many scholars might take exception to the way I categorize mindscapes, three distinct views of schooling and administering can be identified, are worth describing and understanding, and can be evaluated for good fit with the real landscape of practice. The three are the mindscapes of the "Mystics," "Neats," and "Scruffies." Principals and researchers who are Mystics, Neats, or Scruffies have widely different conceptions of the nature of practice and of the relationships between this practice and theoretical knowledge. For Mystics, no relationship whatsoever exists; for Neats, theoretical knowledge is superordinate to practice; and for Scruffies, theoretical knowledge is subordinate to practice. Their respective views can be summarized as follows.

- *Mystics* hold the view that educational administration resembles a nonscience, and, thus, scientific principles gleaned from theory and research have little relevance to practice. Scientific principles and practice are disconnected. Instead, practice is driven by the principal's tacit knowledge, intuitive feel for situations, sixth sense, and other more transcendental factors.
- *Neats* hold the view that educational administration resembles an applied science within which theory and research are directly and linearly linked to practice. The former always determine the latter, and thus knowledge is superordinate to the principal and designed to prescribe practice.
- *Scruffies* hold the view that educational administration resembles a craftlike science within which practice is characterized by interacting reflection and action episodes. Theory and research are only one source of knowledge, which is subordinate to the principal and which is designed to inform but not to prescribe practice.

The mystical end of the continuum is characterized by the belief that no formal knowledge is of use, that the world is hopelessly phenomenological, that everything is relative, that only personal knowledge counts, that all knowing is tacit, that teaching and administrative skills are gifts, and that in the end it is one's intuition or other manifestation of some mysterious sixth sense that counts. The principal functions as a clairvoyant. Although many principals are card-carrying mystics, this view is not at the center of the debate regarding knowledge development and use in the principalship. Therefore, the emphasis in this discussion is on the position of the Neats and Scruffies.

Although its popularity is waning, the Neats' view of applied science remains the dominant metaphor for the study and practice of educational administration. In applied science, knowledge is created through theorizing and research. This knowledge is then used to build and fieldtest models of practice from which universal prescriptions and treatments are generated. These, in return, are communicated to professionals for their use in practice. Applied scientists talk a great deal about knowledge development and utilization chains within which scientific knowledge is used to build practice models and standard practice treatments. Within applied science it is thought that professionals bring to their practice a set of standardized skills linked to a series of scientifically verified standard practice treatments. The professional then searches the context in which she or he works, carefully diagnosing and characterizing contingencies and situations according to predetermined and standardized protocols. Depending on the diagnosis, the appropriate treatment is then applied.

The Neats seek to apply scientific knowledge directly to problems of professional practice. A basic assumption is that a one-to-one correspondence exists between knowledge and practice. Therefore, the Neats seek to establish the one best solution to a problem and the one best way to practice. To them, true facts are supreme. The Neats, for example, accept the research on effective teaching without question. They believe that a generic set of teaching effectiveness behaviors exists that can be applied by all teachers in all situations to all students. The research on effective schools, leadership styles, and conflict-management strategies are viewed similarly as truths to be accepted and applied. Principalship practice is considered to be a research-based technology that can be directly learned and routinely applied. To the Neats, the principal is presumed to function as a highly trained technician.

How does the view of the Neats fit the real world of practice? Not very well. Patterns of school practice are actually characterized by a great deal of uncertainty, instability, complexity, and variety. Value conflicts and uniquenesses are accepted aspects of educational settings. According to Schön (1983), these characteristics are perceived as central to the world of professional practice in all the major professions, including medicine, engineering, management, and education. He concludes: "Professional knowledge is mismatched to the changing characteristics of the situation of practice" (14). Although one may be comfortable in viewing the principalship as a logical process of problem solving with the application of standard techniques to predictable problems, a more accurate view may be a process of "managing messes" (Schön, 1983:16).

In the actual world of schooling, the task of the principal is to make sense of messy situations by increasing understanding and discovering and communicating meanings. Situations of practice are typically characterized by unique events; therefore, uniform answers to problems are not likely to be helpful. Teachers, supervisors, and students bring to their classrooms beliefs, assumptions, values, opinions, preferences, and predispositions. Thus, objective and value-free administrative strategies are not likely to address issues of importance. Uncertainty and complexity are normal aspects in the process of schooling. Intuition becomes necessary to fill in the gaps of what can be specified as known and what cannot. Yet, ordinary intuition will not do. Intuition must be *informed* by theoretical knowledge on one hand and adept understandings of the situation on the other.

Reflective Practice: The Paradigm of the Scruffies

What kind of science is needed that will enable principals to practice successfully in a messy world? The answer is one that resembles a craftlike science, within which professional practice is characterized by interacting reflection and action and episodes. Webster defines *science* tightly as "knowledge covering general truths or the operation of general laws esp. as obtained and tested through scientific method" and loosely as "knowledge attained through study and practice." I use the term loosely. Theory and research are only one source of knowledge, and this knowledge is always subordinate to the principal, teacher, or other professional, serving to inform but not to prescribe practice. Indeed, professional knowledge is *created in use* as principals and teachers think, reflect, decide, and do.

The Scruffies' view of the principalship is that of a science of the practical—a science that stems from theories of practice and that provides principals with practical as well as theoretical mindscapes from which to work. The concept of *reflective practice* is critical to this new science.

Reflective practice is based on the reality that professional knowledge is different from scientific knowledge. Professional knowledge is created in use as professionals who face ill-defined, unique, and changing problems decide on courses of action. Ralph Tyler maintains that researchers don't have a full understanding of the nature of professional knowledge in education. He states:

> Researchers and many academics also misunderstand educational practices. The practice of every profession evolves informally, and professional procedures are not generally derived from systematic design based on research findings. Professional practice has largely developed through trial and error and intuitive efforts. Practitioners, over the years, discover procedures that appear to work and others that fail. The professional practice of teaching, as well as that of law, medicine, and theology, is largely a product of the experience of practitioners, particularly those who are more creative, inventive, and observant than the average. (cited in Hosford, 1984:9)

Scientific studies in the various professions are important. But science, according to Tyler, "explains phenomenon, it does not produce practices" (cited in Hosford, 1984:10). Professionals rely heavily on informed intuition as they create knowledge in use. Intuition is informed by theoretical knowledge on the one hand and by interacting with the context of practice on the other. When teachers use informed intuition, they are engaging in reflective practice. When principals use informed intuition, they too are engaging in reflective practice. Knowing is in the action itself, and reflective professionals become students of their practice. They research the context and experiment with different courses of action. Schön (1983) suggests:

> *They may ask themselves, for example, "what features do I notice when I recognize this thing? What are the criteria by which I make this judgment? What procedures am I enacting when I perform this skill? How am I framing the problem that I'm trying to solve?" Usually, reflection on knowing-in-action goes together with reflection on the stuff at hand. There is some puzzling, or troubling or interesting phenomenon with which the individual is trying to deal. As he tries to make sense of it, he also reflects on the understandings which have been implicit in his action, understandings which he surfaces, criticizes, re-structures and embodies in further action.*
>
> *It is this entire process of reflection-in-action which is central to the "art" by which practitioners sometimes deal with situations of uncertainty, instability, uniqueness, and value conflicts. (50)*

To Schön (1984), reflection-in-action involves "on-the-spot surfacing, criticizing, re-structuring and testing of intuitive understandings of experienced phenomenon; often, it takes the form of a reflective conversation with the situation" (42). Reflection-in-action captures the principal at work as she or he makes judgments in trying to manage a very messy work context.

Life would be simpler if accepting the paradigm of the Scruffies meant the position of the Neats was false. The reality is that both are true. For simple problems that exist in stable environments under determinate conditions, thinking like a Neat will serve principals well. However, for complex problems that exist in turbulent environments under indeterminate conditions, thinking like a Scruffie makes more sense.

The Importance of Craft Knowledge

In his groundbreaking book *School Administration as Craft,* Arthur Blumberg (1989) uses the metaphor *craft* to provide a refreshing and compelling view of the nature of administrative work that can provide the long-missing bridge between what is known in the mind and experience of successful principals and teachers and the practice situations that they face.

To some, *craft* communicates an endeavor that is low level, perhaps even pedestrian. But Blumberg has in mind the accomplished and prized work of *artisans* that stands out from the work of the amateur hobbyist. This distinction between amateurism and artisanship strengthens the use of the craft metaphor, because although principals and other school administrators do not hold a monopoly on exercising management and leadership, their practice should be qualitatively different.

Blumberg explores the craft concept by describing how the mind, heart, and head of the artisan "potter" working with the "clay" produce something useful. Similarly, the craft of administration "is the exercise in individual fashion of practical wisdom toward the end of making things in a school or a school system 'look' like one wants them to look" (46).

Recognizing that there are certain skills involved in any craft, Blumberg focuses on the kinds of know-how that go beyond just being able to employ these skills. It is this know-how that differentiates the artisan from the more pedestrian amateur, the treasured craft item from the run-of-the-mill trinket.

Attributes associated with artisanship are dedication, experience, personal knowledge of the material, mastery of detail, sense of harmony, integration, intimate understanding, and wisdom (Mintzberg, 1987). Artisans, according to Blumberg (1989), develop a special kind of know-how that is characterized as having a refined "nose" for things; a sense of what constitutes an acceptable result in any particular problematic situation; an understanding of the nature of the materials they work with; a mastery of the basic technology undergirding the craft; skill to employ this technology effectively; and, most important, knowing what to do and when to do it. They make pragmatic (and in the case of educational administration, *moral*) decisions and are able to diagnose and interpret what is occurring as they work in any situation.

In summary, reflective principals practice as artisans by bringing together deep knowledge of relevant techniques and competent application of tried-and-true "rules of thumb" with a feel for their practice and a penchant for reflecting on this practice as they create something of practical utility. Craft knowledge represents an anchor equal to and sometimes superior to theoretical knowledge in making up one's theories of practice and informing one's professional practice. The hallmark of the artisan is the ability to reflect on practice.

The Importance of Theoretical Knowledge

To many readers, the foregoing critique of applied science and particularly the emphasis on the mismatch between theoretical knowledge viewed as singular truth and its subsequent ill-fitting application to practice may seem to suggest that research-based theoretical knowledge is useless. Reaching this conclusion would be a mistake. The issue is not the usefulness of theoretical knowledge, but its presumed truthfulness given the idiosyncratic and dynamic nature of administrative problems and situations. In applied science, for example, theoretical knowledge is used to establish a body of "artificial" professional intelligence. Principals would merely have to diagnose problems they face and draw standard treatments to apply from this intelligence. By contrast, reflective practice seeks to establish "augmented" professional intelligence. The principals themselves would be key aspects of this intelligence. Augmented professional intelligence serves to inform, not replace, the intuitions of administrators as they practice.

Mary Kennedy (1984) speaks of two important ways in which theoretical knowledge can be used in practice: *instrumentally* and *conceptually*. When used instrumentally, theoretical knowledge is presumed to be instructive and the decision as to what to do is relatively straightforward. As Kennedy explains, "Whereas the central feature of the instrumental model is the *decision,* the central feature of the conceptual model is the *human information processor* (principal)"; furthermore, "Whereas a decision may follow automatically from the instructions contained in the evidence, information processors (principals) 'interact' with the evidence, interpret its meaning, decide its relevance, and hence determine when and how they will permit the evidence to influence them" (207–208). Her latter point is key. Scruffies believe that because the principal, not the theoretician or the researcher, is in command of the idiosyncratic nature of the situation, she or he must be in control of the available scientific knowledge.

For Scruffies, managing and leading resemble a game of golf in which the distance to the hole is always changing. You know the hole is straight ahead, but you can never be sure just how far away it is. You have a pretty good understanding of the distances that you can get from each club (club payoff), but you cannot choose a club based on where the hole is at the moment. You must guess where the hole will be after you swing. Knowledge of club payoff remains important in this context, but it cannot be used directly. Instead, this knowledge becomes part of one's conceptual framework for making an educated guess in choosing the right club for an assumed distance. In this game, laws exist that determine where the hole will be next, but they cannot be fully understood.

The better golfers are those who develop an intuitive feel for past, current, and likely patterns of appearance of the hole as the game is played. Their play is neither whimsical nor random. Instead, they make mature, educated guesses (in the case of principals, informed professional judgments). These guesses combined with knowledge of club payoff helps them to win. Being familiar with the topographical features of each of the holes to be played, the play of the greens, the texture of the grass and rough, and the idiosyncrasies of each of the sandtraps yields other pieces of information that might or might not come in handy should a hole pop up here rather than there. Having a firm fix on topography and club payoff is not enough if one cannot develop a feel for the patterns that are likely to emerge. However, and equally as important, being pretty good at predicting the patterns but having little understanding of course topography or club payoff will not be of much help.

The key to reflective practice can be found in William James's 1892 message to the teachers of Cambridge, Massachusetts. He pointed out the importance of "an intermediary inventive mind" in making practical application of scientific knowledge. In his words:

> *The science of logic never made a man reason rightly, and the science of ethics . . . never made a man behave rightly. The most such sciences can do is to help us catch ourselves up and check ourselves, if we start to reason or behave wrongly; and to criticise ourselves more articulately after we have made mistakes. A science only lays down lines within which the rules of the art must fall, laws which the follower of the art must not transgress; but what particular thing he shall positively do within those lines is left exclusively to his own genius. (8)*

The idea of reflective practice is relatively new, and much more thinking needs to be given to its development and use in educational administration. It seems clear, nonetheless, that reflective principals are in charge of their professional practice, They do not passively accept solutions and mechanically apply them. They do not assume that the norm is a one best way to practice, and they are suspicious of easy answers to complex questions. They are painfully aware of how context and situations vary, how teachers and students differ in many ways, and how complex school goals and objectives actually are; they recognize that, despite difficulties, tailored treatments to problems must be the norm.

At the same time, reflective professional practice requires that principals have a healthy respect for, be well informed about, and use the best available theory and research and accumulated practice wisdom. All these sources of information help increase understanding and inform practice.

The rub is that no matter how reflective a principal tries to be, effectiveness will remain elusive if still based on traditional management theory. Management theory itself needs to be reinvented, and that is the theme of the next chapter.

References

Blumberg, Arthur. 1989. *School Administration as Craft.* Boston: Allyn and Bacon.

Hosford, Philip L. 1984. "The Problem, Its Difficulties and Our Approaches," in Philip L. Hosford, Ed., *Using What We Know About Teaching.* Alexandria, VA; Association for Supervision and Curriculum Development.

James, William. 1892. *Talks to Teachers on Psychology: And to Students on Some of Life's Ideals.* New York: Holt.

Kennedy, Mary M. 1984. "How Evidence Alters Understanding and Decisions," *Educational Evaluation and Policy Analysis* 6(3), 207–226.

Mintzberg, Henry. 1987. "Crafting Strategy," *Harvard Business Review* July–August 1987, 66–75.

Schön, Donald A. 1983. *The Reflective Practitioner: How Professionals Think in Action.* New York: Basic Books.

Schön, Donald A. 1984. "Leadership as Reflection in Action," in Thomas J. Sergiovanni and John E. Corbally, Eds., *Leadership and Organizational Culture,* 64–72. Urbana-Champaign, IL: University of Illinois Press.

Schön, Donald A. 1987. *Educating the Reflective Practitioner.* San Francisco: Jossey-Bass.

Toward a New Theory of Management for the Principalship

Leadership.

In Chapter 2 it was pointed out that principals have different practical theories about the nature of human rationality, how schools work, and what really matters to people. The mindscapes of Mystics, Neats, and Scruffies were discussed as examples. These mindscapes determine what principals believe about management and leadership and how they practice as a result. Different mindscapes mean different theories. Different theories mean different approaches to management and leadership and different school improvement strategies.

Not all management and leadership mindscapes, however, are equal. Some fit the world of practice better than others. The better the fit, the more successful the practice will be. This chapter compares the assumptions and principles of traditional management theory, the theory of the Neats, with the scruffy context and problems of school practice that principals and teachers face every day, noting where the theory fits and where it doesn't. The framework for a new theory of management is then proposed as a viable candidate for those instances in which traditional management does not fit. *Both traditional and new theories have important roles to play in bringing about quality schooling providing they are appropriately matched to situations of practice.* Deciding when to use each of the theories requires a level of understanding and skill that is not as widespread as it should be in the principalship.

Changing Mindscapes

Traditional management enjoys official sanction in many state capitols and in many university preparation programs for school administrators. It is also the mindscape that dominates much of the literature on school improvement. It's no surprise, therefore, that this mindscape is entrenched in the thinking of many school principals and is difficult to change.

Consider, for example, the case of elementary school principal Jane. Jane now spends from one-third to one-half of her time trying to be an "instructional leader" as prescribed by a recent state law. This law requires that she evaluate every teacher in her building three times a year, using a state assessment instrument composed of a generic list of 50 teaching behaviors gleaned from dozens of independent research reports on "effective teaching." The instrument is several pages long and involves a good deal of paperwork in addition to one hour of classroom observation for each evaluation. Jane takes her responsibilities seriously and estimates that a conscientious job takes about three hours for each evaluation.

Teachers are required to develop "growth plans," which Jane must monitor as well. The growth plans indicate how each teacher intends to improve her or his teaching and thus earn higher evaluation scores. Jane estimates that she spends 270 hours or 33 days a year just conducting the required evaluations. She dreads the many hours it takes to collect, study, and comment on the growth plans and then figure out sensible, albeit efficient, ways to follow up what teachers claim they will do. She notices that the growth plans are often perfunctory in tone, and this bothers her.

Among Jane's other instructional leadership responsibilities are daily monitoring of teachers to ensure that they follow the district-mandated objectives for each of the subjects or courses taught and that they adhere to the proper time allocations as provided by the mandated schedule. Jane can keep tabs on this process by practicing "management by walking around," but is not able by relying on this process alone to demonstrate concretely to her superiors that her school is in compliance. Seeking to avoid a poor evaluation from her supervisors, Jane requires that teachers indicate the objectives they intend to teach on their daily lesson plans, as well as the amount of time they spend teaching each of these objectives. She dutifully collects these lesson plans each Friday and examines them to be sure that teachers are in compliance. As time permits, Jane tries to write comments on the plans that might result in teachers thinking about their lessons more effectively and teaching better.

In Jane's school district, heavy reliance is placed on the use of criteria-referenced tests that are closely linked to the required objectives. These tests are given periodically, and the results must be submitted to the school district's central office and by that office to the state department of education. The results are then published in the newspaper, with statewide comparisons made district by district and district comparisons made school by school. There is enormous pressure for schools to do well on the test comparisons. If the test scores in her school are not high enough, she hears about it from the superintendent's office.

Sometimes Jane gets the impression that the superintendent wants the scores up at any cost and that all that counts is the bottom line. In turn, she puts enormous pressure on her teachers to be sure that the students do well on the tests. All teachers, for example, have been "inserviced" so that their day-by-day teaching should now be based on a popular teaching model made up of a series of specific steps thought to result in better student achievement. In addition to the evaluation system that is now in place and the monitoring of lesson plans and test scores, Jane spends much of her time coaching and monitoring the teachers to be sure that they are using the required teaching techniques.

In her school, Jane supervises a tightly connected "instructional management system" that seeks to link together measurable objectives, a highly specific curriculum, and required, detailed time schedules with a monitoring system of controls to ensure that teachers are doing what they are supposed to be doing and at the right time. Despite this management system, the results have been frustrating. Although there have been modest gains in test scores, particularly with respect to lower-level skills, a number of problems have emerged. The curriculum is becoming increasingly narrow, absentee rates are up, and Jane worries that teachers are using fewer and fewer of their talents and skills. She shudders at the harshness of the term *deskilled,* but is haunted by its imagery nonetheless.

A number of other "unanticipated consequences" from using this particular instructional management system are emerging. Teachers seem to be teaching more and more to the test. Furthermore, Jane is convinced that they are "showboating" the indicators that appear on the required teacher evaluation instrument when she is present and observing, but not using them at other times. She suspects that she is often observing staged lessons that allow for easy display of the indicators in the teachers' efforts to get higher evaluation scores. Higher scores increase their eligibility for merit-pay-ladder advancement, and, thus, Jane does not begrudge them.

Jane wonders what is wrong. Could Murphy's Law be true? Although from a traditional management perspective Jane can provide evidence that she is doing what she is supposed to, that the required instructional management system is in place, and that (at least overtly) teachers are doing what they are supposed to, Jane feels that appearances do not match reality and that things are just not working well. After much painful soul searching she reaches the conclusion that something different must be done.

This conclusion is very disconcerting for Jane. She feels that she is on the verge of experiencing a professional career crisis that resembles the proverbial "midlife crisis." After all, Jane was an outstanding student during her years of graduate study in educational administration. She took the required workshops offered by the state-sponsored Leadership Development Academy and did so well that last summer she was asked to be an academy trainer. She knows how important such management ideas as POSDCoRB are to providing the kind of rational and efficient management needed for schools to work well. She knows how to demonstrate the leadership behaviors learned in a recent workshop, and last summer she developed workshops of her own on conflict management and on how to conduct a successful conference. She has earned a reputation for knowing how to handle people.

On the walls of Jane's office are displayed several plaques containing sayings of widely accepted management principles. Each of the plaques was given to her as an award for completing one of the Leadership Development Academy's workshops. One says, "If you can't measure it, you can't manage it." Another says, "What gets rewarded gets done." Others remind Jane of the importance of having clear objectives, letting people know exactly what is expected of them, and of being a rational and objective manager.

Jane is surrounded by the dimensions, principles, and expressions of traditional management theory, the theory of the Neats. Furthermore, this theory matches well her own mindscape of what management is, how schools are to operate if they are to function well, and the kind of leadership she should provide as a school principal. Finally, this mindscape is nurtured by the system of rewards in place in her school district. The more her practice reflects traditional management theory, the more successful she is assumed to be. It is no wonder Jane experiences dissonance and anxiety from the realization that it doesn't work very well. Changing one's mindscape is a little like changing one's religion.

In recent months, Jane has come to realize that for traditional management to work, schools need to be more tightly structured and predictable than is typically the case and people need to be more passive and uniform than is typical. At first, she responded to this awareness by continuing to do the same things, only doing them better. But gradually she accepted the reality that *when the world cannot be changed to fit your theory, you had better change your theory to fit the world.* This thought made more sense when she read somewhere about the differences between management and leadership. Management is concerned with doing things right, she remembered. Leadership is concerned with doing right things.

Jane realizes that successful principals are both effective managers and effective leaders. But if one has to choose between the two, the only sensible choice is to do right things, even if it means that you are not doing them in the way specified by the system. Arriving at this decision was an important and courageous milestone for Jane. Although anxious at first, she now feels comfortable with the idea that when bureaucratic and moral authority are in conflict, moral authority must always take precedence.

Jane was not known as a reckless person. Indeed, if anything, she was considered to be quite conventional and conservative in the way she did things. Thus, she began to respond to the looseness she found in the structure of schooling by bending rules and interpreting issues in a fashion that always reflected the spirit of the rule but not the letter. When Jane encountered the system tightening up because her supervisors practiced close supervision, or when she was forced by the system to ignore individual differences in people and situations, she would follow the opposite tack by emphasizing the letter of the rule but not the spirit. Perfunctory execution became part of her management repertoire— a skill she realized that teachers often used to advantage when locked into the same predicament.

During the evaluation of teachers using the standardized system, for example, Jane took liberties with the required procedures by not insisting that all the listed teaching behaviors be displayed by teachers, but only the ones that made sense. She would talk to teachers about what they wanted to accomplish in their lessons and how. She was sensitive to and respectful of the differences in personality that determined their teaching styles. She realized, for example, that reticent teachers had a harder time providing the kind of bubbling reinforcement and feedback that "win points" than did their more outgoing counterparts. Together, Jane and the teachers would look over the four-page list of required teaching behaviors, deciding on the eight or ten behaviors that seemed to make the most sense for the particular teaching episode to be evaluated and in light of particular teaching problems identified. The evaluation was then based on this shorter but more meaningful version.

Whenever Jane's supervisors got wind of what was going on and cracked down on her to comply more specifically with the system, Jane shifted her stratagem by routinely evaluating people with dispatch to save as much time as possible for other things. Once the evaluations were complete and the paperwork filed, Jane and her teachers were able to work more meaningfully and in better ways on the improvement of teaching. Jane is learning fast how to provide leadership in the complex, messy, and nonlinear scruffy world. Her mindscapes of management and leadership theory are changing to match the actual landscapes she encounters in practice.

The Limits of Traditional Management Theory

It would be a mistake for Jane to believe that traditional management theory is useless. She should not abandon it but should, rather, learn how to use it to her best advantage. Traditional management theory has its merits and limitations, and it is important for principals to know the difference.

- Traditional management theory is suited to situations of practice that are characterized by linear conditions. However, the usefulness of this theory ends where *nonlinear conditions* begin.
- Traditional management theory is suited to situations of practice that can be tightly structured and connected without causing unanticipated harmful effects. However, the usefulness of this theory ends where *loosely structured* conditions begin.
- Traditional management theory is suited to situations in which the need exists to bring about a routine level of competence and performance. However, the usefulness of this theory ends when the goal is to bring about *extraordinary commitment and performance.*

Linear and Nonlinear Conditions

When deciding on management and leadership strategies, it is important to take into account the extent to which conditions are or are not *linear.* Linear conditions are characterized by:

Stable, predictable environments
Tight management connections
Loose cultural connections
Discrete goals
Structured tasks
Single solutions
Easily measured outcomes
Sure operating procedures
Determinate consequences of action
Clear lines of authority

Under linear conditions, simplicity, clarity, order, and predictability are present. Examples of administrative tasks that typically fit linear conditions include the routing of bus schedules, purchasing books, planning conference times, and other events and activities in which human interactions are simple, incidental, or nonexistent. Yet, even these tasks can quickly become nonlinear. An eight-inch snowstorm can create havoc with a bus schedule.

By contrast, nonlinear conditions are characterized by:

Dynamic environments
Loose management connections
Tight cultural connections
Multiple and competing goals
Unstructured tasks
Competing solutions
Difficult-to-measure outcomes
Unsure operating procedures
Indeterminate consequences of action
Unclear and competing lines of authority

The vast majority of human interactions that take place in schools can be described as nonlinear. James Gleick writes in *Chaos Making a New Science:* "Nonlinearity means that the act of playing the game has a way of changing the rules" (1987:24). In nonlinear situations every decision that is made in response to conditions at the base time (time 1) changes these conditions in such a way that successive decisions also made at time 1 no longer fit. It is difficult, therefore, for a principal to plan a series of steps, commit to a set of stepwise procedures, or otherwise make progressive management and leadership decisions based on the initial assumptions. When the context changes, the original sequence no longer makes sense. One cannot predict the conditions of time 2 until they are experienced.

Under nonlinear conditions, management resembles following a compass when the position of north changes with each step you take. As Cziko (1989) phrases it: "A process demonstrating chaos is one in which strict deterministic causality holds at each *individual* step in an unfolding process, and yet it is impossible to predict the outcome over any *sequence* of steps in the process." In summary, nonlinear relationships between two events lead to consequences that are unpredictable. Furthermore, if the context for action changes, as is often the case in managing, leading, and teaching, the original sequence no longer makes sense.

Take, for example, application of motivation theories in an effort to increase teacher performance. Providing rewards to a teacher might result in a certain amount of motivation at time 1. This relationship may actually be linear, with the amount of motivation increasing proportionally as rewards are provided at times 2 and 3. However, more rewards can result in less motivation if they are no longer valued, if they are viewed as manipulative, or if they are taken for granted. Moreover, individual differences come to play, so that what person A values differs from person B. Person B may tire more quickly of the same rewards than does person A. While person A might feel manipulated as a result of receiving rewards and respond negatively, person B feels attended to and responds positively.

Although the typical textbook version of traditional management theory would have us believe otherwise, the consequences of using the same motivational strategies for different people and under different conditions typically are indeterminate and unpredictable. Their link to people and consequences is nonlinear. This is the case as well for leadership, conflict resolution, and other categories of management behavior. They are all linked to people and events in nonlinear ways. *The fact is that in management and leadership identical situations and strategies give rise to different outcomes and consequences.*

Peter Vaill (1989) aptly describes the nonlinear context for management as "permanent white water." White water is the frothy, turbulent water found in waterfalls, breakers, and rapids. This metaphor was suggested to Vaill by a manager who observed:

> *Most managers are taught to think of themselves as paddling their canoes on calm, still lakes. They are led to believe that they should be pretty much able to go where they want, when they want, using means that are under their control. . . . But it has been my experience that you never get out of the rapids! . . . there are lots of changes going on at once. The feeling is one of continuous upset and chaos. (2)*

Vaill points out that in management "things are only partially under control, yet the effective navigator of the rapids is not behaving randomly or aimlessly" (2). In summary, it is the dynamic nature of unfolding events resembling "permanent white water" that differentiates linear from nonlinear situations. Successful practice in the latter requires the kind of reflection that enables principals and teachers to constantly test what they know against what is happening.

Tight and Loose Structure

Karl Weick (1976) has argued compellingly for viewing schools as loosely coupled organizations. His point is that whereas aspects of schools are connected to each other in such a way that one influences the other, these connections are often confounded by other connections and are rarely characterized by strong and direct influence. As March and Simon (1958:176) point out, loose coupling does not mean that decisions, actions, and programs in effect are unrelated, but that they are only loosely related to each other.

The issue of school goals and purposes provides a good example. It is generally assumed that there is a tight connection between stated goals and the policies, decisions, and actions that take place in an organization. Yet, the problem is that schools have multiple goals and are expected to achieve them. Sometimes the goals conflict with each other such that making progress toward one means losing progress toward another. Always thinking in terms of discrete goals or even discrete multiple goals with each attended to sequentially, therefore, does not fit the special character of schools' unique value systems. Under nonlinear and loosely structured conditions, schools don't achieve goals as much as they respond to certain values and tend to certain imperatives that ensure their survival over time (Parsons, 1951).

Jean Hills (1982) points out that, rather than discrete goal attainment, school administrators bring to their practice what he calls "pattern rationality." Principals, by his way of thinking, respond to "a conception of a pattern development on a number of mutually limiting dimensions with respective gains in a given area having implications for other areas" (1982:7). Successful principals become surfers, skilled at riding the wave of the pattern as it unfolds. They respond to value patterns when discrete goals are in conflict with each other. Important to this concept of pattern rationality is the principal's concern with the costs and benefits of her or his actions.

Teachers respond similarly. Although the literature overwhelmingly portrays teaching as a rational and linear act whereby teaching behaviors and decisions about instructional materials and time are made in response to objectives and intended outcomes, a glimpse into the real world reveals that these connections are much looser and confounding. Goals and outcomes, for example, are selected as often as a result of available materials as are materials selected as a result of goals. Teaching styles and preferences determine objectives as often as objectives determine teaching styles and preferences. Outcomes become goals as often as goals determine outcomes. Teaching, similar to management, is largely nonlinear and indeterminate. Stated goals and objectives are constantly shifting and changing and are often displaced by others once the teaching begins and as it continues. Indeed, teachers are just as likely to discover their goals during and after their teaching than they are to state them beforehand.

Perhaps the most noticeable example of looseness in schools is the connection of teachers to rules. Principal Jane became aware of this reality the hard way as she tried to implement the required teaching evaluation system. When she was in class observing lessons using the instrument, she saw what she was supposed to because the teachers did what they were supposed to. Yet, when she left the classroom, teachers taught in ways that made sense to them and to their colleagues. They were more tightly connected to values, beliefs, and norms than they were to the imposed management system.

Ordinary and Extraordinary Commitment and Performance

The management and leadership needed to bring about "a fair day's work for a fair day's pay" and for transcending this minimum contract to achieve inspired and extraordinary commitment and performance in schools are different (see, for example, Bass, 1985; Burns, 1978; Hertzberg, 1966; Kelly, 1988; Sergiovanni, 1990). Traditional management theory and practice can provide the former but not the latter. Principal Jane noted, for example, that by practicing traditional management she was able to get teachers to do what they were supposed to but could not get *sustained* and *extraordinary* results.

There are two reasons why traditional management theory and practice are limited to achieving minimums, not maximums. First, the theory is based on bureaucratic and personal authority. Relying on rules, mandates, procedures, regulations, and formal expectations to get someone to do something are examples of bureaucratic authority. When this form of authority is used teachers are expected to comply or else face negative consequences. When principals rely on their human relations skills to get people to comply, they are using personal authority. These skills enable principals to successfully trade meeting needs of teachers for compliance with their wishes. Both bureaucratic and personal authority are external. Teachers are motivated to respond for outside reasons rather than be motivated from within.

External authority works and most teachers and students respond to it. But external authority has the tendency to cause people to respond as *subordinates.* Good subordinates always do what they are supposed to but little else. Transcending ordinary competence for extraordinary commitment and performance requires that people be transformed from subordinates to *followers,* which requires a different kind of theory and practice. Subordinates respond to external authority, but followers respond to ideas, values, beliefs, and purposes. Traditional theory encompasses the former but not the latter.

Second, traditional management theory, with its bureaucratic roots, is heavily biased toward standardization and routinization. Though many aspects of schooling should be routinized, traditional theory seeks to routinize that which should be varied as well. For schools to excel, teachers and administrators need to be concerned with uniqueness and specialness in their interactions with each other and with students. The test of their effectiveness is their ability to ensure that every student is successful in achieving high academic, social, and personal goals—a task that cannot be accomplished by applying a standard recipe for organizing, presenting the curriculum, and engaging in teaching and learning. Standardization and routinization may be the formula for simple work that takes place in a stable environment where modest results are acceptable, but it is not the formula for extraordinary commitment and performance.

Toward a New Theory

To overcome the limits of traditional management and leadership, a new theory for the principalship must be developed—a theory more responsive to nonlinear conditions and loose structuring and that can inspire extraordinary commitment and performance. This theory should not replace but subsume the old. The role of traditional management must change, for example, from being the *strategic model* for developing school policies and practices to being a valued, albeit limited, *tactical option* within a new, more broadly based and powerful management theory. In constructing this new theory, many time-honored principles of traditional management will need to be rethought, expanded, and sometimes even inverted *whenever nonlinear and loosely structured conditions or extraordinary performance requirements are present.* The following subsections discuss examples of such principles. This discussion is brief because the purpose is to outline a set of basic ideas that contrast the two theories. Elaborations and further examples illustrating the principles are provided in subsequent chapters.

The Issue of How Schools Are Structured

The Traditional Rule
Schools are managerially tight but culturally loose.

The Problem
This traditional rule assumes that schools are structured and function much like the mechanical workings of a clock made of cogs and gears, wheels, drives, and pins all tightly connected in an orderly and predictable manner. The task of management is to gain

control of and regulate the master wheel and pin. The principal, for example, might put into place a well-oiled instructional delivery system composed of the "right" teacher evaluation system or the "right" alignment system or some other "right" control mechanism that defines in detail what teachers teach, and when and how. Once the master wheel and pin are under control, all the other wheels and pins will move responsively and the principal's intents will be accomplished.

As Jane came to realize, although many aspects of the school are indeed tightly connected in this clockworks fashion, other aspects are not. Furthermore, teachers and students are more tightly connected to values and beliefs than they are to management systems and rules (see, for example, Deal and Kennedy, 1982; March, 1984; Shils, 1961; Weick, 1982). The more typical view of how schools operate is that of clockworks gone awry—cogs, gears, and pins all spinning independently of each other. Although practices based on managerial tightness and cultural looseness can often get people to do what they are supposed to, the rule casts them in roles as subordinates and thus cannot inspire sustained and extraordinary commitment and performance. Furthermore, it is unable to provide the connections needed among loosely connected parts to get the job done well.

The Alternative
Schools are managerially loose but culturally tight

Karl Weick (1986) pointed out "that indeterminancy can be organized not just by rules, job descriptions, and a priori specifications, but also by such things as shared premises, culture, persistence, clan control, improvisation, memory and imitation." Weick continues:

> *In a loosely coupled system you don't influence less, you influence differently. The administrator . . . has the difficult tasks of affecting perceptions, and monitoring and reinforcing the language people use to create and coordinate what they are doing. . . . Administrators model the kind of behavior they desire . . . identify key issues so they can centralize control over a few (not all) issues and help people see them similarly. Leaders in loosely coupled systems have to move around, meet people face-to-face, and to do their influencing by interaction rather than by rules and regulations. . . . Personnel selection is more crucial than in other systems, because the common premises that are selected into that system will guide how the dispersed activities are executed. (10)*

The Issue of Strategic Planning

The Traditional Rule
Clarity, control, and consensus are important to effective management and are achieved by detailed planning. Therefore:

1. *State measurable outcomes* (indicate specifically what is to be accomplished).
2. *Provide behavioral expectations* (decide and communicate who will do what and how it will be done).

3. *Practice monitoring* (compare expected behavior with observed and correct when necessary).

4. *Measure outcomes* (compare observed outcomes with stated and correct when necessary).

The Problem

There are many paradoxes in management, and planning is one of them. By planning in a linear-stepwise way, one assumes that it is possible to control the future, but often one actually loses control. Detailed plans and surefire objectives take over from people, becoming scripts on the one hand that program future actions and self-fulfilling prophecies on the other that determine our destiny *even when we are no longer interested in either the journey or the destiny.* For linear conditions with tight structures, planning as traditionally conceived is a useful management *tactic* that can achieve the anticipated results, but as a *strategy,* traditional planning locks us into a course of action that often does not make sense once events are underway.

Further planning, as described above, has the tendency to result in the "escalation of commitment" to a course of action that sustains itself irrationally long after the original course of action should have been abandoned (Staw, 1984). Sinking huge sums of money into facilities for the high school's interscholastic sports program makes it difficult to de-emphasize sports even when doing so may be a good idea. Commitment to the teacher evaluation system that took so many hours of planning time to develop is likely to remain firm even in light of evidence that the teaching effectiveness research on which it is based is faulty and teacher morale is suffering as a result.

And, finally, the measurement aspects of traditional planning place severe limits on developing powerful strategies that encourage innovation and excellence. By establishing worth as the consistency that exists between stated and observed outcomes, too many worthwhile outcomes not stated or unanticipated don't count. New priorities and new courses of action are missed and innovation is discouraged—hardly conditions for excellence. Citing a study of planning in 75 corporations that appeared in the *Economist,* Peters (1989a) notes that firms without central planners tended to produce better results. A better strategy, Peters suggests, is that of General Bill Creech of the Tactical Air Command: "Organize as we fight . . . organize in accordance with the human spirit" as a way to best use talents of people, to respond to the idiosyncratic nature of situations, and to build esprit and small-group cohesiveness deep into the enterprise (Peters, 1989a). It appears that planning, the sacred cow of traditional management, needs to be understood differently.

The Alternative

Clarity, control, and consensus are important to effective management and are achieved by planning strategically. Therefore:

1. *Be clear about basic directions* (set the tone and charter the mission).

2. *Provide purpose and build a shared covenant.* (What are our shared goals, values, and operating principles?)

3. *Practice tight and loose management* (hold people accountable to shared values but provide them with empowerment and enablement to decide what to do when and how).

4. *Evaluate processes and outcomes* (be sure that decisions and events embody shared values).

The principles that support this alternative rule are examined in some detail in subsequent chapters. Suffice to say here that in a nonlinear and loosely structured world it makes managerial sense to allow people to make decisions in ways that make sense to them providing that the decisions they make embody shared values and commitments.

The Issue of Where to Fit People into the Improvement Planning Process

The Traditional Rule
When it comes to fitting people in:

1. *First emphasize ends* (determine objectives first).
2. *Then ways* (figure out how you will reach your objectives).
3. *Then means* (identify, train, place, and supervise people).

The Problem
Deciding where to fit people into the planning process influences the outcome in important ways (Hayes, 1985). Should one start with people first or fit them in after work requirements are identified? The traditional ends, ways, and means rule is compatible with a "cannonball" theory of management suitable for stable environments where targets don't move. Unfortunately, as Harry Quadracci (Peters, 1989b) points out, we live in a "cruise missile" world. Cannons are excellent weapons for hitting fixed targets under stable conditions; one need only identify the target (ends), take careful aim calculating distance and wind (ways), and give the order to fire to a well-trained crew (means). A hit is virtually guaranteed. However, hitting moving targets is another matter. Moreover, changing one's mind to enable hitting a better target than the initial one after the cannon has been fired is impossible. Yet, in the world of schooling most of our targets are moving and different and more desirable targets are frequently discovered during the course of our actions. Cannons won't do here. Cruise missiles, to continue Quadracci's admittedly surly metaphor, have built into them the capacity to chase shifting targets and indeed to change targets after they are launched.

The Alternative
When it comes to school improvement

1. *First emphasize means* (concentrate on people first, build them up, increase their commitment, link them to purposes, help them to be self-managing).
2. *Then ways* (let them figure out what to do and how).
3. *Then ends* (they will decide on and achieve objectives that are consistent with shared purposes).

Robert H. Hayes (1985), who proposed this alternative rule, believes that it provides the basis for developing strategies that are more responsive to today's complex world. The key to concentrating on means first is to build up the capacity for people to be self-managing and to connect them to shared values and commonly held purposes. Robert E. Kelly (1988) believes that self-management is an essential ingredient in being a good follower. Followers, he maintains, share a number of essential qualities:

- They manage themselves well.
- They are committed to the organization and to a purpose, principle, or person outside themselves.
- They build up their competence and focus their efforts for maximum impact.
- They are courageous, honest, and credible. (144)

Once followership is built up, the other steps in the alternative rule's chain unfold in a manner that inspires performance and brings about extraordinary results. The traditional rule, by contrast, is based on authority and determinism. The likely result is the establishment of subordination rather than followership in the school, with mediocre rather than extraordinary results.

The Issue of Getting and Maintaining Compliance

The Traditional Rule
To manage compliance:

1. *Identify and announce your goals.* (What are your major objectives?)
2. *Use goals to develop work requirements* (decide how the work will be done).
3. *Use work requirements to develop your compliance strategy* (given the above, determine how you will get people to do what they are supposed to do).
4. *Observe involvement and commitment consequences and correct as necessary.* (Are people properly motivated? If not, determine ways to motivate them.)

The Problem
The organizational theorist Amitai Etzioni (1961) noted that one universal requirement of management is the need to obtain and maintain compliance. By compliance he means how schools get teachers and students involved in their work in the first place and how this involvement is maintained over time. A key point in his theory is that the strategy the manager uses to obtain and maintain involvement has a powerful influence on forming the kind of identification and attachment people have for their work and for the school itself, on shaping the goals of the school, and on the kind and character of work that takes place within the school as goals are pursued. *This is so even when goals and work requirements are set first.* Goals and work requirements are ultimately shaped to fit the means that schools use to get and keep teachers involved in their teaching and to get and keep students involved in their learning. These means then influence the kind and degree of involvement with work and school.

Given this influence, it is too chancy to let the involvement strategy evolve naturally as a result of stated goals and work requirements. Some involvement strategies can actually result in the emergence of dysfunctional school goals and work processes with negative effects. Consider, for example, a prison that has as its goal order among the inmates. To achieve this goal it relies on the establishment of closely monitored daily routines and a system of compliance based on punishment for infractions. As a result, prisoners became alienated and would not choose freely to stay in prison. Alienated involvement reinforces the use of rules and punishment to maintain compliance. Changing the goal for this prison from order to rehabilitation will not likely be accomplished without changing what prisoners do and the means for ensuring compliance with the new system. Prisoners will have to come to see the value of rehabilitation, and the activities they engage in will have to be more meaningful to them.

Etzioni (1961) suggests that the strategies an organization or manager uses to get and keep people involved can be grouped into three broad categories:

1. *Coercive* (People, students, and teachers, for example, are forced by the threat of penalties.)
2. *Remunerative* (People are attracted by the promise of rewards such as money, career advancement, good grades, better working conditions, political advantage, enhanced social standing, and having psychological needs met.)
3. *Normative* (People are compelled because they believe what they are doing is right and good and/or because they find involvement intrinsically satisfying.)

Each of the three compliance strategies results in a particular kind of involvement, which in turn shapes the nature and character of school work and school goals. These relationships are illustrated as follows:

	School A	School B	School C
The School's Dominant Compliance Strategy	*Coercion:* Force people by using bureaucratic controls and penalties for infractions	*Remunerative:* Provide people with rewards in exchange for involvement	*Normative:* Bond people to shared values, beliefs, and norms
Resulting Involvement of Teachers and Students	*Indifferent,* often alienated (they won't be involved unless they have to)	*Calculated* (they will be involved as long as they get something of value back in exchange)	*Moral* (they will be involved because they believe it is the right thing to do)
How the Work of Teaching and Learning Gets Done	*Routinely* (the hand works only)	*Instrumentally* (the mind drives the hand)	*Intrinsically* (Mind, hand, and heart work together)
The Resultant Dominant Goal of Management	*Maintain order* by getting and keeping control	*Barter by making the best deal* and monitoring the deal, patching cracks that appear	*Develop and maintain a strong culture*

Because the choice of compliance strategy is so important in determining what happens, the traditional rule needs to be inverted so that the principal and school begin first by deciding on the compliance strategy they will use.

The Alternative
To manage compliance:

1. *First establish your compliance strategy.* (How do we want to involve people in work and keep them involved? Use the strategy that reflects desired involvement.)
2. *Develop complementary work requirements* (What kind of connections will people need to make for them to be properly involved?)
3. *Decide on work strategy* (Given the connections desired, what kind of work designs and settings do we need?)
4. *Evaluate* (What kind of commitment and involvement is observed? Make adjustments in compliance strategy if necessary.)

Moral involvement has the best chance of ensuring and maintaining inspired commitment and performance from students, teachers, and parents. Commitment to moral involvement does not preclude the occasional use of coercive and remunerative compliance, but it does suggest that the overarching framework for compliance must be normative.

The Issue of Developing a Motivational Strategy

The Traditional Rule
What gets rewarded gets done.

The Problem
This rule works—what gets rewarded does get done. But what happens when rewards are not available to principals, teachers, students, or parents? Unfortunately, the rule's flip side is true, too. What does not get rewarded does not get done.

Relying on rewards to obtain compliance leads to calculated involvement (Etzioni, 1961). Furthermore, this rule has a tendency to change other kinds of work involvement to calculated involvement. A student, for example, might be engaged in a learning activity because of its intrinsic interest. No gold stars, grades, or other external rewards are provided for her or his involvement. Once such rewards are introduced, the student's connection to the learning activity has a tendency to change from intrinsic to extrinsic. Take the rewards away and the student is not likely to engage further in the activity (Deci and Ryan, 1985; Greene and Lepper, 1974). By the same token, teachers who are engaged in certain kinds of activities for moral reasons—that is, because they feel a sense of obligation or believe that something is right or important to do—forsake moral involvement for calculated once rewards (or punishments) are introduced.

The Alternative
What is rewarding gets done, gets done well, and gets done without close supervision or other controls. What we believe in and feel obligated to do because of moral commitments gets done, gets done well, and gets done without close supervision or other controls.

Calculated involvement may be able to get people to do what they are supposed to as long as rewards are forthcoming, but it is not a potent enough strategy to inspire motivation and inspire people to become self-managing, to work without direction or supervision, and to remain engaged in their work even when extrinsic rewards are not available. A new theory of management for the principalship needs to subsume such ideas as what-gets-rewarded-gets-done into a broader motivational strategy that recognizes the importance of morality, emotions, and social bonds (Etzioni, 1988:xii). Although often underplayed and sometimes overlooked in traditional motivation theories, what counts most to people are what they believe, how they feel, and the shared norms and cultural messages that emerge from the small groups and communities with which they identify. Some principals, for example, have refused promotion or transfer because they felt a sense of obligation to see projects they initiated through to conclusion. They gave up extrinsic gains such as higher salaries, career advancement, and more prestige because of the obligation and commitment they had to what they were doing. Parents and teachers routinely sacrifice their own self-interests, wants, and needs to advance those of the children they have responsibility for raising.

Following Etzioni (1988), a new theory of management must provide for the development of motivation strategies that are based on all three motivation rules: what is rewarded gets done, what is rewarding gets done, and what is good gets done. In a new management theory, major emphasis would be given to the latter two. The three rules are depicted in the following chart.

The Rules	Why People Behave	Motivational Type	Involvement
What gets rewarded gets done	Extrinsic gain	Instrumental	Calculated
What is rewarding gets done	Intrinsic gain	Expressive	Intrinsic
What is good gets done	Duty/obligation	Moral	Moral

Controlling Events or Probabilities?

Both traditional and new management and leadership theories are about control. Control is intended to reduce ambiguity and indeterminancy, thus increasing reliability and predictability. For example, both clockworks and clockworks-gone-awry theories want the same thing—to get the cogs and gears moving in reliable and predictable ways. But how this control is sought differs depending on the theory one has in mind. The traditional theory seeks to increase control over events and people, which is a *power over* approach to leadership and management. The new theory, by contrast, seeks to control probabilities—the probability that shared goals and purposes are embodied and reached. This is a *power to* approach to management and leadership. Increasing the probability that shared goals and purposes will be realized means giving up control over events and people.

One important key to seeking and maintaining control is to solve the *coordination paradox*. As Mintzberg (1979) points out:

> *Every organized human activity . . . gives rise to two fundamental and opposing requirements: the* division of labor *into various tasks to be performed and the* coordination *of these tasks to accomplish the activity. The structure of an organization can be captured simply as the sum total of ways in which it divides its labor into distinct tasks and then achieves coordination among them. (2)*

Every school faces the same control problem: How should the work of teaching and learning be divided, and, once divided, how should it be coordinated so that things make sense as a whole? Each person has something important to do, but it must be done in coordination with what others are doing if schools are to work well. As is the case with most problems of control, tackling the coordination paradox would be much easier if schooling was largely the linear and tightly structured world of the Neats and if the goal was to achieve a routine level of competence. All one would need to do would be to practice traditional management leadership. However, in a largely nonlinear, loosely structured Scruffy world with the goal of inspired levels of commitment and extraordinary performance, solving the paradox is more complex. Choosing the wrong control strategy can negatively shape the way teaching and learning takes place.

It is useful to think of six basic control strategies that can be used to help solve the coordination paradox: direct supervision, standardizing the work processes, standardizing outcomes, emphasizing professional socialization, emphasizing purposes, and structuring for collegiality and natural interdependence.* Although all six of the strategies might appropriately be used at one time or another, it makes a difference which of the six or which combination is the school's basic strategy for achieving control.

The key in deciding on an appropriate control strategy is whether it fits the kind and amount of complexity found in the work to be done and in the work environment. *This matching of strategy to complexity of work is critical, for if the strategy used does not fit, the level of complexity will change to match the strategy.* This is a variation of the ominous organizational rule: "Form should follow function or function will be shaped to fit the form." Accordingly, a simple control strategy applied to the normally complex work of teaching will simplify this work, with negative effects on what is learned and how it is learned. The six control strategies are summarized in the following paragraphs.

Direct Supervision

The simplest way to control the work of people who have different responsibilities is by having one of those persons take responsibility for the work of others by providing directions, close supervision, inspection, and otherwise executing the well-known plan-

---

*This discussion of control strategies is based largely on the typology proposed by Mintzberg (1979). His typology reflects the conclusions of March and Simon (1958) and Simon (1957). Important to the discussion as presented here is the work of Peters and Waterman (1982) and Weick (1982). See also Sergiovanni (1987b; 1990).

ning, organizing, controlling, directing, motivating, and evaluating linear chain of management functions. In effect, as Mintzberg (1979) points out, one brain coordinates several hands. This simple approach to control works best for simple work that is done in a routine fashion. Direct supervision may be an appropriate control strategy for a fast-food restaurant, but not for schools where the work of teaching and learning is more complex.

Standardizing Work Processes

Mintzberg (1979) refers to standardizing work processes as coordination achieved on the drawing board before the work is actually undertaken. This strategy works best in jobs that are highly determinant and predictable. Work processes are standardized when what needs to be done is specified in great detail and how one does it is scripted. A "one best way" to get the job done is spelled out. A system of monitoring then is put into place to be sure that the best way is followed. Creating very detailed and tightly connected curriculum and teaching as well as evaluating alignment strategies that make up "instructional delivery systems" are examples of standardizing work processes. This strategy might be appropriate for Federal Express or for a fast-food restaurant, but not for schools where the work of teaching and learning is more complex.

Standardizing Outputs

Standardizing outputs is accomplished by requiring everyone to produce similar products or to reach the same level of performance. In schools we do this by relying heavily on standardized test scores, measurable objectives, and other detailed specifications of outcomes as a way to get people to do what they are supposed to do. Standardizing outputs is different from standardizing work processes in that once the output requirements are set, people are essentially free to decide how they are going to accomplish them.

Providing discretion over means is a strength of this strategy. The question, however, is whether output requirements can be standardized and specified in sufficient detail and at the same time not result in undue narrowing of the curriculum and undue neglect of individual differences. Standardizing the outputs ultimately compromises the degrees of freedom people have with respect to work processes. For example, defining quality schooling as levels of gains on standardized tests may dictate how principals and students will spend time, what they will learn, and how they will learn it to the exclusion of other more suitable or better choices. Many of the problems associated with this strategy would be lessened if goals were viewed as values rather than objectives. Instead of designing down from the outcomes that are specified, the strategy would be to design out from shared values, goals, and commitments, leaving the specifics of "outcomes" and processes up to teachers and others. The only requirement would be that the decisions that they make embody the agreed upon values.

Professional Socialization

By relying on professional socialization, one need not standardize either work processes or outputs and still solve the coordination paradox (Mintzberg, 1979). *Professional so-*

cialization refers to the upgrading and standardizing of the knowledge base for teaching and emphasizing one's professional obligations as a teacher. Once a professional level of training and socialization has been accomplished, teachers and other educational workers will presumably know what to do, when they ought to do it, and how to do it. Professional socialization is the way in which more advanced professions such as medicine solve the coordination paradox. As Mintzberg points out, "When an anesthesiologist and a surgeon meet in the operating room to remove an appendix, they need hardly communicate; by virtue of their respective training, they know exactly what to expect of each other" (7). Though professional socialization has much merit, it is less a strategy available to principals for solving the coordination paradox and more a long-term strategy to upgrade the teaching profession itself. As this upgrading occurs, issues of control will become less difficult to resolve.

Purposing and Shared Values

Karl Weick (1982) noted that in schools

> [A]dministrators must be attentive to the "glue" that holds loosely coupled systems together because such forms are just barely systems. In fact, this border-line condition is their strength, in the sense that it allows local adjustment and storage of novel remedies. It is also their point of vulnerability, because such systems can quickly dissolve into anarchy. . . . The effective administrator . . . makes full use of symbol management to tie the system together. People need to be part of sensible projects. Their action becomes richer, more confident, and more satisfying when it is linked with important underlying themes, values, and movements. (675)

Purposing and shared values provide the "glue" that bonds people together in a loosely connected world. Once common purposes and shared values are in place, they become compass points and mileposts for guiding what is to be done and how. As Selznick (1957) observed, "The need for centralization declines as the homogeneity of personnel increases. . . . [W]hen the premises of official policy are understood and widely accepted, centralization is more readily dispensable." (113).

The strategy is to identify shared values and then design what to do throughout the school from these values. Specific goals and purposes remain the responsibility of teachers and others to decide as long as they embody the values. (Purposing and shared values are key themes in the discussion of community that appears in the next chapter and of leadership in Part II.)

Collegiality and Natural Interdependence

Collegiality refers to the extent common work values are shared and teachers work together and help each other as a result of these values. *Natural interdependence* has to do with the extent to which teachers must work together and cooperate to get the job done properly. In both cases the coordination paradox is solved by the process of informal communications and the need for people to cooperate with each other in order for each person to be successful.

Professional socialization, purposing and shared values, and collegiality and natural interdependence are unique in that they are able to solve the coordination paradox even under nonlinear circumstances and under loosely structured conditions. They do this by providing the kind of normative power needed to get people to meet their commitments. Once people are connected to norms, they are internally motivated to do the right thing—they become self-managing. Beyond the benefit of enhancing self-management, the quality of teaching and learning in a school is at stake. A new theory of management for the principalship must give primary attention to professional socialization, shared values, and collegiality and interdependence as control strategies because they match the complexity of teaching and learning at its best. Relying on the other control strategies, by contrast, does not match the complexity of good teaching and learning. The result is that teaching and learning become simplified as they are shaped by the control strategy. As Mintzberg (1979) notes, direct supervision is effective for simple work, but as work becomes more complex, the emphasis needs to shift from direct supervision to standardizing the work, to standardizing the outputs, and finally to emphasizing professional socialization, purposing, colleagueship, and natural interdependence. Relationships between choice of control strategy and the kind of teaching one is likely to receive is shown in Table 3–1.

When professional socialization, purposing and shared values, and collegiality are emphasized, they function as substitutes for leadership. This means that the principal does not have to provide as much direct leadership as would be the case if other control strategy choices were made. Leadership is much less intense and much more informal as issues of control and coordination take care of themselves naturally.

TABLE 3–1 Control Strategies and Consequences

	Direct Supervision	Standardized Work	Standardized Outputs	Professional Socialization	Purposing and Shared Values	Collegiality and Interdependence
Strategy concept	Simple	Simple	Simple	Complex	Complex	Complex
Management system	Complex	Complex	Moderate	Simple	Simple	Simple
Teachers' behavior	Simple	Simple	Moderate	Complex	Complex	Complex
Authority for leadership	Bureaucratic, psychological	Technical-rational, bureaucratic, psychological	Typically technical-rational psychological	Professional	Moral	Professional, moral

Adapted from Thomas J. Sergiovanni, *Moral Leadership.* San Francisco: Jossey-Bass, 1992, p. 97.

Direct supervision, standardizing work, and standardizing outputs are simple ideas that require complex management systems. For these ideas to work, structures must be in place and roles must be identified and delineated. Furthermore, expectations must be explicit and systems of monitoring must be in place to ensure that everything is functioning properly. As this management system becomes more complex, the discretion of teachers is narrowed. As a result, teaching becomes more simplified, routine, and standardized.

Exactly the opposite is the case with socialization, shared values, and collegiality. These are complex ideas that require very simple management systems to implement. Because of this simplicity, they allow teachers to function in complex ways, which enables them to make more responsive decisions that fit the unique circumstances that they face. In short, complex structures result in simple behaviors, and simple structures result in complex behaviors. Moreover, simple ideas require complex systems for implementation and complex ideas require simple systems. In the first case, teaching becomes simplified; in the second place, teaching is more complex. Understanding these seemingly paradoxical relationships is key to building a new and more effective practice of management for the principalship.

The New Theory and School Organization

Good organization provides the administrative structures, arrangements, and coordinating mechanisms needed to facilitate teaching and learning. What are the implications of the new management theory for how we organize schools?

Some Basic Principles of Organizing

Whatever decisions are made about organizing, the new theory suggests that they should reflect the following basic principles:

1. The principle of *cooperation:* Cooperative teaching arrangements facilitate teaching and enhance learning. Furthermore, they help overcome the debilitating effects of the isolation that currently characterizes teaching. In successful schools, organizational structures enhance cooperation among teachers.
2. The principle of *empowerment:* Feelings of empowerment among teachers contribute to ownership and increase commitment and motivation to work. When teachers feel like pawns rather than originators of their own behavior, they respond with reduced commitment, mechanical behavior, indifference, and, in extreme cases, dissatisfaction and alienation. In successful schools, organizational structures enhance empowerment among teachers.
3. The principle of *responsibility:* Most teachers and other school professionals want responsibility. Responsibility upgrades the importance and significance of their work and provides a basis for recognition of their success. In successful schools, organizational structures encourage teacher responsibility.

4. The principle of *accountability:* Accountability is related to empowerment and responsibility. It provides the healthy measure of excitement, challenge, and importance that raises the stakes just enough so that achievement means something. In successful schools, organizational structures allow teachers to be accountable for their decisions and achievements.
5. The principle of *meaningfulness:* When teachers find their jobs to be meaningful, jobs not only take on a special significance but also provide teachers with feelings of intrinsic satisfaction. In successful schools, organizational structures provide for meaningful work.
6. The principle of *ability-authority:* The noted organizational theorist Victor Thompson (1965) stated that the major problem facing modern organizations is the growing gap that exists between those who have authority to act but not the ability needed for their activism to be most effective, and those who have the ability to act effectively but not the authority to do so. This principle seeks to place those who have the ability to act in the forefront of decision making. In successful schools, organizational structures promote authority based on ability. In schools and school districts where it is necessary for authority to be formally linked to one's position in the organizational hierarchy, day-by-day practice is characterized by formal and informal delegation of this authority to those with ability.

As these principles are manifested in the ways in which schools are organized, schools increase their capacity to respond to their problems, principals are able to lead more effectively, teaching is enhanced, and learning increases.

The Language of Theory

The heart of any theory is the language used to describe and implement it. The words we use shape the way we think about management and leadership. Certain aspects of reality are highlighted and other aspects are covered up. For example, when schooling is described as an "instructional delivery system," our mind automatically thinks about such management issues as delivery, targets, and goals; steps, procedures, and schedules that promise the best delivery routes and timetables; the need to provide clear instructions to the deliverers of instruction; monitoring the delivery process; and evaluating to be sure that what is supposed to be delivered is delivered, and on time.

Getting the Words Right

What seems sensible and true can change when the language we use changes. Try thinking about schooling as a "learning community." What issues now come to mind, and how are they different?

Communities, for example, can be thought of as having "centers" that are repositories of shared values that give direction, order, and meaning to community life. The center is the cultural heart of any community. Edward Shils (1961) explains:

> *The center . . . is a phenomenon of the realm of values and beliefs . . . which govern the society. . . . In a sense, society has an official "religion." . . . The center is also a phenomenon of the realm of action. It is a structure of activities, of roles and persons, within the network of institutions. It is in these that the values and beliefs which are central are embodied and propounded. (119)*

Different management issues emerge from the metaphor of school as a learning community. How will this learning community be defined? What relationships among parents, students, teachers, and administrators are needed for us to be a community? What are our shared values, purposes, and commitments? How shall we work together to embody these? What kinds of obligations to the community should members have? How will obligations be enforced? What "wild cultures" exist (e.g., perhaps a student subculture excessively themed to football, beer, music, and sex; or devoted to mediocre academic performance or to stealing hubcaps; or a faculty subculture more concerned with its own welfare than that of the school) that provide competing and work-restricting norms? How can these wild cultures be "domesticated" and thus subsumed under the overall culture that defines our learning community?

The fact that different management issues emerge from different metaphors for schooling suggests that validity in management and leadership is both subjective and objective. The management concepts, rules, and practices that are valid for schools as learning communities are not valid for schools as instructional delivery systems, and vice versa. Validity is subjective between conceptual systems and objective within (Lakoff and Johnson, 1980). The presence of both subjective and objective validity in management is one reason why it's so hard to have a successful argument with someone who uses a language system different from one's own. Furthermore, it is hard to think differently about leadership, management, and schooling unless you are willing to change your own language system—the metaphors and ultimately the mindscapes that create your reality.

The Power of Language

Another important aspect of the language we use is that it can become a source of power that forces others to think in our terms. This is particularly true in instances in which one person has more hierarchical authority than another. As Greenfield (1982) explains: "Language is power. It literally makes reality appear and disappear. Those who control language control thought—and thereby themselves and others" (8). He maintains that language can be used to dominate others by building categories of thinking and logic that they must use whether they want to or not. Getting others to think in your terms is a powerful form of domination. For example, superintendents who use the language of instructional delivery systems in their protocols for evaluating principals force principals to have to defend themselves in those terms no matter how effective they might be otherwise. A similar fate awaits teachers who are evaluated by principals who control the language of evaluation.

Domination is virtually total when one person not only controls the categories that another has to use but also controls the criteria for defining effectiveness. Imagine, for example, two children about to open their lunchboxes at school. One says to the other, "I bet you a soda that the fruit in my box is better than yours." The youngster then sets the criteria for *better* as follows: The redder the fruit and the rounder the fruit, the better. Unfortunately, the other child's lunchpail contains a banana. Had the second child been the one in control of the language criteria, there would be a different winner.

Winning and losing are functions of the language used (Sergiovanni, 1989a). Lakoff and Johnson (1980) summarize the subjective nature of validity as follows:

> *Truth is relative to understanding, which means that there is no absolute stand-point from which to obtain absolute objective truths about the world. This does not mean that there are no truths; it means that truth is relative to our conceptual system, which is grounded in, and constantly tested by, our experiences and those of other members of our culture in our daily interactions with other people and with our physical and cultural environments. (193)*

Although the power of language is very real, it has not received much attention in the management literature.

One test of the adequacy of the language we use in discussing school theory and practice is whether it is beautiful or not. The language of traditional management theory lacks "aesthetic qualities." Such qualities are one important criterion that Kaplan proposes in his monumental book *Conduct of Inquiry* (1961) for validating theories. More pointedly, Mintzberg (1982) describes the language of traditional management theory as being *ugly*. In his words: "If a theory is not beautiful then the odds are good that it is not very useful" (250). Apply this rule, for example, to determine the "usefulness" of such concepts and ideas as instructional delivery system and learning community, instruction and teaching, training and education, POSDCoRB and purposing, objectives and goals, measuring and valuing, monitoring and coaching, bureaucratic and moral, quality control and obligation, and motivate and inspire.

Changing Our Metaphors

Because traditional management theory does not work well in nonlinear and loosely structured situations or under conditions that require extraordinary commitment and performance, a great deal is at stake in developing a new and better-fitting theory. For this to happen, our metaphors for management, leadership, and schooling must change. Subsuming "instructional delivery system" as a tactical option under the more encompassing and strategic "learning community" is an important beginning. What would schools be like if community was indeed the metaphor of choice? That is the topic of the next chapter.

References

Bass, Bernard M. 1985. *Leadership and Performance Beyond Expectations.* New York: The Free Press.

Burns, James MacGregor. 1978. *Leadership.* New York: Harper & Row.

Cziko, Gary A. 1989. "Unpredictability and Indeterminism in Human Behavior: Arguments and Implications for Educational Research," *Educational Researcher* 18(3), 17–25.

Deal, Terrence E., and Allen A. Kennedy. 1982. *Corporate Cultures.* Reading, MA: Addison-Wesley.

Deci, Edward L., and Richard M. Ryan. 1985. *Intrinsic Motivation and Self Determinism in Human Behavior.* New York: Plenum Press.

Etzioni, Amitai. 1961. *A Comparative Analysis of Complex Organizations.* New York: The Free Press.

Etzioni, Amitai. 1988. *The Moral Dimension Toward a New Economics.* New York: The Free Press.

Gleick, James. 1987. *Chaos Making a New Science.* New York: Viking Penguin.

Greene, David, and Mark R. Lepper. 1974. "How to Turn Play Into Work," *Psychology Today* 8(4).

Greenfield, Thomas B. 1982. "Against Group Mind: An Anarchistic Theory of Education," *McGill Journal of Education* 17(Winter).

Hayes, Robert H. 1985. "Strategic Planning—Forward in Reverse?" *Harvard Business Review* Nov.–Dec.

Hertzberg, Frederick. 1966. *Work and the Nature of Man.* New York: World.

Hills, Jean. 1982. "The Preparation of Educational Leaders: What's Needed and What's Next." UCEA Occasional Paper No. 8303. Columbus, OH: University Council for Educational Administration.

Kaplan, Abraham. 1961. *Conduct of Inquiry: Methodology for Behavioral Sciences.* San Francisco: Chandler.

Kelly, Robert E. 1988. "In Praise of Followers," *Harvard Business Review* Nov.–Dec.

Lakoff, George, and Mark Johnson. 1980. *The Metaphors We Live By.* Chicago: University of Chicago Press.

March, James G. 1984. "How We Talk and How We Act: Administrative Theory and Administrative Life," in T. J. Sergiovanni and J. E. Corbally, Eds., *Leadership and Organizational Culture,* 18–36. Urbana: University of Illinois Press.

March, James G., and Herbert A. Simon. 1958. *Organizations.* New York: Wiley.

Mintzberg, Henry. 1979. *The Structuring of Organizations.* Englewood Cliffs, NJ: Prentice-Hall.

Mintzberg, Henry. 1982. "If You're Not Serving Bill and Barbara, Then You're Not Serving Leadership," in James G. Hunt, Una Sekaran, and Chester Schrlesheim, Eds., *Leadership Beyond Establishment Views,* 239–259. Carbondale: Southern Illinois University.

Parsons, Talcott. 1951. *Toward a General Theory of Social Action.* Cambridge, MA: Harvard University Press.

Peters, Tom. 1989a. "Structure vs. Spirit Battle Lines are Drawn," *San Antonio Light,* July 25.

Peters, Tom. 1989b. "Business Can Learn From Military Strategy," *San Antonio Light,* Jan. 24.

Peters, Thomas J., and Robert H. Waterman. 1982. *In Search of Excellence.* New York: Harper & Row.

Selznick, Phillip. 1957. *Leadership in Administration.* New York: Harper & Row.

Sergiovanni, Thomas J. 1987b. *The Principalship: A Reflective Practice Perspective.* Boston: Allyn and Bacon.

Sergiovanni, Thomas J. 1989a. "Science and Scientism in Teaching and Supervision," *Journal of Curriculum and Supervision* 4(2), 93–106.

Sergiovanni, Thomas J. 1990. *Value-Added Leadership: How to Get Extraordinary Performance in Schools.* New York: Harcourt Brace Jovanovich.

Sergiovanni, Thomas J. 1992. *Moral Leadership.* San Francisco: Jossey-Bass.

Shils, Edward A. 1961. "Centre and Periphery," in *The Logic of Personal Knowledge: Essays Presented to Michael Polanyi.* London: Routledge and Kegan Paul.

Simon, Herbert A. 1957. *Administrative Behavior,* 2nd ed. New York: The Free Press.

Staw, Barry. 1984. "Leadership and Persistence," in T. J. Sergiovanni and J. E. Corbally, Eds., *Leadership and Organizational Culture.* Urbana: University of Illinois Press.

Thompson, Victor A. 1965. *Modern Organizations.* New York: Knopf.

Vaill, Peter B. 1989. *Managing as a Performing Art.* San Francisco: Jossey-Bass.

Weick, Karl E. 1976. "Educational Organizations as Loosely Coupled Systems," *Administrative Science Quarterly* (2), 1–19.

Weick, Karl E. 1982. "Administering Education in Loosely Coupled Schools." *Phi Delta Kappan* 27(2), 673–676.

Weick, Karl E. 1986. "The Concept of Loose Coupling: An Assessment," *Organizational Theory Dialogue,* Dec.

Chapter *4*

The School as a Moral Community

The language we use to talk and write about school leadership influences what we think, experience, and do as principals in the real world. Language shapes the theories we have in our minds. These theories determine what is and what isn't; what counts and what doesn't. After a while, this broad picture of accepted truth about how schools work, how to motivate teachers and students, how to connect everything, how to ensure account-ability, and how to lead becomes second nature. The ideas and principles that comprise this picture of truth become taken-for-granted understandings and beliefs that function as our theories of practice. Theories of practice first determine and then affirm what we do. Our practice is continually reinforced by these theories until it becomes so entrenched that little thought is given to changing. As long as the theories are in place, our practice makes sense. If the theories were to change, however, then our practices would no longer make sense.

High school principal Sam, for example, was recently relieved of his position, "demoted" to assistant principal, and transferred to one of the district's junior high schools for violating teacher evaluation procedures. Teachers are required to be evaluated with a state-mandated instrument while teaching a specific, 50-minute lesson. The instrument contains roughly 50 teaching behaviors thought to embody best practice. Teachers are supposed to demonstrate the behaviors as they teach. During evaluation, the principal's job is to make a record of the number of behaviors the teacher demonstrates in the observed lesson, and to note whether the observed behaviors are of exceptional or ordinary quality. The evaluations must be conducted according to a specific timetable, and the appropriate paperwork must be properly completed and appropriately filed.

While evaluating Betty, Sam never got around to formally sitting in her classroom with the required instrument and conducting the evaluation for the required 50 minutes. He did, however, informally visit Betty's classroom on numerous occasions and was well aware of her teaching style. When Betty reminded Sam that the required formal evaluation had never been conducted, he panicked. The deadline had already passed and no paper-work had been sent to the central office. With Betty's permission, Sam completed an evaluation using actual examples of teaching he had observed over the semester. Betty signed the form and Sam sent it up the chain. Sam was disciplined because he completed and filed Betty's evaluation forms without making the required formal observation.

Sam might have gotten away with this "alteration" of procedures, but the central office caught on to what had happened. Violating established teacher evaluation proce-dures was judged to be a serious enough matter to warrant demoting and transferring Sam. Furthermore, two other principals had committed similar violations of teacher evaluation rules and regulations and were disciplined in the same way. Consistent enforcement, the district reasoned, is a cardinal principle of good management. Rules must be universally applicable and consistently enforced with the same consequences—a point reinforced by the district's legal counsel.

A *Sun Times* newspaper columnist expressed approval of the school district's decision to discipline Sam. He pointed out that principals must be held accountable for taking care of school business and "that includes paperwork, too." Removing and transferring Sam, he noted, sends a clear message to the 60 other principals in the district that regulations and rules apply to everyone equally—no "ifs," "ands," or "buts." This stance is necessary, the columnist argued, to ensure that favoritism and politics would not influence school district decisions. The columnist concluded by pointing out that in the future principals will have to "remember their p's and q's if they hope to keep their jobs."

From one perspective it is hard to fault the school district for removing Sam from the principalship and transferring him to an assistant principal's post at another school. After all, violating teacher evaluation procedures is serious business. Rules are rules and they must be followed. Consistency is important to maintain discipline; everyone must be treated the same. Individual circumstances simply cannot be taken into account or the system will fall apart. This is just the way it is—in every respect this is good management. That is, this is what good management is as defined and understood by the theory that now dominates how we think and what we do.

Sam was appointed principal of the high school a year ago. In just one short year, a certain magic had occurred at this school. A second *Sun Times* columnist observed that "a few teachers don't like him because he insists that they help determine the direction of the school." Yet, Sam is known by most of the teachers and nearly all the students as a loving and devoted principal. He is generally recognized throughout the community as an outstanding principal. Another article in the *Sun Times* noted that parents and students credit Sam with transforming morale at the high school by taking a personal interest in students and instilling a positive attitude. The article quotes a student as saying, "He knows most of us on a first-name basis, and he'll call you personally."

In a *Sun Times* editorial entitled "What Are Our Priorities: Paper or People?", it was reported that about 200 parents and students appeared at the school board meeting to show their support for Sam. The editorial stated: "In this day of gangs and dropouts, how many inner-city schools would have such a turnout of students and their families to back a principal? When someone inspires students and helps them care about school, should a paperwork infraction bring that special relationship to a halt?" Given the theory that now defines what school management is and how it works, the answer to that question is yes.

A paperwork infraction should indeed bring this special relationship to a halt. Moreover, because the two other principals got the same treatment for doing the same thing, the school had no choice in this matter.

Receiving a different answer to the question requires a change in the theory itself. If, for example, schools were understood as communities rather than formal organizations, Sam's story would be quite different.* Universal rules and consistent application of rules, for example, are not that important in communities. Each case is more likely to be treated individually. Communities are more likely to place values over rules and to evaluate situations in a more open-ended way than was the case with Sam. Indeed, if schools were understood as learning communities and caring communities Sam might even emerge as a hero rather than a villain. Whether a principal is considered to be a hero or a villain, it seems, is a function of the theory that is used to define and prescribe appropriate practice.

The metaphor of choice for understanding schools is organization. Schools are considered to be formal organizations, professional organizations, organic organizations, and other kinds of organizations. Furthermore, what occurs in schools is understood as organizational behavior.

The term *to organize* provides a good idea about how this metaphor shapes how we think about schools. To organize means to arrange things into a coherent whole. To do this, we have to have a reason for organizing. Then we need to study each of the parts that must be organized. This requires grouping the parts mentally into some kind of logical order. We then need to develop a plan that enables the parts to be arranged properly. As this plan is being followed, it becomes important to monitor our progress and to make any necessary corrections. Finally, when the work is completed, we need to evaluate these organizational arrangements in terms of our original intentions. These principles seem to apply to anything we organize—whether it be our clothes closet, the marine corps, or our schools.

John Meyer (1984) notes that all organizations must develop explicit management structures and procedures in order to give a convincing account to their relevant publics that the proper means-ends chains are in place to accomplish their stated purposes. To do this, schools organize themselves into departments and grade levels, develop job descriptions, construct lock-step curriculum plans, and put into place explicit instructional delivery systems of various kinds. Not only must schools communicate to their relevant publics that they know what they are doing, they must convince everyone that school administrators are in control. They do this with rules and regulations, monitoring and supervision of teachers, and other regulatory means. Not surprisingly, teachers adopt the same schemes to control students.

One assumption that is common to organizations is that hierarchy equals expertise. It is taken for granted that those higher in the hierarchy know more about teaching and learning and other matters of schooling than those lower. This is why each person in a school or school district is evaluated by the person at the next higher level. Those higher in the hierarchy are also trusted with more responsibility—more authority and less supervision than those lower. The implicit corollary is that those at the bottom of the

---

*The argument for changing the metaphor for school from organization to community is summarized from Thomas J. Sergiovanni, *Building Community In Schools* (San Francisco: Jossey-Bass, 1994).

hierarchy must be less concerned. What else could be the reason for why they are given less responsibility, less authority, and more supervision? Organizations, it appears, equate hierarchy with moral superiority.

When formal organizations are first created, people are in control. But as time goes by, organizations have a way of becoming separated from people—functioning independently in pursuit of their own goals and purposes. This separation has to be bridged somehow for things to work. Ties have to exist that connect people to their work and that connect them to each other. In schools understood as organizations, the ties that connect teachers and students to each other and to their work are contractual. Each person acts separately in negotiating a settlement with others and with the school that best meets her or his needs.

Organizations assume that everyone is motivated by self-interest; everyone is out to maximize their gains and cut their losses. Thus, in order for principals to get teachers to do what needs to be done, rewards and punishments must be traded for compliance. Teachers who teach the way they should receive good evaluations. Good evaluations lead to better assignments and improved opportunities for promotion. Teachers who are cooperative are on the school's information loop and are more likely to get picked to attend workshops and conferences. A similar pattern of trading rewards and punishments for compliance characterizes the relationships that exist between students and teachers, and students and their schools.

Leadership in schools that act as formal organizations takes the form of bartering. Principals and teachers, and teachers and students, strike bargains with each other. One gives to the other something in exchange for compliance. As a result, everyone becomes connected to their work for calculated reasons. Students behave and study as long as they receive desired rewards or as long as punishments are stiff and enforceable. Teachers respond pretty much for the same reasons. When rewards are no longer available, or no longer desired, everyone is likely to give less effort in return.

The Community Metaphor

Formal organizations are very much a part of our society, but not all collections of people are formal organizations. Families, neighborhoods, friendship networks, and social clubs, for example, are different. They might more appropriately be thought of as communities. Because of these differences, the practices that make sense in organizations are not appropriate in communities. Communities, too, are concerned with ties and connections. People have to be connected to purposes and to each other for communities to work. Yet, connections in communities are based on commitments not contracts. Teachers, for example, are expected to do a good job not so they can reap rewards from administrators, but because it is important to do so. Discipline policies are norm-based in communities, not rule-based as in organizations. They are not based on trading rewards and punishments for the right behavior, but on what is considered to be right and wrong, obligations and commitments, and moral agreements and social contracts. Students are not bribed to work, but are compelled.

Communities are organized around relationships and the felt interdependencies that nurture them (Blau and Scott, 1962). They create social structures that unify people and that bind them to a set of shared values and ideas. They are defined by their centers of values, sentiments, and beliefs that provide the needed conditions for creating a sense of "we" from "I."

In communities, members live their lives with others who have similar intentions. In organizations, relationships are constructed by others and become codified into a system of hierarchies, roles, and role expectations. Both organizations and communities must deal with issues of control, but instead of relying on external control measures, communities rely more on norms, purposes, values, professional socialization, collegiality, and natural interdependence. As the ties of community become established in schools, they become substitutes for formal systems of supervision, evaluation, and staff development. They become substitutes as well for the management and organizational schemes that seek to "coordinate" what teachers do and how they work together. Finally, they become substitutes for leadership itself.

The ties of community also redefine how empowerment and collegiality are understood. In organizations, empowerment is understood as having something to do with shared decision making, site-based management, and similar schemes. Within communities, empowerment focuses less on rights, discretion, and freedom, and more on commitments, obligations, and duties that people feel toward each other and toward the school. Collegiality in organizations results from administrative arrangements, such as variations of team teaching that force people to work together and team-building skills of principals. In communities, collegiality is something that comes from within. Community members are connected to each other because of felt interdependencies, mutual obligations, and other emotional and normative ties.

A Theory of Community

Community often means different things in different disciplines. Sociologists speak of the African-American community, political scientists of the rural community, theologians of the spiritual community, and psychologists of the emotional community. To capture the spirit of these various uses, this author defines community as follows: Communities are collections of individuals who are bonded together by natural will and who are together bound to a set of shared ideas and ideals. This bonding and binding is tight enough to transform them from a collection of "I"s into a collective "we." As a "we," members are part of a tightly knit web of meaningful relationships. This "we" usually shares a common place and over time comes to share common sentiments and traditions that are sustaining.

The theory of *gemeinschaft* and *gesellschaft* can help us to understand this definition and the forms it might take as schools become communities. *Gemeinschaft* translates to community and *gesellschaft* to society. Writing in 1887, Ferdinand Tonnies (1957) used the terms to describe the shifting values and orientations that were taking place in society as we moved first from a hunting and gathering society, to an agricultural society, and then on to an industrial society. Each of the societal transformations he described resulted in a shift away from *gemeinschaft* toward *gesellschaft;* that is, away from a vision of life as a sacred community toward a more secular society. Although *gemeinschaft* and *gesellschaft* do not exist in pure form in the real world, both are metaphors that bring to mind two "ideal types," two different ways of thinking and living, two different types of cultures, and two alternative visions of life.

Tonnies's basic argument was that as society moves toward the *gesellschaft* end of the continuum, community values are replaced by contractual ones. Among any collection of people, for example, social relationships do not just happen, they are willed. Individuals decide to associate with each other for reasons, and the reasons why they decide to associate are important. In *gemeinschaft,* natural will is the motivating force. Individuals decide to relate to each other because doing so has its own intrinsic meaning and significance. There is no tangible goal or benefit in mind for any of the parties to the relationship. In *gesellschaft,* rational will is the motivating force. Individuals decide to relate to each other to reach some goal, to gain some benefit. Without this benefit the relationship ends. In the first instance, the ties among people are thick and laden with symbolic meaning; they are moral ties. In the second instance, the ties among people are thin and instrumental; they are calculated ties.

The modern formal organization is an example of *gesellschaft.* Within the organization, relationships are formal and distant, having been prescribed by roles and expectations. Circumstances are evaluated by universal criteria as embodied in policies, rules, and protocols. Acceptance is conditional. The more a person cooperates with the organization and achieves for the organization, the more likely she or he will be accepted. Relationships are competitive. Those who achieve more are valued more by the organization. Not all concerns of members are legitimate; legitimate concerns are bound by roles rather than needs. Subjectivity is frowned upon and rationality is prized. Self-interest prevails. It is these characteristics that undergird our present policies with respect to how schools are organized, how teaching and learning take place, how students are evaluated, how supervision is practiced, how principals and students are motivated and rewarded, and what leadership is and how it works. *Gesellschaft* values make sense in getting such formal organizations as a corporation, army, research university, and hospital to work effectively. Applying the same values to the family, rural church, neighborhood, social club, and school, however, raises important epistemological questions. Because, for example, what is considered to be true with respect to school practices depends on the theory that defines it as truth in the first place, we run the risk of creating standards of practice that might otherwise be considered inappropriate.

Gemeinschaft

Gemeinschaft, according to Tonnies, exists in three forms: community by kinship, of place, and of mind. Community by kinship characterizes the special kinds of relationships among people that create a unity that is similar to that found in families and other closely knit collections of people. Community of place characterizes sharing a common habitat or locale. This type of sharing with others for sustained periods of time creates a special identity and a shared sense of belonging that connects people together in special ways. Community of mind emerges from the binding of people to common goals, shared values, and shared conceptions of being and doing. Together, the three forms represent webs of meaning that tie people together by creating a special sense of belonging and a strong common identity.

As schools struggle to become communities, they need to address questions such as the following: What can be done to increase the sense of kinship, neighborliness, and collegiality among the faculty of a school? How can the faculty become more of a professional community where everyone cares about each other and helps each other to grow, to learn together, and to lead together? What kinds of relationships need to be cultivated with parents that will enable them to be included in this emerging community? How can the web of relationships that exist among teachers and between teachers and students be defined so that they embody community? How can teaching and learning settings be arranged so that they are more like a family? How can the school, as a collection of families, be more like a neighborhood? What are the shared values and commitments that enable the school to become a community of mind? How will these values and commitments become practical standards that can guide the lives community members want to lead, what community members learn and how, and how community members treat each other? What are the patterns of mutual obligations and duties that emerge in the school as community is achieved?

Although not cast in stone, community understandings have enduring qualities. These understandings are taught to new members, celebrated in customs and rituals, and embodied as standards that govern life in the community. Furthermore, they are resilient enough to survive the passage of members through the community over time. As suggested by Bellah and his colleagues (1985), enduring understandings create a fourth form of community—community of memory. In time, communities by kinship, of place, and of mind become communities of memory by providing members with memories of common images and common learnings. Being a part of a community of memory sustains us when times are tough, connects us when we are not physically present, and provides us with a history for creating sense and meaning.

The Importance of Relationships

The web of relationships that stand out in communities are different in kind than those found in more *gesellschaft* organizations. They are more special, meaningful, and personalized. They result in a quality of connectedness that has moral overtones. In addition, because of these overtones, members feel a special sense of obligation to look out for each other.

It is generally acknowledged that quality of relationships is an important ingredient in the make-up of a good school. A recent report issued by the Institute for Education and Transformation (1992) at the Claremont Graduate School, for example, points to quality of relationships and other relationship themes as the critical leverage point for school improvement. The quality of relationships determine the quality of the school. Or, in the words of Claremont president John Maguire, "If the relationships are wrong between teachers and students, for whatever reason, you can restructure until the cows come home, but transformation won't take place" (Rothman, 1992:1).

The Claremont researchers spent 18 months studying four culturally diverse schools—two elementary, one middle, and one high school. They interviewed students, teachers, custodians, secretaries, cafeteria workers, parents, and others inside the schools. More than 24,000 pages of data were collected and analyzed. "Our data strongly suggest that the heretofore identified *problems* of schooling (lowered achievement, higher dropout rates, and problems in the teaching profession) are rather *consequences* of much deeper and more fundamental problems" (Institute, 1992:11). These deeper, more fundamental problems pointed to seven major issues that surfaced repeatedly throughout the study. Relationship themes are embedded in each of these issues with relationships themselves being considered most important. The seven issues, as summarized from the institute's report, are presented on the following pages.

1. **Relationships**—*Participants feel the crisis inside schools is directly linked to human relationships. Most often mentioned were relationships between teachers and students. Where positive things about the schools are noted, they usually involve reports of individuals who care, listen, understand, respect others and are honest, open and sensitive. Teachers report their best experiences in school are those where they connect with students and are able to help them in some way. They also report, however, there is precious little time during the day to seek out individual students. . . . Students of color, especially older students often report that their teachers, school staff and other students neither like nor understand them. Many teachers also report they do not always understand students ethnically different than themselves. When relationships in schools are poor, fear, name calling, threats of or incidents of violence, as well as a sense of depression and hopelessness exist. This theme was prominently stated by participants and so deeply connected to all other themes in the data that it is believed this may be one of the two most central issues in solving the crisis inside schools.*

2. **Race, culture, and class**—*A theme which ran through every other issue, like that of relationships, was that of race, culture and class. This is a theme with much debate and very little consensus. Many students of color and some Euro-American students perceive schools to be racist and prejudiced, from the staff to the curriculum. Some students doubt the very substance of what is being taught. . . . Teachers are tremendously divided on such issues. Some are convinced that students are right about racism, others are not. . . . Students have an intense interest in knowing about one another's culture but receive very little of that knowledge from home or school.*

3. **Values**—*There are frequently related conversations in the U.S. that suggest people of color and/or people living in economically depressed areas hold different basic values than others, and that it is these differences which create conflicts in schools and society. While cultural differences clearly do exist in the expression or prioritization of values, our data hold no evidence that people inside schools have significantly different fundamental values. Our data suggest that parents, teachers, students, staff and administrators of all ethnicities and classes, value and desire education, honesty, integrity,*

*beauty, care, justice, truth, courage and meaningful hard work. Participants'
writings and transcripts of discussions are filled with references to basic
values. However, very little time is spent in classrooms discussing these
issues and a number of restrictions exist against doing so. In the beginning
of our research many participants initially assumed other participants held
different values. The more we talked, the more this assumption was challenged. Students desire a network of adults (parents and teachers) with
whom they can "really talk about important things," and want to have these
conversations about values with one another.*

4. **Teaching and learning**—*Students, especially those past fifth grade, frequently report that they are bored in school and see little relevance of
   what is taught to their lives and their futures. Teachers feel pressure to teach
   what is mandated and sometimes doubt its appropriateness for their students. Teachers also are often bored by the curriculum they feel they must
   teach. . . . Students from all groups, remedial and advanced, high school to
   elementary, desire both rigor and fun in their schoolwork. They express
   enthusiasm about learning experiences that are complex but under-
   standable, full of rich meanings and discussions of values, require their own
   action, and those about which they feel they have some choice.*

5. **Safety**—*Related to disconnected relationships and not knowing about one
   another's differences is the issue of safety. Very few participants on campus
   or parents feel schools are safe places. This is particularly true in our middle
   school and high school. Teachers, students and staff fear physical violence.
   The influence of drugs, gangs and random violence is felt by students.
   Students feel physically safest inside classrooms and least safe in large
   gatherings between classes or traveling to or from school.*

6. **Physical environment**—*Students want schools that reflect order, beauty,
   space and contain rich materials and media. The desire for clean, aestheti-
   cally pleasing and physically comfortable spaces is expressed by all. The
   food served to students is a persistent complaint. Many would like foods
   more typical of their homes and home cultures. The lack of any significant
   personal space such as lockers is problematic to students and also leads to
   feelings of being devalued. The depressed physical environment of many
   schools, especially those in lower socioeconomic areas, is believed by participants to reflect society's lack of priority for these children and their
   education.*

7. **Despair, hope, and the process of change**—*Many participants feel a hopelessness about schools that is reflected in the larger society and in the music
   and art of our youth. Paradoxically, hope seemed to emerge following
   honest dialogues about our collective despair. Participants are anxious for
   change and willing to participate in change they perceive as relevant. We
   have strong indications that change inside schools might best be stimulated
   through participatory processes. In these self-driven research processes,
   participants came to openly discuss their hopes and dreams. Through this
   process, we understood there were shared common values around which we
   could begin to imagine a more ideal school. (12–16)*

The problematic relationships described in the report are the kinds of relationships that seem inevitably to evolve whenever schools are viewed as formal organizations. Furthermore, it is not likely that relationships will improve in schools unless this view is abandoned in favor of community.

The Pattern Variables

The sociologist Talcott Parsons (1951) used Tonnies's concepts of *gemeinschaft* and *gesellschaft* to describe different types of social relationships. He argued that any relationship can be described as a pattern that comprises five pairs of variables that represent choices between alternative value orientations. The parties to this relationship, for example, have to make decisions as to how they will orient themselves to each other. When taken together, these decisions represent a pattern giving rise to Parsons's now famous "pattern variables." The pairs of variables that comprise this pattern are now familiar to us:

  affective–affective-neutrality
  particularism–universalism
  diffuseness–specificity
  ascription–achievement
  collective orientation–self-orientation

In schools, for example, principals, teachers, and students have to make decisions about how they will perform their respective roles in relationship to others. Teachers have to decide: Will relationships with students be similar to a professional expert who treats students as if they were clients (affective-neutrality)? Or, will relationships be similar to a parent, with students treated as if they were family members (affective)? Will students be given equal treatment in accordance with uniform standards, rules, and regulations (universalism)? Or, will students be treated more preferentially and individually (particularism)? Will role relationships and job descriptions narrowly define specific topics for attention and discussion (specificity)? Or, will relationships be considered unbounded by roles and thus more inclusive and holistic (diffuseness)? Will students have to earn the right to be regarded as "good" and to maintain their standing in the school (achievement)? Or, will students be accepted completely, simply because they have enrolled in the school (ascription)? Do we decide that a certain distance needs to be maintained for professional interests and concerns to remain uncompromised (self-orientation)? Or, do we view ourselves as part of a student–teacher "we" that compels us to work intimately with students in identifying common interests, concerns, and standards for decision making (collective orientation)?

Parsons believed that the five pairs of pattern variables, when viewed as polar opposites on a continuum, can be used to evaluate the extent to which social relationships in an enterprise resemble communities or resemble more *gesellschaft*-like organizations. For example, although no school can be described as emphasizing one or another of the variables all the time or as never emphasizing any of the variables, schools can be fixed on this continuum based on the relative emphasis given to each of the polar opposites.

This fixing across several pairs of variables can provide us with a kind of cultural "DNA" (a pattern of variables in Parsons's language) that can be used to place the school on a *gemeinschaft–gesellschaft* continuum. (See Appendix 4–1 for an assessment that can be used to evaluate your school on this continuum.)

In addition to Parsons's five variables, two other "polar opposites" are worth considering: substantive and instrumental, and altruistic love and egocentric love. Substantive and instrumental speak to the issue of means and ends. In organizations a clear distinction is made between means and ends communicating an instrumental view of human nature and society. In communities these distinctions are blurred; ends remain ends, but means are also considered ends.

Altruistic love and egocentric love address the issue of motivation. Like Tonnies, Mary Rousseau (1991) believes that it is the motives that bring people together that are key in determining whether community will be authentically achieved. To her it is altruistic love that is the deciding factor. Altruistic love is an expression of selfless concern for others that stems from devotion or obligation. It is more cultural than psychological. Egocentric love, more characteristic of organizations, is self-gratifying. Relationships are implicit contracts for the mutual exchange of psychological satisfactions.

Taken together, the seven pairs of variables portray different ties for connecting people to each other and for connecting them to their work. In school as community:

- Relationships are both close and informal.
- Individual circumstances count.
- Acceptance is unconditional.
- Relationships are cooperative.
- Concerns of members are unbounded and, therefore, considered legitimate as long as they reflect needs.
- Subjectivity is okay.
- Emotions are legitimate.
- Sacrificing one's self interest for the sake of other community members is common.
- Members associate with each other because doing so is valuable as an end in itself.
- Knowledge is valued and learned for its own sake, not just as a means to get something or go somewhere.
- Children are accepted and loved because that's the way one treats community members.
- The bonding of relationship ties helps the school become a community by kinship and a community of place.
- The binding of idea ties helps the school become a community of mind.

In time, these collective sentiments bring people together as a community of memory and sustain them even when they become separated from each other.

Finding the Right Balance

It would be a mistake to take an either-or stance when selecting a framework for understanding schools. Doing so would create a false dichotomy between *gemeinschaft* and *gesellschaft.* Still, the use of ideal types is useful. The use of polar opposites along a common continuum is a strategy with a long tradition in sociology. *Gemeinschaft* and *gesellschaft* represent ideal types that do not exist in the real world in pure forms. They are, as Weber (1949) pointed out, polar mental representations that can help us categorize and explain on the one hand and track movement along a common continuum on the other. Thus, schools are never *gemeinschaft* or *gesellschaft;* they possess characteristics of both.

Although most schools are currently too *gesellschaft* and we need a realignment in favor of *gemeinschaft,* it is important to recognize that the *gesellschaft* perspective is both valuable and inescapable. We live, after all, in a *gesellschaft* world—a society characterized by technical-rationality, which has brought us many gains. Without *gesellschaft* we would not have a successful space program or heart transplant technology. Nor would we have great universities, profitable corporations, and workable governmental systems. There would be no hope of cleaning up the environment, and as a nation we would not be able to defend ourselves.

Yet, we need to decide which theory should dominate which spheres of our lives. Most everyone will agree that the family, the extended family, and the neighborhood should be dominated by *gemeinschaft* values. The corporation, the research laboratory, and the court system, however, might well lean more toward *gesellschaft* values. In modern times, the school has been solidly ensconced in the *gesellschaft* camp with unhappy results. It's time that the school was moved from the *gesellschaft* side of the ledger to the *gemeinschaft.*

Implications for School Management and Leadership

What are the implications of a theory of community for how we understand schools and how we arrange teaching and learning? With community as the theory, we would have to restructure in such a way that the school itself is not defined by brick and mortar, but by ideas and relationships. Creating communities by kinship and of place, for example, might well mean the dissolution of the high school as we now know it into several small schools rarely exceeding 300 or so students. The importance of creating sustained relationships would require that students and teachers stay together for longer periods of time. Teaching in 50-minute sessions would have to be replaced with longer blocks of time. The curriculum would have to be retaught to accommodate a new schedule. Elementary schools would have to give serious consideration to organizing themselves into smaller and probably multi-age families. Discipline problems would no longer be based on psychological principles but moral ones, which would require abandoning such taken-for-granted notions as having explicit rules linked to clearly stated consequences that are uniformly applied in favor of the development of social contracts, constitutions, and normative codes. Inservice and staff development would move from the administrative side of the ledger to the teacher side as part of their ongoing commitment to practice at the edge of their craft. Extrinsic reward systems would have to disappear. The number of specialists would likely be reduced and pull-outs would be less common as families of teachers and students, similar to families of parents and children, take fuller responsibility for solving their own problems. Finally, all these changes would necessitate the invention of new standards of quality, new strategies for accountability, and new ways of working with people—that is, the invention of a new educational administration.

These and other issues associated with changing the metaphor for the school from formal organization to community are explored in subsequent chapters. Important to those discussions is the changing nature of the principal's role and the need to develop a new definition of what leadership is and how it works. It is argued that as community takes hold in schools, the principal emerges as a true leader.

References

Bellah, Robert N., Richard Madsen, William M. Sullivan, Ann Swidler, and Steven M. Tipton (1985). *Habits of the Heart: Individualism and Commitment in American Life.* New York: Harper & Row.

Blau, Peter M. and W. Richard Scott. 1962. *Formal Organizations: A Comparative Approach.* San Francisco: Chandler Publishing Co.

Institute for Education and Transformation. 1992. "Voices from the Inside. A Report on Schooling from Inside the Classroom, Part I: Naming The Problem," Claremont, CA: The Claremont Graduate School.

Meyer, John. 1984. "Organizations as Ideological Systems" in T. J. Sergiovanni and J. E. Corbally, Eds., *Leadership and Organizational Culture,* pp. 85–114. Urbana: University of Illinois Press.

Parsons, Talcott. 1951. *The Social System.* Glencoe, IL: Free Press.

Rothman, R. Dec. 2, 1992. "Study 'From Inside' Finds a Deeper Set of Problems," *Education Week 12*(13).

Rousseau, Mary F. 1991. *Community: The Tie That Binds.* New York: University Press of America.

Sergiovanni, Thomas J. 1994. *Building Community in Schools.* San Francisco: Jossey-Bass.

Tonnies, Ferdinand. 1957. *Community and Society (Gemeinschaft und Gesellschaft).* (C. P. Loomis, trans. and ed.) New York: Harper & Row. (Originally published 1887.)

Weber, Max. 1949. *The Methodology of the Social Sciences.* (Edward A. Shils and Henry A. Finch, trans.) Glencoe, IL: Free Press.

Appendix 4–1   Profiles of Community: Assessing
Organizational and Community Values

The quality and kind of relationships that exist in a school provide an indication of the extent to which a school is oriented toward community values. Though no school can be described as emphasizing community values all of the time or never emphasizing community values, schools can be fixed on *gemeinshcaft-gesselschaft* continuum based on the relative emphasis given to each of the polar opposites.*

Below the five pairs of pattern variables posed by Parsons (1951) and two other pairs that are closely related to the original five are discussed by asking you to participate in a thought exercise. The variables are represented in the form of a schedule arranged as polar opposites. Think of a school you know well. As the variables are discussed, use each of the pairs to describe three kinds of relationships in that school: the way teachers relate to students; the way teachers relate to each other; and the way administrators relate to teachers. In each case place a mark on the line scale in the schedule somewhere between the polar opposites that best places the relationship.

1. *Affective vs. affective-neutrality:* The parties that comprise the relationship are always interested in each other or are always disinterested. Actions toward each other are always determined by emotions (i.e., feelings of kinship, duty, or love) or are always devoid of feelings. In the first instance teachers always relate to students as if they were teaching their own children. In the second instance teachers always relate to students as skilled technicians who apply objective treatments to students who are clients. Principals are emotionally involved as they work with and relate to teachers. Or, principals adopt an emotionally detached, neutral attitude.

	Affective											Affective-neutrality
Teacher–student	5	4	3	2	1	0	1	2	3	4	5	
Among teachers	5	4	3	2	1	0	1	2	3	4	5	
Administrator–teachers	5	4	3	2	1	0	1	2	3	4	5	

2. *Collective orientation vs. self-orientation:* The parties that comprise the relationship are always motivated by common interests or are always motivated by self interest. In the first instance any particular action or situation is always evaluated in terms of its collective significance as defined by agreed upon values that comprise a public moral code. In the second instance any particular action or situation is always evaluated in terms of personal significance by a private standard. Teachers, for example, always choose to help each other get ready for "teacher evaluations" or to plan for the new year as a reflection of their commitment to a shared sense of success. Or, teachers always choose to face "teacher evaluations" or to plan for the

*From Thomas J. Sergiovanni, *Building Community in Schools.* (San Francisco: Jossey-Bass, 1994).

Appendix 4–1 *(Continued)*

new year individually and privately as they compete with each other in pursuit of more personal gains. Principals are concerned with being sure that the best decisions are made even if lines of authority have to be compromised. Or, principals are concerned with maintaining proper lines of authority and thus insist on making decisions.

	Collective orientation											Self-orientation
Teacher–student	5	4	3	2	1	0	1	2	3	4	5	
Among teachers	5	4	3	2	1	0	1	2	3	4	5	
Administrator–teachers	5	4	3	2	1	0	1	2	3	4	5	

3. *Particularism vs. universalism:* The parties that comprise the relationship always size up situations and make decisions on the basis of the specifics that define that situation or always on the basis of general protocols and rules. Actions are governed entirely by the particulars of the relationship itself or actions are governed entirely by the universal norms of the system itself. In the first instance teachers always take into consideration the unique circumstances that define a discipline problem and then always create a unique resolution based on this consideration. (Thus, the same discipline problem may be handled differently on different occasions.) In the second instance discipline problems are always categorized by predetermined protocols and then always dealt with according to universal rules. (Thus, the same discipline problem is always handled the same way whenever it appears.) Teachers judge students in accordance with particular and specific standards. The standards vary with students. Teachers judge the abilities of students by universal standards. The standards do not vary with the students.

	Particularism											Universalism
Teacher–student	5	4	3	2	1	0	1	2	3	4	5	
Among teachers	5	4	3	2	1	0	1	2	3	4	5	
Administrator–teachers	5	4	3	2	1	0	1	2	3	4	5	

4. *Ascription vs. achievement:* The parties that comprise the relationship always value each other for who and what they are regardless of their achievements or always value each other for what they accomplish. Each always accepts the other as an absolute or acceptance is always contingent on one's achievements. In the first instance students are always accepted, considered "good" and loved regardless of how well they do in school and how much they achieve. In the second instance acceptance, attributions of being a good person and love are always contingent upon and distributed based on the extent to which students are cooperative and achieve.

Appendix 4–1   *(Continued)*

Teachers accept each other, help each other, and respect each other because they are members of the same school faculty. Or, teachers accept, help, and respect each other differentially, in accordance with perceptions of relative worth and relative achievement.

Ascription												Achievement
Teacher–student	5	4	3	2	1	0	1	2	3	4	5	
Among teachers	5	4	3	2	1	0	1	2	3	4	5	
Administrator–teachers	5	4	3	2	1	0	1	2	3	4	5	

5. *Diffuseness vs. specificity:* The parties that comprise the relationship always view each other in less defined ways that allow for broad interaction and for concern that is widely defined or always view each other in ways defined more narrowly by roles, role expectations and preset work requirements. In the first instance everything about the person is always relevant on any given occasion. In the second instance relevance is always determined by role requirements and the requirements of the task at hand. Principals always view teachers as whole persons to be engaged fully. Or, principals always view teachers as cases to be treated in accordance with proper role definitions and expectations. Teachers are bonded to each other as total personalities who comprise a "family." Teachers relate to each other in more limited ways as defined by their jobs.

Diffuseness												Specificity
Teacher–student	5	4	3	2	1	0	1	2	3	4	5	
Among teachers	5	4	3	2	1	0	1	2	3	4	5	
Administrator–teachers	5	4	3	2	1	0	1	2	3	4	5	

One important characteristic that differentiates one school from another is the relationship that exists between means and ends. In some schools a fairly clear distinction is made between means and ends. This distinction communicates an instrumental view of human nature and society. In other schools, by contrast, the distinctions are blurred. Ends remain ends but means too are considered as ends.

6. *Substantive vs. instrumental:* The partners that comprise the relationship always view means as ends equal to ends or always make a clear distinction between means and ends. In the first instance discipline policies and rules are always considered to be moral standards to be celebrated in their own right. [In the second instance, discipline policies and rules] are always considered as means to manage the behavior of students. The subjects taught are viewed entirely as knowledge to be valued

Appendix 4–1 *(Continued)*

and enjoyed, or are always viewed as content to be mastered in order to get good grades and high test scores. In the first instance principals emphasize improving the quality of the teacher's workplace because that is a good thing to do. In the second instance principals work to improve the quality of the teachers' workplace as a way to motivate them to perform. In the first instance students are fed because loving, compassionate people feed hungry children. In the second instance the purpose of the school breakfast program is to relieve the hunger that keeps children from learning. Students study only because they value knowledge as an end in itself or only to win approval, get promoted, or perhaps to qualify for the driver's education program.

	Substantive										Instrumental
Teacher–student	5	4	3	2	1	0	1	2	3	4	5
Among teachers	5	4	3	2	1	0	1	2	3	4	5
Administrator–teachers	5	4	3	2	1	0	1	2	3	4	5

7. *Altruistic love vs. egocentric love:* Sometimes relationships between and among people are governed by altruistic love and at other times by egocentric love. Egocentric love is emotionally and physically self-gratifying. When egocentric love is the motive, each of the parties to the relationship enter into an implicit contract with the other for the exchange of needs and satisfactions that benefit both. Teachers, for example, develop special relationships with students, expecting in return cooperation and greater effort. Teachers help each other so that each will be more effective. Principals "love" their teachers for similar reasons.

Webster defines altruism as benevolent concern for the welfare of others, as selflessness. Love, in this case, is defined as deep devotion and good will that comes from and contributes to feelings of brotherhood and sisterhood. Altruistic love is an expression of selfless concern for others that stems from devotion or obligation. The emphasis is on giving without concern for what one gets in return.

Strictly speaking altruistic love and egocentric love are not opposite poles of the same continuum. But arranging them in this way is still useful for our purposes. Place your school on the continuum between the two to show the relative emphasis given to each.

	Altruistic love										Egocentric love
Teacher–student	5	4	3	2	1	0	1	2	3	4	5
Among teachers	5	4	3	2	1	0	1	2	3	4	5
Administrator–teachers	5	4	3	2	1	0	1	2	3	4	5

Appendix 4–1 (Continued)

Now use the score sheet that follows to summarize your ratings. By drawing in the profile lines, you will have an idea of where your school is on the *gemeinschaft-gesselschaft* continuum.

Score Sheet: Profiles of Community

Teachers' relationships with students

                    5   4   3   2   1   0   1   2   3   4   5

Gemeinschaft   **Gesselschaft**
1. affective . . . . affective-neutrality
2. collective orientation . . . . self-orientation
3. particularism . . . . universalism
4. ascription . . . . achievement
5. diffuseness . . . . specificity
6. substantive . . . . instrumental
7. altruistic love . . . . egocentric love

Relationships among teachers

                    5   4   3   2   1   0   1   2   3   4   5

1. affective . . . . affective-neutrality
2. collective orientation . . . . self-orientation
3. particularism . . . . universalism
4. ascription . . . . achievement
5. diffuseness . . . . specificity
6. substantive . . . . instrumental
7. altruistic love . . . . egocentric love

Administrators' relationships with students

                    5   4   3   2   1   0   1   2   3   4   5

1. affective . . . . affective-neutrality
2. collective orientation . . . . self-orientation
3. particularism . . . . universalism
4. ascription . . . . achievement
5. diffuseness . . . . specificity
6. substantive . . . . instrumental
7. altruistic love . . . . egocentric love

Part II

Providing Leadership

The Forces of Leadership and the Culture of Schools

Principals are important! Indeed, no other school position has greater potential for maintaining and improving quality schools. These assertions are bolstered by findings that emerge from research and from more informal observation of successful schools. It is clear that when schools are functioning especially well and school achievement is high, much of the credit typically belongs to the principal. A recent governmental study, for example, reached the following conclusions (U.S. Senate, 1972):

> *In many ways the school principal is the most important and influential individual in any school. . . . It is his leadership that sets the tone of the school, the climate for learning, the level of professionalism and morale of teachers and the degree of concern for what students may or may not become. . . . If a school is a vibrant, innovative, child-centered place; if it has a reputation for excellence in teaching; if students are performing to the best of their ability one can almost always point to the principal's leadership as the key to success. (305)*

Although principals are important, their mere presence does not automatically result in the required leadership being provided. Often circumstances prevent principals from becoming the leaders they want to be. Consider, for example, what one principal has to say about constraining circumstances:

> *I go almost every year to conventions for principals, and there's always a speech telling us we need to be educational leaders, not managers, It's a great idea. And yet the system doesn't allow you to be an educational leader. Everyone wants the power to run schools in one way or another—the central office, the union, the board, the parents, the special-interest groups. What's left for the principal to decide isn't always very much. There's so little we have to control or to change.*

> *The power, the authority, is somewhere else, though not necessarily the respon-sibility. (Boyer, 1983:219)*

Still, many principals are able to rise above these and other difficulties. Key to realizing the potential for leadership in the principalship is to recognize that schools provide opportunities for expressing a *unique* form of leadership. These opportunities spring from special characteristics that schools possess.

The work of schooling is considered by most people to be important; teachers are typically a highly educated and committed group of workers; teaching itself has the potential to provide teachers with variety, interest, and challenge; schools can be fun and exciting places to work; frequently schools take on strong identities stemming from an agreed set of purposes and an agreed-upon mission; and being part of such strong identity schools can be highly motivating and exhilarating to teachers and students. Successful principals understand these unique characteristics of schools as organizations and have learned how to use them as a basis for generating forceful school leadership.

As a result of their research Blumberg and Greenfield (1980) conclude that "princi-pals who lead seem to be highly *goal oriented* and to have a keen sense of *goal clarity*" (246). They point out that successful principals are alert to opportunities or create oppor-tunities favoring their ability to affect what is going on in the school. Although they rely heavily on operational goals of a long-term nature, they emphasize day-by-day actions as well. They have a good sense of themselves, feel secure as individuals and as principals at work, and are able to accept failure as failure of an idea rather than of them as persons. These principals have a high tolerance for ambiguity and are able to work in loosely structured environments. With respect to authority, they test the limits of the boundaries they face and do not make premature assumptions about what they can or cannot do. They are sensitive to the dynamics of power existing in the school district and school commu-nity, and they are accomplished in establishing alliances and in building coalitions that enable them to harness this power on behalf of the school. Approaching problems from an analytical perspective, they are able to remove themselves from the situation; that is, they do not become consumed by the problems and situations they face.

In this chapter, the intent is to focus beneath these descriptions and to examine principal leadership as a set of forces available for improving and maintaining quality schooling. Suggestions are provided as to how principals can use these forces.

The Forces of Leadership

Leadership can be viewed metaphorically as comprising a set of forces. Each of the "forces" can be used by the principal to push the school forward toward effectiveness or to prevent it from being pushed back. Different forces have different consequences for school effectiveness.

Five "forces of leadership"—technical, human, educational, symbolic, and cultural—are discussed in the following subsections. All five are important. Technical, human, and educational are foundational forces that must be provided to ensure that schools will work. Symbolic and cultural are stretcher forces that help schools rise to levels of extraordinary commitment and performance.

The Technical Force

The first force available to principals is the power of leadership derived from using sound management techniques. This force is concerned with the technical aspects of leadership. When expressing the technical force, principals can be thought of as assuming the role of "management engineers," who emphasize such concepts as planning and time management, contingency leadership theories, and organizational structures. As management engineers, principals provide planning, organizing, coordinating, and scheduling to the school and are skilled at manipulating strategies and situations to ensure optimum effectiveness. The technical leadership force is very important because its presence, competently articulated, ensures that the school will be managed properly.

Proper management is a basic requirement of all organizations if they are expected to function properly day by day and to maintain support from external constituents. School boards and other segments of the public will not tolerate inefficient and poorly managed schools. Furthermore, it is clear from the research that poorly managed enterprises can have debilitating effects on workers. Ray C. Hackman (1969:158), for example, found that "poor organization of work" resulted in such negative feelings among workers as frustration and aggression, anxiety, personal inadequacy, and even social rejection. It is apparent that workplaces need to be characterized by a degree of order and reliability that provides security for people *and* that frees them to focus wholeheartedly on major purposes and central work activities. The technical force of leadership serves this important need.

The Human Force

The second force available to principals is the power of leadership derived from harnessing the school's social and interpersonal potential—its human resources. This force is concerned with human aspects of leadership. Principals expressing this force can be thought of as assuming the role of "human engineer," emphasizing human relations, interpersonal competence, and instrumental motivational techniques. As human engineers, principals provide support, encouragement, and growth opportunities for teachers and others.

It is hard to imagine a school functioning properly without the strong presence of this human force of leadership. Schools are, after all, human intensive, and *the interpersonal needs of students and teachers are of sufficient importance that, should they be neglected, schooling problems are likely to follow.* High student motivation to learn and high teacher motivation to teach are prerequisite for quality schooling and must be effectively addressed by principals. This force is so fundamental that the development of human resources appears as either the dominant or underlying theme of each of this book's chapters.

The Educational Force

The third force available to principals is the power of leadership derived from expert knowledge about matters of education and schooling. This force is concerned with educational aspects of leadership. At one time educational aspects were dominant in the literature of educational administration and supervision. Principals were considered to be instructional leaders, and emphasis on schooling characterized university training programs. In the latter part of the 1950s and during the 1960s, advances of management and social science theory in educational administration and supervision brought to center stage technical and human aspects of leadership; indeed, educational aspects were often neglected. As a result, the principalship was often viewed as a school management position separate from teaching. During this period, the original meaning of principal as "principal teacher" became lost. John Goodlad (1978) has been a persistent critic of the displacement of educational aspects of leadership in favor of the technical and human. He states:

> *But to put these matters (technical and human) at the center, often for understandable reasons of survival and expediency, is to commit a fundamental error which, ultimately, will have a negative impact on both education and one's own career. Our work, for which we will be held accountable, is to maintain, justify, and articulate sound, comprehensive programs of instruction of children and youth. (326)*

He states further: "It is now time to put the right things at the center again. And the right things have to do with assuring comprehensive, quality educational programs in each and every school in our jurisdiction" (331).

Matters of education and schooling are again in the forefront. This new emphasis on the educational force of leadership is a happy result of recent school effectiveness and teaching effectiveness research and of other reports of research, such as Goodlad's *A Study of Schooling* (1983). Recent national policy studies on the present status and future of education, such as the Carnegie Foundation for the Advancement of Teaching's report *High School: A Report on Secondary Education in America* (Boyer, 1983), have also contributed to enhancing this renewed emphasis on educational aspects of leadership. The following statement from Boyer's book (1983) regarding the preparation of principals is representative of current thought:

> *new preparation and selection programs are required. Principals cannot exercise leadership without classroom experience. Specifically, we recommend that the preparation pattern for principals follow that of teachers. Without a thorough grounding in the realities of the classroom, principals will continue to feel uncomfortable and inadequate in educational leadership roles. Moreover, they will continue to lack credibility in instructional matters with their teachers. (223)*

When expressing the educational force, the principal assumes the role of "clinical practitioner" who brings expert professional knowledge and bearing to teaching, educational program development, and supervision. As clinical practitioner, the principal is adept at diagnosing educational problems; counseling teachers; providing for supervision, evaluation, and staff development; and developing curriculum.

Sometimes the educational force takes the form of principal as strong instructional leader, and at other times as knowledgeable colleague or leader of leaders who engages with teachers on an equal basis on matters of teaching and learning. The first expression of this educational force might be appropriate for new teachers, teachers with less than fully developed competencies, or teachers with doubtful commitment. The second expression is appropriate for more mature, competent, and committed teachers. Although instructional leadership might be appropriate for a particular circumstance or for a limited period of time, the overall goal is for principals to become leaders of leaders. As leadership builds, the principal strives to help the school become a community of leaders.

Technical, human, and educational forces of leadership—brought together in an effort to promote and maintain quality schooling—provide the critical mass needed for basic school competence. A shortage in any of the three forces upsets this critical mass, and less effective schooling is likely to occur. Studies of excellence in organizations suggest that despite the link between technical, human, and educational aspects of leadership and basic competence, the presence of the three does not guarantee excellence. Excellent organizations, schools among them, are characterized by other leadership qualities represented by symbolic and cultural forces of leadership.

The Symbolic Force

The fourth force available to principals is the power of leadership derived from focusing attention of others on matters of importance to the school. This force is concerned with the symbolic aspects of leadership. When expressing this force, the principal assumes the role of "chief," emphasizing selective attention or the modeling of important goals and behaviors, and signaling to others what is important and valuable in the school. Touring the school; visiting classrooms; seeking out and visibly spending time with students; downplaying management concerns in favor of educational concerns; presiding over ceremonies, rituals, and other important occasions; and providing a unified vision of the school through proper use of words and actions are examples of principal activities associated with this force.

The providing of *purposing* to the school is a major aspect of symbolic leadership. Peter Vaill (1984) defines purposing as "that continuous stream of actions by an organization's formal leadership which has the effect of inducing clarity, consensus, and commitment regarding the organization's basic purposes." Leaders of the high-performing organizations he studied had in common the ability to provide purposing.

The symbolic force of leadership derives much of its power from the needs of persons at work to have a sense of what is important and to have some signal of what is of value. Students and teachers alike want to know what is of value to the school and its leadership; they desire a sense of order and direction, and they enjoy sharing this sense with others. They respond to these conditions with increased work motivation and commitment.

To understand the symbolic force we need to look beneath the surface of what the principal does to what this behavior means. In symbolic leadership, what the principal stands for and communicates to others by his or her actions and words is important. In addition, providing meaning to teachers, students, and parents and rallying them to a common cause are the earmarks of effectiveness. As Louis Pondy (1978) suggests:

> *What kind of insights can we get if we say that the effectiveness of a leader lies in his ability to make activity meaningful for those in his role set—not to change*

behavior but to give others a sense of understanding what they are doing, and especially to articulate it so they can communicate about the meaning of their behaviors? (94)

The noted administrative theorist James G. March (1984) echos Pondy's thoughts as follows:

Administrators manage the way the sentiments, expectations, commitments and faiths of individuals concerned with the organization fit into a structure of social beliefs about organizational life. Administrative theory probably underestimates the significance of this belief structure for effective organizations. As a result, it probably underestimates the extent to which the management of symbols is a part of effective administration. If we want to identify one single way in which administrators can affect organizations, it is through their effect on the world views that surround organizational life; and those effects are managed through attention of the ritual and symbolic characteristics of organizations and their administration. Whether we wish to sustain the system or change it, management is a way of making a symbolic statement. (32)

Technical aspects of leadership are managing structures and events; human aspects are managing psychological factors such as needs; and educational aspects are managing the substance of our work. By contrast, symbolic aspects are managing sentiments, expectations, commitments, and faith itself. Because symbolic leadership affects the faith that people have in the school, it provides the principal with a powerful force for influencing school events.

The Cultural Force

The fifth force available to principals is the power of leadership derived from building a unique school culture and refers to cultural aspects of leadership. It is clear from reviews of the successful schools literature that the building of a *culture* that promotes and sustains a given school's conception of success is key. When expressing this cultural force, the principal assumes the role of "high priest," seeking to define, strengthen, and articulate those enduring values, beliefs, and cultural strands that give the school its unique identity over time. As high priest, the principal is engaged in legacy building, and in creating, nurturing, and teaching an organizational saga (Clark, 1972) that defines the school as a distinct entity with an identifiable culture. The words *clan* and *tribe* come to mind as a way to think about how the school might be depicted and function.

   Leadership activities associated with the cultural view include articulating school purposes and mission; socializing new members to the school; telling stories and maintaining or reinforcing myths, traditions, and beliefs; explaining "the way things operate around here"; developing and displaying a system of symbols (as exemplified in the fourth force) *over time;* and rewarding those who reflect this culture. The net effect of the cultural force of leadership is to bond students, teachers, and others together and to bind them to the work of the school as believers. The school and its purposes become revered, and in some respects they resemble an ideological system dedicated to a sacred mission.

As persons become members of this strong and binding culture, they are provided with opportunities for enjoying a special sense of personal importance and significance. Their work and their lives take on a new importance, one characterized by richer meanings, an expanded sense of identity, and a feeling of belonging to something special—all of which are highly motivating conditions (Peters and Waterman, 1982).

Culture can be described as the collective programming of the mind that distinguishes the members of one school from another (Hofstede, 1980:13). Cultural life in schools is constructed reality, and school principals can play a key role in building this reality. School culture includes values, symbols, beliefs, and shared meanings of parents, students, teachers, and others conceived as a group or community. Culture governs what is of worth for this group and how members should think, feel, and behave. The "stuff" of culture includes a school's customs and traditions; historical accounts; stated and unstated understandings, habits, norms, and expectations; common meanings; and shared assumptions. The more understood, accepted, and cohesive the culture of a school, the better able it is to move in concert toward ideals it holds and objectives it wishes to pursue. Ultimately, the intent of cultural leadership is to transform the school from an organization inhabited by a collection of "I"s to a moral community—themes described in Chapter 4.

Practicing Symbolic and Cultural Leadership

Culture building and practicing the art of purposing in schools are the essentials of symbolic and cultural leadership forces. The expression of these forces requires vision and an understanding of the semantics of daily activities.

Expressing Symbolic Leadership

When principals are expressing symbolic aspects of leadership, they are typically working beneath the surface of events and activities; they are seeking to tap deeper meanings, deeper values. As Robert J. Starratt (1973) suggests, leaders seek to identify the roots of meaning and the flow and ebb of daily life in schools so that they can provide students, teachers, and members of the community with a sense of importance, vision, and purpose above the seemingly ordinary and mundane. Indeed, they work to bring to the school a sense of drama in human life that permits persons to rise above the daily routine that often characterizes their day-by-day activities. Symbolic leaders are able to see the significance of what a group is doing and indeed could be doing. They have a feel for the dramatic possibilities inherent in most situations and are able to urge people to go beyond the routine, to break out of the mold into something more lively and vibrant. Finally, symbolic leaders are able to communicate their sense of vision by words and examples. They use language symbols that are easily understood but that also communicate a sense of excitement, originality, and freshness. These efforts provide opportunities for others in the school to experience this vision and to gain a sense of purpose, feeling that they share in the ownership of the school enterprise.

Lieberman and Miller (1984) found that principals often practiced symbolic leadership as opportunists and under serendipitous circumstances. They note, for example,

> *when complimenting a teacher for a well-constructed and well-taught lesson, an administrator is making a statement that excellence is recognized and rewarded.*

When meeting with a teacher whose classroom is in revolt, the principal is expressing concern about what happens behind the closed doors of the classroom and signals a change from previous administrators who gave high marks to a teacher needing improvement. When attending department meetings that focus on curricular issues, the principal is supporting dialogue and informed action. All of these events and actions may be defined as educational leadership—not rational, linear, and planned; but ad hoc, responsive and realistic. Educational leadership happens, when it happens at all, within the cracks and around the edges of the job as defined and presently constituted. (76)

Warren Bennis (1984) finds that compelling vision is the key ingredient of leadership among heads of the highly successful organizations he studied. *Vision* refers to the capacity to create and communicate a view of a desired state of affairs that induces commitment among those working in the organization. Vision becomes the substance of what is communicated as symbolic aspects of leadership are emphasized. Tom Davis, principal of the John Muir School in the St. Louis area, speaks of vision as follows:

I think the first thing I think I'd do real well is I have a vision about what the school should be and about what this school should be in particular . . . And I think that's essential to a number of things. I think it's important to inspire staff, both emotionally and intellectually. I think it needs to serve that function. Explicitly, I function to bring back the broader vision, the broader view . . . to bear on all the little pieces. That's something I work at very hard . . . so, because I've got all these semi-autonomous, really capable human beings out there, one major function is to keep it all going in one direction.

He continues:

So the vision . . . has to inform the board, the parents, and staff—all the relationships. It's a whole community, so it all has to be part of it. The vision has to include not only a vision of what you do with children, but what you do in the process of doing it with children. It has to be all of one fabric. (Prunty and Hively, 1982:66)

Lieberman and Miller (1984) speak of the power of the principal as the school's "moral authority," who by actions, statements, and deeds makes symbolic statements. In describing this power from case study notes involving student discrimination, they state:

Principals can maintain neutrality and let things progress as they always have; even that is a moral statement. Or they may take an active stance, threatening the assumptions of staff members and moving a school in more progressive or more regressive directions. Principals condone or condemn certain behaviors and attitudes; they model moral precepts as they go about the job. When the administrators at Albion took the side of minority students in the lunchroom radio incident, they gave a clear message to faculty that discrimination by race was not to be tolerated. A powerful message was transmitted. Had there been administrative apathy, an equally powerful point would have been made. (76)

Principals are cast into powerful symbolic roles whether they intend it or not and whether they like it or not. Inaction, in certain circumstances, can be as powerful a symbolic statement as is action.

The Semantics of Cultural Leadership

To understand and practice symbolic and cultural leadership, the emphasis needs to be on the semantics of leadership, not the phonetics. What the leader does represents the phonetics. What the leader's actions and behaviors mean to others represents the semantics. Focusing on semantics helps in the understanding that very often it is the little things that count. One does not have to mount a white horse and charge forward in a grand dramatic event in order to be a symbolic leader. Simple routines and humble actions properly orchestrated can communicate very important messages and high ideas.

Saphier and King (1985), for example, point out that the content of symbolic and cultural leadership need not be different from that of technical, human, and educational leadership. In their words, "Cultures are built through the everyday business of school life. It is the way business is handled that both forms and reflects the culture. . . . Culture building occurs . . . through the way people use educational, human and technical skills in handling daily events or establishing regular practices" (72). David Dwyer reaches a similar conclusion. In describing his research (Dwyer, Lee, Rowan, and Bossert, 1983), Dwyer notes:

> *Another fundamental characteristic of these principals was the routine nature of their actions. Instead of leaders of large-scale or dramatic innovation, we found men and women who shared a meticulous attention to detail. We observed an attention to the physical and emotional elements of the school environment, school-community relations, the teaching staff, schoolwide student achievement, and individual student progress. Their most essential activities included forms of monitoring, information control and exchange, planning, direct interaction with students, hiring and staff development, and overseeing building maintenance. (1984:37)*

It is through such routines that the principal focuses attention, demonstrates commitments, and otherwise "embarks on a slow but steady campaign to create a consensus of values and beliefs in a setting" (Dwyer, 1989:22). Appendix 5–1 shows how Frances Hedges, one of the principals studied by Dwyer and his colleagues, managed to practice symbolic and cultural leadership by tending to both routine and varied aspects of her work.

Reeves and Reitzug (1992) have used the forces of leadership framework as the basis for describing how symbolic leadership is practiced by principals. They studied the principal of an 800-student elementary school. Both the school and the principal were considered to be exemplary by the district's teachers and administrators. As the researchers sorted the observed leadership behaviors into the forces category, they were able to develop a taxonomy of symbolic leadership forms. The taxonomy appears as Table 5–1. This taxonomy might be helpful in sorting the behaviors of Frances Hedges. The relationships between the five leadership forces and successful schooling are summarized in Table 5–2.

TABLE 5–1 Taxonomy of Symbolic Leadership Forms

Technical	Human	Educational
Planning	Consideration	Diagnosing educational problems
Coordinating	Support	Coaching/counseling teachers on
Scheduling	Concerns	instructional matters
Budgeting	Individuality	Supervision of instruction
Accounting	Autonomy	Evaluation of instruction
Initiating structure	Encouragement	Program development
forms management	Reinforcement	Curriculum development
	Growth opportunities	Staff development
	Building morale	Discussing instructional program
	Shared decision making	Providing growth opportunities
	Conflict management	
	Discipline	
	Team building	
	Counseling	

Symbolic/Culture

Actions	Language	Artifacts
Way time is spent	Conversations	Documents
Where energy is committed	Questions asked	Agendas
Meetings attended	Topics discussed	Handbooks
Where meetings are located	Announcements	Letters
Which items result in follow-up	Feedback given	Memos
Presiding over ceremonies, rituals	Gestures	Mission/vision
Things rewarded	Nonverbal communication	statements
Downplaying one type of activity	Stories	Newsletters
(e.g., management) in favor of	Jokes	Policy books
another (e.g., educational)	Myths	School philosophies
Modeling	Legends	Slogans
Touring school	Favorite sayings	Teacher bulletins
Visiting classrooms	Slogans	Grant proposals
Spending time with students, staff	Recurring phrases	Written correspondence
Rituals	Rumors	Other documents
Rites of passage	Content of documents	School products
Ceremonies	Songs sung	Badges, pins, buttons
Way that resources are acquired	Books read	Displayed objects
What resources are requested		Bulletin boards
Way that resources are expanded		
Decisions made		*Artifacts (intangible)*
Materials distributed		
Gifts given		Heroes
Procedures/policies developed		Cultural network

From Ulrich C. Reitzug and Jennifer Esler Reeves. 1992. " 'Miss Lincoln Doesn't Teach Here': A Descriptive Narrative and Conceptual Analysis of a Principal's Symbolic Leadership Behavior," *Educational Administration Quarterly* 28(2), 192.

TABLE 5–2 The Forces of Leadership and Excellence in Schooling

Force	Leadership Role Metaphor	Theoretical Constructs	Examples	Reactions	Link to Excellence
Technical	"Management engineer"	Planning and time management strategies Contingency leadership theories Organizational structure	Plan, organize, coordinate, and schedule Manipulate strategies and situations to ensure optimum effectiveness	People are managed as objects of a mechanical system. They react to efficient management with indifference but have a low tolerance for inefficient management.	Presence is important to achieve and maintain routine school competence but not sufficient to achieve excellence. Absence results in school ineffectiveness and poor morale.
Human	"Human engineer"	Human relation supervision Psychological theories of motivation Interpersonal competence Conflict management Group cohesiveness	Provide needed support Encourage growth and creativity Build and maintain morale Use participatory decision making	People achieve high satisfaction of their interpersonal needs. They like the leader and the school and respond with positive interpersonal behavior. A pleasant atmosphere exists that facilitates the work of the school.	
Educational	"Clinical practitioner"	Professional knowledge and bearing Teaching effectiveness Educational program design Clinical supervision	Diagnose educational problems Counsel teachers Provide supervision and evaluation Provide inservice Develop curriculum	People respond positively to the strong expert power of the leader and are motivated to work. They appreciate the assistance and concern provided.	Presence is essential to routine competence. Strongly linked to, but still not sufficient for, excellence in schooling. Absence results in ineffectiveness.

Continued

TABLE 5–2 *(Continued)*

Force	Leadership Role Metaphor	Theoretical Constructs	Examples	Reactions	Link to Excellence
Symbolic	"Chief"	Selective attention Purposing Modeling	Tour the school Visit classrooms Know students Preside over ceremonies and rituals Provide a unified vision	People learn what is of value to the leader and school, have a sense of order and direction, and enjoy sharing that sense with others. They respond with increased motivation and commitment.	Presence is essential to excellence in schooling though absence does not appear to negatively affect routine competence.
Cultural	"High priest"	Climate, clan, culture Tightly structured values —loosely structured system Ideology "Bonding" motivation theory	Articulate school purpose and mission Socialize new members Tell stories and maintain reinforcing myths Explain SOPs Define uniqueness Develop and display a reinforcing symbol system Reward those who reflect the culture	People become believers in the school as an ideological system. They are members of a strong culture that provides them with a sense of personal importance and significance and work meaningfulness, which is highly motivating.	

From Thomas J. Sergiovanni. 1984. "Leadership and Excellence in Schooling," *Educational Leadership* 41(5), 12.

The Dynamic Aspects of School Culture

Appendix 5–2, a "Primer on School Culture," provides an overview of school culture and its dimensions. Included are discussions of why culture is an integral and unavoidable part of school life, the levels of school culture, how culture can be developed, and the dark side of school culture.

All schools have cultures, but successful schools seem to have strong and functional cultures aligned with a vision of quality schooling. Culture serves as a compass setting to steer people in a common direction; it provides a set of norms defining what people should accomplish and how, and it is a source of meaning and significance for teachers, students, administrators, and others as they work. Strong and functional cultures are *domesticated* in the sense that they emerge deliberately—they are nurtured and built by the school leadership and membership.

Once shaped and established in a school, strong culture acts as a powerful socializer of thought and programmer of behavior. Yet, the shaping and establishment of such a culture don't just happen; they are, instead, a negotiated product of the shared sentiments of school participants. When competing points of view and competing ideologies exist in the school, deciding which ones will count requires some struggling. Principals are in an advantageous position to strongly influence the outcome of this struggle. They are, for example, in control of the communications system of the school and thus can decide what information to share and with whom. Furthermore, they control the allocation of resources and are able to reward desirable (and sanction undesirable) behavior. Bates (1981) elaborates on the principal's influence in shaping school culture:

> The culture of the school is therefore the product of conflict and negotiation over definitions of situations. The administrative influence on school language, metaphor, myths and rituals is a major factor in the determination of the culture which is reproduced in the consciousness of teacher and pupils. Whether that culture is based on metaphors of capital accumulation, hierarchy and domination is at least partly attributable to the exercise of administrative authority during the negotiation of what is to count as culture in the school. (43)

Can a culture emerge in a school based on agreements to disagree, on the maintenance of ambiguity over certainty, and on norms of variety and playfulness rather than order? Key for the concept of culture is the importance of collective ideology, shared values and sentiments, and norms that define acceptable behavior. The actual substance of culture is, by contrast, less important. Thus, not all schools with strong cultures are characterized by "harmony." Indeed, agreeing to disagree may well be the core value of a given school culture. This is often the case with respect to colleges and universities and to school research and development enterprises.

School Culture Building

Culture building requires that school leaders give attention to the informal, subtle, and symbolic aspects of school life. Teachers, parents, and students need answers to questions such as these: What is this school about? What is important here? What do we believe in? Why do we function the way we do? How are we unique? How do I fit into the scheme of things? Answering these questions imposes an order on one's school life that is derived from a sense of purpose and enriched meanings. Purpose and meaning are essential in helping the school become a community of mind. As Greenfield (1973) states:

> *What many people seem to want from schools is that schools reflect the values that are central and meaningful in their lives. If this view is correct, schools are cultural artifacts that people struggle to shape in their own image. Only in such forms do they have faith in them; only in such forms can they participate comfortably in them. (570)*

What is the purpose of leadership conceived as a cultural force? "The task of leadership is to create the moral order that binds them [leaders] and the people around them," notes Thomas B. Greenfield (1984:159). James Quinn (1981) states: "The role of the leader, then, is one of orchestrator and labeler: taking what can be gotten in the way of action and shaping it—generally after the fact—into lasting commitment to a new strategic direction. In short, he makes meanings" (59). Leadership as culture building is not a new idea but one that is solidly embedded in our history and well known to successful school and other leaders. In 1957, Phillip Selznick wrote:

> *The art of the creative leader is the art of institution building, the reworking of human and technological materials to fashion an organism that embodies new and enduring values. . . . To institutionalize is to* infuse with value *beyond the technical requirements of the task at hand. The prizing of social machinery beyond its technical role is largely a reflection of the unique way it fulfills personal or group needs. Whenever individuals become attached to an organization or a way of doing things as persons rather than as technicians, the result is a prizing of the device for its own sake. From the standpoint of the committed person, the organization is changed from an expendable tool into a valued source of personal satisfaction. . . . The institutional leader, then,* is primarily an expert in the promotion and protection of values. *(28)*

In 1938, the noted theorist Chester Barnard stated the following about executive functions: "The essential functions are, first to provide the system of communications; second, to promote the securing of essential efforts; and third, to formulate and define purpose." He continued: "It has already been made clear that, strictly speaking, purpose is defined more nearly by the aggregate of action taken than by any formulation in words" (vii).

Successful Schools and Central Zones

One of the findings revealed in the successful schools literature and in the community-building literature is that these schools have central zones comprising values and beliefs that take on sacred characteristics. Indeed, it might be useful to think of them as having an official "religion" that gives meaning and guides appropriate actions. As repositories of values, these central zones are sources of identity for teachers and students from which their school lives become meaningful. The focus of cultural leadership, then, is on developing and nurturing these central zone patterns so that they provide a normative basis for action within the school.

In some respects the concept of central zone suggests that successful schools are tightly structured. This means that they are closely organized in a highly disciplined fashion around a set of core ideas spelling out the way of life in the school and governing the way in which people should behave. This is in contrast to recent developments in organizational theory that describe schools as being loosely structured entities (these developments were discussed in Part 1). Cohen, March, and Olsen (1972), for example, speak of educational organizations as being "organized anarchies." Similarly, Karl Weick (1982) uses the phrase "loose coupling" to describe the ways in which schools are organized. Indeed, Weick believes that one reason for ineffectiveness in schools is that they are managed with the wrong theory in mind.

Contemporary thought, Weick argues, assumes that schools are characterized by four properties: the existence of a self-correcting rational system among people who work in highly interdependent ways; consensus on goals and the means to obtain these goals; coordination by the dissemination of information; and predictability of problems and responses to these problems. He notes that, in fact, *none* of these properties is a true characteristic of schools and how they function. Principals in loosely coupled schools, he argues, need to make full use of symbol management to tie the system together. In his words: "People need to be part of sensible projects. Their action becomes richer, more confident, and more satisfying when it is linked with important underlying themes, values and movements" (675). He further states: "Administrators must be attentive to the 'glue' that holds loosely coupled systems together because such forms are just barely systems" (675). Finally, he notes that

> the administrator who manages symbols does not just sit in his or her office mouthing clever slogans. Eloquence must be disseminated. And since channels are unpredictable, administrators must get out of the office and spend lots of time one on one—both to remind people of central visions and to assist them in applying these visions to their own activities. The administrator teaches people to interpret what they are doing in a common language. (676)

Some commentators on the successful schools literature point out that these schools are not loosely coupled or structured at all but instead are tightly coupled (Cohen, 1983). A more careful study of this literature leads one to believe that successful schools are *both* tightly coupled and loosely coupled, an observation noted as well by Peters and Waterman (1982) in their studies of America's best-run corporations. There exists in successful schools a strong culture and clear sense of purpose that defines the general thrust and nature of life for their inhabitants. At the same time, a great deal of freedom is given to teachers and others as to how these essential core values are to be honored and realized. This combination of tight structure—around clear and explicit themes representing the core of the school's culture—and of autonomy—so that people can pursue these themes in ways that make sense to them—may well be a key reason why these schools are so successful.

The combination of tight structure and loose structure matches very well three important human characteristics associated with motivation to work, commitment, enthusiasm, and loyalty to the school:

1. The need for teachers, students, and other school workers to find their work and personal lives meaningful, purposeful, sensible, and significant
2. The need for teachers, students, and other school workers to have some reasonable control over their work activities and affairs and to be able to exert reasonable influence over work events and circumstances
3. The need for teachers, students, and other school workers to experience success, to think of themselves as winners, and to receive recognition for their success

People are willing to make a significant investment of time, talent, and energy in exchange for enhancement and fulfillment of these three needs (Hackman and Oldham, 1980; Peters and Waterman, 1982). The concept of combined tight and loose coupling in schools is developed further in Part III of this book as the importance of school goals and purposes is discussed. In the language of community, focusing on central zones of values, shared conceptions, covenants, and other idea structures are key to building a community of mind.

References

Barnard, Chester I. 1938. *The Functions of the Executive.* Cambridge, MA: Harvard University Press.

Bates, Richard. 1981. "Management and the Culture of the School," in Richard Bates and Course Team, Eds., *Management of Resources in Schools: Study Guide I,* pp. 37–45. Geelong, Australia: Deakin University.

Bennis, Warren. 1984. "Transformation Power and Leadership," in Thomas J. Sergiovanni and John E. Corbally, Eds., *Leadership and Organizational Culture,* Urbana-Champaign: University of Illinois Press.

Blumberg, Arthur, and William Greenfield. 1980. *The Effective Principal: Perspectives on School Leadership.* Boston: Allyn and Bacon.

Boyer, Ernest. 1983. *High School: A Report on Secondary Education in America.* New York: Harper & Row.

Clark, Burton R. 1972. "The Organizational Saga in Higher Education." *Administrative Science Quarterly* 17(2), 178–184.

Cohen, Michael. 1983. "Instructional Management and Social Conditions in Effective Schools," in Allan Odden and L. Dean Webb, Eds., *School Finance and School Improvement: Linkages in the 1980's,* Yearbook of the American Educational Finance Association.

Cohen, Michael D., James G. March, and Johan Olsen. 1972. "A Garbage Can Model of Organizational Choice," *Administrative Science Quarterly* 17(1), 1–25.

Dwyer, David. 1984. "The Search for Instructional Leadership: Routines and Subtleties in the Principal's Role," *Educational Leadership* 41(5).

Dwyer, David. 1989. "School Climate Starts at the Curb." *School Climate—The Principal Differ-ence.* Monograph Series #1. The Connecticut Principals' Academy. Hartford, CT. pp. 1–26.

Dwyer, David, Ginny Lee, Brian Rowan, and Steven Bossert. 1983. *Five Principles in Action: Perspectives on Instructional Management.* San Francisco: Far West Laboratory for Educa-tional Research and Development.

Goodlad, John L. 1978. "Educational Leadership: Toward the Third Era," *Educational Leadership* 23(4), 322–331.

Goodlad, John L. 1983. *A Study of Schooling.* New York: McGraw-Hill.

Greenfield, Thomas B. 1973. "Organizations as Social Inventions: Rethinking Assumptions About Change," *Journal of Applied Behavioral Science* 9(5).

Greenfield, Thomas B. 1984. "Leaders and Schools: Willfullness and Non-Natural Order in Organi-zation," in Thomas J. Sergiovanni and John E. Corbally, Eds., *Leadership and Organizational Culture.* Urbana-Champaign: University of Illinois Press.

Hackman, Ray C. 1969. *The Motivated Working Adult.* New York: American Management Associa-tion.

Hackman, J. Richard, and Greg R. Oldham. 1980. *Work Redesign.* Reading, MA: Addison-Wesley.

Hofstede, G. 1980. *Cultures Consequences.* Beverly Hills, CA: Sage Publications.

Lieberman, A., and L. Miller. 1984. *Teachers, Their World, and Their Work.* Arlington, VA: Association for Supervision and Curriculum Development.

March, James G. 1984. "How We Talk and How We Act: Administrative Theory and Administrative Life," in Thomas J. Sergiovanni and John E. Corbally, Eds., *Leadership and Organizational Culture,* 18–35. Urbana-Champaign: University of Illinois Press.

Peters, Thomas J., and Robert H. Waterman, Jr. 1982. *In Search of Excellence.* New York: Harper & Row.

Pondy, Louis. 1978. "Leadership Is a Language Game," in Morgan W. McCall, Jr. and Michael M. Lombardo, Eds., *Leadership: Where Else Can We Go?* Durham, NC: Duke University Press.

Prunty, John J., and Wells Hively. 1982. "The Principal's Role in School Effectiveness: An Analysis of the Practices of Four Elementary School Leaders." National Institute of Education (G 8-01-10) and CEMRL, Inc., Nov. 30, 1982.

Quinn, James B. 1981. "Formulating Strategy One Step at a Time," *Journal of Business Strategy,* Winter.

Reeves, Jennifer Esler, and Ulrich C. Reitzug. 1992. "'Miss Lincoln Doesn't Teach Here': A Descriptive Narrative and Conceptual Analysis of a Principal's Symbolic Leadership Behav-ior," *Educational Administration Quarterly* 28(2), 185–219.

Saphier, John, and Matthew King. 1985. "Good Seeds Grow in Strong Cultures," *Educational Leadership* 42(6), 67–74.

Selznick, Phillip. 1957. *Leadership and Administration: A Sociological Interpretation.* New York: Harper & Row.

Starratt, Robert J. 1973. "Contemporary Talk on Leadership: Too Many Kings in the Parade?" *Notre Dame Journal of Education* 4(1), 5–14.

United States Senate, Select Committee on Equal Educational Opportunity. 1972. "Revitalizing the Role of the School Principal," in *Toward Equal Educational Opportunity,* Senate Report No. 92-0000, 305–307.

Vaill, Peter B. 1984. "The Purposing of High Performing Systems," in Thomas J. Sergiovanni and John E. Corbally, Eds., *Leadership and Organizational Culture,* 85–104. Urbana-Champaign: University of Illinois Press.

Weick, Karl E. 1982. "Administering Education in Loosely Coupled Schools," *Phi Delta Kappan* 27(2), 673–676.

Appendix 5–1 Frances Hedges and Orchard Park Elementary School

The year 1982 marked Orchard Park Elementary School's 35th year in the city of Hillsdale. Surrounding the school were rows of white, grey, pale green and pastel yellow houses, whose neatly trimmed yards were, by late summer, straw-colored from lack of water. The neighborhood itself was quiet, but the noises from a nearby freeway attested to its urban setting. The community's only distinctive landmark was an old church which occupied a large corner lot adjacent to the school. Its three onion-shaped spires had for years cast a sense of permanence over the entire community.

"Permanent," however, would be a somewhat misleading description of the area. Prior to 1960, white, middle-class families of Italian descent predominated in the neighborhood. Over the next few years increasing numbers of ethnic minorities moved out of the city's poorer neighborhoods to areas like Orchard Park's community, seeking better schools and better living conditions. As a result, Orchard Park's neighborhood lost its homogeneity, and some of its quiet, as a number of racial conflicts marred the community's tranquility. The school also was affected, and staff had to find a way to adapt the program to the needs of the newer students.

The new student body at Orchard Park Elementary School was characterized by a diversity of racial groups from various ethnic backgrounds. District records showed that as many as 10 different language groups were represented in the school's student population. Fifty-nine percent of the students were black; 13 percent reflected Spanish heritage; 16 percent were Asian (Chinese, Filipino, Samoan, Laotian, and Vietnamese); and 11 percent were white. Other ethnic groups composed the remaining one percent. The majority of the students' families were of low- or lower-middle income status. These students were energetic and active, frequently exhibiting aggressive behavior that stemmed more from overexuberance than from any other motivation. Groups at play were observed to be multiethnic and solicitous of affection and approval from teachers and the principal. Warm hugs exchanged between staff members and students were common occurrences on the playground.

Orchard Park employed 25 teachers, the majority of whom were very experienced. There were few signs of negativism, criticism or conflict among these teachers despite the fact that their instructional approaches differed markedly. Generally, they were supportive of the school and particularly of the principal. One teacher told us that there was only one reason for staff turnover at Orchard Park—retirement. Further evidence of their satisfaction with the status quo came at the end of the year of our study. The staff, together with the community, rallied to prevent the transfer of their principal and came together to hold a "Principal Appreciation" gathering to honor Hedges' leadership.

The center of attention at that ceremony, Frances Hedges, was a 60-year-old black woman who had served at Orchard Park for six and a half years. She conveyed to all who met her a sense of elegance through her well-matched clothes, golden earrings, oversized

Excerpted from David Dwyer (1989), "School Climate Starts at the Curb," *School Climate—The Principal Difference,* Hartford: The Connecticut Principals' Academy.

Appendix 5–1 *(Continued)*

glasses and neatly fashioned white hair. Her appearance contrasted to the casual style adhered to by most of her staff; she was easily distinguished as the person in charge.

Long before coming to Orchard Park, Hedges had attended a teachers' college in her hometown, originally intending to become a child psychologist. But economic considerations prevented her from pursuing this goal. Instead, she spent 21 years as a classroom teacher, mostly in the district that includes Orchard Park. After receiving a Masters Degree in educational administration, she gradually climbed to her current position by working as a reading resource teacher, a district program coordinator, and a vice principal.

Hedges' manner with staff and students was personable. Whether discussing professional matters or just making small talk, she conveyed warmth and friendliness through smiles and laughter. She was generous with compliments to both students and teachers. She also communicated often and comfortably through touches, hugs and embraces. As a result, she frequently was referred to by both students and teachers as Orchard Park's "mother figure."

Hedges' way of acting was consistent with her philosophy. She strongly adhered to what she termed "humanistic" beliefs about education. She explained:

My philosophy is that if we are warm and humane and nurturing, we maximize the learning of children. There is just no way to separate out those basic needs.

Believing that she was "acutely sensitive to . . . children's needs as well as adults' needs," Hedges strove to keep everyone in her learning community "reasonably happy" and worked to help everyone strengthen their self-concepts.

Attending to the basic needs of children logically led to Hedges' attention to safety and order in her school. She was a strict disciplinarian and never hesitated to reprimand children for misbehavior. Her harsh words, however, always would be followed by her efforts to help children understand their mistakes and become more responsible for their own behavior. She said:

I believe that if we are really going to change the behavior of children, we can't just say "stop that," without going a step further and really having some kind of dialogue about what took place, why, and what are the options.

Her philosophy of education also included tenets about instruction. She strongly believed in the importance of academics, particularly reading. She pronounced:

Reading is by far our number one priority. I believe that if children don't know how to read, they really cannot make it in this world.

Thus, Hedges' beliefs about education were related to her concerns for both the social and academic well-being of her students. It came as no surprise to find that her goals for the school reflected those convictions.

Appendix 5–1   (Continued)

Hedges' primary goal at Orchard Park was to build a program conducive to the emotional and social growth of her students. She wanted her staff both to instill in each child a love for learning and to foster an awareness of social responsibility. She was adamant that her staff actively seek to strengthen students' self-concepts. These goals, she believed, were pre-eminent. They were a foundation upon which successful academic experiences could be built.

The principal's concern for the academic growth of her students was always stated from a "whole-child" perspective. Delineating her academic goals, she said:

We work very hard to try to make sure that in the six or seven years that boys and girls are in elementary school, that they leave this school operating at grade level or above. . . . I'd like to see them at grade level for at least their last two years so that they can go into junior high school as much stronger and more confident children.

Hedges actively promoted both her social and academic goals to her faculty. During the year of our study with her, she utilized a district mandate to develop and implement an integrated, three-year instructional plan as a major vehicle to communicate her goals and develop her staff's commitment to them. Evidence that she had been very successful in this aspect of her work accumulated as we interviewed teachers about their beliefs and goals. In virtually all instances, their statements echoed Hedges' own.

How did Frances Hedges bring about the warm and productive climate at Orchard Park? Hedges demonstrated a propensity for direct, face-to-face interaction with participants in her setting. In total, 51 percent of her activities were verbal exchanges of varying length. The other glaring fact in the Orchard Park story is that her routine actions directly affected the climate at Orchard Park, making it conducive to teaching and learning.

Both the value she placed on students' emotional well-being and her goal to improve students' self-esteem contributed to a vision of school climate as an important end in itself. In addition, her beliefs about schools and schooling linked climate to instruction in several ways: she considered students' emotional well-being as an important precursor to their learning; she regarded an orderly, disciplined environment as a necessary condition for teaching and learning to take place; and she believed that the improvement of teachers' instructional practices was best achieved in a setting that built on the positive aspects of their skills. Thus, she strove to maintain an environment that contributed to the happiness, safety, and productivity of all participants.

We see in many of Hedges' routine actions the keys to the development and maintenance of Orchard Park's social milieu. Her actions, as she supervised students in the building and on the playgrounds, attended simultaneously to the need to maintain safety and order at the school and to build students' self-esteem. She monitored their conduct and corrected them when necessary, exchanging her views about responsible behavior and reinforcing school rules. She constantly reminded students to pick up trash, bus their trays in the cafeteria, play in the correct areas of the playyard, walk instead of run in the

Appendix 5–1   *(Continued)*

hallways, refrain from pushing and shoving, and be quiet in the corridors and auditorium. She utilized these same actions to carry out her more social goals: she frequently stopped to talk to students, expressing delight at seeing them or remarking about the clothes they were wearing. Children often approached her to describe important events in their lives. Many of these brief interactions were concluded with a hug exchanged between the principal and the youngster.

An additional strategy Hedges used in her supervision of students was to model appropriate behavior. She might, for example, pick up a piece of trash and deposit it in a container or take a food tray to the cafeteria kitchen as she reminded students of the rules, often mentioning that they should keep the school as tidy as they would their homes.

Hedges' desire to counsel students played a large part in her interactions with children, especially those who had committed some infraction of school rules. We witnessed many instances of her counselor-like approach as she dealt with students whom she had seen misbehaving or who had been sent to her for fighting, stealing, acting inappropriately in class, or failing to complete their school work. In all instances, she carefully took the time to listen to what the students had to say about their behavior. Hedges explained this strategy in terms of her humanistic philosophy:

> *If you don't do something, [children] feel . . . that their problems are falling on deaf ears. I tell the staff all the time, "You really do have to take the time out, let a child explain what happened, and be willing to at least listen, whether it's what that particular child wants, or not . . . it's just that someone has listened."*

Students were aware that Hedges would act vigorously and appropriately if they misbehaved as well as listen to their problems. When infractions were serious, Hedges would tell students that she was going to phone their parents to report incidents . . . she always followed through. As a result Orchard Park's students understood that their principal was serious about discipline and true to her word.

We mentioned earlier the importance that Hedges placed on building on the positive aspects of people in the school. This approach was most apparent in her dealings with problem students as she implemented special plans to communicate to them that, despite misbehavior, they were still worthy human beings and could act responsibly. We observed one instance in which Hedges appointed the worst offenders in the school as "Chair Captains" and allowed them to pick their own squads who would help set up and take down chairs in the auditorium. The youngsters saw this as an important and enjoyable responsibility that gave them status among their peers. In another instance, Hedges urged that a child who had a particularly negative attitude toward school be assigned to the traffic detail. His teacher remarked that this made a dramatic improvement in the boy's classroom behavior and attitude.

When infractions were serious, Hedges often assigned offenders work projects around the school that would contribute to the school's overall welfare. She tenaciously

Appendix 5–1   *(Continued)*

pursued alternatives to suspension. One teacher reported of the principal's efforts to deal with problem students:

> *[Hedges] has a relationship with almost all of the children that regularly act out, the ones that are really on your blacklist . . . if it's your child that's constantly acting out, you would almost want her to say, "Doggone! Let's give up on that kid." But she never really does.*

Hedges not only worked creatively with problem students but encouraged growth in responsibility among all students at Orchard Park. For example, she taught leadership to all members of the school's student council.

Orchard Park's teachers also were encouraged to promote positive social values in the school through classroom activities. In an unusual departure from Hedges' policy of permitting a good deal of staff autonomy concerning the selection of classroom materials, for example, she established a schoolwide focus on her social goals through the introduction of a set of self-esteem materials. At the first faculty meeting of the year, Hedges presented the materials and asked staff members to use them as a regular part of their programs. Although the use of these materials was not systematically monitored, her message was clear to her staff. Subsequently, teachers were observed using an array of esteem-building activities in their classrooms, including magic circle activities, life box materials, and art projects to stimulate discussions about feelings and attitudes.

Thus Hedges aggressively pursued a positive school climate at Orchard Park. By demonstrating her values in her daily interactions and conversations, Hedges encouraged an environment in which staff members shared her child-centered approach. Participants in the setting directly and indirectly exhibited their satisfaction: there was very little vandalism by students in the school, teachers felt lucky to be at the school and left only because of retirement, and the district held a waiting list of teachers anxious to join this faculty.

Hedges also directly or indirectly manipulated such important elements of the organization as class size and composition, scheduling, staff assignments, the scope and sequence of curriculum, the distribution of instructional materials, and even teaching styles. On the surface, a principal actively and successfully engaged in shaping the conditions for and of instruction in a school seems perfectly natural—principals are supposed to be instructional leaders, right? But we also know that teachers enjoy and expect autonomy in matters related to classroom instruction. It is not uncommon for teachers to actively or passively resist principals' instructional improvement campaigns.

Hedges was able to transcend this problem for two reasons. First, her own 21 years of experience as a classroom teacher and reading specialist legitimated her expertise in the eyes of her faculty. The second ingredient to Hedges' success at influencing her staff's classroom practices was her ability to establish a culture of instruction at the school, facilitated by the emphasis she placed on building on people's strengths and emphasizing the positive. Thus, experience coupled with style enabled her to provide infor-

Appendix 5–1 *(Continued)*

mation to teachers without alienating them. Her staff regarded her as competent and nonthreatening. They not only accepted her suggestions, but actively sought her advice and counsel.

While there many strategies that Hedges used to influence instruction both directly and indirectly at the school, the most potent and pervasive was the informal classroom visit. Hedges monitored instruction by regularly dropping into teachers' classrooms. These visits provided opportunities to make suggestions that did not carry the onus that might accompany recommendations made as the result of formal classroom evaluations. On many of Hedges' informal visits, we observed her assisting teachers by working with students and making brief constructive and supportive comments to her staff.

These often-repeated behaviors were key features in her strategy to reduce teachers' anxieties about her visits. She mentioned that she spent time building positive rapport with teachers before providing suggestions for changes in their instructional patterns:

> *I operate with the idea that we really are all a team. If I can just . . . give [the staff] enough strokes on those positives, then I can get [at] those areas that are not so well done.*

When Hedges did feel a need to comment on teachers' deficiencies, she did so in a low-key, nonthreatening manner without embarrassing, confronting, or demeaning them.

Hedges also promoted a norm of teacher-to-teacher sharing because she did not see herself as the only source of instructional expertise in the school. She often advised teachers to talk with their colleagues for assistance or ideas. Frequently this required Hedges to organize opportunities for staff members to get together. For example, she commonly arranged for the school's reading specialist to help teachers create reading centers in a classroom or help classroom teachers evaluate those students who required remedial instruction. There were many instances of Hedges arranging meetings between teachers who were successful with new methods and teachers who were less successful. In this way, she served as a "linking agent" or "information broker." Because Hedges' classroom visits were regular, her recommendations were timely and the staff found them very helpful. Hedges also used classroom visits as opportunities to impress upon children the importance she attached to academic success. By publicly complimenting students on their individual or group successes, she not only strengthened their self-esteem, but created an ethos about learning that children would want to share. . . .

Her philosophy is marked by simple tenets: all people are fundamentally good; everyone can learn and grow in a warm and nurturing environment; any successful enterprise is the result of teamwork and everyone can and must contribute to the whole. From experience, Hedges adds to these beliefs a strongly held value regarding the importance of reading as an essential skill that children must master to realize their highest potential. These humane attributes are wrapped in her tough-minded awareness about the importance of setting limits and making children and staff responsible for their own behavior.

Appendix 5–1   *(Continued)*

Hedges leads her school by continually communicating her beliefs to parents, students, and staff members through her routine actions. By constant word and deed she demonstrates how the vision she holds of the "good" school must work. Mostly she proceeds through patient, subtle suggestions and reminders. Occasionally, she mandates changes or additions to organizational structures, procedures, and curricula. But the key to her success is the relentless pursuit of her goals and her talent in getting others to adopt those goals.

Over years at Orchard Park, staff have experimented with procedures and techniques Hedges has recommended. They have been continually bombarded with her rationale. As they experience success, the procedures and rationales become embedded in their own experiences and slowly alter their own beliefs. Slowly, a working consensus about the "right" way to teach and run a school emerges. As those beliefs fade into assumptions and become habituated, an organizational culture is born. Its progenitor, its patient nurseryman, was Frances Hedges.

Appendix 5–2   *A Primer on School Culture*

In every school there are observable behavioral regularities defined by the rules of the game for getting along. These rules are norms that define for people what is right and correct to do, what is acceptable, and what is expected. Norms are expressions of certain values and beliefs held by members of the work group. When trying to understand how norms emerge and work, the metaphor of culture can be helpful. Some experts may debate whether schools really have cultures or not, but the issue is less the reality of culture and more what can be learned by thinking about schools as cultures. The metaphor school culture helps direct attention to the symbols, behavioral regularities, ceremonies, and even myths that communicate to people the underlying values and beliefs that are shared by members of the organization.

External Adoption and Internal Integration

Edgar Schein believes that the term *culture* "should be reserved for the deeper level of *basic assumptions* and *beliefs* that are shared by members of an organization, that operate unconsciously, and that define in a basic 'taken-for-granted' fashion an organization's view of itself and its environment" (Schein, 1985:6). The concept of culture is very important, for its dimensions are much more likely to govern what it is that people think and do than is the official management system. Teachers, as suggested earlier, are much more likely to teach in ways that reflect the shared assumptions and beliefs of the faculty as a whole than they are in ways that administrators want, supervisors say, or teacher evaluation instruments require.

Following Argyris (1964), Merton (1957), and Parsons (1951), Schein (1985) points out that schools and other organizations must solve two basic problems if they are to be effective: external adoption and survival and internal integration. The problems of *external adoption and survival* are themed to:

Appendix 5–2 *(Continued)*

1. Mission and strategy (how to reach a shared understanding of the core mission of the school and its primary tasks)
2. Goals (developing a consensus on goals that are linked to the core mission)
3. Means (reaching consensus on the managerial and organizational means to be used to reach goals)
4. Standards (reaching consensus on the criteria to be used to determine how well the group is doing in fulfilling its goals and whether it is meeting its commitments to agreed-upon processes)
5. Correction (reaching consensus on what to do if goals are not being met)

The problems of *internal integration* are themed to:

1. Developing a common set of understandings that facilitates communication, organizes perceptions, and helps to categorize and make common meanings.
2. Developing criteria for determining who is in and out and how one determines membership in the group.
3. Working out the criteria and rules for determining who gets, maintains, and loses power.
4. Working out the rules for peer relationships and the manner in which openness and intimacy are to be handled as organizational tasks are pursued.
5. "Every group must know what its heroic and sinful behaviors are; what gets rewarded with property, status and power; and what gets punished in the form of withdrawal of the rewards and, ultimately, excommunication" (Schein, 1985:66).
6. Dealing with issues of ideology and sacredness: "Every organization, like every society, faces unexplainable and inexplicable events, which must be given meaning so that members can respond to them and avoid the anxiety of dealing with the unexplainable and uncontrollable" (Schein, 1985:66).

As issues of external adoption and internal integration are solved, schools and other organizations are better able to give full attention to the attainment of their goals and have the means for allowing people to derive sense and meaning from their work lives—to see their work as being significant. In summarizing his stance, Schein (1985) notes that culture is *"a pattern of basic assumptions—invented, discovered or developed by a given group as it learns to cope with its problems of external adaptation and internal integration—that has worked well enough to be considered valid and, therefore, to be taught to new members as the correct way to perceive, think, and feel in relation to those problems"* (9). Because the assumptions have resulted in decisions and behaviors that have worked repeatedly, they are likely to be taken for granted. This point is important because the artifacts of culture, such as symbols, rites, traditions, and behaviors, are different from the actual content and substance of culture; the basic assumptions that govern what is thought to be true, what is right, and for all intents and purposes, what is reality for the school. As mentioned in earlier discussions of culture, the central zone that Shils (1961) speaks of is

Appendix 5–2 *(Continued)*

composed of assumptions, values, and beliefs. The values and beliefs are often manifest, but the assumptions are typically tacit.

Levels of Culture

Because assumptions and basic beliefs are typically tacit, they are inferred from manifestations of cultures such as the school's climate (Dwyer, 1989) and the rites and rituals of the school's organizational life (Deal, 1985). To account for both, it is useful to think about dimensions of school culture as existing at at least four levels (Dyer, 1982; Schein, 1981; Schein, 1985). The most tangible and observable level is represented by the *artifacts* of culture as manifested in what people say, how people behave, and how things look. Verbal artifacts include the language systems that are used, stories that are told, and examples that are used to illustrate certain important points. Behavioral artifacts are manifested in the ceremonies and rituals and other symbolic practices of the school. The interpersonal life of the school as represented by the concept of school climate is an important artifact of culture.

Less discernible but still important is the level of *perspectives.* Perspectives refer to the shared rules and norms to which people respond, the commonness that exists among solutions to similar problems, how people define the situations they face, and the boundaries of acceptable and unacceptable behavior. Often, perspectives are included in statements of the school's purposes or its covenant when these include ways in which people are to work together as well as the values that they share.

The third level is that of *values.* Values provide the basis for people to judge or evaluate the situations they face, the worth of their actions and activities, their priorities, and the behaviors of people with whom they work. Values not only specify what is important but often the things that are not important. In schools the values are arranged in a fashion that represents the covenant that the principal, teachers, and others share. As discussed in Chapter 8, this covenant might be in the form of an educational or management platform, statements of school philosophy, mission statements, and so forth.

The fourth level is that of *assumptions.* Assumptions are "the tacit beliefs that members hold about themselves and others, their relationships to other persons, and the nature of the organization in which they live. Assumptions are the nonconscious underpinnings of the first three levels—that is, the implicit, abstract axioms that determine the more explicit system of meanings" (Lundberg, 1985:172).

Identifying the Culture of Your School

The four levels of culture provide a framework for analyzing the culture of a school. Because assumptions are difficult to identify firsthand, they often must be inferred from what is found at the artifacts, perspectives, and values levels. Much can be learned from examining the school's history. Terence E. Deal (1985) points out, for example, that

Appendix 5–2 *(Continued)*

[e]ach school has its story of origin, the people or circumstances that launched it, and those who presided over its course thereafter. Through evolutionary development—crises and resolutions, internal innovations and external pressures, plans and chance occurrences—the original concept was shaped and reshaped into an organic collection of traditions and distinctive ways. Throughout a school's history, a parade of students, teachers, principals, and parents cast sustaining memories. Great accomplishments meld with dramatic failures to form a potentially cherishable lore. (615)

The following questions might be helpful in uncovering a school's history:

How does the school's past live in the present?

What traditions are still carried on?

What stories are told and retold?

What events in the school's history are overlooked or forgotten?

Do heroes and heroines exist among teachers and students whose idiosyncrasies and exploits are still remembered?

In what ways are the school's traditions and historical incidents modified through reinterpretation over the years? Can you recall, for example, a historical event that has evolved from fact to myth?

Believing that an organization's basic assumptions about itself can be revealed through its history, Schein (1985) suggests that the organization's history be analyzed by identifying all major crises, crucial transitions, and other times of high emotion. For each event identified, reconstruct how management dealt with the issue, how it identified its role, and what it did and why. Patterns and themes across the various events identified should then be analyzed and checked against current practices. The next step is to identify the assumptions that were behind the actions taken in the past and check whether those assumptions are still relevant for present actions.

To uncover beliefs, ask what are the assumptions and understandings that are shared by teachers and others, though they may not be explicitly stated. These may relate to how the school is structured, how teaching takes place, the roles of teachers and students, what is believed about discipline, and the relationship of parents to the school. Sometimes assumptions and understandings are written down somewhere in the form of a philosophy or other value statements. Whether that is the case or not, beliefs can best be understood by being inferred from examples of current practices.

According to Schein, one important set of basic assumptions revolves around the theme of what is believed about human nature and how these beliefs then affect policies and decisions. To address this issue, he suggests that an attempt be made to identify organizational heroes and villains, successful people, and those who are less successful, and compare the stories that are told about them. He recommends as well that recruitment selection and promotion criteria be examined to see if indeed they are biased toward selecting a certain type of person into the organization and promoting that type. An analysis of who gets rewarded and who gets punished can also be revealing. Do patterns emerge from this sort of analysis? Are there common assumptions about people that begin to emerge?

Values can be identified by asking what things the school prizes. That is, when teachers and principals talk about the school, what are the major and recurring value themes underlying what they say? When problems emerge, what are the values that seem to surface as being relied on in developing solutions?

Norms and standards can be identified by asking what are the oughts, shoulds, do's, and don'ts that govern the behavior of teachers and principals, and examining what behaviors get rewarded and what behaviors get punished in the school. What are the accepted and recurring ways of doing things, the patterns of behavior, the habits and rituals that prevail?

Corwith Hansen (1986) suggests that teachers discuss the following questions when seeking to identify the culture of their school: Describe your work day both in and outside of the school. On what do you spend your time and energy? Given that most students forget what they learn, what do you hope your students will retain over time from your teaching? Think of students whom you are attracted to—those whom you admire, respect, or enjoy. What common characteristics do these students share? What does it take for a teacher to be successful in your school? What advice would you give to new teachers who want to be successful? What do you remember about past faculty members and students in your school? If you were to draw a picture or take a photo or make a collage that represented some aspect of your school, what would it look like? How are students rewarded?

The Dark Side of School Culture

The benefits of a strong school culture are clear. Culture represents an effective means of coordination and control in a loosely connected and nonlinear world. Its covenant or center of purposes and shared values represents a source of inspiration, meaning, and significance for those who live and work in the school. These qualities can lead to enhanced commitment and performance that are beyond expectations. As a result, the school is better able to achieve its goals.

Yet, there is a dark side to the concept of school culture, as well. Weick (1985) points out, for example, that

> *a coherent statement of who we are makes it harder for us to become something else. Strong cultures are tenacious cultures. Because a tenacious culture can be a rigid culture that is slow to detect changes and opportunities and slow to change once opportunities are sensed, strong cultures can be backward, conservative instruments of adaptation. (385)*

Furthermore, the presence of a strong norm system in a school can collectively program the minds of people in such a way that issues of reality come into question. If this is carried to the extreme, the school might come to see reality in one way but its environment

Appendix 5–2   (Continued)

in another. Finally, there is the question of rationality. As commitment to a course of action increases, people become less rational in their actions. Strong cultures are committed cultures, and in excess, commitment takes its toll on rational action.

Schein points out that as organizations mature, the prevailing culture becomes so entrenched that it becomes a constraint on innovation. Culture preserves the glories of the past and hence becomes valued as a source of self-esteem and as a means of defense rather than for what it represents and the extent to which it serves purposes (Schein, 1985).

The Importance of a Loyal Opposition

If the purposes and covenants that constitute cultural centers are highly dynamic and fluid, school cultures are likely to be weak and ineffectual. By the same token, if they are cast in granite they can squelch individuality and innovation. The alternative is to build a resilient culture—one that can bend to change here and there, but not break; that can stretch in a new direction and shrink from an old, but still maintain its integrity; a culture that is able to bounce back and recover its strength and spirit, always maintaining its identity. Key to resiliency is the cultivation of a small but energetic loyal opposition made of

> *people with whom we enjoy an honest, high-trusting relationship but who have conflicting visions, goals or methods. . . . The task of the (loyal opposition) is to bring out the best in us. We need to be grateful for those who oppose us in a high-trust way, for they bring the picture of reality and practicality to our plans. (Block, 1987:135–136)*

Block believes that it is important when working with the loyal opposition that the leader communicate the extent to which they are valued. Leaders can do this, in his view, by reaffirming the quality of the relationship and the fact that it's based on trust. They should be clear in stating their positions and the reasons why they hold them. They should also state in a neutral way what they think positions of the loyal opposition are. The leader reasons as follows:

> *We disagree with respect to purpose, goals, and perhaps even visions. Our task is to understand their position. Our way of fulfilling that task is to be able to state to them their arguments in a positive way. They should feel understood and acknowledged by our statement of their disagreement with us. (Block, 1987:137)*

With this kind of relationship in place, the leadership and the loyal opposition are in a position to negotiate differences in good faith.

References

Argyris, Chris. 1964. *Integrating the Individual and the Organization.* New York: Wiley.

Block, Peter. 1987. *The Empowered Manager.* San Francisco: Jossey-Bass.

Appendix 5–2 *(Continued)*

Deal, Terrance E. 1985. "The Symbolism of Effective Schools," *The Elementary School Journal* 85(5).

Dyer, W. G., Jr. 1982. *Patterns and Assumptions: The Keys to Understanding Organizational Culture.* Office of Naval Research, Technical Report TR-O NR-7.

Dwyer, David C. 1989. "School Climate Starts at the Curb," in *School Climate—The Principal Difference.* Hartford: The Connecticut Principals' Academy.

Hall, John W. 1972. "A Comparison of the Halpin and Croft's 'Organizational Climates' and Likert and Likert's 'Organizational Systems,' " *Administrative Science Quarterly* (17), 586–590.

Hansen, Corwith. 1986. "Department Culture in a High-Performing Secondary School." Unpublished dissertation, Teachers College, Columbia University.

Likert, Rensis. 1961. *New Patterns of Management.* New York: McGraw-Hill.

Likert, Rensis. 1967. *The Human Organization: Its Management and Value.* New York: McGraw-Hill.

Lundberg, Craig C. 1985. "On the Feasibility of Cultural Intervention in Organizations," in Peter J. Frost, Larry F. Moore, Meryl Reis Louis, Craig C. Lundberg, and Joanne Martin, *Organizational Culture.* Beverly Hills, CA: Sage Publications.

Merton, Robert K. 1957. *Social Theory and Social Structure.* New York: The Free Press.

Parsons, Talcott. 1951. *The Social System.* New York: The Free Press.

Schein, Edgar H. 1981. "Does Japanese Management Style Have a Message for American Managers?" *Sloan Management Review,* 24(1), 55–68.

Schein, Edgar H. 1985. *Organizational Culture and Leadership.* San Francisco: Jossey-Bass.

Shils, Edward A. 1961. "Centre and Periphery," in *The Logic of Personal Knowledge: Essays Presented to Michael Polanyi.* London: Routledge and Kegan Paul.

Weick, Karl E. 1985. "The Significance of Culture," in Peter J. Frost, Larry F. Moore, Meryl Reis Louis, Craig C. Lundberg, and Joanne Martin, *Organizational Culture.* Beverly Hills, CA: Sage Publications.

Chapter 6

The Stages of Leadership: A Developmental View

In Chapter 5 we examined leadership as a set of forces that principals can use to maintain and improve schools. In this chapter we are concerned with the leadership strategies and tactics that principals can use as they work firsthand with teachers and others. Four leadership strategies are identified (Sergiovanni, 1990, 1994).

1. *Bartering*: Principals and teachers strike a bargain within which the leader gives to those led something they want in exchange for what the leader wants. The emphasis in bartering is on trading wants and needs for cooperation and compliance. This approach works best when the principal and teachers do not share common goals and interests—when their stakes in the school are different.

2. *Building*: Principals provide the climate and interpersonal support that enhances teachers' opportunities for fulfillment of individual needs for achievement, responsibility, competence, and esteem. The emphasis in building is less on trading and more on providing the conditions that enable teachers to experience psychological fulfillment. Once a minimum level of common effort has been achieved, this approach is recommended to shift the emphasis from extrinsic to intrinsic rewards.

3. *Bonding*: Principals and teachers develop together a set of shared values about the relationships they want to share and the ties they want to create so that together they can become a community of learners and leaders—a community of colleagues. The emphasis in bonding is on relationships characterized by mutual caring and the felt interdependence that comes from mutually held obligations and commitments. This approach strives to shift the emphasis from what the principal provides to obligations and commitments teachers feel toward each other.

4. *Binding*: Here principals and teachers together commit themselves to a set of shared values and ideas that ties them together as a "we." The emphasis in binding is on developing common commitments and conceptions about purposes, teaching and

learning, and the relationships that bring people together as a community of mind. Binding is recommended as a means to establish the moral authority that enables people to become self-managing.

Taken together the strategies can be thought of as developmental stages, each suited to different levels of school competence and excellence. The stages are summarized as follows (Sergiovanni, 1990:31):

Stage	Leadership by	Results
1. Initiation (getting started)	Bartering (push)	Has value (helps achieve competence)
2. Uncertainty (muddling through)	Building (support)	Adds value (increases readiness for excellence)
3. Transformative (breakthrough)	Bonding (inspire)	Adds value (helps achieve excellence)
4. Routinization (promoting self-management)	Binding (sustain)	Adds value (promotes self-management)

When viewed as developmental stages the emphasis is not on which leadership strategy is best, but which of the strategies makes most sense given the stage of school improvement in question. Leadership by bartering, for example, makes most sense in schools that are not working very well. Leadership by bonding, by contrast, makes sense when basic competence is not the issue and when a healthy interpersonal climate has been established. Each of the stages and leadership strategies will be elaborated on later in this chapter, but first it is important to differentiate between leadership for competence and leadership for excellence.

Leadership for Competence and Leadership for Excellence

Principals are responsible for gaining control over the likelihood that the school's basic requirements for competence are met and for helping the school and its members transcend competence by inspiring extraordinary commitment and performance. One of the shortcomings of traditional management and its leadership practices is that they can help teachers and schools achieve a basic level of competence but cannot sustain this competence without constant monitoring. Furthermore, traditional management and leadership are not able to encourage people and schools to transcend competence, allowing for commitment and performance beyond expectations (Bass, 1985; Burns, 1978).

In recent years the leadership practices based on traditional management have been augmented by findings from social science that suggest a more progressive human resources leadership practice (Argyris, 1964; Likert, 1967; McGregor, 1960; Miles, 1965; Sergiovanni and Starratt, 1971, 1988). This practice seeks to enhance and uplift the intrinsic motivational structure of people, allowing them to experience higher levels of need fulfillment. The results attributed to this human resources leadership have been salutary. Given the right psychological conditions, commitment and performance exceed expectations (see, for example, Herzberg 1966 and Maslow 1954).

Human resources leadership, however, has serious limitations. Because it relies on psychological contracts that barter need fulfillment for compliance and commitment, it is limited by the conditions of its psychological contract. Teachers, for example, respond enthusiastically as long as participation in work is psychologically fulfilling. When it isn't, commitment and performance become routine. These shortcomings make the cultivation of self-management among teachers difficult.

The challenge for principals is to provide the leadership needed to achieve a basic level of competence and then to transcend this competence to get extraordinary commitment and performance not only when rewards are available but when they are not. Sustained commitment and performance require an approach to leadership that connects people to work for moral reasons. Moral reasons emerge from the purposes, values, and norms that form the cultural center of the school. This center bonds people together in a common cause. For this reason the leadership that is required is referred to as *bonding leadership*. Bonding leadership is key in cultivating self-management among teachers. The three approaches to leadership can be summarized as follows.

1. *Traditional leadership* practices emphasize hierarchy, rules, and management protocols and rely on bureaucratic linkages to connect people to work by forcing them to respond as subordinates.

2. *Human resource leadership* practices emphasize leadership styles, supportive climates, and interpersonal skills and rely on psychological linkages to motivate people to work by getting them to respond ultimately as self-actualizers.

3. *Bonding leadership* practices emphasize ideas, values, and beliefs and rely on moral linkages to compel people to work by getting them to respond as followers.

Traditional leadership practices rely heavily on bureaucratic values as their source of authority. Teachers (and students, too) are expected to comply with the rules and to follow the provided scripts or face the consequences. In a sense, they trade compliance to avoid problems with the system. Bureaucratic authority has a place even in the most progressive of schools. Yet, when this source of authority is central, the following implicit assumptions are made:

Teachers are subordinates in a hierarchically arranged system.

Principals are trustworthy, but you cannot have a lot of trust in subordinates.

The goals and interests of teachers and principals are not the same; therefore, principals must be watchful.

Hierarchy equals expertise; thus, principals know more about everything than do teachers.

External accountability works best. (Sergiovanni and Starratt, 1993:25)

The consequences of relying on a leadership based primarily on bureaucratic authority have been carefully documented in the literature. Without proper monitoring, principals wind up being loosely connected to bureaucratic systems complying only when they have to (Sergiovanni, 1990–1991; Weick,1976). When this monitoring is effective, teachers respond as technicians who execute predetermined scripts and whose performance becomes narrowed. They become, to use the jargon, "de-skilled" (McNeil, 1986; Rosenholtz, 1989; Wise, 1979). When teachers are not able to use their full talents and when they are caught in the drudgery of routine, they become separated from their work, viewing teaching as a job rather than a vocation and treating students as cases rather than persons.

At least on the surface very few people advocate a leadership practice based primarily on bureaucratic authority. Also, on the surface, few accept the implicit assumptions that are behind this practice. Not many principals, for example, believe that teachers as a group are not trustworthy and do not share the same goals and interests about schooling as they do. Even fewer would accept the idea that hierarchy equals expertise, and, thus, they know more about everything than do teachers. Even so, most principals are likely to feel that teachers are subordinates in a hierarchically arranged system and that external monitoring works best. For this reason, supervision based on external monitoring persists. Principals still rely heavily on "expect and expect," predetermined standards, inservicing teachers, and direct supervision.

Human resources leadership practices rely heavily on personal expertise and skill in motivating and manipulating people as their source of authority. Essentially the idea is to figure out which psychological buttons to push when motivating teachers, and if the right ones are chosen, then teachers willingly trade compliance with the principal's wishes for getting needs met. When principals place personal authority at the center of their leadership practice, the following implicit assumptions are made:

> The goals and interests of teachers and principals are not the same. As a result, each must barter with the other so that both get what they want by giving something that the other party wants.
>
> Teachers have needs and if these needs are met at work, their work gets done as required in exchange.
>
> Congenial relationships in pleasant interpersonal climates make teachers easier to work with and more apt to cooperate with the principal.
>
> Principals must be experts at reading the needs of teachers and otherwise handling them in order to barter successfully for their cooperation and commitment. (Sergiovanni and Starratt, 1993:27)

The typical reaction of teachers to personal authority is to respond when rewards are available, but not otherwise. Teachers become involved in their work for calculated reasons, and as such, their performance is difficult to sustain over time without continually renegotiating the bartering arrangement.

Bonding leadership practices rely heavily on moral values as their source of authority. Moral authority is derived from obligations and duties that teachers feel toward each other and toward the school as a result of their connection to widely shared values, ideas, and ideals. When moral authority is in place, teachers respond to shared commitments and to the felt interdependence that comes from the sense of "we" that is created. As moral authority becomes the center of a principal's practice, the school is transformed into a moral community. Moral authority, for example, is the central tenant of the discussion on building community that appears in Chapter 4. The sources of authority and their relationship to leadership practice are summarized in Table 6–1.

The Stages of Leadership

In 1978, James MacGregor Burns proposed a theory of leadership that has shaped the way leadership practice is now understood. According to Burns, leadership is exercised when persons with certain motives and purposes mobilize resources so as to arouse and satisfy the motives of followers. He identified two broad kinds of leadership: transactional and transformative. Transactional leadership focuses on basic and largely extrinsic motives and needs; transformative leadership focuses on higher-order, more intrinsic, and ulti-

TABLE 6–1 The Sources of Authority for Leadership and Practice

Source	Assumptions when use of this source is prime	Leadership/supervisory strategy	Consequences

Bureaucratic authority
  Hierarchy
  Rules and
   regulations
  Mandates
  Role expectation
 	
Teachers are expected to comply or face consequences.
	Teachers are subordinates in a hierarchically arranged system.
	
	Supervisors are trustworthy, but you cannot trust subordinates very much.
	
	Goals and interests of teachers and supervisors are not the same; thus, supervisors must be watchful.
	
	Hierarchy equals expertise; thus, supervisors know more than do teachers.
	
	External accountability works best.
		"Expect and inspect" is the overarching rule.
		
		Rely on predetermined standards to which teachers must measure up.
		
		Identify their needs and "in-service" them.
		
		Directly supervise and closely monitor the work of teachers to ensure compliance.
		
		Figure out how to motivate them and get them to change.
			With proper monitoring teachers respond as technicians executing predetermined scripts. Their performance is narrowed.

Personal authority
  Motivation
   technology
  Interpersonal
   skills
  Human relations
   leadership
 	
Teachers will want to comply because of the congenial climate provided and to reap rewards offered in exchange.
	The goals and interests of teachers and supervisors are not the same but can be bartered so that each gets what they want.
	
	Teachers have needs, and if those needs are met at work, the work gets done as required in exchange.
	
	Congenial relationships and harmonious interpersonal climates make teachers content, easier to work with, and more apt to cooperate.
		Develop a school climate characterized by congeniality among teachers and between teachers and supervisors.
		
		"Expect and reward."
		
		"What gets rewarded gets done."
			Teachers respond as required when rewards are available but not otherwise. Their involvement is calculated and performance is narrowed.

Continued

TABLE 6–1 *(Continued)*

Source	Assumptions when use of this source is prime	Leadership/supervisory strategy	Consequences
Moral authority Felt obligations and duties derived from widely shared community values, ideas, and ideals Teachers respond to shared commitments and felt interdependence.	Schools are professional learning communities. Communities are defined by their center of shared values, beliefs, and commitments. In communities: What is considered right and good is as important as what works and what is effective. People are motivated as much by emotion and beliefs as by self-interest. Collegiality is a professional virtue.	Identify and make explicit the values and beliefs that define the center of the school as community. Translate the above into informal norms that govern behavior. Promote collegiality as internally felt and morally driven interdependence. Rely on ability of community members to respond to duties and obligations. Rely on the community's informal norm system to enforce professional and community values.	Teachers respond to community values for moral reasons. Their practice becomes collective and their performance is expansive and sustained.

Adapted from Thomas J. Sergiovanni. 1992. "Moral Authority and the Regeneration of Supervision," in Carl Glickman, Ed., *Supervision in Transition,* pp. 203–214. ASCD Yearbook. Association for Supervision and Curriculum Development, © Thomas J. Sergiovanni. All rights reserved. See also T. J. Sergiovanni, 1992. *Moral Leadership,* pp. 30–42. San Francisco: Jossey-Bass.

mately moral motives and needs. This latter point is important to understanding Burns's theory. Burns (1978:20) described transformational leadership, for example, as a process within which "leaders and followers raise one another to higher levels of morality and motivation." Transformative leadership is in two stages, one concerned with higher-order psychological needs for esteem, autonomy, and self-actualization, and the other with moral questions of goodness, righteousness, duty, and obligation.

 In his groundbreaking examination of the moral dimension in management and motivation, Amitai Etzioni (1988) provides a compelling case for moral authority as a source of motivation and basis for management. Etzioni acknowledges the importance of extrinsic and intrinsic motivation, but points out that ultimately what counts most to people is what they believe, how they feel, and the shared norms and cultural messages that emerge from the groups and communities with which they identify. Morality, emotion, and social bonds, he maintains, are far more powerful motivators than are the extrinsic concerns of transactional leadership and the intrinsic psychological concerns of the early stages of transformative leadership.

In transactional leadership, leader and followers exchange needs and services in order to accomplish *independent* objectives. It is assumed that leader and followers do not share a common stake in the enterprise, and thus some kind of bargain must be struck. This bargaining process can be viewed metaphorically as a form of *leadership by bartering*. The wants and needs of followers and the wants and needs of the leader are traded and a bargain is struck. Positive reinforcement is given for good work, merit pay for increased performance, promotion for increased persistence, a feeling of belonging for cooperation, and so forth.

In transformative leadership, by contrast, leaders and followers are united in pursuit of higher-level goals that are common to both. Both want to become the best. Both want to shape the school in a new direction. When transformative leadership is practiced successfully, purposes that might have started out being separate become fused.

Initially, transformative leadership takes the form of *leadership by building*. Here the focus is on arousing human potential, satisfying higher-order needs, and raising expectations of both leader and follower in a manner that motivates both to higher levels of commitment and performance. Leadership by bartering responds to physical, security, social, and ego needs. Leadership by building responds to esteem, achievement, competence, autonomy, and self-actualizing needs. The human resources management and leadership literature referred to earlier in this chapter provides compelling evidence supporting the efficacy of leadership by building.

Burns points out that ultimately transformative leadership becomes moral because it raises the level of human conduct and ethical aspiration of both leader and led. When this occurs, transformative leadership takes the form of *leadership by bonding*. Here the leader focuses on arousing awareness and consciousness that elevate school goals and purposes to the level of a shared covenant that bonds together leader and follower in a moral commitment. Leadership by bonding responds to such intrinsic human needs as a desire for purpose, meaning, and significance in what one does. The key concepts associated with transformative leadership by bonding are cultural and moral leadership.

Leadership by bartering, building, and bonding, when viewed sequentially, make up the stages of leadership for school improvement referred to earlier. Bartering provides the push needed to get things started; building provides the push needed to deal with uncertainty and to create the psychological support system necessary for people to respond to higher levels of need fulfillment; and bonding provides the inspiration needed for performance and commitment that are beyond expectations.

School improvement initiatives become real only when they are institutionalized as part of the everyday life of the school. To this effort, *leadership by binding* is the fourth stage of school improvement. *Binding* seeks to routinize school improvements, thus conserving human energy and effort for new projects and initiatives. The key is connecting people to a set of ideas and ideals about the work of the school. This binding of ideas provides guidelines as to what to do and helps people become self-managing.

When practicing leadership by binding, the principal *ministers* to the needs of the school and works to serve others so that they are better able to perform their responsibilities. In addition to manager, minister, and servant, the leader functions as a "high priest" by protecting the values of the school. The high priest function is an expression of the cultural force of leadership discussed in Chapter 5.

Each of the stages of leadership can be thought of as comprising distinct school improvement strategies. However, tactically speaking, bartering, building, bonding, and binding can be thought of as leadership styles to be used simultaneously for different purposes or people within any of the stages. A recalcitrant teacher, for example, may well require leadership by bartering regardless of one's overall strategy.

Leadership by bartering is an especially effective strategy when the issue is one of competence. However, once competence has been achieved, one needs to look to leadership by building and bonding for the strategies and tactics that will help transcend competence to inspire commitment and extraordinary performance. The stages of leadership and their relationship to school improvement are summarized in Exhibit 6–1.

EXHIBIT 6–1   The Stages of Leadership and School Improvement

Leadership Type	Leadership Styles	Stages of School Improvement	Leadership Concepts	Involvement of Followers	Needs Satisfied	Effects
Value (transactional) leadership	Leadership as "bartering"	*Initiation* (push) Exchanging human needs and interests that allow satisfaction of independent (leader and follower) but organizationally related objectives.	Management skills Leadership style Contingency theory Exchange theory Path-goal theory	Calculated	Physical Security Social Ego	Continual performance contingent on parties keeping the bargain struck. "A fair day's work for a fair day's pay."
Value-added (transformational) leadership	Leadership as "building"	*Uncertainty* (muddle through) Arousing human potential, satisfying higher needs, raising expectations of both leader and followers that motivate to higher levels of commitment and performance.	Empowerment Symbolic leadership "Charisma"	Intrinsic	Esteem Competence Autonomy Self-actualization	Performance and commitment are sustained beyond external conditions. Both are beyond expectations in quantity and quality.

EXHIBIT 6–1   *(Continued)*

Leadership Type	Leadership Styles	Stages of School Improvement	Leadership Concepts	Involvement of Followers	Needs Satisfied	Effects
	Leadership as "bonding"	Transformative (breakthrough) Arousing awareness and consciousness that elevate organizational goals and purposes to the level of a shared covenant and that bond together leader and followers in a moral commitment.	Cultural leadership Moral leadership Covenant Building followership	Moral	Purpose Meaning Significance	
	Leadership as "binding"	*Routinization* (promoting self-management) Turning improvements into routines so that they become second-nature. Ministering to the needs of the school, being of service, guarding the values. Connecting people to an idea structure that guides what to do.	Procedures Institutional leadership Servant leadership Leadership by outrage Kindling outrage in others	Automatic	All needs are supported	Performance remains sustained.

Adapted from Thomas J. Sergiovanni. 1990. *Value-Added Leadership: How to Get Extraordinary Performance in Schools,* pp. 39–40. New York: Harcourt Brace Jovanovich.

Operationalizing Charismatic Leadership

Transformational leadership in the form of leadership by building, bonding, and binding sounds similar to the concept of *charisma*. This similarity can be troublesome because depending on how charisma is defined, one could conclude that the ability to successfully practice leadership by building, bonding, and binding is based on specific endowed gifts of birth and personality. If this is the case, then some principals have it and others don't, and those who don't can't get it. This is the conclusion to be reached if one accepts the metaphysical definition that comes from the Greek language in which *charisma* means the ability to perform miracles, to predict the future, and to possess divinely inspired gifts.

In recent years the social science literature has moved away from considering charisma as having something to do with "divine personality" to more ordinary definitions themed either to one's ability to influence and inspire others or to attributions of this ability. Instead of worrying about a mysterious charismatic personality, the emphasis is on identifying behaviors that encourage people to *attribute* charismatic qualities to the leader.

Leaders thought to be charismatic have the ability to touch some people in meaningful ways. As a result, these people respond to their leaders and to the ideas and values that they stand for with unusual commitment and effort. The typical result is performance that is beyond expectations.

There is growing consensus that this charismatic leadership does not exist as something concrete or objective but is a perception—indeed an attribute that cannot be separated from followership. Followers attribute charisma to the leader. Furthermore, no leader is thought to be charismatic by everyone. There needs to be a connection between what the leader does and the meanings, if any, that followers derive. For example, to many Americans, Presidents Kennedy and Reagan were considered to be charismatic in the sense that they touched people in meaningful ways—but not necessarily the same people. By the same token, large numbers of Americans view Presidents Kennedy and Reagan negatively—but not necessarily the same people. Conger (1989:23–24) points out that in order for leadership behaviors to "induce the perception of charisma, their specific character has to be seen by followers as *relevant* to their situation. If followers do not think their leader's formulation of a strategic vision matches their own aspirations, they are less likely to perceive him or her as a charismatic leader."

According to attribution theory (i.e., Kelly, 1973), followers search for the meaning of the leader's behavior. We attribute a set of generalizations to the leader based on what we see and hear and what we think it means to us. We might conclude, for example, that Bill is a wishy-washy principal, Terry is a manager but little else, and that Mary is the kind of principal who is a real leader. Our conclusions result from our own needs, our values, our conceptions of what good leadership is, and our own experiences. If there is a match between the behaviors we observe and what we think they mean, then the attribution is a positive one. If not, it is negative. These attributions result in different kinds of commitments to the leader and different levels of effort. After an exhaustive survey of the literature on charismatic leadership and attribution theory, Yukl (1989:205) concludes: "Charisma is believed to result from follower perceptions of leader qualities and behavior. These perceptions are influenced by the context of the leadership situation and the follower's individual and collective needs."

Behavioral Dimensions of Charisma

Conger and Kanungo (1987, 1988) have proposed a theory that identifies the leadership behaviors that influence followers to attribute charismatic qualities to a leader. The dimensions identified do not constitute a personality type but rather a set of leadership behaviors that can be duplicated by principals with varying personalities. Moreover, independent of the charismatic issue, the leadership behaviors result in extraordinary levels of commitment and performance (Conger, 1989). Conger and Kanungo (1987, 1988) propose that followers are more likely to attribute charisma to leaders

> who advocate a vision that challenges the status quo but still is close enough to be accepted by followers.

> who demonstrate convincingly that they are willing to take personal risks, incur high costs and even make self-sacrifices to achieve their vision.

> who act in unconventional ways in implementing the vision.

> whose vision and actions are timely in the sense that they are sensitive to the values, beliefs, and needs of followers on the one hand and to the opportunities inherent in the situation at hand on the other.

> who respond to existing dissatisfaction or, if needed, who create dissatisfaction in the status quo.

> who are able to communicate confidence in themselves and their proposals and who are enthusiastic about the future prospects for successful implementation of proposals.

> who rely on expert power to influence others by demonstrating that they know what they are talking about and can propose solutions that help others to be successful. (summarized from Yukl, 1989:208–209)

According to Conger (1989), the behavioral dimensions of charismatic leadership are manifested in four stages. Stage one involves sensing leadership opportunities and formulating a vision. The leader detects unexploited opportunities and deficiencies or problems in the current situation and formulates a vision that responds. Key to stage one is being sensitive to the needs of followers and other constituents. Success of the proposed vision depends on whether it helps followers and others satisfy their own needs.

Stage two involves communicating the vision in a fashion that makes it clear that the current situation is unacceptable and the proposed vision is an attractive alternative. If the proposed alternative is responsive to the needs of followers and other constituents then it is likely to be accepted even though it represents a radical departure from the present. As Conger (1989) points out, "Since the vision is a perspective shared by the followers and promises to meet their aspirations, it tends to be very acceptable despite its radical departure from the present situation" (29).

Stage three involves building trust with followers and other constituencies by demonstrating sincerity and commitment to the proposed vision. As Conger (1989) explains, "Thus the leader must build exceptional trust among subordinates in himself and in the goals he articulates. The charismatic leader does this through personal risk taking, unconventional expertise, and self-sacrifice. These qualities set the charismatic leader apart from others" (33).

Stage four involves demonstrating the means to achieve the vision through modeling, empowering others, and the use of unconventional tactics.

One of the ways to test the efficacy of the ideas Conger and Kanungo propose is to examine leaders you know from personal experience whom you consider to possess charismatic qualities. To what extent do they exhibit the behavioral dimensions just described? As you review the dimensions, which one seems to function as the lynchpin that holds the others together?

Charismatic leaders, bonding leaders, and transformative leaders share one common quality; *the ability to respond to the needs of followers.* They are able to help others reach higher levels of need fulfillment, to extract more meaning from their work lives, and to see that what they are doing is something special and significant. When these needs are addressed, followers invariably respond with higher levels of commitment, effort, and performance.

Why Leadership by Bonding and Binding Works

Bonding and binding leadership works because:

- They are aligned with a realistic view of how schools actually work; thus its practices are practical.
- They are based on a theory of human rationality that enhances both individual and organizational intelligence and performance.
- They respond to higher-order psychological and spiritual needs that lead to extraordinary commitment, performance, and satisfaction.

In Chapter 4, it was pointed out that traditional management assumes schools, school districts, and state systems of schooling are "managerially tight and culturally loose." According to this theory, what counts in improving schools is management connections, not people. When this is the case, the operation of schools represents the mechanical workings of a clock comprising cogs and gears, wheels, drives, and pins, all tightly connected in an orderly and predictable manner. This is the "Clockworks I" theory or mindscape of management.

Clockworks I leaders believe that the purpose of leadership is to gain control and regulate the master wheel and the master pin of their clockworks organization. This is sometimes done by introducing highly refined management systems to ensure that teachers will teach the way they are supposed to and students will be taught what they are supposed to learn. Unfortunately, this rarely happens, at least not on a sustained and continuous basis and not without excessive monitoring and other enforcement efforts. When such a system does work, it gets people to do what they are supposed to, but no more (leadership by bartering).

Weick's (1976) observations and those of March (1984) provide an image of schools that function like a clockworks gone awry—a theory of cogs, gears, and pins all spinning independently of each other. Regulating for the main gear and pin as a management strategy doesn't work because they are not connected to any of the other parts. Instead, the leader must rely on "cultural cement" to provide the necessary connections for coordination and control. The ingredients for cultural cement are the norms, values, beliefs, and purposes of people. Weick (1982:675) advises school leaders to ". . . . be attentive to the 'glue' that holds loosely coupled systems together because such forms are just barely systems." March (1984:32) similarly advises:

> *If we want to identify one single way in which administrators can affect organizations, it is through their effect on the world views that surround organizational life; those effects are managed through attention to the ritual and symbolic characteristics of organizations and their administration. Whether we wish to sustain the system or change it, management is a way of making a symbolic statement.*

Leadership by bonding and binding can provide the necessary cultural cement that holds people and organizations together.

Theories of school management and leadership are based on different images of human rationality. When a school leader chooses a theory from which to practice, a particular image of rationality is assumed whether or not it fits the real world. A better fit between theory and practice will occur by starting the other way around. First choose the image of rationality that fits the real world, and then find a theory that fits that image of rationality.

Shulman (1989) provides three images of human rationality. All three are true to a certain extent, but some are more true than others. It makes a difference which of the three or which combination of the three provides the strategic basis for one's leadership practice. The three are provided below. Using a total of 10 points, distribute points among the three to indicate the extent to which you believe each to be true.

1. Humans are rational; they think and act in a manner consistent with their goals, their self-interests and what they have been rewarded for. If you wish them to behave in a given way, make the desired behavior clear to them and make it worth their while to engage in it.
2. Humans are limited in their rationality; they can make sense of only a small piece of the world at a time and they strive to act reasonably with respect to their limited grasp of facts and alternatives. They must, therefore, construct conceptions or definitions of situations rather than passively accept what is presented to them. If you wish them to change, engage them in active problem solving and judgment, don't just tell them what to do.
3. Humans are rational only when acting together; since individual reason is so limited, men and women find opportunities to work jointly on important problems, achieving through joint effort what individual reason and capacity could never accomplish. If you want them to change, develop ways in which they can engage in the change process jointly with peers. (Shulman, 1989:171)

The first image of rationality fits traditional management theories and leadership by bartering practices very well. The second and third images, by contrast, are better accommodated by the clockworks-gone-awry view of management and leadership by building and bonding. Within the second and third images, rationality is achieved by helping people make sense of their world. As sense builds, some of the limits on rationality are overcome. The ability to make sense builds when people are able to construct their own definitions of situations and are involved with the leader in active problem solving. The limits, however, are typically too great for anyone to do it alone. Thus, a key strategy for sense building is the pooling of human resources and the fostering of collegial values in an effort that expands individual reason and capacity to function successfully.

Leadership as bartering responds to physical, security, social, and ego needs of people at work. In his well-known motivation-hygiene theory, Herzberg (1966) pointed out that these needs and the job factors that accommodated them had less to do with commitment and performance beyond expectations than with meeting ordinary basic job requirements. He pointed out that should the needs not be met, worker performance and commitment are likely to fall below a satisfactory level. But when the needs are met, all that results is that workers meet basic job requirements. However, when such job factors as opportunities for achievement, challenge, responsibility, recognition for one's accomplishment, and opportunities to demonstrate competence were present, then such higher-order needs as esteem, competence, autonomy, and self-actualization were likely to be met. These factors and needs are related to leadership by building. They are the bridges that leader and followers must cross together as they move from ordinary performance to performance that is beyond expectations.

The strength of leadership by bonding and binding is the ability to focus on arousing awareness and consciousness to elevate school goals and purposes to the level of a shared covenant that bonds leader and followers together and binds them to a set of ideas that comprise moral commitments. Leadership by bonding and binding responds to such higher-order needs as the desire for purpose, meaning, and significance in what one does.

Idea-Based Leadership

When values and beliefs become institutionalized into the everyday management life of the school, then management know-how, hierarchical authority, interpersonal skill, and personality are ultimately transcended as the leader becomes one who administers to the needs of the school and its members. The principal doesn't become less important, only differently important. On the one hand she or he becomes the guardian of the values of the school's covenant, and on the other hand a capable administrator who works hard to help others meet their commitments to the school. Once at this stage, leadership and followership become very, very close. As pointed out earlier, followers manage themselves well by thinking for themselves, exercising self-control, accepting responsibility and obligation, and believing in and caring about what they are doing (Kelly, 1988:144). Both followers and leaders are attracted to and compelled by the same things: ideas, values, and commitments. Thus, over time, leaders seek to restructure the chain of command so that followers are not connected to leaders in a hierarchical sense, but so that both leaders and followers respond to the same ideas, values, and commitments.

Traditional chain of command	*New chain of command*
(hierarchical authority)	*(moral authority)*
Leaders	*Ideas, values, commitments*
↓	↓
Followers	*Leaders as followers and*
	followers as leaders

When this happens, hierarchical authority and authority derived from one's personality give way to purpose and management. The leader is neither boss nor messiah but administrator.

The authority vested in the leader as boss is organizational and hierarchical; the authority vested in the leader as messiah is charismatic and interpersonal; and the authority vested in the leader as administrator is obligatory, stemming from the obligations that come from serving shared values and purposes (Sergiovanni, 1990:150).

School principals are responsible for "ministering" to the needs of the schools they serve, as defined by the shared values and purposes of the school's covenant. They minister by furnishing help and by being of service to parents, teachers, and students. They minister by providing leadership in a way that encourages others to be leaders in their own right. They minister by highlighting and protecting the values of the school. The principal as minister is one who is devoted to a cause, mission, or set of ideas and accepts the duty and obligation to serve this cause. Ultimately, her or his success is known by the quality of the followership that emerges in the school. The quality of followership is a barometer that indicates the extent to which moral authority has replaced bureaucratic. When moral authority drives leadership practice, the principal is at the same time a leader of leaders, follower of ideas, minister of values, and servant to the followership.

References

Argyris, Chris. 1964. *Integrating the Individual and the Organization.* New York: Wiley.

Bass, Bernard. 1985. *Leadership and Performance Beyond Expectations.* New York: Harper & Row.

Burns, James MacGregor. 1978. *Leadership.* New York: Harper & Row.

Conger, Jay A. 1989. *The Charismatic Leader.* San Francisco: Jossey-Bass.

Conger, Jay A., and Rabindra N. Kanungo. 1987. "Towards a Behavioral Theory of Charismatic Leadership in Organizational Settings," *Academy of Management Review* 12(4), 637–647.

Conger, Jay, and Rabindra N. Kanungo. 1988. "Behavioral Dimensions of Charismatic Leadership," in J. A. Conger and R. N. Kanungo, Eds., *Charismatic Leadership.* San Francisco: Jossey-Bass.

Etzioni, Amitai. 1988. *The Moral Dimension Toward a New Theory of Economics.* New York: The Free Press.

Herzberg, Frederick. 1966. *Work and the Nature of Man.* Cleveland: The World Publishing Company.

Kelly, H. H. 1973. "The Process of Causal Attribution," *American Psychologist* 28(2), 107–128.

Likert, Rensis. 1967. *The Human Organization: Its Management and Value.* New York: McGraw-Hill.

March, James G. 1984. "How We Talk and How We Act: Administrative Theory and Administrative Life," in T. J. Sergiovanni and J. E. Corbally, Eds., *Leadership and Organizational Culture.* Urbana: University of Illinois Press.

Maslow, Abraham. 1954. *Motivation and Personality.* New York: Harper & Row.

McGregor, Douglas. 1960. *The Human Side of Enterprise.* New York: McGraw-Hill.

McNeil, Linda. 1986. *Contradictions of Control: School Structure and School Knowledge.* New York: Routledge and Kegan Paul.

Miles, Raymond E. 1965. "Human Relations or Human Resources?" *Harvard Business Review* 43(4), 148–163.

Rosenholtz, Susan. 1989. *Teachers' Workplace: The Social Organization of Schools.* New York: Longman.

Sergiovanni, Thomas J. 1990. *Value-Added Leadership: How to Get Extraordinary Performance in Schools.* San Diego, CA: Harcourt Brace Jovanovich.

Sergiovanni, Thomas J. 1990–1991. "Biting the Bullet: Rescinding the Texas Teacher Appraisal system," *Teacher Education in Practice* 6(2), 89–93.

Sergiovanni, Thomas J. 1994. *Building Community in Schools.* San Francisco: Jossey-Bass.

Sergiovanni, Thomas J., and Robert J. Starratt. 1971. *Emerging Patterns of Supervision: Human Perspectives.* New York: McGraw-Hill.

Sergiovanni, Thomas J., and Robert J. Starratt. 1988. *Supervision: Human Perspectives,* 4th ed. New York: McGraw-Hill.

Sergiovanni, Thomas J., and Robert J. Starratt. 1993. *Supervision: A Redefinition*, 5th ed. New York: McGraw-Hill.

Shulman, Lee. 1989. "Teaching Alone, Learning Together: Needed Agenda for New Reforms," in T. J. Sergiovanni and J. H. Moore, Eds., *Schooling for Tomorrow: Directing Reforms to Issues that Count.* Boston: Allyn and Bacon.

Weick, Karl E. 1976. "Educational Organization as Loosely Coupled Systems," *Administrative Science Quarterly* 21.

Weick, Karl E. 1982. "Administering Education in Loosely Coupled Schools," *Phi Delta Kappan* 26.

Wise, Arthur E. 1979. *Legislated Learning: The Bureaucratization of the American Classroom.* Berkeley: University of California Press.

Yukl, Gary A. 1989. *Leadership in Organizations,* 2nd ed. Englewood Cliffs, NJ: Prentice-Hall.

Becoming a Community of Leaders

The idea of community has appeal to most principals, and many schools are quick to label themselves as caring communities and learning communities. But yet, when the conversation shifts to a discussion of school as a community of leaders, many principals begin to feel uncomfortable. The literature, for example, frequently encourages us to provide strong and direct leadership in making schools effective. As a result, leadership is part of an interaction influence system within which the leader, acting alone, interacts with others in an effort to influence what they think and do.

As discussed in Chapter 6, we have come to understand this approach as leadership by bartering. Leader and led strike bargains within which the leader gives to the led something they want in exchange for something the leader wants. Within this view, leaders may have lofty visions and may want to do the right thing, but exercising leadership still means controlling events and people in a way that makes events transpire the way leaders think they should. Progressive leaders, however, are not supposed to be dictatorial. Instead, they are encouraged to share some of *their* responsibility for leadership with others and delegate some of *their* authority to others. When they do this, so it is believed, the likelihood that others will respond better and thus be more likely to do what the leader thinks is good for the school is increased.

Struggling to make the school a community changes all of this. Leadership by bartering may be necessary in the beginning, but then the emphasis shifts to leadership by building, bonding, and binding. In creating community, what matters most is what the community shares together, what the community believes in together, and what the community wants to accomplish together. It is this shared idea structure, this community of mind, that becomes the primary source of authority for what people do. Together, principals and teachers become followers of the dream and are committed to making it real. Within this view, leadership is nothing more than a means to make things happen. Because not only the principal but all of the followers have an equal obligation to embody community values, principals and teachers must share equally together in the obligation to lead.

Practical Issues

Striving to make the school a community of leaders is a good idea that doesn't need much justification. After all, most will agree the more that leadership is cultivated in a school, the more likely it is that everyone will get a chance to use their talents fully and the more committed everyone is likely to be. Furthermore, in a democracy such as ours, the more that leadership is shared and expressed, the better it is presumed to be. Exercising leadership for the good of everyone is considered to be one of the responsibilities of citizenship. An additional consideration is that, given today's complex world, shared leadership is necessary for schools to work well.

In their review of the literature on school improvement, Lieberman and Miller (1986) reached a similar conclusion. They found that any effort to improve schools must be grounded in the social realities of the classroom as revealed in the lives of teachers and their work. This is the same conclusion they reached in their 1978 epic, "The Social Realities of Teaching." In their words:

> *What we have rediscovered are some tried and true notions that have become enriched and expanded over time. Among them:*
>
> *Working with people rather than working* on *people.*
>
> *Recognizing the complexity and craft nature of the teacher's work.*
>
> *Understanding that there are unique cultural differences in each school and how these affect development efforts.*
>
> *Providing time to learn.*
>
> *Building collaboration and cooperation, involving the provisions for people to do things together, talking together, sharing concerns.*
>
> *Starting where people are, not where you are.*
>
> *Making private knowledge public, by being sensitive to the effects of teacher isolation and the power of trial and error.*
>
> *Resisting simplistic solutions to complex problems; getting comfortable with reworking issues and finding enhanced understanding and enlightenment.*
>
> *Appreciating that there are many variations of development efforts; there is no one best way.*
>
> *Using knowledge as a way of helping people grow rather than pointing up their deficits.*
>
> *Supporting development efforts by protecting ideas, announcing expectations, making provisions for necessary resources.*

Sharing leadership functions as a team, so that people can provide complementary skills and get experience in role taking.

Organizing development efforts around a particular focus.

Understanding that content and process are both essential, that you cannot have one without the other.

Being aware of and sensitive to the differences in the worlds of teachers and other actors within or outside of the school setting. (Lieberman and Miller, 1986:108–109)

Lieberman and Miller's list suggests that successful school improvement efforts depend on reaching into the invisible aspects of school life and tapping the energy and commitment of teachers up close. Teachers have to take initiative, accept responsibility, and become active leaders. Together, principal and teachers must become a community of leaders.

New Leadership Values for the Principalship

Becoming a community of leaders requires adopting new leadership values such as purposing, followership, empowerment, accomplishment, collegiality, intrinsic motivation, quality control, simplicity, reflection, and outrage. Together the values provide the substance for practicing leadership by bonding and by binding. They are considered in the following subsections in the form of leadership principles.

Purposing and Shared Values

Harvard Business School professor Abraham Zaleznik (1989) believes that the failure of management is the substitution of process for substance. The importance of management processes to school effectiveness should not be underestimated, but such processes are not substitutes for substance. It is important, for example, to know how to get from A to B, and sound management can help, however, the substance of administrative leadership is concerned with whether B is better than A and why. Furthermore, having determined the direction, substance is the means by which one brings together divergent human resources, inspires commitment, and achieves extraordinary performance.

Management processes alone turn workers into *subordinates*. Substances, by contrast, build *followership.* Subordinates comply with management rules and procedures and with the leader's directives; the job gets done. Followers, however, respond to ideas, ideals, values, and purposes; as a result, the job gets done well.

In his classic book *The Functions of the Executive* (1938), Chester Barnard stated: "The inculcation of belief in the real existence of a common purpose is an essential executive function" (87). The inculcation of belief comes from the embodiment of purposes as leaders act and behave, or, in the words of Peter Vaill, from *purposing*. He defines purposing as "that continuous stream of actions by an organization's formal leadership which has the effect of inducing clarity, consensus and commitment regarding the organizations basic purposes" (1984:91). Vaill (1984) conducted extensive studies of high-performing systems (HPS) from a broad spectrum of American society. He examined the characteristics held in common by these systems and the kind of leadership found within them. Key to success was the presence of purposing. "HPS's are clear on their broad purposes and on near-term objectives for fulfilling these purposes. They know why they exist and what they are trying to do. Members have pictures in their heads which are strikingly congruent" (86). He continues, "Commitment to these purposes is never perfunctory. . . . [M]otivation as usually conceived is always high" (86).

Purposing is a key characteristic found by others who have studied successful schools in the United States. This research establishes the importance of shared goals and expectations and approved modes of behavior that create a strong school culture. Important to this culture are the norms and values that provide a cohesion and identity and that create a unifying moral order from which teachers and students derive direction, meaning, and significance. One example is Joan Lipsitz's (1984) study of four successful middle schools. She found that the four schools achieved unusual clarity about the purposes of intermediate schooling and the students they teach, and made powerful statements, both in word and in practice, about their purposes. There was little disagreement about what they believed and little discrepancy between what they said they were doing and what they were actually doing.

It is through purposing and the building of shared values and agreements that a school culture emerges.

> *The concept of culture refers to the total way of life in a society, the heritage of accumulated social learnings that is shared and transmitted by the members of that society. To put it another way a culture is a set of shared plans for living, developed out of necessities of previous generations, existing in the minds of the present generation, taught directly or indirectly to new generations. (White, 1952:15)*

Purposing involves both the vision of the leader and a set of agreements that the group shares. Warren Bennis (1984) describes vision as "the capacity to create and communicate a compelling vision of a desired state of affairs, a vision . . . that clarifies the current situation and induces commitment to the future" (66). Vision is an important dimension of purposing and without it the very point of leadership is missed, but the vision of the school must also reflect the hopes and dreams, the needs and interests, the values and beliefs of everyone who has a stake in the school—teachers, parents, and students. In the end it is what the school stands for that counts. In successful schools, consensus runs deep. It is not enough to have worked out what people stand for and what is to be accomplished. A binding and solemn agreement needs to emerge that represents a value system for living together and that provides the basis for decisions and actions. This binding and solemn agreement represents the school's covenant.

When both vision and covenant are present, teachers and students respond with increased motivation and commitment and their performance is beyond expectations. The affirming of values that accompanies purposing is a motivational force far more powerful than the bureaucratic and psychological transactions that characterize leadership by bartering and building. They become the very basis upon which we construct our reality and from which we derive sense and meaning. As Gardner (1986) points out,

> *A great civilization is a drama lived in the minds of people. It is a shared vision; it is shared norms, expectations and purposes. . . . If we look at ordinary human communities, we see the same reality: A community lives in the minds of its members—in shared assumptions, beliefs, customs, ideas that give meaning, ideas that motivate. (7)*

Building Followership

In his book *Every Employee a Manager,* Scott Meyers (1971) observed that the more managementlike jobs were, the more readily workers accepted responsibility and responded with increased motivation. By *managementlike,* he meant having the freedom to plan, organize, and control one's life, and to make decisions, to accept responsibility, and to be held accountable for one's actions in light of this responsibility. Every employee as a manager is a goal of leadership by bonding because it contributes to leadership density. *Leadership density* refers to the extent to which leadership roles are shared and leadership itself is broadly based and exercised. To understand leadership density one needs to understand how closely leadership and followership are linked and what the differences are between being a good follower and a good subordinate. Good followers manage themselves well. They think for themselves, exercise self-control, and are able to accept responsibility and obligation, believe in and care about what they are doing, and be self-motivated; therefore, they are able to do what is right for the school, do it well, do it with persistence, and most importantly do it without close supervision (Kelly, 1988). Followers are committed people—committed perhaps to a set of purposes, a cause, a vision of what the school is and can become, a set of beliefs about what teaching and learning should be, a set of values and standards to which they adhere, a conviction.

By contrast, good subordinates do what they are supposed to but little else. They want to know specifically what is expected of them, and with proper monitoring and supervision will perform accordingly. They are dependent on their leaders to provide them with goals and objectives and the proper ways and means to achieve them. They want to know what the rules of the game are and will play the game as required to avoid problems. For them and their leaders, life is comfortable and easy. For the school and the children they teach, excellence escapes and mediocrity becomes the norm.

Subordinates are not committed to causes, values, or ideas, but respond instead to authority in the form of rules, regulations, expectations of their supervisors, and other management requirements. This is a crucial distinction. Subordinates respond to authority; followers respond to ideas. The standard dictionary definition of a follower is one who is in the service of a cause or of another person who represents a cause; a follower is one who follows opinions and teachings—a disciple. Because followership is linked to ideas, it is difficult for principals to help others transcend subordinateness for followership in schools, without practicing leadership by purposing.

The concept of followership proposes a number of paradoxes. It turns out that effective following is really a form of leadership (Kelly, 1988). Commitment to a cause and the practice of self-management are hallmarks of good leadership and they are hallmarks of good followership as well. The successful leader then is one who builds up the leadership of others and who strives to become a leader of leaders. A successful leader is also a good follower—one who follows ideas, values, and beliefs. When followership is established, bureaucratic and psychological authority are transcended by moral authority. A new kind of hierarchy emerges in the school, one that places purposes, values, and commitments at the apex and teachers, principals, parents, and students below in service to these purposes.

Enabling Others to Function Autonomously on Behalf of Shared Purposes

There are three dimensions to enablement: (1) empowering principals, teachers, parents, and others by giving them the discretion they need to function autonomously on behalf of school goals and purposes; (2) providing them with the support and training they need to function autonomously; and (3) removing the bureaucratic obstacles that keep them from being autonomous.

Bonding leaders practice the principle of power investment. They distribute power among others in an effort to get more power in return. They know that it is not power over people and events that counts, but power over the likelihood that accomplishments and shared goals and purposes will be realized. To gain control over the latter they recognize that they need to delegate or surrender control over the former. In a nonlinear and loosely connected world they are resigned to the reality that delegation and empowerment are unavoidable.

Except for the most routine of jobs, the major problem facing management in America today is the gap existing between ability and authority (Thompson, 1961). Those who have the authority to act typically don't have the necessary technical ability, and those with the ability to act typically don't have the necessary authority. Leadership by empowerment can remedy this situation by lending to those with the ability the necessary authority to act.

Empowerment without purposing is not what is intended by this value. The two must go hand in hand. When directed and enriched by purposing and fueled by empowerment, teachers and others respond not only with increased motivation and commitment but with surprising ability as well. They become smarter, using their talents more fully and growing on the job. Thus, the first question that bonding leaders ask when thinking about empowerment is: Empowered to do what? The empowerment rule that they follow is *everyone is free to do the things that make sense to them providing the decisions they make about what to do embody the values that are shared.* Furthermore, the best empowerment strategy is not to focus on teachers or to focus on any other particular role group, but to think about empowering the school site. It is principals, teachers, and parents, bonded together in a common cause, who are given the necessary discretion that they need to function effectively. Empowerment is the natural complement to accountability. One cannot hold teachers, parents, and schools accountable without giving them the necessary responsibility to make the decisions that they think are best. The mistake of equating empowerment with freedom must be avoided. Empowerment has to do with obligation and duty. One is not free to do what he or she pleases, but free to make sensible decisions in light of shared values.

Viewing Leadership as Power to Accomplish

Successful leaders know the difference between power *over* and power *to*. There is a link between leadership and power, and indeed leadership is a special form of power—power to influence. There are, however, two conceptions of power: power over and power to. Power over is controlling and is concerned with "how can I control people and events so that things turn out the way I want?" Power over is concerned with dominance, control, and hierarchy. One needs to be in a position of dominance, control, and hierarchy to exercise power over. One needs to have access to rewards and punishments, "carrots," and "bully" sticks. In reality, however, most principals don't have many carrots or bully sticks. Furthermore, people don't like carrots or bully sticks and resist power over leadership both formally and informally. Thus, this approach is rarely effective.

The concept of power over raises certain ethical questions relating to dominance and manipulation. Power to, however, is not instrumental but facilitative. It is power to do something, to accomplish something, and to help others accomplish something that they think is important. In power to, far less emphasis is given to what people are doing and far more emphasis is given to what they are accomplishing.

Putting Collegiality First

When combined with purposing, leadership density, and enablement, collegiality is an important strategy for bringing about the kinds of connections that make schools work and work well in a nonlinear and loosely structured world. Too often, however, collegiality is confused with congeniality (Barth, 1986). *Congeniality* refers to the friendly human relationships that exist among teachers and is characterized by the loyalty, trust, and easy conversation that result from the development of a closely knit social group. *Collegiality*, by contrast, refers to the existence of high levels of collaboration among teachers and between teachers and principal and is characterized by mutual respect, *shared work values*, cooperation, and specific conversations about teaching and learning. When congeniality is high, a strong, informal culture aligned with social norms emerges in the school; however, the norms may or may not be aligned with school purposes. Sometimes the norms contribute to and at other times interfere with increased commitment and extraordinary performance. By contrast, when collegiality is high, a strong, professional culture held together by shared work norms emerges in the school. The norms are aligned with school purposes, contributing consistently to increased commitment and extraordinary performance.

Recent research independently reported by Little (1981) and Rosenholtz (1989) provides compelling support for the importance of collegiality and building a professional culture of teaching on the one hand and in enhancing commitment and performance on the other. Both researchers found that the kind of leadership principals provided influences the collegial norm structure of the school. Rosenholtz found that teachers in high collegial schools described their principals as being supportive and as considering problems to be schoolwide concerns that provided opportunities for collective problem solving and learning. Teachers and principals in less collegial schools, by contrast, reported being isolated and alienated. In her research, Little found that norms of collegiality were developed when principals clearly communicated expectations for teacher cooperation; provided a model for collegiality by working firsthand with teachers in improving the school; rewarded expressions of collegiality among teachers by providing recognition, release time, money, and other support resources; and protected teachers who were willing to go against expected norms of privatism and isolation by engaging in collegial behaviors. Although norms of collegiality can be enhanced within traditionally organized school structures, these structures provide obstacles that prevent optimal expression of this value. For collegiality to be fully expressed, schools will need to be restructured differently than is currently the case (one teacher working in a self-contained classroom with the same group of students following a locked, fixed schedule).

Emphasizing Intrinsic Motivation

Traditional management theory is based on the principle "what gets rewarded gets done." It makes sense to base motivational strategies and practices on this principle; however, when this principle becomes the overriding framework for making decisions about how to lead and how to encourage and reward good performance, typically the result is the opposite of that which is anticipated. In the long run, the job just doesn't get done. The problem with "what gets rewarded gets done" is that it results in calculated involvement of people with their work. When rewards can no longer be provided, the work no longer will be done. Work performance becomes contingent on a bartering arrangement rather than being self-sustaining because of moral principle or a deeper psychological connection. A better strategy on which to base our efforts is "what is rewarding gets done." When something is rewarding, it gets done even when "no one is looking"; it gets done even when extrinsic rewards and incentives are scarce or nonexistent; it gets done not because somebody is going to get something in return but because it's important. The power of intrinsic motivation is well documented in both research and practice and is a key element in bonding leadership.

Understanding Quality Control

Perhaps on no issue do ordinary and highly successful leaders differ more than in their beliefs about and concepts of quality control. To ordinary leaders, quality control is considered to be a management problem solvable by coming up with the right controls such as scheduling, prescribing, programming, testing, and checking. Although successful leaders recognize that such managerial conceptions of quality control have their place, they are likely to view the problem of quality control as being primarily cultural rather than managerial. Quality control, they have come to learn, is in the minds and hearts of people at work. It has to do with what teachers and other school employees believe, their commitment to quality, their sense of pride, the extent to which they identify with their work, the ownership they feel for what they are doing, and the intrinsic satisfaction they derive from the work itself. It is for this reason that quality control is not viewed so much as planning, organizing, scheduling, and controlling as it is viewed as purposing, enablement, leadership density, collegiality, and intrinsic motivation as means to build identity and commitment.

Valuing Simplicity

Highly successful principals believe in lean, action-oriented, uncomplicated organizational structures. To them, "small is beautiful" and "simple is better." Smallness has the advantage of encouraging primary group relationships among teachers and students, providing more readily for empowerment, and increasing one's identity and feeling of belongingness. Simplicity is action-oriented and to the point. It places emphasis on what needs to be accomplished and how best to do it without undue emphasis on protocols and procedural matters.

Reflection in Action

Leaders of highly successful schools view with suspicion quick fixes, sure-fire remedies, and one-best-way prescriptions for teaching and learning, supervising, and evaluating. Instead, they bring to their work a more complex view of schooling (see, for example, Brandt, 1985; Glatthorn, 1984; Joyce and Weil, 1980). No single model of teaching is sufficient to address all the aims of schooling. The issue, for example, is not didactic and informal versus structured and direct, but costs and benefits of various approaches to teaching and learning. What is gained and what is lost by using a particular approach? Given one's present situation, are the gains worth the losses? Similarly, no single method of supervision and evaluation is sufficient for all teachers and all situations.

Successful principals resist accepting a direct link between research and practice. They recognize instead that the purpose of research is to increase one's understanding and not to prescribe practices (Tyler, 1984). Paying close attention to theory and research, they heed well the success stories emerging from practice, but they have a conceptual rather than an instrumental view of such knowledge (Kennedy, 1984). Knowledge viewed instrumentally is evidence for directly prescribing action. Knowledge viewed conceptually is information for informing thought and enhancing professional judgment—the prerequisites for action.

Leadership by Outrage

The standard prescription that emerges from traditional management is that leaders should be cool, calculated, and reserved in everything they say or do. Studies of successful leaders (e.g., Lipsitz, 1984; Peters and Waterman, 1982; Sergiovanni, 1990; Vaill, 1984) reveal quite a different image. Indeed, successful leaders typically bring to their practice a sense of passion and risk that communicates to others that if something is worth believing in then it's worth feeling strongly about. In his extensive studies of successful leaders, Peter Vaill (1984) found that their leadership practice was characterized by *time-feeling and focus.* Successful leaders put in extraordinary amounts of time, have strong feelings about the attainment of the system's purposes, and focus their attention and energies on key issues and variables. These characteristics are key contributors to building purposing in the enterprise. According to Vaill,

> *Purposing occurs through the investment of large amounts of micro- and macro-Time, through the experience and expression of very strong Feeling about the attainment of purposes and importance of the system, and through the attainment of understanding of the key variables in the system success (Focus). All leaders of high-performance systems have integrated these three factors at a very high level of intensity and clarity. (1984:103)*

Vaill noted that feeling was the important link between time and focus. His successful leaders cared deeply about the welfare of their particular enterprise, its purposes, structure, conduct, history, future security, and underlying values and commitments. They cared deeply enough to show passion; and when things were not going right, this passion often took the form of outrage.

Leadership by outrage is a symbolic act that communicates importance and meaning and that touches people in ways not possible when leadership is viewed only as something objective and calculated. Leaders use outrage to highlight issues of purpose defined by the school's shared covenant, and this outrage adds considerable value to their leadership practice.

The linking of outrage to purposes is very important. Bonding leaders, for example, know the difference between real toughness and merely looking tough or acting tough. Real toughness is always principle-value based. Bonding leaders expect adherence to common values but promote wide discretion in how these values are to be implemented (they practice enablement and emphasize followership). They are outraged when they see these values ignored or violated. The values of the common core represent nonnegotiables that comprise cultural strands that define a way of life in the school. No matter how free people may be to do and decide, they are expected to embody the values that are shared and make up the school's covenant. When this is not the case, outrage is expressed.

Kindling Outrage in Others

Outrage is not owned by the principal alone. When purposes are established, followership is understood, enabling is provided, collegiality is in place, and leadership by outrage is modeled by the designated leader; then, expressing outrage becomes an obligation of every person connected with the school. When the ideals and commitments that are shared are compromised, outrage is expressed. Bonding leaders work hard at *kindling outrage in others.*

The Worth of the Leadership Values

None of the leadership values considered alone is powerful enough to make the difference in bringing about quality schooling. Indeed, a critical connectedness exists among them, and leadership is best understood as comprising interdependent parts. Practicing enabling leadership in the form of individual empowerment, for example, without practicing leadership that emphasizes purposing and the building of a covenant of shared values is more likely to result in laissez faire management than in quality schooling. Furthermore, emphasizing management at the expense of leadership by providing controls and regulations, by emphasizing authority, by attempting to regulate the flow and work of schooling will not allow the practice of convincing and meaningful empowerment. A school that builds a covenant of shared values composed of technical statements of objectives, targets, and outcomes that fail to inspire; that are lacking in symbolic representations; and that do not allow principals, parents, teachers, and students to derive sense and meaning from their school lives will not likely be characterized by extraordinary commitment and performance.

In a major breakthrough, Rost (1991) offers a definition of leadership that can help to connect its practice to community building. "Leadership is an influence relationship among leaders and followers who intend real changes that reflect their mutual purposes" (102). This definition contains four key elements—all of which, Rost argues, must be present for relationships between and among people to be called leadership. If any one of the four is missing, then these relationships might better be thought of as management or some other expression—they may have merit, but they just aren't leadership. The four elements are as follows:

1. The relationship is based on influence.
2. Leaders and followers are the people in this relationship.
3. Leaders and followers intend real change.
4. Leaders and followers develop mutual purposes.
   (Rost, 1991:102–103).

Rost points out that conceiving of leadership as an influence relationship means that it is interactive and multidirectional. Leadership does not exist if influence is just top down. Furthermore, influence, in his definition, means the use of persuasion and not rewards and punishments or position and legal power. It is not leadership if a person orders, requires, seduces, or threatens another's compliance.

Rost also proposes that for something to be called leadership, both followers and leaders must be doing the leadership. They need not be equal in the relationship nor must everyone be leading all the time, but in any given period of time or for any given episode, both share the burdens and obligations of leadership.

Furthermore, for leader and followers to intend real changes, leadership acts must be purposeful; they must be motivated not by personal gain or by bureaucratic requirements, but by a desire to better serve purposes. Finally, the purposes themselves must be shared by both leaders and followers. In the ideal, they are developed together.

Rost's definition relies on the importance of compelling ideas and shared commitment to these ideas. Furthermore, the roles of followers and leaders are blurred. With shared ideas as the source of authority, everyone is a follower first, and when anyone takes the initiative to lead, followership becomes redefined as leadership. Leadership flourishes when leaders and followers view each other as being credible. The stronger this credibility, the more likely people will allow themselves to be influenced by leadership acts, no matter what their source.

To Rost and Smith (1992:199), credibility can be thought of as encompassing five "C"s: *character*, defined as honesty, trust, and integrity; *courage,* defined as the willingness to change and to stand up for one's beliefs; *competence,* defined in both technical and interpersonal senses; *composure,* defined as being graceful under pressure and displaying emotion appropriately; and *caring,* defined as being concerned with the welfare of others.

The credibility of the "C"s suggests that certain relationship requirements must be met before leadership can be fully and widely expressed in a school—before the school, in other words, can become a community of leaders. Not surprisingly, the relationship requirements are *gemeinschaft.* How open are we to each other? Do we have the courage to speak, to express our true feelings, to ask for help, and to stand up for what we believe? Can we speak knowledgeably about teaching and learning? Are we sensitive to the views of others? Do we care about each other, our work, and the students we serve? How do we embody this caring? Becoming a community of leaders means that not only does everyone share in the obligations and responsibility of leadership in an effort to facilitate the work of the school, but everyone shares in the obligations and responsibilities of caring. Not only does leadership involve doing, but it involves being. Are we willing to care enough to accept responsibility together for the burdens of leadership?

References

Barnard, Chester. 1938. *The Functions of the Executive.* Cambridge, MA: Harvard University Press.

Barth, Roland. 1986. "The Principal and the Profession of Teaching," *Elementary School Journal* 86(4).

Bennis, Warren. 1984. "Transformative Power and Leadership," in Thomas J. Sergiovanni and John E. Corbally, Eds., *Leadership and Organization Culture* (pp. 64–71). Urbana: University of Illinois.

Brandt, Ron. 1985. "Toward a Better Definition of Teaching," *Educational Leadership* 42(8).

Gardner, John. 1986. "The Tasks of Leadership." Leadership Papers No. 2. Leadership Studies Program. Independent Sector, Washington, DC. March.

Glatthorn, Alan. 1984. *Differentiated Supervision.* Alexandria, VA: Association for Supervision and Curriculum Development.

Joyce, Bruce, and Marsha Weil. 1980. *Models of Teaching,* 2nd ed. Englewood Cliffs, NJ: Prentice-Hall.

Kelly, Robert E. 1988. "In Praise of Followers," *Harvard Business Review,* Nov.–Dec.

Kennedy, Mary. 1984. "How Evidence Alters Understanding and Decisions," *Educational Evaluations and Policy Analysis* 6(3), 207–226.

Lieberman, Ann, and Lynne Miller. 1978. "The Social Realities of Teaching," *Teachers College Record.* 80(1), 54–68.

Lieberman, Ann, and Lynne Miller. 1986. "School Improvement: Themes and Variations" in Ann Lieberman, Ed., *Rethinking School Improvement.* New York: Teachers' College Press.

Lipsitz, Joan. 1984. *Successful Schools for Young Adolescents.* New Brunswick, NJ: Transaction Books.

Little, Judith. 1981. *School Success and Staff Development in Urban Desegregated Schools.* Boulder, CO: Center for Action Research.

Meyers, Scott. 1971. *Every Employee a Manager.* New York: McGraw-Hill.

Peters, Thomas J. and Robert H. Waterman. 1982. *In Search of Excellence.* New York: Harper & Row.

Rosenholtz, Susan. 1989. *Teacher's Workplace: A Social-Organizational Analysis.* New York: Longman.

Rost, Joseph. 1991. *Leadership for the Twenty-first Century.* New York: Praeger.

Rost, Joseph, and A. Smith. 1992. "Leadership: A Post-Industrial Approach," *European Management Journal* 10(2).

Thompson, Victor. 1961. *Modern Organization: A General Theory.* New York: Knopf.

Tyler, Ralph. 1984. Quoted in Philip L. Hosford, "The Problem, Its Difficulties, and Our Approaches," in P. L. Hosford, Ed., *Using What We Know about Teaching.* Alexandria, VA: Association for Supervision and Curriculum Development.

Vaill, Peter B. 1984. "The Purposing of High-Performance Systems," in T. J. Sergiovanni and J. E. Corbally, Eds., *Leadership and Organizational Culture.* Urbana: University of Illinois Press.

White, Robert W. 1952. *Lives in Progress: A Study of the Natural Growth of Personality.* New York: Dryden Press.

Zaleznik, Abraham. 1989. *The Managerial Mystique: Restoring Leadership in Business.* New York: Harper & Row.

Part **III**

Building Community

Chapter 8

Characteristics of Successful Schools

Since the beginning of schooling in America the relationship between quality of schools and quality of learning for students has been accepted as an article of faith. However, with the 1964 publication of Benjamin Bloom's *Stability and Change in Human Characteristics* and the 1966 publication of James Coleman's and his colleague's *Equality of Educational Opportunity,* this faith was broken. Many teachers and principals joined the general public in a widespread acceptance of the belief that schools were not very important.

Coleman's study suggested that social inequality, poverty, and segregated schooling were key elements in determining inadequate levels of learning for many students and that improving learning would require the correction of these social factors. Regardless of one's race or region, it was the home environment (social class and income of parents, exposure to books, need for achievement, and modeling differentials) that was far more important in explaining differences in student-learning outcomes than were school facilities, teacher salaries, or even the curriculum itself.

Bloom's classic work on the development of educational capacity reinforced the primacy of nonschool over school factors in determining the amount and extent of student learning. He noted, for example:

> by about 4, 50% of the variation in intelligence at age 17 is accounted for . . . in terms of intelligence measured at age 17; from conception to age 4, the individual develops 50% of his mature intelligence; from ages 4 to 8 he develops another 30%; and from ages 8 to 17, the remaining 20%. . . . We would expect the variations in the environments to have relatively little effect on the I.Q. after age 8, but would expect such a variation to have marked effect on the I.Q. before that age, with the greatest effect likely to take place between the ages of about 1 to 5. (Bloom, 1964:68)

As these ideas became accepted, principals and teachers came to believe that the home or basic educational capacity, not the school, accounted for major differences in student achievement. Some principals and teachers welcomed this news, seeing within it a legitimate excuse for their own results. After all, they reasoned, the research shows clearly that poor student performance is linked to conditions beyond control of the school.

The 1980s provided quite a different picture as to the relationship between schooling and quality of learning for students. The belief that schooling does make a difference became once more the accepted stand. Quality schooling indeed leads to quality learning, and an important key to quality schooling is the amount and kind of leadership that school principals provide directly and promote among teachers and supporting staff.

These assertions are supported by hundreds of studies on school effectiveness and success. For example, a classic study conducted in 1978 by Gilbert Austin and his colleagues compared 18 high achieving and 12 low achieving schools carefully selected from among all schools in Maryland, using that state's accountability data. Schools selected were considered "outliers" for scoring outside the average statistical band of test scores for all Maryland schools. This research indicated that one difference between high and low achieving schools was the impact of the principal. In higher achieving schools, principals exerted strong leadership, participated directly and frequently in instructional matters, had higher expectations for success, and were oriented toward academic goals. It seems clear from this study, and many others like it, that quality of schooling is greatly influenced by direct leadership from the principal.

Direct principal leadership, however, is only part of the answer to establishing successful schools. Many experts and many supporting studies point out that equally significant—perhaps even most significant—is the amount and quality of leadership density that exists in schools. *Leadership density* refers to the total leadership available from teachers, support staff, parents, and others on behalf of the school's work. Of course, the principal plays a key role in building and maintaining leadership density. In this sense, principal leadership can be understood as an enabling process. Principals practice enabling leadership when they help teachers, students, and staff to function better on behalf of the school and its purposes, to engage more effectively in the work and play of the school, and to promote the achievement of the school's objectives. It is crucial to build up the leadership capacity of others, and in this sense the principal is a leader of leaders.

Effectiveness and School Success

Are *effective* and *good* schools the same? The terms are often used interchangeably to describe the same school or to communicate the same level of accomplishment, but this can cause confusion. *Effectiveness* has both common and technical meanings. It is commonly understood to mean the ability to produce a desired effect. Thus, in a sense, any school that produces effects desired by some group would be considered effective by that group. Yet, technically speaking, within educational circles, school effectiveness has taken on a specific and special meaning. An effective school is understood to be a school whose students achieve well in basic skills as measured by achievement tests. The dimensions of management, teaching, and leadership that are included in the school effectiveness model have been convincingly linked to this limited view of effectiveness, but not to broader, higher order, and more qualitative intellectual and academic views of effectiveness.

The question remains, what is a good school? How does one know such a school when it is seen? Can "goodness" be defined? Just how does one determine if a school is doing a good job or not?

Such questions usually receive quick answers. For example:

- Graduates of good high schools get jobs or are admitted to college in larger numbers.
- Test scores of students are at or above average for similar groups of students.
- High school teachers remark that incoming students from the junior high are well prepared.
- Students spend approximately two hours each evening on homework.
- A survey of the number of books checked out of the school library during the last year reveals that students in that school check out more books than students in other area schools.
- The average salary of former students 10 years after graduation is high.
- Attendance at school is up.
- Teachers agree as to what the purposes of schooling are.
- Discipline problems are on the decline.
- Students select tougher courses.
- Teachers report that students are working harder.
- Students report that teachers are working harder.
- Surveys indicate that students are satisfied with their school.
- Parents indicate that if they had to choose between sending their children to this or another school, they would choose this one.
- Faculty members carefully plan lessons.
- Tax referenda are passed.
- The North Central Association Accrediting Team praises the school.
- Faculty members are available to students.
- The Christmas play, the Chanukkah program, and other seasonal pageantry are well attended year after year, and parents report being pleased with the results.
- The school has a winning football team.
- Faculty members work together, share ideas, and help one another.
- The number of Merit Scholars is increasing.
- Teacher turnover is low.
- The number of students referred to mental health services is low when compared with similar schools.
- More students study foreign languages.
- More students study art.
- More students study physics.
- Morale of faculty is high.

This list of responses could easily be extended. Clearly, the problem of defining a good school is more complex than it seems at first appearances. Indeed, educators and parents alike often have difficulty in coming to grips with an adequate description, definition, or list of criteria.

The problem of determining goodness and differentiating it from effectiveness is compounded by the fact that often schools look "effective," but may not be "good." In complying with a new state law, for example, the Texas Education Agency recently rated every school and school district into one of five categories: exemplary, recognized, acceptable, low-performing, or unacceptable. Ratings were based on how well students scored on state achievement tests, drop-out statistics, and other indicators. Schools rated at the top of the list are presumed to be effective and those at the bottom ineffective. But what about goodness? Are those at the top good schools solely because of their high ratings? Some certainly are, but others are probably not. If, for example, the faculty of a random sample of 100 schools in the top third of the rankings was switched with a similar group from the bottom third, and schools were reevaluated a year later, it is not likely that we would see much shifting in the rankings. Many schools in the top group are not there because they provide superior teaching, have better faculties, or improved educational programs; instead, they are there simply because the values of the home are more closely aligned with the values of the school. As Comer and his colleagues (N.A.K. Production Associates, 1993) pointed out, "In general, children whose parents are part of the social mainstream have the best opportunities for success in school, because the values and social skills they acquired from their parents and care-givers are consistent with those of the school, its teachers and administrators" (6). They compellingly argue that "mainstream children—those from social networks where the attitudes, values and behavior most closely resemble those of the school, and its teachers and administrators,—have the best chance of meeting the expectations of the school" (9). Mainstream students, for example, are more likely to thrive in the competitive environment the school provides, respond to a pattern of schooling that prizes individuality over community and competition over cooperation, accept docile roles as recipients of an instructional delivery system, look and act the way teachers want them to, learn how to be test savvy, and show up for school even if it's boring. The reason is that these expectations of the school are mirrored in the culture of the family. These same expectations are less likely to be reinforced in the families of students in schools whose ratings are in the lower third.

Good schools, as Comer and his associates so compellingly argue, do not expect families and students to bear all of the burdens of alignment with the values of the school. Instead, they work hard to align themselves with the values of the home. They are committed to respond with empathy and to respect those values. In short, many, but not all, of the schools in that upper third of Texas's rankings can be considered good; there are also many good schools in the lower third.

Nonetheless, intuitively, "goodness" is a known quality no matter how difficult it is to precisely articulate its essence. Joan Lipsitz (1984), for example, found that the principals of the good schools she studied had difficulty in articulating what it was that made their schools special or what the dimensions of goodness were. "You will have to come and see my school" was the typical and predictable response.

Similarly, we know good schools when we experience them, although we cannot always specify their precise components. In good schools, things "hang together"; a sense of purpose exists, rallying people to a common cause; work has meaning and life is significant; teachers and students work together and with spirit; and accomplishments are readily recognized. To say that good schools have high morale or achieve higher test scores or send more students to college—and to leave it at that—is to miss the point. Goodness is all of this and more.

Should we expect more from our schools than the satisfaction of knowing that they are performing "up to the standard" and that students are competent performers as measured by such typical indicators as test scores? The situation is sufficiently poor in some schools that, if they were indeed to achieve such a modest standard, it would be cause for celebration. Most surveys indicate that basic skill learning and developing fundamental academic competence (the indicators of effectiveness common to the school effectiveness literature) are paramount school goals in the minds of parents and teachers. But the question of goodness does not end with this emphasis. Pushed a bit further, most parents and teachers provide a more expansive view of school success. Educational goals typically espoused by parents include developing a love of learning, critical-thinking and problem-solving skills, aesthetic appreciation, curiosity and creativity, and interpersonal competence. Parents want a complete education for their children (see, for example, Goodlad, 1983). Indeed, our society requires a complete education for its youth if it is to survive and flourish. What is needed is that our young become cultured and educated citizens, able to participate fully in our economic and social society, not just trained workers with limited potential for such participation. These aspirations include all of America's youth, including urban and rural poor and minority students, for whom the more limited definitions of school effectiveness are often applied.

How Researchers Identify Effective Schools

Researchers investigating the characteristics of effective schools typically rely on such important student outcome data as test scores. The outlier concept, as used in the Austin (1978) study cited earlier, is an example. Schools having students who perform significantly higher than the statistical average are compared with schools having students whose scores are within or below this average range. The now famous Edmonds (1979) and Brookover and Lezotte (1979) studies of more and less effective elementary schools serving primarily urban, poor, and minority students are examples of this approach. Effectiveness in these schools was determined by pupil performance on standardized tests of reading and math skills.

Student achievement in basic skills is undoubtedly the most popular criterion for determining an effective school. One reason for its popularity is the ease with which one is able to define and measure school effectiveness. However, the reliance on test scores to identify effective schools is not without its critics. Rowan, Dwyer, and Bossert (1982), for example, feel that effectiveness is too often narrowly defined:

> *The use of achievement scores as the sole criteria for judging school effectiveness is common. For example, virtually all the studies in the effective schools tradition employ this unidimensional criterion. Yet as Steers (1975) pointed out in his general discussion of measures of organizational effectiveness, most*

theorists and participants in organizations view effectiveness as a multidimensional construct. By viewing school effectiveness as a unidimensional phenomenon, current research neglects a number of interesting and important issues. For example, numerous constituencies view the purpose of schooling as broader than simple academic training. Citizenship training, development of self-esteem, independence training, and the development of self-discipline exist as important alternative goals. By focusing exclusively on academic achievement, much of the literature on school effectiveness has ignored the relationship between achieving effectiveness in academic outcomes and achieving effectiveness among these other dimensions. We urge more attention to the relationship between these various criteria, a process that would require the development of a multidimensional view of school effectiveness. (8)

Some researchers provide a more expansive definition of school effectiveness. Joan Lipsitz (1984) used the following six general criteria in identifying the successful middle schools she studied:

1. *These schools contain safe and orderly environments where student achievement is up to or exceeds expectations. More specifically, scores on standardized achievement tests are above or approach the county mean or the mean of some other comparative reference group; low absenteeism and turnover rates among students and staff exist; vandalism and victimization are not frequent occurrences or indeed are nonexistent; there is lack of destructive graffiti; and low suspension rates for students exist.*
2. *These schools respond appropriately to the developmental levels of students. Basic skills and other intellectual objectives are considered important, but are best pursued in a healthy psychological environment for students.*
3. *Teachers and students in these schools pursue competency in learning.*
4. *These schools are accepted within the context of the local community and its expectations.*
5. *These schools enjoy a reputation for excellence in the community.*
6. *These schools function well in response to or despite national issues such as desegregation, busing, and other problems. (11)*

Characteristics of Successful Schools

It is fashionable to talk about the correlates of effective schools. Many school districts and even states settle on a particular list of such correlates (e.g., strong instructional leadership from the principal, academic focus on the basic skills, safe and orderly environment, high expectations for students, close monitoring of instruction by supervision and testing) to apply uniformly to all schools. Recent research and reasoned thought, however, suggest that *correlates* may be too strong a designation, and uniform application of any particular list may be hazardous for the long-term health of the school. The research and thought, however, do provide us with a number of insights in the form of general characteristics that can help us decide what counts in our own unique situation.

Research Revelations

The seminal work of Brookover and Lezotte (1979), Brookover and colleagues (1979), and Edmonds (1979) consistently reveals that effective schools are characterized by high agreement among staff as to goals and purposes, a clear sense of mission, and the active presence of purposing. Studies by Bossert and his colleagues (1982) and by Greenfield (1982) reveal that goal orientation and the articulation and modeling of school purposes by principals are also common characteristics.

Blumberg and Greenfield's (1980) research reveals that successful principals are pro-active and direct behaviors at building and articulating a vision of what the school is and can become. This notion of vision is supported, as well, by the case study research of Prunty and Hively (1982) and of Newberg and Glatthorn (undated). Nearly all these studies, as well as that of Rutter and his colleagues (1979), identify the concept of ethos (shared goals and expectations and associated approved modes of behavior) or strong school culture as being an important characteristic. Important to this culture are norms and values that provide for cohesion and identity and that create a unifying moral order or ideology from which teachers and students derive direction, meaning, and significance.

Of particular significance in understanding the depth of detail that characterizes life in successful schools is the research of Joan Lipsitz (1984). In summarizing her case studies of four successful middle schools, she reaches the following conclusions about principal leadership and school characteristics.

- The four schools achieved unusual clarity about the purposes of intermediate schooling and the students they teach.
- The schools made powerful statements, both in word and in practice, about their purposes. There is little disagreement within them and little discrepancy between what they say they are doing and what they are actually doing. As a result, everyone can articulate what the school stands for.
- These are confident schools. Each one stands for something special, whether it is being the best in the country, desegregation, diversity, or the arts. Each has a mission and knows what it is and in each case it is both academic and social.
- In every case, a principal . . . took hold of the possible for definition and proclaimed it within the school and throughout the community. Each school became special.
- Made to feel like chosen people, staff and students have banded together in their specialness and achieved accordingly. The sense of definition that comes from the exclusivity felt by each school is important in keeping staff morale high and retaining parent support. More important, though, is the sense of purpose it gives the young adolescents. It helps bind them to the school.
- Each of the four schools has or has had a principal with a driving vision who imbues decisions and practices with meaning, placing powerful emphasis on why things are done as well as how. Decisions are not made just because they are practical but for reasons of principle.
- Through their vision and practicality they articulate for their schools . . . a collective ideology that defines an organization's identity and purposes. The principals make these schools coherent, binding philosophy to goals, goals to programs, and programs to practices.

- The principals see their major function to be instructional leadership. It is their job to sustain their faculty's commitment. They set standards for performance and establish the norms and taboos for adult–child relationships.
- The major contribution of the principal is to make the schools larger than one person. They institutionalize their vision in program and organizational structure.
- The principals are good enough to leave a legacy behind: their staff, a powerfully defined school, an educated community and a tradition of excitement, sensitivity, and striving for excellence.
- Most striking is the level of caring in these schools.
- Most striking is the lack of adult isolation in these schools. . . . Common planning and lunch periods, team teaching encourage constant communication and allow for high levels of companionship.
- . . . teachers have high expectations for *themselves* and . . . they believe that they are capable of making a difference in their students' learning.
- Each school's principal has been a driven, energetic worker, committed to establishing the best possible school environment for the age group.
- The principals' authority is derived from their acknowledged competence. They are authoritative, not authoritarian leaders, although one often senses that a strain of authoritarianism is being kept carefully in tow.
- While the particulars of school governance differ from school to school, the schools have in common highly autonomous teachers. They understand how the whole school works, and in most cases they know why.
- These driven, possessive, and sometimes defiant principals are critical to the continued excellence and support of their schools; but they are not alone responsible for their schools' success, nor are they indispensable.*

Duttweiler's (1988, 1990) review of the more recent literature (Purkey and Smith, 1982; Roueche and Baker, 1986; Stedman, 1987; Wayson, 1988; Wimpelberg, Teddlie, and Stringfield, 1989) reveals a much more comprehensive picture of what constitutes an effective school than that provided by earlier studies. Although Duttweiler continues to use the word effective to describe these schools, she has redefined the term. The following characteristics emerge from her synthesis (Duttweiler, 1990: 72–74).

Effective Schools Are Student-Centered

Effective schools make an effort to serve all students, create support networks to assist students, involve students in school affairs, respect and celebrate the ethnic and linguistic differences among students, and have student welfare as a first priority. They use community volunteers, parents, teacher aides, and peer tutors to provide close, personal attention to students. They involve students in many of the activities of running a school. Student needs are given priority over other concerns. An atmosphere of cooperation and trust is created through a high level of interaction between students and teachers.

*The conclusions from Joan Lipsitz's work are verbatim statements drawn from Chapter 7, "The Challenge of the Schools" (Lipsitz, 1984): 267–323. Published by permission of Transaction, Inc. from *Successful Schools for Young Adolescents,* copyright © 1984 by Transaction, Inc.

Effective Schools Offer Academically Rich Programs

Student development and the provision of a well-rounded academic program are the primary goals. Effective schools address higher as well as lower order cognitive objectives, provide an enriched environment through a variety of options, have an active co-curricular program, provide in-depth coverage of content, and appropriately monitor student progress and provide feedback.

Effective Schools Provide Instruction that Promotes Student Learning

Effective schools have a distinctive normative structure that supports instruction. They design their programs to ensure academic success and to head off academic problems. Teachers and administrators believe that all students can learn and feel responsible for seeing that they do. Teachers and administrators believe in their own ability to influence students' learning. Teachers communicate expectations to students, provide focused and organized instructional sessions, adapt instruction to student needs, anticipate and correct student misconceptions, and use a variety of teaching strategies. In general, effective schools set high standards, closely and regularly monitor performance, and recognize and reward effort and success.

Effective Schools Have a Positive School Climate

Effective schools have a clear organizational personality, characterized by stated missions, goals, values, and standards of performance. They have a sense of order, purpose, and direction fostered by consistency among teachers; an atmosphere of encouragement in which students are praised and rewarded; a work-centered environment; and high optimism and expectations for student learning. Teachers and principals commit themselves to breaking down institutional and community barriers to equality. They create a learning environment that is open, friendly, and culturally inviting. Using community resources, they acknowledge the ethnic and racial identity of their students. They provide encouragement and take a positive approach to discipline. Administrators model the behaviors that they say are important.

Effective Schools Foster Collegial Interaction

Effective schools strive to create professional environments for teachers that facilitate the accomplishment of their work. Teachers participate in decisions affecting their work, have reasonable control or autonomy to carry out work, share a sense of purpose and community, receive recognition for contributions to the organization, and are treated with respect and dignity by others in the workplace. Teachers work together as colleagues to carry out instruction, to plan curriculum, and to refine teaching practices.

Effective Schools Have Extensive Staff Development

The teacher evaluation system is used to help teachers improve their skills. Inservice is practical, on-the-job training tailored to meet the specific needs of staff members. The emphasis is on the exchange of practical teaching techniques and on making training an integral part of a collaborative educational environment. Teachers and administrators conduct inservice programs and are provided with ample staff-development opportunities to help them develop further. Administrators and teachers are encouraged to reflect on their practices.

Effective Schools Practice Shared Leadership

Instructional leadership does not depend solely on the principal. School administrators understand and use a leadership style appropriate for professionals; solve problems through collaboration, team, or group decision making; know their staff members and delegate authority; communicate and build cohesiveness; and use their positions to recognize and reward accomplishments of both staff and students. While no single leadership style dominates, common leadership features include setting and maintaining direction for the school and facilitating the work of teachers by adopting a wide range of supportive behaviors. Involvement in decision making is a critical element. Involvement begins with members of the school community developing the goals, mission, and values of the school. Decisions are made with input from those to be affected by the decision.

Effective Schools Foster Creative Problem Solving

Staff members in effective schools are unwilling to accept defeat or settle for mediocrity. They turn their problems into challenges, design solutions, and implement them. They go about their tasks with commitment, creativity, persistence, and professionalism. Resources such as time, facilities, staff expertise, and volunteers are used to maximum advantage to facilitate the process of teaching and learning.

Effective Schools Involve Parents and the Community

There is a partnership linkage between the school and the community. Effective schools establish a variety of methods for communicating as well as working with parents and the community. They involve parents and community members in the teaching and learning activities of the school, include them in the decision-making process, have them serve as resources to extend the efforts of the school, and depend on them to be advocates as well as to provide good public relations for the school. They make sure that parents are involved in all aspects of their children's learning. Effective schools are contributory partners to the community they serve. They teach young people that they have a responsible part to play in society and that their contributions are valued and needed.

To this list, Stedman (1987) adds ethnic and racial pluralism, student responsibility for school affairs, and shared governance with parents and teachers. Stedman's conclusions are interesting because they rely on studies of successful schools conducted in the 1960s and early 1970s as well as more recent studies, and thus provide a more "longitudinal" view.

Although lists of general characteristics are helpful, they should not be readily translated into specific prescriptions for management and leadership practice. What needs to be done to increase effectiveness and how one does it are situationally specific. What works for a failing school, for example, will not necessarily work for a competent school. What works for low socioeconomic status schools will not necessarily work for middle socioeconomic status schools. The early school-effectiveness studies, for example, pointed out the importance of strong instructional leadership by the principal.

The principal's job, according to this view, is to establish procedures and criteria for evaluating teachers, observe classrooms regularly and meet with teachers to discuss and improve classroom practices, and reward teachers for excellence in teaching. Furthermore, every effort must be made to ensure that what the teacher teaches is aligned with carefully delineated purposes, and both purposes and content are aligned with tests. Directing and monitoring the affairs of teaching and learning are essential to the principal's role.

Clearly, such principalship behaviors and expectations make sense in many situations but not in others. Being a strong instructional leader may be a good idea in schools where teachers are poorly trained or lacking in commitment, but it is not a good idea in schools where competence and commitment are not issues. In some schools, for example, teachers know more than the principal about matters of teaching and learning. To persist in providing strong instructional leadership in such a situation locks in teachers as instructional followers or subordinates and puts a cap on the total amount of leadership available in the school to promote better teaching and learning.

A number of researchers (e.g., Gersten, Carnine, and Green, 1982; Pajak and Glickman, 1989) have found that the leadership provided by lead teachers, assistant principals, grade-level heads, central office supervisors, department chairpersons, and teams of teachers are often the most critical factors in improving teaching and learning. What seems crucial to school improvement is not so much who provides the leadership but how much leadership there is. To that end, the principal as leader of leaders may well be a more appropriate role where competence and commitment are not issues than would the role of instructional leader.

In summary, indiscriminate application of school-effectiveness research findings and, in particular, the development of generic lists of correlates or indicators that are subsequently applied uniformly to schools pose serious questions about the proper use of research and can result in negative, unanticipated consequences for teaching and learning. Wimpelburg, Teddlie, and Stringfield (1989) put it more bluntly: "It is patently foolish to attempt 'effective schools' changes in schools that are wholly different from the settings in which the 'effective schools' correlates were isolated" (103). Lists of effectiveness characteristics as proposed by knowledgeable researchers remain useful if viewed as general indicators. They are not so much truths to be applied uniformly, but understandings that can help principals and others make more informed decisions about what to do and how in improving schools.

References

Austin, Gilbert. 1978. "Process Evaluation: A Comprehensive Study of Outlines." Baltimore: Maryland State Department of Education. ERIC: ED 160 644.

Bloom, Benjamin S. 1964. *Stability and Change in Human Characteristics.* New York: Wiley.

Blumberg, Arthur, and William Greenfield. 1980. *The Effective Principal: Perspective on School Leadership.* Boston: Allyn and Bacon.

Bossert, Steven T., D. D. Dwyer, B. Rowan, and G. V. Lee. 1982. "The Instructional Management Role of the Principal," *Educational Administration Quarterly* 18(3), 34–64.

Brookover, Wilbur B., C. Brady, P. Flood, J. Schweigen, and J. Wisenbater. 1979. *School Systems and School Achievement: Schools Can Make a Difference.* New York: Praeger.

Brookover, Wilbur B., and Lawrence W. Lezotte. 1979. "Changes in School Characteristics Coincident with Changes in School Achievement." East Lansing: Institute for Research on Teaching, Michigan State University.

Coleman, James, Ernest Q. Campbell, Carol J. Hobson, James McParland, Alexander M. Mood, Frederick D. Weinfeld, and Robert L. York. 1966. *Equality of Educational Opportunity.* Vol. 2. Washington, DC: U.S. Government Printing Office, OE-38001.

Duttweiler, Patricia Cloud. 1988. "New Insights from Research on Effective Schools," *Insights.* Austin, TX: Southwest Educational Development Laboratory. No. 4.

Duttweiler, Patricia Cloud. 1990. "A Broader Definition of Effective Schools: Implications from Research and Practice," in T. J. Sergiovanni and J. H. Moore, Eds., *Target 2000: A Compact for Excellence in Texas's Schools.* Austin: Texas Association for Supervision and Curriculum Development.

Edmonds, Ronald. 1979. "Some Schools Work and More Can," *Social Policy* 9(2), 28–32.

Gersten, Russell, Douglas Carnine, and Susan Green. 1982. "The Principal as Instructional Leader: A Second Look," *Educational Leadership* 40(Dec.), 47–50.

Goodlad, John. 1983. *A Place Called School.* New York: McGraw-Hill.

Greenfield, William. 1982. *A Synopsis of Research on School Principals.* Washington, DC: National Institute for Education.

Lipsitz, Joan. 1984. *Successful Schools for Young Adolescents.* New Brunswick, NJ: Transaction.

N.A.K. Production Associates and Association for Supervision and Curriculum Development. March 29, 1993. *Creating Learning Communities: The Comer Process.* Teleconference Coordinators Handbook.

Newberg, Norman A., and Allan A. Glatthorn. Undated. "Instructional Leadership: Four Ethnographic Studies of junior High School Principals." Washington, DC: National Institute for Education (G-81-008).

Pajak, Edward F., and Carl D. Glickman. 1989. "Dimension of School District Improvement," *Educational Leadership* 46(8), 61–64.

Prunty, John J., and Wells Hively. 1982. "The Principal's Role in School Effectiveness: An Analysis of the Practices of Four Elementary School Leaders." Washington, DC: National Institute for Education (G-8-01-10) and CEMRL, Inc.

Purkey, S. C., and M. S. Smith. 1982. "Synthesis of Research on Effective Schools," *Educational Leadership* (40)3, 64–69.

Roueche, J. E., and G. A. Baker. 1986. *Profiling Excellence in America's Schools.* Arlington, VA: American Association of School Administrators.

Rowan, Brian, David C. Dwyer, and Steven T. Bossert. 1982. "Methodological Considerations in Studies of Effective Principals." Paper presented at American Educational Research Association, New York.

Rutter, M., B. Maughan, P. Mortimore, J. Ouston, and A. Smith. 1979. *Fifteen Thousand Hours: Secondary Schools and Their Effects on Children.* Cambridge, MA: Harvard University Press.

Stedman, Lawrence C. 1987. "It's Time We Changed the Effective Schools Formula," *Phi Delta Kappan* 69(3), 215–227.

Wayson, W. W. 1988. *Up From Excellence: The Impact of the Excellence Movement on Schools.* Bloomington, IN: Phi Delta Kappan Foundation.

Wimpelberg, Robert K., Charles Teddlie, and Samuel Stringfield. 1989. "Sensitivity to Context: The Past and Future of Effective Schools Research," *Educational Administration Quarterly* 25(1), 82–108.

$$Chapter \quad 9$$

Becoming a Community
of Mind

In Chapter 4, community was defined as collections of individuals who are bonded together by natural will and who are together bound to a set of shared ideas and ideals. This bonding and binding is tight enough to transform them from a collection of "I"s into a collective "we." As a "we," members are part of a tightly knit web of meaningful relationships. This "we" usually shares a common place and over time comes to share sentiments and traditions that are sustaining.

When this definition of community is applied to schools, they become transformed from formal organizations to caring, learning, and inquiring communities. Key to this transformation is building new kinds of relationships among people. This requires restructuring living and learning environments in ways that enhance the identity of teachers and students with each other, with the work of the school, and with the school itself. The aim is to build new connections among people and between them and their work that are idea- and norm-based, and to sanctify and ritualize these connections in ways that make them traditions rich in meaning and significance. As connections build, schools become communities by relationship, of place, of mind, and of memory.

Among the four dimensions of community, none is more important than the struggle to create a community of mind that bonds everyone together in special ways and binds them to a shared ideology. Schools cannot become caring communities unless caring is valued and unless a norm system develops that points the way toward caring, rewards caring behaviors, and frowns on noncaring behaviors. Nor can schools become learning or inquiring communities without valuing these respective images and without developing norm systems that guide their quest for embodying these images.

Community emerges from a network of shared ideologies. Ideologies are coherent sets of beliefs that tie people together and that explain their work to them in terms of cause and effect relationships (Trice and Beyer, 1984). Ideologies are the means by which we make sense of our lives, find a direction, and commit ourselves to courses of action. In communities, ideologies shape what principals and teachers believe and how they practice. They influence, as well, the norm structure and behavior of students.

The Importance of Goals

Goals are an important part of a school's community of mind. Nonetheless, disagreement exists among those who study schools as to how the term *goals* should be defined and understood, and even as to whether goals actually make a difference in the decisions that principals and teachers make about schooling. Many prominent organizational theorists doubt whether organizations actually have goals; for example, Perrow (1981) states: "The notion of goals may be a mystification, hiding an errant, vagrant, changeable world" (8). He continues:

> *Do organizations have goals, then, in the rational sense of organizational theory? I do not think so. In fact, when an executive says, 'This is our goal' chances are that he is looking at what the organization happens to be doing and saying, 'Since we are all very rational here, and we are doing this, this must be our goal.' Organizations in this sense, run backward; the deed is father to the thought, not the other way around. (8)*

Other organizational theorists have commented that schools are loosely structured (Bidwell, 1965; Weick, 1976), suggesting that parts tend to operate independently of one another. Teachers, for example, work alone in classrooms; their work is not visible to others. Close supervision under these circumstances is difficult, and continuous evaluation of teaching is impossible. No mechanism exists to ensure that school mandates, such as stated goals, are reflected in actual teaching. Coordination of the work of several teachers is difficult to achieve.

Because direct supervision and tight coordination are not possible in loosely structured schools, principals need to rely on the management of symbols to rally teachers to a common cause. Although schools may be loosely structured in the way they are organized, effective schools combine this loosely structured characteristic with a tightly structured core of values and beliefs. This core represents the cultural cement that bonds people together, gives them a sense of identity, and provides them with guidelines for their work.

But are symbols the same as goals? At one level, symbols and goals share common characteristics and similar functions. Weick's view is that symbols are more like *charters* than goals. They tell people *what* they are doing and *why* they are doing it. They reveal to people the importance and significance of their work. Goals, however, provide direction and are devices for telling people when and how well they are doing things (Weick, 1982:676).

The more generally goals are stated, the closer they approximate symbols. As goals become more precise, they tend to lose symbolic value and to resemble instrumental objectives designed to program daily school activities. They serve less to provide a sense of purpose or to instill a feeling of significance and more to guide what teachers should be doing at a given moment. Goals as symbols sacrifice precision, detail, and instrumentality to gain significance and meaning. They seek to capture the spirit of teachers at work. Objectives, however, sacrifice significance and meaning in an attempt to gain instrumental power over what teachers are doing at a given moment and to provide ready measures of how well they are performing these tasks.

Experts who describe schools as being loosely structured maintain that instrumental control is difficult to achieve. Behind closed classroom doors, they argue, teachers follow the beat of a different drummer—selecting learning materials and deciding on what and how to teach not in response to objectives, but in response to available materials, their own intuitions and abilities, their perceptions of student needs, time constraints, and other situational characteristics. Tight school structures, they maintain, simply cannot reach into the classroom and challenge this de facto autonomy of the teacher no matter how detailed such structures might be or how eloquently they might be described. Because the influence of direct control is blunted by de facto teacher autonomy, the significance of goal-symbols as a means of influence in schools is increased.

Goals as Patterns

Jean Hills (1982) points out that in the real world, school administrators rarely find themselves in a position where they can pursue goals one at a time. The problem they face is that schools have multiple goals. Furthermore, sometimes the goals conflict with each other. Making progress toward one goal may mean losing progress toward another. Always thinking in terms of discrete goals or even discrete multiple goals with each attended to sequentially by the principal, therefore, does not fit the special character of the school's unique value system. Under loosely structured conditions, schools don't achieve goals as much as they respond to certain values and tend to certain imperatives that ensure their survival over time.

Parsons (1951), for example, identified four imperatives that must be balanced against each other in such a way that each is maximized in order for the school or any other institution to survive. The neglect of any of these imperatives causes the other to decline, which means trouble for the school. The "pattern variables," as Parsons refers to them, are goal attainment; internally maintaining day-to-day stability and functions; adopting to external demands, concerns, and circumstances; and, finally, tending to the cultural patterns and norms that hold the school together over time. External adoption, for example, often threatens internal stability and upsets cultural patterns. Maintaining cultural patterns often interferes with goal attainment, and so forth.

Rather than discrete goal attainment, Hills points out that school administrators bring to their practice what he calls "pattern rationality." They behave in response to "a conception of pattern development on a number of mutually limiting dimensions with respective gains in a given area having implications for others" (1982:7). Successful principals become surfers, skilled at riding the wave of the pattern as it unfolds. They respond to value patterns when discrete goals are in conflict with each other. Important to the concept of pattern rationality is that administrators be concerned with the costs and benefits of their actions.

Goals as Symbols

School boards, state departments of education, and other groups and institutions expect schools to have goals. Goal statements are, therefore, necessary to symbolically portray the school as being rational and therefore legitimate to outsiders. Rational schools are supposed to have goals and purposes and are supposed to pursue them deliberately. Schools, for example, are expected to behave rationally by accrediting agencies, state governments, the local press, the local school board, and other groups. Thus, stated goals and purposes are necessary to obtain legitimacy from these and other groups.

It is clear that some discrepancy exists between stated goals and what schools actually do. This gap is more evident as goals take the form of actual intents (specifying exactly what we will accomplish) than the form of beliefs (specifying what is important and valued). Statements of beliefs provide the language necessary to bond people together in a common cause, to provide them with a sense of direction, and to establish a standard by which they can evaluate their actions and from which meanings for their actions can be derived. The more successful the school, the stronger is this bonding and the stronger is the link between beliefs, decisions, and actions.

Findings from the successful schools research parallel those of Peters and Waterman (1982) in their studies of excellent business corporations. In their words: "Every excellent company we studied is clear on what it stands for, and takes the process of value shaping seriously. In fact, we wonder whether it is possible to be an excellent company without clarify of values and without having the right sorts of values" (280). They continue:

> *Virtually all of the better performing companies we looked at in the first study had a well-defined set of guiding beliefs. The less well-performing institutions, on the other hand, were marked by one of two characteristics. Many had no set of coherent beliefs. The others had distinctive and widely discussed objectives, but the only ones that they got animated about were the ones that could be quantified (the financial objectives, such as earnings per share and growth measures). (281)*

Thomas Watson, Jr. (1963) in describing his many years of experience at the helm of IBM, highlights the importance of goals and symbols as statements of beliefs as follows:

> *I firmly believe that any organization, in order to survive and achieve success, must have a sound set of beliefs on which it premises all its policies and actions. Next, I believe that the most important single factor in corporate success is faithful adherence to these beliefs. And, finally, I believe that if an organization is to meet the challenge of a changing world, it must be prepared to change everything about itself except those beliefs as it moves through corporate life. In other words, the basic philosophy, spirit, and drive of an organization have far more to do with its relative achievements than do technological or economic resources, organizational structure, innovation, and timing. All these things weigh heavily in success. But they are, I think, transcended by how strongly the people in the organization believe in its basic precepts and how faithfully they carry them out. (4–6)*

Corporations, of course, are different from schools. They are generally considered to be more quantitative, impersonal, and instrumental. Schools, by contrast, are much more human-intensive. Although values are important to both, they are presumed to be more central to the inner workings of schools. Thus, providing examples from the corporate world illustrating the importance of goals, values, and beliefs should serve as notice to principals and other educators that such statements are even more important to schools.

Statements of belief provide the common cement, bonding people together as they work on behalf of the school. Operationally, such beliefs form an *education platform* for the school and principal. Educational platforms should be thought of as encompassing the defining principles and beliefs that guide the actions of individuals and that provide a basis for evaluating these actions. Leaders of successful schools have well-defined educational platforms from which they operate. Indeed, successful schools contain fairly well-developed educational platforms serving as guides to teachers and others as they live and work in the school. Platforms are not objectives or specifications of what exactly is to be accomplished; instead, they contain guiding principles from which individuals decide what to do and how to do it. The more loosely structured the school, the more important is the concept of educational platform in bringing about cohesion and concerted action. Platforms are the means by which mission statements and broad goals and purposes are articulated into practice.

When taken together, platforms, mission statements, and broad goals and purposes constitute a covenant of shared values that functions as the cultural center of the school—the repository of that which is held sacred by all.

The Legacy of Economics

Many readers will wonder whether teachers, to say nothing of students, will respond in sacred ways to a "covenant of shared values." After all, current management thought is inclined toward contractual models of motivation and commitment that involve bartering of wants and needs for compliance. Of all the social science disciplines, management theory and practice have been most influenced by classical economics. It comes as no surprise, therefore, that most of our management principles and leadership practices emphasize bureaucratic and psychological authority at the expense of moral authority.

A key concept in classical economics is the "utility function," which is used to explain virtually *all* consumer behavior. In simple language, the reasoning is as follows. Human beings are by their very nature selfish. They are driven by a desire to maximize their self-interest and thus continually calculate the costs and benefits of their actions, choosing courses of action that either make them winners (they get rewards) or keep them from losing (they avoid punishment). So dominant is this view and so pervasive is the concept of the utility function that such emotions as love, loyalty, outrage, obligation, sense of duty, belief in the goodness of something, dedication to a cause, and a desire to help make things better count very little in determining a course of action. For the most part, classical economics views these emotions as mere currency that one uses to get something. The soldier hero, for example, storms the hill and sacrifices life not out of a sense of duty or obligation, but to gain a medal or receive honors, even if given posthumously. A loving relationship is a contract within which two people exchange sentiments and commitments in order to gain benefits and services not as easily available outside such a relationship.

Another important concept underlying economic theory is that it is the individual that counts, not the group or community to which she or he belongs. The individual is the prime decision maker who calculates costs and benefits and chooses courses of action that are personally beneficial. The decisions of groups or societies are acknowledged but explained merely as the aggregate of many individual decisions.

Like management, the field of economics is undergoing a radical change, challenging its basic assumptions and developing new understandings that explain human behavior more fully. Amitai Etzioni (1988), for example, provides compelling evidence that people are driven not only by self-interest but by values and emotions as well. Values have to do with what people believe to be morally right, and emotions are the pleasure or intrinsic satisfaction they derive from doing something. Furthermore, the idea of the individual decision maker determining all human behavior is now thought to be suspect. Individuals typically make decisions that reflect collective attributes and processes in response to the norms and values of the groups and communities with which they identify. As Etzioni (1988:4) explains:

> *The neoclassical assumption that people render decisions rationally . . . is replaced by the assumption that people typically select means, not just goals, first and foremost on the basis of their values and emotions. Far from always "intruding on" or "twisting" rational deliberations, values and emotions render some decision making more effective, This holds not just for social behavior, such as courtship, but also for economic behavior, say relationships with one's employees or superiors. . . .*
>
> *The neoclassical assumption that the individual is the decision-making unit is changed here to assume that social collectivities (such as ethnic and racial groups, peer groups at work, and neighborhood groups) are the prime decision-making units. Individual decision-making often reflects, to a certain extent, collective attributes and processes. Individual decisions do occur, but largely within the context set by various collectivities.*

The new economics does not dismiss the important roles of self-interest or individual decision making in understanding why people decide to behave the way they do, but it enlarges this view by including two other powerful reasons—emotions and values. This discovery matches very well the evidence that emerges from studies of successful schools and other enterprises reviewed in Chapter 8 and the leadership practices that contribute to success reviewed in Chapters 5, 6, and 7. These studies and practices reveal that schools and other enterprises have something that metaphorically might be described as "cultures." As pointed out in Chapter 3, at the heart of any culture is what the noted sociologist Edward A. Shils (1961) calls the "central zone." He believes that all societies and organizations within societies have central zones that provide a sense of order and stability and a source for the development of norms that gives meaning and significance to the lives of people. The school's central zone represents a repository for the emotions and values that become the basis for moral authority.

Centers evolve naturally in schools in response to human needs, but if left unattended they can take the form of "wild cultures." Wild cultures are driven by emotions and values that may or may not be compatible with school goals, may or may not be supportive of improved teaching and learning, may or may not be growth oriented, and may or may not be good for students. One of the jobs of the principal is to try to unravel and make manifest the wild culture so that it can be examined and understood. Doing so helps those involved come to grips with what is in relation to the values and beliefs that are desired. The idea is to "domesticate" this culture so that it emerges as a system of shared values and beliefs that define for all a way of life that is committed to quality teaching and learning. The goal of domestication is to create community.

When domesticated, the center that defines the school culture becomes the basis for collective decision making and the basis for moral action. The actions and behaviors of parents, teachers, students, and others are driven less by self-interest and more by what the school community considers to be right and good. In this chapter, *center* is referred to as the *covenant* of shared values that determines for the school what is right and good, points to the school's mission, defines obligations and duties, and spells out what must be done to meet commitments.

Purposing Is the Lynchpin

Key to domesticating the culture of the school along the lines of community is the building of a covenant of shared values that replaces more implicit and informal norms. Abraham Zaleznik (1988) believes that "the failure of American management is the substitution of process for substance." He attributes this substitution to an exaggerated belief that schools can be improved by perfecting management systems, structures, and programs and by emphasizing human relationships in order to better control what people do. Too often, process and relationship means become ends in themselves, resulting in vacuous school improvement strategies (Sergiovanni and Duggan, 1990).

To Zaleznik, "leadership is based on a compact that binds those who lead and those who follow into the same moral, intellectual and emotional commitment" (1988:15). Purposing is what principals do to develop this compact. Purposing involves both the vision of the leader and the covenant that the group shares.

Vision in school leadership needs to be understood differently than the way it emerges from the corporate sector. Peters and Austin (1985), for example, point out that vision should start with a single person and suggest that one should be wary of "committee visions." There is some truth to this observation, but there are problems as well. Principals and superintendents have a responsibility and obligation to talk openly and frequently about their beliefs and commitments. They are responsible for encouraging a dialogue about what the school stands for and where it should be headed. Vision, however, should not be construed as a strategic plan that functions like a road map charting the turns needed to reach a specific reality that the leader has in mind. It should, instead, be viewed more as a compass that points the direction to be taken, that inspires enthusiasm, and that allows people to buy into and take part in the shaping of the way that will constitute the school's mission (Bricker, 1985). The fleshing out of this vision requires the building of a shared consensus about purposes and beliefs that creates a powerful force bonding people together around common themes. This bonding provides them with a sense of what is important and some signal of what is of value. *With bonding in place the school is transformed from an organization to a community.*

Often overlooked is the importance of the personal visions of teachers. As Roland Barth (1986) points out:

> *All of us who entered teaching brought with us a conception of a desirable school. Each of us had a personal vision and was prepared to work, even fight, for it. Over time our personal visions became blurred by the visions, demands, and requirements of others. Many teachers' personal visions are now all but obliterated by external prescriptions. (478)*

Vision is a noun that describes what principals and others bring to the school. *Purposing* is a verb that points to what principals do to bring about a shared consensus tight enough and coherent enough to bond people together in a common cause and to define them as a community, but loose enough to allow for individual self-expression.

Purposes in Action

Purposes let people know where the school is going, why, and how. Sometimes purpose statements contain bedrock beliefs that comprise value assumptions about the nature of people. The following four beliefs, for example, are based on Purkey and Novak's (1988) proposal for an approach to schooling they call *invitational education:*

1. Teachers, parents, students, and everyone else with whom the school works are able, valuable, and responsible and should be treated accordingly.
2. Education should be a collaborative, cooperative activity.
3. Teachers, parents, students, and everyone else with whom the school works possess untapped potential in all areas of human endeavor.
4. Human potential can best be realized by places, policies, and processes that are designed to invite development and by the actions and behaviors of people who are intentionally inviting.

When adopted, the four beliefs become a policy platform from which decisions are made about how to organize the school and its curriculum, how people are to work together, and the tone of teaching that is expected. The first belief, for example, frames policies about success and failure. If principal and teachers believe that every parent is worthy of respect and can learn, then they will find ways for parents to improve their parenting skills, to learn about how to help their children at home with their lessons, and so forth. Excuses such as "they are barely literate themselves" and "they don't speak English" would not be acceptable. This formula applies as well to student success.

Similarly, the second belief frames policies in the direction of cooperation rather than competition. Good policies and practices in a school committed to those beliefs are those that do things *with* people rather than *to* people. They give parents, teachers, and students voices, and they listen to these voices. Similar guidelines for action can be derived from beliefs three and four.

Sometimes purposes take the form of a set of common principles that combine beliefs with understandings and expectations. "The Common Principles" of the Coalition of Essential Schools, a national effort to restructure secondary schools founded by Theodore Sizer, is an example of this approach. Sizer believes that no two good schools are quite alike. Instead, each should be a creation of its unique school-community. Thus, advocating common principles rather than proposing a model to be emulated makes sense. The principles of the coalition are as follows:

1. *An Essential school should focus on helping adolescents learn to use their minds well. Schools should not attempt to be "comprehensive" if such a claim is made at the expense of the school's central intellectual purpose.*

2. *The school's goals should be simple: that each student master a limited number of essential skills and areas of knowledge. While these skills and areas will, to varying degrees, reflect the traditional academic disciplines, the program's design should be shaped by the intellectual and imaginative powers and competencies that students need, rather than by "subjects" as conventionally defined. The aphorism "less is more" should dominate. Curricular decisions should be guided by the aim of thorough student mastery and achievement rather than by an effort merely to "cover content."*

3. *The school's goals should apply to all students, although the means to these goals will vary as those students themselves vary. School practice should be tailor made to meet the needs of every group or class of adolescents.*

4. *Teaching and learning should be personalized to the maximum feasible extent. Efforts should be directed toward a goal that no teacher have direct responsibility for more than 80 students. To capitalize on personalization, decisions about the course of study, the use of students' and teachers' time, and the choice of teaching materials and specific pedagogics must be unreservedly placed in the hands of the principal and staff.*

5. *The governing practical metaphor of the school should be student-as-worker, rather than the more familiar metaphor of teacher-as-deliverer-of-instructional-services. A prominent pedagogy will be coaching, to provoke students to learn how to learn and thus to teach themselves.*

6. *Students entering secondary school studies should be those who can show competence in language and elementary mathematics. Students of traditional high school age but not yet at appropriate levels of competence to enter secondary school studies should be provided intensive remedial work to help them meet these standards. The diploma should be awarded upon a successful final demonstration of mastery for graduation—an "exhibition." This exhibition by the student of his or her grasp of the central skills and*

knowledge of the school's program may be jointly administered by the faculty and by higher authorities. The diploma is awarded when earned, so the school's program proceeds with no strict age grading and with no system of credits collected by time spent in class. The emphasis is on the students' demonstration that they can do important things.

The tone of the school should stress values of unanxious expectation ("I won't threaten you but I expect much of you"); of trust (until abused); and of decency (the values of fairness, generosity, and tolerance). Incentives appropriate to the school's particular students and teachers should be emphasized, and parents should be treated as essential collaborators.

7. The principal and teachers should perceive themselves as generalists first (teacher and scholars in general education), and specialists second (experts in one particular discipline). Staff should expect multiple obligations (teacher-counselor-manager), and demonstrate a sense of commitment to the entire school.

8. Ultimate administrative and budget targets should include, in addition to total student loads per teacher of 80 or fewer pupils, substantial time for collective planning by teachers, competitive salaries for staff, and an ultimate per pupil cost not to exceed that at traditional schools by more than 10 percent. To accomplish this, administrative plans might include the phased reduction or elimination of some services now provided for students in many traditional comprehensive secondary schools. (Sizer, 1989:2–4)

Sometimes the substance of a school's covenant comprises a commitment to a set of ideals and beliefs or "theory" about the nature of schooling. This is the case in the Key School in the Indianapolis, Indiana, School District. This school is organized around Howard Gardner's (1983) theory of multiple intelligences. Gardner proposes that people are possessed by seven relatively autonomous intellectual competencies: linguistic and mathematical (the two now emphasized almost exclusively in schools), musical, spatial, bodily-kinesthetic, and two personal intelligences (one focusing on self-understanding and the other on the understanding of others). The Key School gives all seven of these intelligences equal emphasis through the use of an interdisciplinary curriculum. Belief in a common approach to teaching and a common conception of human potential is the core element that bonds together the Key School faculty into a common cause.

"Expeditionary learning" (Outward Bound USA Convenor, 1992) is another example of how school purposes can provide the kind of idea structure that gives direction and guides decisions that schools make. Those involved in this movement seek to transform schools into centers of expeditionary learning. They believe that learning is an expedition into the unknown that requires bringing together personal experience and intellectual growth to promote self-discovery and construct knowledge. Schools committed to the expeditionary learning approach are not provided with scripts to implement but with design principles and components. As is the case with the essential schools movement, the design principles and components serve to inform the decisions that schools make. The principles, along with a handful of key program components that provide a standard for how the principles should be implemented, appear in Table 9–1.

TABLE 9–1   Expeditionary Learning Outward Bound® Design Principles and Components

Principles

1. **The Primacy of Self-Discovery:** Learning happens best with emotion, challenge and the requisite support. People discover their abilities, values, "grand passions," and responsibilities in situations that offer adventure and the unexpected. They must have tasks that require perseverance, fitness, craftsmanship, imagination, self-discipline and significant achievement. A primary job of the educator is to help students overcome their fear and discover they have more in them than they think.

2. **The Having of Wonderful Ideas:** Teach so as to build on children's curiosity about the world by creating learning situations that provide matter to think about, time to experiment, and time to make sense of what is observed. Foster a community where students' and adults' ideas are respected.

3. **The Responsibility for Learning:** Learning is both a personal, individually specific process of discovery and a social activity. Each of us learns within and for ourselves and as a part of a group. Every aspect of a school must encourage children, young people, and adults to become increasingly responsible for directing their own personal and collective learning.

4. **Intimacy and Caring:** Learning is fostered best in small groups where there is trust, sustained caring and mutual respect among all members of the learning community. Keep schools and learning groups small. Be sure there is a caring adult looking after the progress of each child. Arrange for the older students to mentor the younger ones.

5. **Success and Failure:** All students must be assured a fair measure of success in learning in order to nurture the confidence and capacity to take risks and rise to increasingly difficult challenges. But it is also important to experience failure, to overcome negative inclinations, to prevail against adversity and to learn to turn disabilities into opportunities.

6. **Collaboration and Competition:** Teach so as to join individual and group development so that the value of friendship, trust, and group endeavor is made manifest. Encourage students to compete, not against each other, but with their own personal best and with rigorous standards of excellence.

7. **Diversity and Inclusivity:** Diversity and inclusivity in all groups dramatically increases richness of ideas, creative power, problem-solving ability, and acceptance of others. Encourage students to investigate, value and draw upon their own different histories, talents and resources together with those of other communities and cultures. Keep the schools and learning groups heterogeneous.

8. **The Natural World:** A direct and respectful relationship with the natural world refreshes the human spirit and reveals the important lessons of recurring cycles and cause and effect. Students learn to become stewards of the earth and of the generations to come.

9. **Solitude and Reflection:** Solitude, reflection, and silence replenish our energies and open our minds. Be sure students have time alone to explore their own thoughts, make their own connections and create their own ideas. Then give them opportunity to exchange their reflections with each other and with adults.

10. **Service and Compassion:** We are crew, not passengers, and are strengthened by acts of consequential service to others. One of a school's primary functions is to prepare its students with the attitudes and skills to learn from and be of service to others.

Continued

TABLE 9–1   *(Continued)*

Components

1. **Schedule, Structure, Teacher–Student Relationships:** Implementing Expeditionary Learning will require a complete reconsideration of the relationships among staff and students, as well as the schools' arrangements of time and space. Schools should be prepared to eliminate the fifty minute period as the basic scheduling unit and to replace it with a schedule organized to accommodate learning expeditions that may engage students full-time for periods of days, weeks, or months.

    Interdisciplinary learning expeditions will replace subject-separated classes. Tracking will be eliminated; Teachers will work with the same group of students for periods of several years.

2. **Curriculum:** Expeditionary Learning engages the learner in situations that provide not only context but consequence. The curriculum makes intellectual learning and character development of equal importance and encourages self-discovery.

3. **Assessment:** Expeditionary Learning uses real-world performance as the primary way to assess effectiveness in teaching and learning. The International Baccalaureate is used as a framework for establishing world-class standards.

4. **Staff Development:** Expeditionary Learning depends upon and invests in the ongoing development and renewal of staff. An apprenticeship model, flexibility in hiring or reassignment, and a substantial investment in year round staff growth is required.

5. **Linkages to Community and Health Service Organizations:** To provide necessary support to students and their families, expeditionary centers will develop working relations with the appropriate service agencies.

6. **Budget:** Expeditionary Learning achieves its goals through reorganization of existing resources and should not require significant additional funding after an initial period of transition.

From Expeditionary Learning Outward Bound® (1993) *The Expeditionary Learning Reader* Expeditionary Learning: Cambridge, MA. Vol. 1. The above principles have been informed by Kurt Hahn's "Seven Laws of Salem," by Paul Ylvisaker's "The Missing Dimension," and by Eleanor Duckworth's *"The Having of Wonderful Ideas" and Other Essays on Teaching and Learning* (New York: Teachers College Press, Columbia University, 1987).

Characteristics of Purpose Statements

There is no recipe for developing a covenant of shared values. it is a "personal" statement that is developed and owned by a particular school-community. There are, however, some general characteristics of covenants that might be helpful to school communities as they seek to develop ones that are useful and meaningful:

1. They should be clear enough so that you know you are achieving them.
2. They should be accessible enough so that they can be achieved with existing resources.
3. They should be important enough to reflect the core values and beliefs that are shared by those with a stake in the school.

4. They should be powerful enough that they can inspire and touch people in a world that is managerially loose and culturally tight.

5. They should be focused and few in number so that it is clear as to what is important and what isn't.

6. They should be characterized by consonance. The purposes should "hang together" as a group. It should be clear that contradictory purposes can be managed.

7. They should be difficult enough to evoke challenge and cause people to persevere, to persist.

8. They should be resilient enough to stand the test of time and thus not be easily changed.

9. They should be flexible enough to be changed after careful consideration.

Taken together, a good set of purposes should encourage cooperation within the school, and not competition. Cooperative purposes encourage people to work together by allowing each member to share in what the group achieves or attains. Everyone benefits when anyone is successful. Competitive purposes, by contrast, pit one person against another. Each member receives rewards independent of the success of the group and contingent only on her or his own performance, regardless of how well the group does.

Is Outcomes-Based Education a Model?

To what extent are such ideas as vision, purposing, and covenant similar to statements of outcome and to designs for schooling linked tightly to outcomes? The answer to this question depends on one's interpretation of "outcome-based education."

The strategies adopted by the essential schools, the expeditionary learning movements, and the Key school, for example, resemble the popular outcomes-based education (OBE) movement in some ways.* However, designing out from values and OBE strategies are not the same. The OBE approach typically requires the identification and specification of measurable student performance outcomes. These outcomes (often called "exit outcomes") are competencies that students must demonstrate before completing a particular lesson, unit, course, or school year. Completion, in some cases, is a requirement for graduation. Instead of emphasizing *designing out* from values, OBE emphasizes *designing down* from performance outcomes. According to Spady, OBE means "organizing for results: basing what we do instructionally on the outcomes we want to achieve...." (Spady, 1988: 5).

Outcomes-based education offers a number of advantages. Prime among them is that the strategy is inclusive. Advocates firmly believe that all students can learn and will learn given the right (i.e., OBE) circumstances. OBE, for example, is often accompanied by mastery learning as an instructional process. Mastery learning begins with identifying well-defined learning objectives. Well-organized learning units that are closely aligned

*The following discussion of outcomes-based education is drawn from Chapter 5, "Building A Purposeful Community" and Chapter 6, "Using Curriculum to Build Community," in Thomas J. Sergiovanni. 1994. *Building Community In Schools.* San Francisco: Jossey-Bass.

with these objectives are then constructed. Monitoring systems are often developed to be sure that teachers teach the prescribed curriculum. The curriculum is then taught directly by teachers. Tests are used to determine the extent to which students have achieved the objectives. Throughout, students are provided with regular feedback, guidance, and direction, not only to let them know what it is they must learn and how, but to provide them with whatever extra help they might need to master the material. Usually time is not an issue; students are allowed as much time as they need to master the material. To Spady (1988), OBE "means having all students learn well, not just the fastest, the brightest, or the most advantaged" (4).

Despite OBE's commitment to inclusiveness in learning, the strategy can present some problems. The strategy is linear as curriculum is designed down from performance outcomes. Yet, sound curriculum choices and decisions about effective teaching and learning practices are anything but linear. They are as likely to emerge *in use* as teachers practice as they are to be set ahead of time. Furthermore, teachers are not just concerned with instructional objectives and outcomes but other kinds of teaching and learning circumstances as well. Instructional objectives and outcomes are typically outlined before teaching begins and defined in behavioral terms. What is the student expected to do or know at the end of teaching? Certainly the use of instructional objectives and outcomes makes sense for certain kinds of teaching and learning circumstances, but it may not make sense for other kinds.

Because OBE learning outcomes are typically universal and set beforehand, students often have very little to say about what they will learn. Thus, the outcomes do not always reflect unique characteristics and interests of all students. Furthermore, once the curriculum is aligned to the outcomes, teachers are required to teach directly to them. This process includes frequent measuring of the extent to which outcomes are being reached and reteaching as necessary until the outcomes are mastered.

In a sense, the outcomes and the linear chain of events that follow can become scripts that limit the decisions teachers make. Once outcomes are set by the school, teachers are not free to select their own. Initially, they may have autonomy over means, but this autonomy may be elusive. Over time, choices as to what to teach, when, and how can become increasingly limited by the outcomes toward which one must teach.

Both Discipline and Discretion are Key

Shared purposes, covenants, design principles, and other agreements should provide enough discipline to ensure that focus, clarity, and harmony characterize what teachers do. This discipline, however, must be achieved without taking away the discretion teachers need to make decisions in light of the unique circumstances that they face. A good idea structure, in other words, doesn't tell people what to do but informs the decisions they make about what to do. One way to achieve both discipline and discretion is by striking a balance among instrumental, problem solving, and expressive outcomes (Eisner, 1969, 1979) as curriculum experiences are planned. Instructional outcomes are set beforehand and in fairly specific ways. They are stated in terms of what the student is supposed to be able to do as a result of teaching. Curriculum and teaching decisions are made by designing down from the instructional outcomes. Problem-solving outcomes are shaped by the decisions made about problems that students must solve and exhibitions they must master and perform. Expressive outcomes are discovered during and after the teaching of trusted subject matter and the use of trusted teaching activities—trusted means that they are known for their ability to stimulate learning.

In a sense, instructional outcomes represent baseball strike zones. Teaching to them represents the pitching of learning into a particular strike zone. Balls and strikes must be called to keep track of how effective the teaching is in achieving the outcomes. For example, in teaching a lesson or unit on the jury system, we might state the following instructional outcomes: (1) the student will be able to differentiate between the roles and functions of various principles in a jury trial (e.g., prosecuting attorney, defense attorney, bailiff, types of witnesses); (2) the student will be able to write two coherent paragraphs that describe the differences in rules of evidence for civil trials as opposed to criminal trials. If the student performs according to the specified behaviors, then we have a strike. If she or he does not, then it's a ball. When a ball is called, the teaching pitches do not count, even though what the student learns may be as important or more important than the instructional outcome that was stated. The student, for example, may not be able to differentiate the rules of evidence as required, but is able to detect flaws in arguments better than before. The student may not be able to differentiate the various roles very well, but she or he has a greater appreciation for the fairness and effectiveness of the judicial system. Sorry, it's still a ball. The learning doesn't count because it does not fit into the strike zone.

In the real world of teaching, good teachers often change their minds as they teach. Sometimes they chase a student's ideas and wind up at a place different than originally intended. The strike zone that counts for them moves to another position; however, the strike zone that counts officially stands still, converting perfectly sound and sensible strikes into balls.

When using only instructional outcomes, the curriculum intended, the curriculum taught, and the curriculum learned must always be aligned with each other. Thus, once outcomes are set (discipline), teachers have increasingly less say over the taught and learned curriculum (discretion). It often makes sense to insist that students be able to demonstrate exactly what they are supposed to demonstrate. Thus, instructional outcomes have an important role to play, but so do problem solving and expressive outcomes. Balance is needed among the three if both discipline and discretion are to be achieved.

Problem-solving outcomes are harder to nail down in a specific way beforehand, but they are hardly serendipitous. By carefully crafting a problem, we can increase the likelihood that certain kinds of outcomes will emerge. As Eisner (1979) explains,

> *The problem-solving objective differs in a significant way from the behavioral [instructional] objective. In the problem-solving objective, the students formulate or are given a problem to solve—say to find out how deterrents to smoking might be made more effective, or how to design a paper structure that will hold two bricks sixteen inches above a table, or how the variety and quality of food served in the school cafeteria could be increased within the existing budget. (101)*

It's not enough just to state the problem; certain criteria need to be provided that set a standard for how the problem will be solved. The more specific the criteria, the more the range of outcomes becomes narrowed. The forms of the solution, however, remain infinite. With instructional outcomes, both questions and answers are set ahead of time. With problem-solving objectives, the question is set but the answer is not definite.

Problems-based learning provides a happy balance between discipline and discretion for both teachers and students. Teachers might agree, for example, on the problems that students will solve in a given unit, course, or grade level. However, because no single answer or no one solution exists for the typical problem, teachers have flexibility in making choices about what will be studied, what materials will be used, what teaching approaches to use, what learning settings to invent, and so forth. Furthermore, students have discretion; within the parameters of the problem, they decide how they will learn and what they will learn. As teachers monitor learning, they make decisions that shape what students are doing and that are shaped by what students are doing. Despite discretion, a certain coherence and focus is maintained by the parameters the problem provides.

Problem-solving outcomes play a major role in organizing the curriculum, arranging learning experiences, teaching, and evaluating in schools that are committed to the principles of both the Coalition of Essential Schools and expeditionary learning. These schools rely heavily on exhibitions of mastery as the construct for organizing the curriculum, for teaching and learning, and for evaluating.

Expressive outcomes, according to Eisner (1969), are what one ends up with, whether intended or not, after being engaged in a learning experience. "Expressive outcomes are the consequences of curriculum activities that are intentionally planned to provide a fertile opportunity for personal purposing and experiences" (26). The emphasis is on the activity itself, the learning experience that the student will be engaged in, and the content or the subject matter, not the specifics of what the student will learn as a result of this engagement.

Although expressive outcomes are not anticipated prior to the actual teaching, they represent valued learnings nonetheless. Good teachers, for example, know and trust the potential of certain ideas, activities, and experiences to promote learning. They know that when students engage in them good things happen. Although the teacher cannot say exactly what students will get out of the experience, she or he has always found that they learned a great deal when engaging in the learning activity.

Instructional outcomes, problem-solving outcomes, and expressive outcomes all have important roles to play in curriculum planning. When brought together, they allow teachers to make decisions that reflect the discipline necessary for purposeful community building. Furthermore, this discipline is achieved without compromising the discretion needed to make informed decisions in light of the ambiguities found in the typical teaching and learning situation. Discretion increases the likelihood that effective teaching and learning decisions will be made and that effective caring decisions will be made. Discretion allows the building of an inquiring community as teachers puzzle together over what decisions make the most sense. In addition, discretion embodies professional community by allowing teachers to take control of their practice.

Redefining the Outcomes-Based Movement

In summary, many of the ideas associated with the outcome-based movement as it is now understood are useful. This movement, however, is plagued by two major problems. One is a tendency to align outcome thinking with "instructional delivery models" that are too explicit, that rely almost exclusively on instructional outcomes, and that subsequently reduce teacher discretion and narrow student learning.

Diez (1993) believes that this problem can be remedied by redefining the term *outcome* as follows:

> [outcome refers to] Individual student performance, over time, giving evidence of the development of integrated, complex abilities. This view of outcomes sets up an interest in the process of development as well as in the end product. It calls for demonstrations in multiple modes and contexts, ways that integrate knowledge dispositions (attitudes, beliefs, values, etc.), and performance. Multiplicity of modes and contexts of demonstration is important because student learning outcomes are most powerful when they are seen as transferable—e.g., outcomes like problem-solving, critical thinking, or communication abilities that cut across the content areas. (2)

Diez's definition places problem-solving outcomes and expressive outcomes on an equal footing with instructional outcomes.

The second problem is that focusing only on "outcomes" ignores other issues that should play important roles in developing an idea structure for a school. An idea structure, for example, should include values and commitments that inform what people do and provide a moral basis for their actions. Furthermore, an idea structure should include commitments that teachers make to each other as to how they want to live their lives together and how they want to relate to their students. This problem can be remedied by paying less attention to "designing down from outcomes" and more attention to "designing out from values."

Appendix 9–1 provides an inventory of assumptions that school faculties can use to begin a conversation about what they believe and what they don't believe about teaching and learning and about the nature of school knowledge. The assumptions they settle on can become values used to "design out" to how they relate with students, how teaching and learning is planned and practiced, and how curriculum and evaluation decisions are made.

Providing the Necessary Leadership

Shared goals and purposes, agreed-upon covenants, and other statements of what is believed are the nerve center of a successful school. They provide the necessary signals, symbols, substance, and direction needed for coordinated action on behalf of quality in schooling. The clarity and coherence they provide cannot be duplicated by close supervision, management controls, and other regulatory measures, for these latter practices require a much tighter connection among school parts, roles, and activities than is typically found in schools. Loosely structured schools achieve coordinated action by creating a powerful normative system that serves to socialize newcomers and to provide reinforcement to those already socialized. Furthermore, this normative system provides a source of meaning and direction to those who live and work in the school.

Principal leadership in tight value and loose decision-making schools is more complicated than first seems apparent. It requires the balancing of both flexible and resilient leadership styles. Effective principals display a great deal of resiliency when concerned with the school's goal structure, educational platform, and overall philosophy. At the same time, they display a great deal of flexibility when concerned with the everyday articulation of these values into teaching and learning practices and designs. Before continuing with this discussion, let's examine the Style Flexibility Index (SFI) and the Style Resilience Index (SRI) shown in Exhibits 9–1 and 9–2. The items in these indexes were suggested by W. J. Reddin's (1970) discussion of style flexibility and style resilience. Respond to each of the indexes and obtain flexibility and resilience scores. Keep in mind that both indexes suggest only how you might be perceived on these dimensions by others with whom you work.

EXHIBIT 9–1   Style Flexibility Index

Think of occasions, situations, and incidents when you as school principal were interacting directly with teachers about *day-to-day and week-to-week decisions involving instructional materials, subject-matter content, classroom organization, and the provision of teaching and learning.* As a result of this interaction, indicate how teachers would describe you, using the 10 paired statements provided below.

	10 9 8 7 6 5 4 3 2 1	
Other-directed	_____	Dogmatic
Sensitive	_____	Unresponsive
Collaborating	_____	Rejecting
Reality-oriented	_____	Status-oriented
Interdependent	_____	Authority-oriented
Involved	_____	Inhibited
Team player	_____	Uncooperative
Colleague-oriented	_____	Control-oriented
Open-minded	_____	Close-minded
Practical	_____	Intolerant
	10 9 8 7 6 5 4 3 2 1	

Scoring: Sum the scores given to each of the 10 scales of the Style Flexibility Index. Scores will range from a low of 10 to a high of 100. The higher the score, the more flexible one is perceived to be. An improved indication of style flexibility would be obtained by having teachers actually describe their principal.

EXHIBIT 9–2   Style Resilience Index

Think of occasions, situations, and incidents when you as principal were interacting directly with teachers about *general goals and purposes, educational platform, and overall philosophy of the school.* As a result of this interaction, indicate how teachers would describe you, using the 10 paired statements provided below.

	10 9 8 7 6 5 4 3 2 1	
Clear goals		Inconsistent
Fulfills commitments		Uncommitted
Willpower		Avoids conflict
Individualistic		Conforming
Decisive		Indecisive
Reliable		Disorganized
Self-confident		Avoids rejection
Simplifies issues		Ambiguous
Persistent		Yielding
Tough-minded		Wavering
	10 9 8 7 6 5 4 3 2 1	

Scoring: Sum the scores given to each of the 10 scales of the Style Resilience Index. Scores will range from a low of 10 to a high of 100. The higher the score, the more flexible one is perceived to be. An improved indication of style resilience would be obtained by having teachers actually describe their principal.

Now let's examine the concepts of flexibility and resilience. Flexibility is perhaps best understood by understanding its relationship to drifting. As leadership concepts, both flexibility and drifting comprise the same behaviors. Yet, expressions of these behaviors might result in effectiveness in one situation and ineffectiveness in another. When the behavior expressed matches the situation, the principal will be viewed as being highly flexible. When the exact same behavior is expressed in inappropriate situations, the principal is viewed as drifting.

Reddin (1970) points out that style flexibility in leadership is characterized by high ambiguity tolerance, power sensitivity, an open belief system, and other-directedness. Highly flexible principals are comfortable in unstructured situations, are not control-oriented, bring to the work context very few fixed ideas, and display a great deal of interest in the ideas of others. These characteristics are very desirable when articulated within the loosely structured discretionary space of schools, but in matters of the school's goal structure and educational platform, flexibility by the principal is often viewed negatively by teachers and others. When this is the case, the principal's style can be described as drifting rather than flexible. Drifting suggests a lack of direction and an absence of commitment to a purpose or cause.

Rigidity is the concept that Reddin suggests to understand counterproductive expressions of resilience. The resilient leadership style is characterized by willpower, tough-mindedness, self-confidence, and self-discipline. Principals of effective schools display these qualities when dealing with aspects of the school's value core. Expressing these same qualities, when dealing with the day-to-day decisions that teachers make in classrooms as they work with students, would result in the principal's being perceived as rigid. The two dimensions of resilience and flexibility are illustrated in Figure 9–1 in the form of a leadership grid. Note that, at the base of the grid, resiliency ranges from a low score of 0 to a high of 100. Plot your score from the Style Resilience Index on this dimension of the grid. To the left is the flexibility dimension, ranging from 0 to 100. Plot your score from the Style Flexibility Index on this dimension.

High resiliency scores combined with low flexibility scores would place one in the lower right-hand corner of the grid and represent the Rigid style. A flexibility score of 80 combined with a resiliency score of 30, however, would place one in the upper left-hand quadrant of the grid, representing the Drifting leadership style. High scores on both flexibility and resilience would place one in the upper right-hand quadrant—the Balanced leadership style. Low scores on both dimensions would place one in the lower left

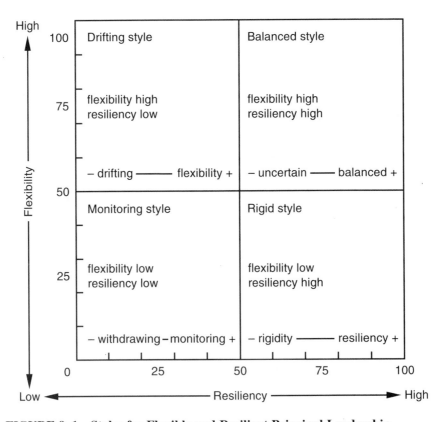

FIGURE 9–1   Styles for Flexible and Resilient Principal Leadership

quadrant—the Monitoring style, Let's examine each of the four styles with reference to principals as they manage issues of tight and loose coupling in schools.

The Drifting style can work when important values are not at stake and might be appropriate for issues common to the school's loosely structured, high discretionary area. However, when principals are flexible in dealing with the school's core of values, they appear to teachers to be drifting and are not viewed as able to provide necessary purposing and direction.

The Rigid style can work for issues relating to the school's core of values. Using this style with teachers on issues of providing for daily teaching and learning, however, is likely to be viewed negatively. Instead of appearing resilient, principals will be seen as autocratic and their style as rigid.

The Monitoring style can work in instances in which jobs can be programmed in such detail that the emphasis is less on persons and goals and more on monitoring the work flow, thus ensuring reliability. Teacher-proof designs for schooling support the Monitoring style. The enforcement of school rules and providing drill-practice work in teaching and learning might be examples appropriate for the Monitoring style. When principals use this style excessively or in the wrong instances, they are viewed as having withdrawn their concern for people as individuals and for goals and purposes.

The Balanced style provides flexible leadership in the articulation of the school's values, goals, and platform as teachers work day by day. At the same time, this style provides resilient leadership with respect to the promotion and maintenance of important values. This approach characterizes principal leadership found in successful schools. The concept of balanced leadership characteristic of successful schools should be the cornerstone of one's management platform and is an important dimension of reflective practice in the principalship.

References

Barth, Roland. 1986. "The Principal and the Profession of Teaching," *Elementary School Journal* 86(4).

Bidwell, Charles E. 1965. "The School as a Formal Organization," in James G. March, Ed., *Handbook of Organization,* 972–1022. Chicago: Rand McNally.

Bricker, H. 1985. As quoted in Robert H. Hayes, "Strategic Planning Forward in Reverse?" *Harvard Business Review,* Nov.–Dec.

Diez, Mary E. 1993. "Briefs," *American Association of Colleges for Teacher Education* (14) 12.

Eisner, Elliot. 1969. "Instructional and Expressive Educational Objectives: Their Formulation and Use In Curriculum," in W. James Popham, Ed., *Curriculum Evaluation: Instructional Objectives.* AERA Monograph Series. Chicago: Rand-McNally.

Eisner, Elliot. 1979. *The Educational Imagination: On the Design and Evaluation of School Programs.* New York: Macmillan.

Etzioni, Amitai. 1988. *The Moral Dimension Toward a New Economics.* New York: The Free Press.

Gardner, Howard. 1983. *Frames of Mind: The Theory of Multiple Intelligences.* New York: Basic Books.

Hills, Jean. 1982. "The Preparation of Educational Leaders: What's Needed and What's Next?" UCEA occasional paper No. 8303. Columbus, OH: University Council for Educational Administration.

Outward Bound USA Convenor. 1992. "Expeditionary Learning: A Design for New America's Schools." A proposal to the New American Schools Development Corporation. Greenwich, CN: Author.

Parsons, Talcott. 1951. *Toward a General Theory of Social Action.* Cambridge, MA: Harvard University Press.

Perrow, Charles. 1981. "Disintegrating Social Sciences," *New York University Education Quarterly* 10(2), 2–9.

Peters, Thomas J., and Robert H. Waterman, Jr. 1982. *In Search of Excellence: Lessons from America's Best-Run Companies.* New York: Harper & Row.

Peters, Tom, and Nancy Austin. 1985. *A Passion for Excellence.* New York: Random House.

Purkey, William W., and J. M. Novak. 1988. *Education: By Invitation Only.* Bloomington, IN. Phi Delta Kappan Foundation.

Reddin, W. J. 1970. *Managerial Effectiveness.* New York: McGraw-Hill.

Sergiovanni, Thomas J., and Brad Duggan. 1990, "Moral Authority: A Blueprint for Managing Tomorrow's Schools," in T. J. Sergiovanni and J. H. Moore, Eds., *Target 2000: A Compact for Excellence in Texas's Schools.* The 1990 Yearbook of the Texas Association for Supervision and Curriculum Development. San Antonio, TX: Watercress Press.

Shils, Edward A. 1961. "Centre and Periphery," in *The Logic of Personal Knowledge: Essays Presented to Michael Polanyi.* London: Routledge and Kegan Paul.

Sizer, Theodore R. (1989). "Diverse Practice, Shared Ideas: The Essential School," in H. J. Walberg and J. J. Lane, *Organizing for Learning Toward the 21st Century.* Reston, VA: National Association of Secondary School Principals.

Spady, William G. 1988. "Organizing for Results: The Basis of Authentic Restructuring and Reform," *Educational Leadership* 47. 4–10.

Trice Harrison, M., and Ganice M. Beyer. 1984. "Studying Organizational Cultures Through Rites and Ceremonials," *Academy of Management Review* 9(4), 653–669.

Watson, Thomas J., Jr. 1963. *A Business and Its Beliefs: The Ideas That Helped Build IBM.* New York: McGraw-Hill.

Weick, Karl. 1976. "Educational Organizations as Loosely Coupled Systems," *Administrative Science Quarterly* 21(2), 1–19.

Weick, Karl. 1982. "Administering Education in Loosely Coupled Systems," *Phi Delta Kappan* 27(2), 673–676.

Zaleznik, Abraham. 1988. Quoted in Doran P. Levin, "G.M. Bid to Rejuvenate Leadership." *The New York Times.* Sept. 3.

Appendix 9–1   Assumptions about Learning and Knowledge

Instructions: Make somewhere along each line a mark that best represents your own feelings about each statement.

Example: School serves the wishes and needs of adults better than it does the wishes and needs of children.

strongly agree	agree	no strong feeling	disagree	strongly disagree

I. Assumptions about Children's Learning

Motivation

    Assumption 1: Children are innately curious and will explore their environment without adult intervention.

strongly agree	agree	no strong feeling	disagree	strongly disagree

    Assumption 2: Exploratory behavior is self-perpetuating.

strongly agree	agree	no strong feeling	disagree	strongly disagree

Conditions for Learning

    Assumption 3: The child will display natural exploratory behavior if he is not threatened.

strongly agree	agree	no strong feeling	disagree	strongly disagree

    Assumption 4: Confidence in self is highly related to capacity for learning and for making important choices affecting ones learning.

strongly agree	agree	no strong feeling	disagree	strongly disagree

    Assumption 5: Active exploration in a rich environment, offering a wide array of manipulative materials, will facilitate children's learning.

strongly agree	agree	no strong feeling	disagree	strongly disagree

From Roland S. Barth (1971), "So You Want to Change to an Open Classroom," *Phi Delta Kappan* 53(2), 98–99.

Appendix 9–1   *(Continued)*

Assumption 6: Play is not distinguished from work as the predominant mode of learning in early childhood,

| strongly agree | agree | no strong feeling | disagree | strongly disagree |

Assumption 7: Children have both the competence and the right to make significant decisions concerning their own learning.

| strongly agree | agree | no strong feeling | disagree | strongly disagree |

Assumption 8: Children will be likely to learn if they are given considerable choice in the selection of the materials they wish to work with and in the choice of questions they wish to pursue with respect to those materials.

| strongly agree | agree | no strong feeling | disagree | strongly disagree |

Assumption 9: Given the opportunity, children will choose to engage in activities which will be of high interest to them,

| strongly agree | agree | no strong feeling | disagree | strongly disagree |

Assumption 10: If a child is fully involved in and is having fun with an activity, learning is taking place.

| strongly agree | agree | no strong feeling | disagree | strongly disagree |

Social Learning

Assumption 11: When two or more children are interested in exploring the same problem or the same materials, they will often choose to collaborate in some way.

| strongly agree | agree | no strong feeling | disagree | strongly disagree |

Assumption 12: When a child learns something which is important to him, he will wish to share it with others.

| strongly agree | agree | no strong feeling | disagree | strongly disagree |

Appendix 9–1 *(Continued)*

Intellectual Development
  Assumption 13: Concept formation proceeds very slowly.

strongly agree	agree	no strong feeling	disagree	strongly disagree

  Assumption 14: Children learn and develop intellectually not only at their own rate but in their own style.

strongly agree	agree	no strong feeling	disagree	strongly disagree

  Assumption 15: Children pass through similar stages of intellectual development, each in his own way and at his own rate and in his own time.

strongly agree	agree	no strong feeling	disagree	strongly disagree

  Assumption 16: Intellectual growth and development take place through a sequence of concrete experiences followed by abstractions.

strongly agree	agree	no strong feeling	disagree	strongly disagree

  Assumption 17: Verbal abstractions should follow direct experience with objects and ideas, not precede them or substitute for them.

strongly agree	agree	no strong feeling	disagree	strongly disagree

Evaluation
  Assumption 18: The preferred source of verification for a child's solution to a problem comes through the materials he is working with.

strongly agree	agree	no strong feeling	disagree	strongly disagree

  Assumption 19: Errors are necessarily a part of the learning process; they are to be expected and even desired, for they contain information essential for further learning.

strongly agree	agree	no strong feeling	disagree	strongly disagree

Appendix 9–1   *(Continued)*

Assumption 20: Those qualities of a person's learning which can be carefully measured are not necessarily the most important.

strongly agree	agree	no strong feeling	disagree	strongly disagree

Assumption 21: Objective measures of performance may have a negative effect upon
learning.

strongly agree	agree	no strong feeling	disagree	strongly disagree

Assumption 22: Learning is best assessed intuitively, by direct observation.

strongly agree	agree	no strong feeling	disagree	strongly disagree

Assumption 23: The best way of evaluating the effect of the school experience on the
child is to observe him over a long period of time.

strongly agree	agree	no strong feeling	disagree	strongly disagree

Assumption 24: The best measure of a child's work is his work.

strongly agree	agree	no strong feeling	disagree	strongly disagree

Assumptions about Knowledge

Assumption 25: The quality of being is more important than the quality of knowing;
knowledge is a means of education, not its end. The final test of an education is what a
man *is,* not what he *knows.*

strongly agree	agree	no strong feeling	disagree	strongly disagree

Assumption 26: Knowledge is a function of one's personal integration of experience
and therefore does not fall into neatly separate categories or "disciplines."

strongly agree	agree	no strong feeling	disagree	strongly disagree

Appendix 9–1   *(Continued)*

Assumption 27: The structure of knowledge is personal and idiosyncratic; it is a function of the synthesis of each individual's experience with the world.

strongly agree	agree	no strong feeling	disagree	strongly disagree

Assumption 28: Little or no knowledge exists which is essential for everyone to acquire.

strongly agree	agree	no strong feeling	disagree	strongly disagree

Assumption 29: It is possible, even likely, that an individual may learn and possess knowledge of a phenomenon and yet be unable to display it publicly. Knowledge resides with the knower, not in its public expression.

strongly agree	agree	no strong feeling	disagree	strongly disagree

Chapter *10*

Teaching, Learning, and Community

Just a few years ago it seemed that the issue of defining effective teaching and understanding how students learn was settled. We had in hand a body of knowledge based on "effective teaching" research and on associationist and behaviorist learning principles that provided a crystal clear picture of how students learn and of what teachers needed to do to maximize this learning. Included in this picture were beliefs that learning was an individual matter involving the accumulation of bits and pieces of knowledge and skills. This learning could be facilitated by providing lots of direct teaching and guided practice, and could be motivated by providing the right rewards.

   Things are different today. Whereas the effective teaching findings of the 1970s and early 1980s cannot be summarily dismissed, more recent research provides a different picture of how students learn and of what good teaching is. This research is based on constructivist cognitive psychology and on cultural views of human being and learning.

Comparing the Theories

The implications for curriculum building, supervision, staff development, and leadership practice of these two different views of teaching and learning—constructivist cognitive psychology and cultural views of human being and learning—are important. Theories create the realities that we have to deal with. As theories change, so do the realities. In the image of teaching based on the effective teaching research and behaviorist psychology, the emphasis in curriculum building is on explicitness and on alignment of what will be learned with preset objectives, with approaches to teaching, and with assessment strategies. Supervision becomes a process of monitoring the various parts of this alignment and making the needed corrections. Staff development becomes training, and leadership becomes a process of planning, organizing, motivating, and evaluating the work of others.

Within the constructivist cognitive view of teaching and learning, the emphasis is on emergent curriculum, collegial supervision, teacher development as inquiry and reflection, and leadership as community building. In both cases it is the theory of teaching and learning that determines what good practice is. If we want to change existing practice we will first have to change what we believe is true about teaching and learning.

Exhibit 10–1 lists seven pairs of beliefs about teaching and learning.* As you read the pairs distribute 10 points to reflect the extent to which you think each is true. If, for example, you think belief *1a* and belief *1b* are equally true, give them each five points. If you think belief *1a* is absolutely true and *1b* is absolutely false, assign 10 points to *a* and none to *b,* and so forth.

By totaling the points you assigned to the *a* statements and to the *b* statements, you can get an idea of the extent to which you agree with each of the two theories of teaching and learning.

The choices we make about the beliefs we hold determine, for example, what is considered effective supervisory practice. The rating, inspecting, and inservicing practices that now account for what principals are expected to do are based on beliefs about teaching and learning implied by the *a* statements of each pair. This supervision takes the form of tightly linking teachers to detailed objectives, to curriculum content scripts, to teaching schedules, and to corresponding evaluation schemes that rely on checking to be sure that teachers are following the approved script. Effective teaching is expressed as research-validated generic behaviors. These behaviors often comprise lists that principals use in observing teachers.

The beliefs implied by the *b* statements are based on constructivist cognitive psychological principles that suggest different teaching and supervisory practices. Harriet Tyson (1990) describes some of these differences:

> *School structures and routines should be shaped more by students' needs than by the characteristics of the disciplines, and less by teachers' and administrators' need for control and convenience. Young children learn best when they become active workers rather than passive learners. They make more progress, and are much more interested in schoolwork, when they are permitted to work together in groups to solve complex tasks, allowed to engage in class discussions and taught to argue convincingly for their approach in the midst of conflicting ideas and strategies. Even young children can do these things well with a little encouragement . . . many children, particularly those with little home support, learn best in a more familial school atmosphere. (22)*

Believing that teaching is not the same as telling, Tyson (1990) concludes that

> *Generic pedagogy, which has spawned generic in-service training programs and generic teacher evaluation systems, overlooks the intimate and necessary*

---

*The assumptions are summarized from James Nolan and Pam Francis, "Changing Perspectives in Curriculum and Instruction," in Carl Glickman, Ed., *Supervision in Transition,* 1992 Yearbook of the Association for Supervision and Curriculum Development, 44–59. Alexandria, VA: Association for Supervision and Curriculum Development. The inventory itself is from Thomas J. Sergiovanni and Robert J. Starratt. 1993. *Supervision: Redefinition,* 5th ed., p. 114. New York: McGraw Hill.

EXHIBIT 10–1   Beliefs About Teaching and Learning

1. (a) Learning is a process of accumulating isolated bits of
   information and skills.   (a) _____
   (b) Learning involves active construction of meaning and
   understanding.   (b) _____ = 10
2. (a) Students are empty vessels who receive and store
   information that is taught.   (a) _____
   (b) Students' prior understandings influence what they learn
   during instruction.   (b) _____ = 10
3. (a) Learning is defined as a change in student
   behavior.   (a) _____
   (b) Learning is defined as a change in a student's cognitive
   structure and world view.   (b) _____ = 10
4. (a) Teaching and learning involves interactions between
   teachers and students.   (a) _____
   (b) Teaching and learning involves active construction of
   meaning by students.   (b) _____ = 10
5. (a) Students are individual learners and motivation should be
   competitively based.   (a) _____
   (b) Learning in cooperation with others is important in
   motivating students and in enhancing outcomes.   (b) _____ = 10
6. (a) Teachers must work hard at delivering instruction to
   students to be successful.   (a) _____
   (b) Teachers must arrange for students to do the work of
   learning.   (b) _____ = 10
7. (a) Thinking and learning skills are generic across content
   areas and context.   (a) _____
   (b) Thinking and learning skills are content- and
   context-specific.   (b) _____ = 10
                                                                                            _____
                                                                                              70

---

connection between a discipline and teaching methods. Powerful, subject-specific and topic-specific pedagogy, most of it in mathematics and science, is becoming available. These new techniques make the battles over relative importance of content knowledge and pedagogical knowledge seem futile. Effective teaching requires both kinds of knowledge, developed to a high degree, and applied flexibly and artistically to particular topics and students. (24)

Much of the new research on teaching leads to the conclusion that teaching is much more than script-following and supervision is much more than making sure that those scripts are followed (Brandt, 1993; Marzano, 1992; Resnick and Klopfer, 1989). Two recent issues of *Educational Leadership* (April, 1992; April, 1993) provide readable and compelling summaries of this research.

Implications for Supervision

The *b* beliefs about teaching and learning provide a different image of how supervision should be thought about and practiced. According to Nolan and Frances (1992):

1. *Teachers will be viewed as active constructors of their own knowledge about teaching and learning;*
2. *Supervisors will be viewed as collaborators in creating knowledge about teaching and learning;*
3. *The emphasis in data collection during supervision will change from almost total reliance on paper and pencil observation instruments [designed] to capture the events of a single period of instruction to the use of a wide variety of data sources to capture a lesson as it unfolds over several periods of instruction;*
4. *There will be greater emphasis on content specific knowledge and skills in the supervisory process; and*
5. *Supervision will become more group oriented rather than individually oriented. (58)*

This image suggests new roles and responsibilities for teachers. They will, for example, become more active as participants in knowledge and collaborators in creating new knowledge about teaching and learning. They must assume roles not only as co-supervisors with principals and other administrators, but also as co-supervisors with other teachers. They must join together with their principals to help the school become a learning and inquiring community. These themes will be further developed in Chapter 11. The sections below briefly review the research on effective teaching and then compare this research with the new insights that have emerged from constructivist cognitive psychology.

Research on "Effective Teaching"

Without question the early research on effective teaching contributed to our understanding, provided a base upon which to build new insights into effective teaching, and still provides some useful ideas for certain teaching and learning situations. The findings are apt to sound familiar to experienced teachers and might even be considered applications of common sense. This research showed that certain teacher behaviors were related to student gains on both criterion- and norm-referenced tests. Examples of the behaviors most frequently cited by this research are:

Provide classroom rules that allow pupils to take care of personal and procedural needs without having to check with the teacher.

Communicate high expectations to students.

Begin each class by reviewing homework and by reviewing material covered in the previous few classes.

Make objectives of teaching clear to students.

Teach directly the content or skills that will be measured on the tests.

After teaching, asses student comprehension by asking questions and by providing practice.

Provide opportunities for successful practice and monitor this practice by moving around the classroom.

Be sure that students are directly engaged in academic tasks.

Assign homework.

Hold review sessions weekly and monthly.

An important question is: How applicable are these teaching behaviors? For example, are they likely to be as effective in teaching complex subject matter that requires interpretation and teaching higher-order thinking skills as they are for teaching simple subject matter and basic skills? Are they equally effective for teaching music, physics, reading, arithmetic, or more advanced mathematics? Effective teaching researchers would answer no. They never intended that research findings be applicable to all situations. Consultants, workshop providers, and policymakers, however, were often quick to answer yes. In their enthusiasm to find simple answers to complex questions they tended to consider the findings as generic and thus applicable to all situations.

How teaching effectiveness was defined created another problem. Definitions of effectiveness, similar to theories, create realities. With different definitions we get different effective teaching practices. Some teacher evaluation instruments, for example, define effective teaching as the display of behavior associated with the research on direct instruction. Other instruments define effectiveness as the embodiment of constructivist teaching and learning principles. "Effectiveness," in each case, is a function of how effectiveness is defined originally.

Most of the studies that led to the effective teaching findings were concentrating on the teaching of basic skills in reading and arithmetic in the early grades of elementary schools. Whether these teaching behaviors are appropriate for higher-level learning in reading and mathematics or for learning in other areas such as history or music, is an open question. The indicators of teaching effectiveness are neither objective nor independent, but are directly linked to how researchers define effectiveness.

Process-Product Research

The original teaching effectiveness researchers limited their analysis to linking teaching behaviors to outcomes such as achievement test scores. The teaching behaviors were known as processes and the outcomes as products, which gave rise to the name process-product research. The behaviors of teachers that correlated with high student outcomes were considered to be effective. This approach provided a limited definition of teacher productivity. A more valid definition identifies the teacher as just one of several inputs into the process of producing student outcomes. Furthermore, it focuses on a teacher's contribution to learning rather than some arbitrary and absolute standard applied uniformly to all students. Productivity, in other words, is a relative, not an absolute, term. Thus, it is very possible for teacher *a* to be more productive than teacher *b,* even though at an absolute level teacher *b*'s students score higher on tests than do teacher *a*'s (Schlock, Cowart, and Staebler, 1993).

The lessons learned from the process-product effective teaching research are important. This research tells us that some teachers elicit greater gains in student achievement on tests than others because of differences in how they teach; because they expect more from students, emphasize mastery, provide more opportunities to learn, and manage their classrooms well; and because they spend a great deal of time actively teaching their students (Brophy, 1992). Teachers who do these things are likely to be much more effective than teachers who don't. Nonetheless, because this research focused on basic aspects of teaching that differentiated least effective teachers from others, it does not highlight the critical, albeit more subtle, points of teaching that distinguish outstanding teachers.

The New Research

What does the new research tell us? This research points out that learning requires knowledge, which comes in many forms. Some knowledge is limited and other knowledge is generative. Limited knowledge does not lead anywhere, it is simply accumulated, stored, and recalled. Generative knowledge, however, leads to more learning, new learning, more expansive learning, and the transfer of learning. Generative knowledge is used to create new knowledge. It is knowledge that can be used to understand new situations, to solve unfamiliar problems, to think and reason, and to continue to learn. Constructivist cognitive research reveals that before knowledge becomes generative in the minds of students, they must elaborate and question what they learn, be able to examine new information in relationship to other information, and build new structures of knowledge.

A further distinction is made between "declarative knowledge" and "procedural knowledge." Declarative knowledge refers to subject-matter content and procedural knowledge refers to processes such as how to think, and how we solve problems, and how we synthesize. Knowing what a virus is, how democracy works, what Federalist Paper No. 10 is about, what the Civil Rights Act includes, and who wrote *The Great Gatsby* are examples of declarative knowledge. Using coordinates to fix a position on a map, finding words in a dictionary, proofreading an essay, synthesizing existing information into new wholes, differentiating fact from fiction, and using a problem-solving strategy are examples of procedural knowledge.

Whether declarative knowledge turns out to be limited or generative depends on how content and thinking skills are taught. Are they taught separately or at the same time? Joining the two is needed to create a curriculum that emphasizes thinking. Subject matter becomes the primary site for developing problem solving and reasoning. As Resnick and Klopfer (1989) explain,

"In this vision of the Thinking Curriculum, thinking suffuses the curriculum. It is everywhere. Thinking skills and subject-matter content are joined early in education and pervade instruction. There is no choice to be made between a content emphasis and a thinking-skills emphasis. No depth in either is possible without the other. (6)

Teaching for Understanding

In the new research, the emphasis is on teaching subject matter for understanding and on generative use of knowledge. In order for knowledge to be understood and used, students must be involved in its active construction. This means not just telling and explaining, but providing students with opportunities to answer questions, to discuss and debate meanings and implications, and to engage in authentic problem solving in real contexts. According to Brophy (1992):

> *Early in the process, the teacher assumes most of the responsibility for structuring and managing learning activities and provides students with a great deal of information, explanation, modelling and cuing. As students develop expertise, however, they can begin regulating their own learning by asking questions and by working on increasingly complex applications with increasing degrees of autonomy. The teacher still provides task simplification, coaching, and other "scaffolding" needed to assist students with challenges that they are not ready to handle on their own. Gradually, this assistance is reduced in response to gradual increases in student readiness to engage in self-regulated learning. (6)*

Relying on the research of Anderson (1989) and Prawat (1989), as well as his own work, Brophy (1992) identifies the following principles of good subject-matter teaching:

1. *The curriculum is designed to equip students with knowledge, skills, values, and dispositions useful both inside and outside of school.*
2. *Instructional goals underscore developing student expertise within an application context and with emphasis on conceptual understanding and self-regulated use of skills.*
3. *The curriculum balances breadth with depth by addressing limited content but developing this content sufficiently to foster understanding.*
4. *The content is organized around a limited set of powerful ideas (key understandings and principles).*
5. *The teacher's role is not just to present information but also to scaffold and respond to students' learning.*
6. *The students' role is not just to absorb or copy but to actively make sense and construct meaning.*
7. *Activities and assignments feature authentic tasks that call for problem solving or critical thinking, not just memory or reproduction.*
8. *Higher-order thinking skills are not taught as a separate skills curriculum. Instead, they are developed in the process of teaching subject-matter knowl-*

> edge within application contexts that call for students to relate what they are
> learning to their lives outside of school by thinking critically or creatively
> about it or by using it to solve problems or make decisions.
> 9. *The teacher creates a social environment in the classroom that could be de-
> scribed as a learning community where dialogue promotes understanding. (6)*

The Classroom as Learning Community

Two characteristics of Brophy's principles stand out. One is the importance of helping the classroom become a social community and the other is the power of learning through engagement in real work. Much of the earlier literature on effective teaching makes the assumption that teaching and learning is a rather solo affair and focuses primarily on the individual learner. Constructivist cognitive psychology points out the importance of social relationships and the need for classrooms to become learning communities and communities of inquiry. Much of the new research, for example, points to the value of cooperative living and learning within the classroom as a learning community.

In a learning community, knowledge exists as something that is both individually owned and community owned at the same time. The two feed off each other. A particular student's own individual growth and accumulated knowledge contributes to the shared growth and accumulated knowledge that exists in a classroom as a whole. As this accumulated knowledge expands, so does individual knowledge. This view of shared knowledge is based on several assumptions.

> *First, learning is an active process of knowledge construction and sense-making
> by the student. Second, knowledge is a cultural artifact of human beings: we
> produce it, share it, and transform it as individuals and as groups. Third,
> knowledge is distributed among members of a group, and this distributed knowl-
> edge is greater than the knowledge possessed by any single member. (Leinhardt,
> 1992:23)*

Authentic Learning

Perhaps the most basic lessons that the constructivist cognitive research teaches are the importance of relating new learning to prior knowledge and the importance of immersing teaching in the world of real or "authentic" learning. Generative learning—learning that is understood and can be used to create new learning—doesn't just take place in a vacuum. It is always contextual. What is learned depends on one's prior knowledge; learning takes place best when bridges or scaffolds are developed that link the new with the old.

Sometimes prior knowledge interferes with learning or encourages one to learn the wrong thing. Students, for example, often bring misconceptions or naive theories and notions to their studies. Linking new ideas to prior knowledge that is wrong may result in the further accumulation of faulty learning. This problem highlights the importance of personalized learning, intimate settings for learning, and acknowledging the social nature of learning. Teachers have to get "up close" to understand where kids are coming from. This doesn't happen when the old tell-teach-practice-reteach practices are used.

The importance of authentic learning and the provision of "cognitive apprenticeships" to promote it cannot be underestimated. Students learn best by doing, and doing is best when it is lifelike—when it involves engagement with real or near real problem solving. Effective learning settings allow for learners to use shared knowledge to solve problems, allow students to practice their skills in real life settings, and allow for the integration of abstract and practical learning activities. These are the conditions that increase the likelihood that teaching will be for understanding and that students will indeed be learning.

An Integrated View

Taking the new research on teaching and learning seriously means making some changes in the way we have thought about organizing the classroom, planning for teaching, and arranging the curriculum. The key will be changing from a coverage mentality to a mastery mentality. As Gardner explains,

> *The greatest enemy of understanding is coverage. As long as you are determined to cover everything, you actually ensure that most kids are not going to understand. You've got to take enough time to get kids deeply involved in something so they can think about it in lots of different ways and apply it—not just at school but at home and on the street and so on. (Brandt, 1993:7)*

Furthermore, we will have to rely far less on textbooks that provide the broad stroke and more on other materials that provide in-depth coverage of fewer topics. The curriculum will have to be revisited and serious inquiries made to identify essential and nonessential material, the fundamental structures of the disciplines that are generative by their very nature, and the aspects of the curriculum that comprise more limited or dead-end knowledge. Learning will have to emphasize solving problems. The curriculum will need to be more emergent as teachers and students, representing a community of learners, make decisions about what to do and when and how as they are involved in the process of thinking and learning.

Robert Marzano (1992:154–155) offers a "dimensions of learning" framework that is comprised of five sets of questions he believes teachers need to answer as they plan for teaching and learning. Exhibit 10–2 lists the dimensions and questions.

Answers to the questions in dimension 1 lay the groundwork for developing the kind of social relationships that provide students with shared meaning, shared funds of knowledge, and a shared basis for creating new knowledge. The remaining dimensions focus on teaching strategies and skills and decisions about knowledge.

Marzano (1992) recommends two broad strategies for teaching: presentation strategies and workshop strategies. Presentation strategies help students acquire and integrate new knowledge whether it be declarative or procedural, and thus help with the second dimension of learning. They also help extend and refine knowledge that helps with the third dimension of learning.

EXHIBIT 10–2   Dimensions of Learning

Dimension 1

1. What will be done to help students develop positive attitudes and perceptions about the learning climate?
   a. What will be done to help students feel accepted by the teacher and their peers?
   b. What will be done to help students perceive the classroom as a comfortable and orderly place?
2. What will be done to help students develop positive attitudes and perceptions about classroom tasks?
   a. What will be done to help students perceive classroom tasks as valuable?
   b. What will be done to help students believe they can perform classroom tasks?
   c. What will be done to help students understand and be clear about classroom tasks?

Dimension 2

Declarative Knowledge:

1. What are the general topics?
2. What are the specifics?
3. How will students experience the information?
4. How will students be aided in constructing meaning?
5. How will students be aided in organizing the information?
6. How will students be aided in storing the information?

Procedural knowledge:

1. What skills and processes do students really need to master?
2. How will students be aided in constructing models?
3. How will students be aided in shaping the skill or process?
4. How will students be aided in internalizing the skill or process?

Dimension 3

1. What information will be extended and refined?
2. What activities will be used to help students extend and refine knowledge?

Dimension 4

1. What are the big issues?
2. How many issues will be considered?
3. Who will structure the tasks?
4. What types of products will students create?
5. To what extent will students work in cooperative groups?

Dimension 5

1. Which mental habits will be emphasized?
2. Which mental habits will be introduced?
3. How will the mental habits be reinforced?

Presentation strategies incorporate many of the features of the original teaching effectiveness research. Examples are the importance of stimulating interest in the topic to be learned, relating the new information to existing information, providing clear goals and directions to students, modeling important activities, and providing closure. Yet, instead of viewing these functions in a linear stepwise fashion with one following the other, and instead of insisting that each of the functions be a part of every presentation type of teaching, the five are understood differently. Marzano points out that not all need to be part of every presentation nor do they need to be performed in any set order. The five functions might be depicted then, not as a linear list, but as follows:

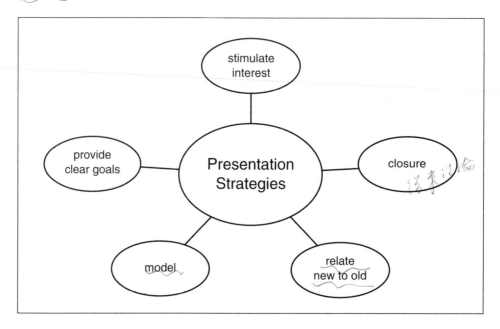

Students and teachers, for example, might begin a new unit with the end, with modeling what is to be learned, or with an activity that stimulates interest, and then move to one or another of the functions in any way that makes sense.

Marzano recommends workshop strategies for the questions included in dimension 4 of his learning framework. The metaphor of workshop suggests teaching is more student directed and activity oriented. A "workshop lesson" would generally begin with a mini lesson designed to provide guidance and give assistance to students as they begin to work on projects. Mini lessons provide students with essential information, resources, and so forth. The major block of teaching would be the *activity.* Here, students work individually, in pairs, or in small groups on projects. Finally, there would be a *sharing period* that allows students to discuss a variety of topics and issues. "The hallmark of a sharing period is that the students and teacher freely discuss their learning as students work on their projects" (Marzano, 1992:162).

Manager and Executive Roles of Teaching

One way to understand different theories of teaching is to examine various roles that teachers assume. What are the roles that teachers must assume, for example, when teaching for understanding and when their classrooms function as learning communities? How do these roles differ from those that are assumed when teachers function in accordance with the prescriptions of the earlier effective teaching research? Four roles are described in Table 10–1. They are manager, executive, mediator, and leader.

When teachers function as managers, they execute fairly specific teaching steps according to well-defined and structured protocols. When this role dominates, teaching begins to resemble a pipeline, with the role of the teacher to manage the flow of information through this line. Objectives are defined specifically for the student, students are motivated by extrinsic means, and both students and teachers are subordinate to a structured teaching system. Furthermore, two different teachers are likely to teach in the same way. The managerial role can be effective for teaching basic skills and simple subject-matter content, but it is inadequate for teaching higher-order thinking skills, teaching for understanding, and encouraging the mastery of generative knowledge.

When assuming the role of executive, the teacher uses the research on teaching and principles of learning to make proper decisions in light of the situations, but within a fairly set framework for teaching. There is, for example, an executive plan for teaching, and effective teaching parallels this plan. The teacher makes important decisions about subject-matter content, grouping for and pacing of instruction, student assignments, and other teaching and learning considerations. Objectives are defined for the student by the teacher, and motivation is typically extrinsic. Students are not partners in the teaching, but objects of the teaching. Teachers are active decision makers who are very much in control providing that they follow the established teaching protocols and the approved executive plan. The executive role is workable for teaching straightforward kinds of subject-matter content and can be suitable as well for teaching basic skills, however, this role does not provide a powerful enough conception of what teaching is and how it works to encourage teaching for understanding, to build community, and to develop learning based on generative knowledge.

Mediator and Leader Roles of Teaching

The remaining two roles, mediator and leader, are more consistent with the principles of teaching and learning implied by the constructivist cognitive research. They are associated with higher-level learning and with the development in students of attitudes and commitments to learning as something that is worthwhile. Decision making is more collaborative as students assume increasing responsibility for making learning decisions and for doing the actual work of learning.

As mediator, the teacher uses reciprocal teaching strategies that enable students to process new information and new learning in light of their own personal meanings, experiences, and prior learnings. The idea is not to define what the nature or the value of a particular learning experience is, but to have the student search for this value. The emphasis is on helping students make sense of learning encounters by constructing new meanings, by linking new to prior learnings, and by helping students interact with information and ideas. At times, teachers decide the actual learning outcomes, but a balance is sought between teacher-determined and student-determined outcomes. The

TABLE 10–1 Roles of Teaching

Roles	Description	Characteristics	Strengths
Teacher as manager	The Teacher executes explicit teaching steps according to highly structured protocols associated with direct instruction. The teacher manages student behavior accordingly.	Teaching is conceived as a pipeline. The role of the teacher is to manage the flow of information through the line. Objectives are defined for the student. Motivation is typically extrinsic. Both teacher and students are subordinate to the structured teaching protocols. Reliability in teaching, therefore, is very high.	Very effective for teaching basic skills and effective for teaching simple subject-matter content.
Teacher as executive	The teacher uses research on effective teaching and psychological principles of learning to make proper teaching decisions in light of situations faced but within a set framework which provides decision-making rules. Within this framework, for example, the teacher makes important decisions about subject-matter content, grouping for and pacing of instruction, student assignments, and other instructional features. Decisions are typically made beforehand in the form of an executive plan for teaching. Effective teaching results when this plan is followed.	Teaching is conceived as executive decision making which requires that situations be diagnosed and that established teaching principles be applied correctly. Objectives are typically defined for the student. Motivation is typically extrinsic. Students are subordinate to the system (that is, they are viewed as objects of teaching rather than partners to the teaching). Teachers are active decision makers and are in control, provided that they follow the established teaching protocols.	Very effective for teaching simple subject-matter content and effective for teaching basic skills.
Teacher as mediator	The teacher uses reciprocal and interactive teaching strategies which enable students to process new information and new learnings in light of their own personal meanings and experiences and prior learnings. Emphasis is on helping students make sense of learning encounters by constructing new understandings and by linking new to prior learnings.	Teaching is conceived as a mediating process within which students, with the help of teachers, interact with information and ideas in terms of personal meanings and previous learnings. Though at times teachers decide the actual learning outcomes of teaching, a balance is sought between teacher-determined and student-determined outcomes. The intent is to move away from students as absorbers of information to students as processors, synthesizers, creators, and users of information; from students being dependent upon the learning system provided to students using the learning system provided. Motivation is frequently intrinsic.	Very effective for teaching analysis, problem-solving, and higher-order skills; complex concepts, higher levels of comprehension, and having students extend what is learned for application to new situations.

TABLE 10–1 *(Continued)*

Roles	Description	Characteristics	Strengths
Teacher as leader	The teacher models the importance of subject matter and learning intents by the manner and enthusiasm with which teaching is provided. Modeling dimensions include time (teaching reflects a great deal of effort), feeling (the teacher cares deeply about the content, learning outcomes, and students), and focus (teaching reflects a deep understanding of the subject taught: the whys as well as the whats, the structure of knowledge; and a focus on key issues and dimensions of importance.	Teaching is conceived as a sacred activity which reflects a reverence for the importance of knowledge and of learning as ends in themselves. Through modeling students find teaching and learning to be meaningful and significant and respond with higher levels of motivation and commitment.	Very effective for communicating the importance, meaning, and significance of subject matter and learning intents; for promoting learning attitudes and values in students.

From Thomas J. Sergiovanni and Robert J. Starratt. 1993. *Supervision: A Redefinition* 5th Ed., pp. 124–125. New York: McGraw-Hill. Reprinted by permission of McGraw-Hill.

curriculum is emergent as decisions about what is worth learning are made as teaching and learning progresses. The purpose of this kind of teaching is to move students away from being absorbers of information to being processors, synthesizers, creators, and users of information; from being dependent on the learning system provided to using the learning system. Motivation is frequently intrinsic. The mediator role is very effective for teaching for understanding, for encouraging community building, and for helping students accumulate generative knowledge.

In many respects the role of teacher as leader is the most important of the four. Its purpose is to instill in students a love for, commitment to, and appreciation of learning that carries them not only through their school years, but throughout their lives. Here the teacher models the importance of subject matter and learning intents by the manner and enthusiasm with which teaching is provided. When this role is successfully implemented, teaching and learning are conceived as sacred activities that reflect a reverence for knowledge as an end in itself.

On the surface it appears that teachers are active when assuming the managerial and executive roles, and passive when assuming mediator and leader roles, however, when we look deeper, we find that just the opposite is true. Mediator and leader roles require careful and skilled planning, diligent arrangement of the learning environment, close personal relationships with students, and intimate knowledge of the work that they do. Together these requirements provide a more active and deeper involvement in teaching and learning than is the case when managerial and executive roles are assumed. These roles, by contrast, involve a lot of "show biz" that in reality requires only superficial involvement in students' learning and lives.

Getting Started

When teachers become acquainted with the new constructivist cognitive research on teaching, they admit that it makes sense, but wonder how one gets started. As suggested by the mediating and leadership roles, a great deal of attention needs to be given to arranging the learning environment and organizing the classroom in a way that is more compatible with teaching for understanding, building a learning community, and accumulating generative knowledge. Indeed, how one organizes the classroom may be a critical lever. In the appendices of this chapter, some suggestions for getting started are provided. Appendix 10–1, "Suggestions For Organizing," provides a number of ideas that can be used by teachers either one at a time or in combination. Appendix 10–2, "Planning and Organizing in a Learning Community," provides an example of how one teacher of a combined grades 4 and 5 classroom organizes for learning in a manner consistent with the new research on teaching.

References

Anderson, L. 1989. "Implementing Instructional Programs to Promote Meaningful, Self-Regulated Learning," in J. Brophy, Ed., *Advances In Research on Teaching, Vol. 1,* pp. 311–343. Greenwich, CN: JAI.

Brandt, Ron. 1993. "On Teaching for Understanding: A Conversation With Howard Gardner," *Educational Leadership* 50(7), 4–7.

Brophy, Gere. 1992. "Probing the Subtleties of Subject-Matter Teaching," *Educational Leadership* 49(7), 4–8.

Educational Leadership 49(2), April, 1992.

Educational Leadership 50(7), April, 1993.

Leinhardt, Gaea. 1992. "What Research on Learning Tells Us About Teaching," *Educational Leadership* 49(7), 20–25.

Marzano, Robert J. 1992. *A Different Kind of Classroom: Teaching with Dimensions of Learning.* Alexandria, VA: Association for Supervision and Curriculum Development.

Nolan, James, and Pam Francis. 1992. "Changing Perspectives in Curriculum and Instruction," in Carl Glickman, Ed., *Supervision in Transition,* Yearbook of the Association for Supervision and Curriculum Development, 44–59. Alexandria, VA: Association for Supervision and Curriculum Development.

Prawat, R. 1989. "Promoting Access to Knowledge, Strategy, and Disposition in Students: A Research Synthesis," *Review of Educational Research* 59, 1–41.

Resnick, Lauren B., and Leopold E. Klopfer. 1989. *Toward the Thinking Curriculum: Current Cognitive Research,* Yearbook of the Association for Supervision and Curriculum Development. Alexandria, VA: Association for Supervision and Curriculum Development.

Schlock, M.D. 1987. "Teacher Productivity: What Is It? How Might It Be Measured? Can It Be Warranted?" *Journal of Teacher Education (37)5,* 59–62.

Schlock, Mark D., Bill Cowart, and Bonnie Staebler. 1993. "Teacher Productivity Revisited: Definition, Theory, Measurement, and Application," *Journal of Personnel Evaluation in Education (7)2,* 179–196.

Tyson, Harriet. March 1990. "Reforming Science Education/Restructuring the Public Schools: Roles for the Scientific Community," 22, 24. Prepared as a background paper for the New York Academy of Sciences and the Institute for Educational Leadership Forum on Restructuring K–12 Education. New York: Academy of Sciences.

Appendix 10–1 Suggestions for Organizing

Classroom Organization Patterns

Assuming that a teacher is starting with a fairly traditional approach to school subjects and teacher-initiated activities, there are a number of organizational arrangements for the classroom that can be employed, either singly or in combination.

1. Learning centers can be organized in which single knowledge areas are represented by various kinds of materials and problems to solve or activities to carry out. These can be tailored to individual students or to levels in the developmental sequence and should be varied enough to accommodate a range of learning styles and individual interests on the part of the children.
2. Individual and small group contracts between students and the teacher can be established, outlining objectives to be pursued and work to be completed over given periods of time in one or more knowledge areas. Contracts work best when they are worked out cooperatively between students and teachers.
3. Individual, small group, or whole class projects can be organized within single knowledge areas or on problems that cut across several areas. These projects can be set up in learning centers or they can involve a wider range of activities and locations including those outside the school and classroom. The duration of such projects can be anywhere from one or two days to more than a month.
4. Individual, small group, or whole class projects can be developed involving the concurrent study of selected topics or themes from the points of view of a number of disciplines.
5. One or two time periods during each day can be set aside for students to work in a manner different from the traditional way. This can be in single subject areas or a kind of "free activity" period for work on electives such as art, music, movement, and crafts as well as in regular areas such as history, mathematics, and language.
6. The teacher can select one subject or knowledge area to be approached from a direction utilizing teacher-pupil planning, contracts, and projects focused on problems or themes. Sometimes an area that is not a regular part of the standard curriculum makes a good place to start—for example, movement, art, group dynamics, self-knowledge, or music.

There are several keys to reorganizing classroom work. Among them are *cooperative planning* among teachers and students in light of mutually understood aims and objectives; careful *record keeping* by teachers and students of aims, actual activities carried out and materials used, and evaluation results; and allowance for as much *individual initiative* on the part of teachers and students in determining the time, place, and manner of their learning as they can currently handle.

The learning center can be viewed as an intermediate step on the road to the organization of more free-wheeling and flexible activities and experiences. As an alternative to textbooks and workbooks, a learning center can offer students a specific place to

Appendix 10–1   *(Continued)*

go within the classroom and specific directions for daily work without the usual restrictions. Each center can offer the teacher a way of evolving individualized activities for students which are valid developmentally and in relation to the ways of knowing of relevant disciplines on a day-to-day or weekly basis without having to produce a whole year's program in advance. Student work contracts are a variation on the learning center idea, since they can detail places to go and resources to tap, thus giving the student the task of assembling materials and ideas he needs, instead of having the teacher collect all the required items for him. Students can help create learning centers and materials for other students to use.

Student initiative and autonomy, as important as they are, cannot be created by teacher fiat; students will need to learn how to take responsibility for promoting their own development. With a good deal of prior structuring, children with little experience can start off by handling small tasks with short time spans and gradually take over more and more responsibility on their own. A teacher might, for example, group her students into three types: "people-to-people" students who have to be under direct adult supervision most of the time; "learning station" students whose days are organized largely around learning station activities; and "autonomous" students who are on their own during those parts of the day when students are carrying out individual and small group activities, but who meet regularly with the teacher to plan and to discuss their work. People-to-people students would be aware that they could move up to working in centers on their own and, ultimately, to independent functioning as they acquire the necessary competence and are able to accept the necessary responsibility.

Appendix 10–2 *Planning and Organizing in a Learning Community*

In this appendix Joan Primeaux describes how she organizes her classroom for learning and strives to build a learning community. Primeaux teaches a multi-age class of fourth and fifth graders in the Olive-Mary Stitt School in Arlington Heights, Illinois.

Grouping

When I think of my mixed-age class, I think of the advantage I have over the single-age class I used to teach. My mixed-age class consists of children who are different ages, have different interests, and different levels of abilities (developmentally, emotionally, and academically). Although these levels exist in all classrooms, the range is broader in a mixed-age class. I take advantage of this composite by using my own version of cooperative groups.

Our class is a democratic class made up of 28 fourth and fifth graders arranged in seven cooperative groups which are labeled for management purposes with the seven continents. These groups are heterogeneously mixed. Fourth and fifth graders, boys and girls, developmental, emotional, and academic levels are evenly distributed. These cooperative groups stay together and work from one activity to another throughout the day. Seats are changed each month, giving everyone a chance to eventually work together.

The only subject are for which I group differently is instructional reading, also called literature discussion groups. These groups consist of award-winning novels and reader response journals. I begin these groups by describing four choices. I read the reviews, show the print, talk about the awards they've won, and read a sample, which leads to a brief discussion of the author's style. Following this presentation, the novels are displayed for one week while the children "shop" around. The children decide which novel interests them most, and they self-select. Discussion groups, led by me, are based on written and verbal reader response. These groups last for about three weeks and continue to change throughout the year.

I also group flexibly when needed. For example, if a group or an individual needs practice with handwriting or multiplication facts, I often form a group consisting of children who have mastered the skill with children who haven't. The children are never separated into grade level groups. Because of this, it's possible for a fifth grader to be working on fourth grade work and fourth graders to be working on fifth grade work at any given time. Since the activities are planned to be open-ended, the children often work beyond their grade level.

Planning

All subject areas are planned around a theme, usually taken from a content area. Integrating all subject areas around a content area theme is an efficient way to teach. It's also a motivational way to provide for the application of skills and concepts. Letter writing skills may be learned by writing to a wildlife organization instead of practicing the skills in isolation. While planning, I use our district curriculum guide as a resource to make sure that I at least include grade level skills and concepts. Since I keep this class for two years, I know these children well, I can tailor the activities to areas of interest and leave the activities open-ended to either remediate or enrich. Since I don't use a teacher's guide, evaluation is also up to me. I can either accept a child where he is or challenge him. The activities are generally hands-on, research-based, and process oriented. Process oriented activities, such as creative writing, requires and unlimited amount of time. A finished product is not required by the end of work time.

Typical Day—Plan Your Own Day
Unit Topic: Japan
A typical day in our class would be . . .

8:50–9:15	Daily oral language and mini- math/attendance, pledge, etc.
9:15–9:45	Magic Circle (class meeting)—review of day's activities, sharing, discussing, compliment a classmate, etc.
9:45–10:15	30 min. worth of activities
10:20–10:40	Recess
10:45–11:15	30 min. worth of activities
11:15–12:00	Literature discussion groups
12:00–1:00	Lunch
1:00–1:20	Silent reading
1:20–2:20	60 min. worth of activities
2:20–2:40	Recess
2:40–3:10	30 min. worth of activities
3:10–3:30	Read aloud, *The Big Wave,* by Pearl S. Buck
3:30	Dismissal

After Magic Circle, each cooperative group plans its own day. From the activities list on the board, the children arrange their activities and fit them into the blocks of time scheduled for the day. A typical activities list would be

Activities:	Time it Should Take
Science—Japan's Land—Erupt a volcano and record Predict/Observe/Conclude	40 minutes
Math—Convert and compare yen to cents	40 minutes
Creative Writing—fly to Japan List/rough draft/edit/conference/final copy/Author's Chair	55 minutes

Appendix 10–2 *(Continued)*

Graphic Organizer—Japan's land Earthquakes and volcanoes	55 minutes
Computer—Division or Multiplication practice	20 minutes

Choices for 5 or 10 min. activities—origami, Japanese words, classroom charts.

Computer Schedule

9:45–10:05	Africa
10:05–10:20	Asia
then	
10:40–10:50	Asia
10:50–11:10	Europe
1:20–1:40	Antarctica
1:40–2:00	Australia
2:00–2:20	North America
2:40–3:00	South America

Using the scheduling information above, the group Africa may arrange their day like this:

Name of Group: Africa
Plan Your Own Day!

Activities	Time to Begin	Time to Stop
Computer	9:45	10:05
Graphic Organizer	10:05	11:00
Math	11:00	11:15
then	1:20	1:50
Creative Writing	1:50	2:20
Science	2:40	3:20

Our literature discussion groups' time is set and is never interrupted. I arrange computer times which vary each day. Our schedule allows for two children to work at our two classroom computers for at least 20 minutes each day.

The children begin working once they've arranged their schedule. During work time, I monitor, redirect, question, and assess as I move from group to group. I encourage discussion and require participation. Cooperative groups serve two purposes in our room. Sometimes the group members only support each other as they work individually, such as in creative writing. And sometimes members rely on each other as needed, such as when conducting a science experiment.

Evaluation

Once an activity time is up, or when the activity is complete, all members of the group raise their hands to signal me to check their work. I check for accuracy or completion or

Appendix 10–2   (Continued)

both. All group members must receive a red checkmark before moving on to the next activity. This system requires the children to budget their time and stay on task. It provides me with immediate feedback for the children and me. The children know their work is acceptable or know they need to go back and make corrections.

As I assess, I think about remediation or extensions I can make for that moment and for the next day. Working one day at a time allows me to focus on individual needs. At the end of the unit, the children are sometimes tested. More often, they create a project or develop a museum which they share with parents and invited guests.

Part IV

The Development of
Human Resources

Teacher Development and Supervision

How should principals help teachers learn more about themselves and their work? What should principals do to help teachers improve their teaching practice? Answers to these questions depend on the views that principals have about good teaching, how learning environments should be developed, what curriculum decisions make sense, and how the school should be organized for effective learning. If a principal's view corresponds to the process-product effective teaching research discussed in Chapter 10, one answer would make most sense. If, however, a principal's view corresponds to the newer cognitive research on teaching, then a different set of decisions would make sense. There is a link between how principals want teachers to teach and how to help them learn to teach in that way.

Below are some of the principles of teaching that emerged from the earlier research on teaching:

Learning is the mastery of culturally defined meanings.

Meanings are mastered in small, isolated pieces. Complex ideas are "task analyzed" and broken down into manageable parts.

Meaning is an individual thing.

Motivation to learn is largely external, what is rewarded is learned.

Learners differ in the time needed to learn, but typically respond to learning in the same way.

Verbal and mathematical learning should get nearly exclusive attention because they match definitions of intelligence that are embedded in the school's current curriculum and they count the most in present assessment schemes.

Useful knowledge and skill is best learned by direct teaching.

Learning is facilitated by mastering the basic skills and by recalling desired concepts and content.

These principles emphasize uniformity, consumption, memorization, and replication. The best way to get teachers to follow these principles is to use them in training. Principals should carefully develop (or purchase carefully developed) training programs for teachers. Teachers should then be given practice in using the training they receive. As follow-up, principals will need to provide supervision to be sure that the training is practiced. Reteach, remove, or reward are the consequences of this supervision.

Now let's examine some of the principles of teaching and learning that are based on the constructivist research:

Learning is a process of making sense with the construction of personal meanings.

Meanings are constructed by comparing existing understandings and developing connections among ideas, concepts, and blocks of information.

Meanings are norm-referenced and thus are constructed in social contexts and are influenced by the views of others.

Motivation to learn is in part related to an individual's goals and aspirations, and in part influenced by an individual's connections to others and the resulting group norms that emerge.

Learners differ in the time needed to learn the same thing and in the cognitive processes needed to learn.

Learners differ in the kind of aptitudes and intelligences they bring to learning and are predisposed to learn when strengths are emphasized.

Knowledge and skills are best learned in situations and under circumstances that resemble how they will actually be used.

Learning is facilitated by emphasizing the mastery of generative knowledge, which helps learners to acquire new knowledge on their own.

In this image of teaching and learning, students are not consumers of knowledge but constructors, and the personal meanings they bring to learning are critical determinates of what will be learned and how well it will be learned. Helping teachers to learn to teach or to improve their teaching along these lines requires a shift in our understanding of teacher development. This view of teaching cannot be mastered by emphasizing consumption, memorization, and replication. Training just won't do. Instead, principals will need to *emphasize* professional development and renewal improvement strategies. Training, professional development, and renewal strategies are described and contrasted in Table 11–1.

The term *emphasize* is key. All three strategies have important roles to play, but not all three strategies are equal. If we value teaching for understanding, the development of thinking, and the mastery of generative knowledge, then we will need to give less attention to training models and more attention to professional development and renewal models.

TABLE 11–1 Models of Teacher Development

	Training	Professional	Renewal
Assumptions	Knowledge stands above the teacher.	The teacher stands above knowledge.	Knowledge is in the teacher.
	Knowledge is, therefore, instrumental. It tells the teacher what to do.	Knowledge is, therefore, conceptual. It informs the teacher's decisions.	Knowledge is, therefore, personal. It connects teachers to themselves and others.
	Teaching is a job and teachers are technicians.	Teaching is a profession and teachers are experts.	Teaching is a calling and teachers are servants.
	Mastery of skills is important.	Development of expertise is important.	Development of personal and professional self is important.
Roles	Teacher is consumer of knowledge.	Teacher is constructor of knowledge.	Teacher is internalizer of knowledge.
	Principal is expert.	Principal is colleague.	Principal is friend.
Practices	Emphasize technical competence.	Emphasize clinical competence.	Emphasize personal and critical competencies.
	Build individual teacher's skills.	Build professional community.	Build caring community.
	Through training and practice.	Through problem solving and inquiry.	Through reflection and reevaluation.
	By planning and delivering training.	By emphasizing inquiry, problem solving, and action research.	By encouraging reflection, conversation, and discourse.

Training Models

Training models of teacher development have important roles to play. They resemble traditional in-service programs that are well known to teachers and principals and need little elaboration. They are best suited when a problem can be defined as a deficit in knowledge of some kind, for example, teachers don't know about something or need to improve their skills in some area. Outside or inside experts do the training. Training is linked to clear objectives and relies on conventional well-executed instruction. Teachers, for example, might be introduced to various ways in which interest centers can be set up, methods for evaluating student portfolios, new techniques for using simulation for teaching world history, tips on how to monitor student progress, or some basic teaching skills that help keep students "on task." Teachers generally assume passive roles. Techniques most often used are oral presentations, illustrated presentations, demonstrations, and observations of good practice. Effective training programs provide opportunities for teachers to practice what it is that they learn. They receive coaching as they actually begin to use what they learned in their classrooms.

Professional Development Models

Although training has its place, most observers believe that it should no longer be the primary model for teacher development. Implementing lists of do's and don'ts, standard skill repertoires, and other scripts is not the way to help teachers to teach for understanding, to develop student thinking, and to promote generative knowledge. Instead, teachers need to learn how to think on their feet, inventing their practice as they go.

The relationship between teachers and the knowledge base for teaching is understood differently in professional development than in training. Professional development assumes that teachers are superordinate to the research on teaching. Unlike technicians who are trained to apply research findings, professionals view research as knowledge that informs the decisions that they make. Professionals create their practice in use.

Professional development approaches emphasize providing teachers with a rich environment loaded with teaching materials, media, books, and devices. With encouragement and support, teachers interact with this environment and with each other through exploration and discovery. Thelan (1971) suggests that the most useful teacher development programs are characterized by "intensity of personal involvement, immediate consequences for classroom practice, stimulation and ego support by meaningful associates in the situation, and initiating by teacher rather than outside" (72–73). Judith Warren Little (1993), a thoughtful commentator on teacher development, proposes six principles that she believes should guide the design of professional development experiences for teachers.

1. *Professional development offers meaningful intellectual, social and emotional engagement with ideas, with materials, and with colleagues both in and out of teaching.*
2. *Professional development takes explicit account of the context of teaching and the experience of teachers. Focused study groups, teacher collaboratives, long-term partnerships, and similar models of professional development afford teachers a means of locating new ideas in relation to their individual and institutional histories, practices, and circumstances.*
3. *Professional development offers support for informed dissent. In the pursuit of good schools, consensus may prove to be an over-stated virtue. . . . dissent places a premium on the evaluation of alternatives and the close scrutiny of underlying assumptions.*
4. *Professional development places classroom practice in the larger context of school practice and the educational careers of children. It is grounded in a big-picture perspective on the purposes and practices of schooling, providing teachers with a means of seeing and acting upon the connections among students' experience, teachers' classroom practice, and school-wide structures and cultures.*
5. *Professional development prepares teachers (as well as students and their parents) to employ the techniques and perspectives of inquiry. . . . it acknowledges that the existing knowledge is relatively slim and that our strength may derive less from teachers' willingness to consume research knowledge*

> *than from their capacity to generate knowledge and to assess the knowledge claimed by others.*
>
> ✓ 6. *The governance of professional development ensures bureaucratic restraint and a balance between the interests of individuals and the interests of institutions. (138–139)*

Little offers the principles as alternatives to training models that when used excessively provide teachers with shallow and fragmented content and subject them to passive roles as they participate in scripted workshops. The principles are anecdotes to the "one-size-fits-all" problem that training too often presents. Furthermore, she argues that the principles challenge the view that teaching is a narrowly defined technical activity. Little believes that today's emphasis on teacher in-service is dominated by "a district-subsidized marketplace of formal programs over which teachers exert little influence or in which they play few leadership roles" (139). In professional development models, the teacher's capacities, needs, and interests are paramount. They are actively involved in contributing data and information, solving problems, analyzing, and so forth. Principals are involved as colleagues. Together, principals and teachers work to develop a common purpose themed to the improvement of teaching and learning. Together, principals and teachers work to build a learning and inquiring community.

Renewal Models

Both training and professional development models share the purpose of helping teachers to improve their practice. Frances Bolin, Judith Falk, and their colleagues (1987) point out that although improvement may be a legitimate goal, it is not powerful enough to tap the potential for teachers to grow personally and professionally. Bolin (1987), for example, writes

> *What would happen if we set aside the question of how to improve the teacher and looked instead at what we can do to encourage the teacher? . . . asking how to encourage the teacher places the work of improvement in the hands of the teacher. It presupposes that the teacher desires to grow, to be self-defining, and to engage in teaching as a vital part of life, rather than as unrelated employment. This leads to looking at teaching as a commitment or calling, a vocation . . . that is not adequately contained in the term* profession *as it has come to be used. (11)*

Bolin believes that when the emphasis shifts from improving teachers to encouraging them, then both training and professional development give way to renewal. In her view, renewal is not driven so much by professional problems as by a teacher's commitment to teaching as a vocation. Renewal implies doing over again, revising, making new, restoring, reestablishing, and revaluing as teachers individually and collectively reflect on not only their practice but themselves and the practice of teaching that they share in the school.

In training, the emphasis is on building each individual's teaching skills by planning and delivering instruction. In development, the emphasis is on building professional community by helping teachers to become inquirers, problem solvers, and researchers of their own practice. In renewal, the emphasis is on building a caring community by encouraging teachers to reflect and to engage in conversation and discourse.

Teacher Development and Types of Teacher Competence

Nancy Zimpher and Kenneth Howey (1987) describe four major types of teaching competence that can help sort out when each of the approaches—training, development, and renewal—might make the most sense. The four types of competence depicted and discussed in Table 11–2 are technical, clinical, personal, and critical. Teaching as an expression of technical competence is probably the most popular of the four. It remains the area that receives the most attention in teacher education programs and in school district and state mandated teacher evaluation instruments. An example of an emphasis on technical competence is focusing on lists of teaching behaviors as found in the earlier process-product teaching effectiveness research. Technical competence is important to successful teaching and learning, but once technical competence is ensured, primary attention should be given to developing the clinical, personal, and critical competencies of teachers.

When addressing clinical competence, the emphasis is on helping teachers become better problem solvers who are able to frame problems and issues and come to grips with solutions. The purpose of teacher development in this case is to enhance inquiry, encourage reflection, build problem-solving skills, and help teachers make more informed decisions about their practice.

When the emphasis is on personal competence, the intent is to help teachers understand and interpret their own teaching in a manner that provides them meaning and significance. Personal competence is enhanced as teachers increase their awareness and understand more fully their teaching practice.

Critical competence is concerned with issues of value and with the hidden meanings underlying teaching practice. Critical competence is developed as teachers are able to differentiate between effective and good practice, take ethical stands, and be concerned with worth and purpose.

Although training can help enhance the teacher's technical competence, it seems not to be powerful enough to enhance the other three types. Clinical competence seems best addressed by professional development models. Professional development can also help build personal competence, with renewal models being most appropriate for enhancing personal and critical competence.

Reflecting on Supervision

Teacher development and supervision go hand in hand. Principals have a responsibility to help teachers improve their practice and to hold them accountable for meeting their commitments to teaching and learning. These responsibilities are usually referred to as supervision. Done well, supervision enhances teacher development.

TABLE 11–2 Zimpher and Howey: Framework for Examining Four Types of Teaching Competence

	Technical Competence	Clinical Competence	Personal Competence	Critical Competence
Conception of the Teacher	Determines in advance what is to be learned, how it is to be learned, and criteria by which success is to be measured	Instructional problem solver; clinician frames and solves practical problems; takes reflective action; inquirer	Understanding of self, self-actualized person who uses self as effective and humane instrument	Rational, morally autonomous, socially conscious change agent
Focus of Supervision	Mastery of methods of instruction: specific skills (how to ask good questions); how to apply teaching strategies; how to select and organize curriculum content; how to structure the classroom for learning what techniques to use to maintain control	Reflective decision making and action to solve practical problems (what should be done about disruptive behavior) as well as reconsideration of intents and practices to take action to solve practical problems	Increase self-awareness, identity formation, and interpretive capacities, e.g., self confrontation; values clarification; interpersonal involvement; small-group processes; develop personal style in teaching role	Reflective decision making and action to form more rational and just schools, critique of stereotypes/ideology, hidden curriculum, authoritarian/permissive relationships, equality of access, responsibilities, and forms of repressive social control
Conception of the Supervisor	Technical expert/master provides for skill development and efficient/effective use of resources in classroom; translator of research theory into technical rules for application in classrooms	Fosters inquiry regarding the relationship of theory and practice; fosters reflection about the relationship of intents and practice and reconsideration/modification of intent/practice in light of evaluation of their conscience	Expert in interpersonal competence and theories of human development; nondirective participant: warm and supportive learning environment, responsiveness to teacher-defined needs and concerns, wisdom in guiding free exploration of teaching episodes, diagnosing theories-in-use	Collaborator in self-reflective communities of practitioner-theorists committed to examining critically their own/institutional practices and improving them in interests of nationality and social justice; provides challenges and support as do other participants in dialogue
Type of Theoretical Knowledge	Technical guidelines from explanatory theory; analytic craft knowledge about what constitutes "good" practice	Synthesis of normative, interpretive, and explanatory knowledge to form intellectually and morally defensible practical judgments about what to do in a particular situation	Analytic and interpretive theory to understand and make explicit reasons underlying symbolic interaction essentially those which occur in the class	Critical theory of education; unite philosophical analysis and criticism and causal and interpretive science

Continued

TABLE 11–2 *(Continued)*

	Technical Competence	Clinical Competence	Personal Competence	Critical Competence
Mode of Inquiry	Applied science, functional and task analysis, linear problem solving to determine how to accomplish given ends	Practical action research to articulate concerns, plan action, monitor action, and reflect on processes and consequences to improve our teaching practices; rationale-building	Phenomenological, ethnographic, hermeneutic analysis and interpretation; analyze elements of teaching episodes	Collaborative action and reflection to transform the organization and practice of education; group inquiry regarding conditions of communicative interaction and social control
Level of Reflectivity	Specific techniques needed to reach stated objectives involve instrumental reasoning; means-end (if, then) relative to efficiency/effectiveness	Practical reasoning and judgment relative to what should be done (best course of action under the circumstances)	Interpretation of intended meaning of verbal and nonverbal symbols and acts; introspection relative to self-awareness/ identity	Critical self-reflection/ reflexivity and social critique to uncover contradictions/inadequacies and different conceptions of educational practice as values with society

The authors wish to acknowledge the major contribution of Sharon Strom in the development of this framework.
From Zimpher, Nancy L. and Kenneth R. Howey. 1987. "Adapting Supervisory Practices to Different Orientations of Teaching," *Journal of Curriculum and Supervision (2) 2,* 104–105.

A first step in building a practical and meaningful supervisory program is willingness by the principal and by teachers to face up to, struggle with, and accept a more complex view of supervision and evaluation. Required next is dealing with the negative stereotypes of supervision emerging from its history of hierarchy, dominance, and control.

From the start it should be clear that no one-best-way strategy, model, or set of procedures for supervision makes sense. Instead, a differentiated system of supervision more in tune with growth levels, personality characteristics, needs and interests, and professional commitments of teachers is needed. Such a system is proposed in the next chapter, "Options for Supervision."

Supervision and Evaluation

When the focus of supervision is on teaching and learning, evaluation is an unavoidable aspect of the process. The literature is filled with reports and scenarios highlighting the disdain with which teachers regard evaluation (see, for example, Blumberg, 1980). One reason for such attitudes is that evaluation has been too narrowly defined in both purpose and method. Evaluation is, and will remain, a part of supervision, and this reality cannot be ignored. Attempts to mask evaluation aspects of supervision by avoiding use of the term, by denying that evaluation occurs, or by declaring that evaluation is reserved only for the annual administrative review of one's teaching performance will not be helpful. Such claims are viewed suspiciously by teachers and for good reason—evaluation cannot be avoided. We are constantly evaluating everything that we experience, and our experiences with teachers and their teaching is no different.

Evaluation can be less of a problem if we expand its meaning within supervision. Evaluation, for example, is often defined narrowly as a process for calculating the extent to which teachers measure up to *preexisting standards*. Standards might be a program goal or teaching intent, or perhaps a list of "desirable" teaching competencies or performance criteria. Broader conceptions of evaluation include describing what is going on in a particular classroom, discovering learning outcomes actually achieved, and assessing their worth. In broader conceptions, the focus of evaluation is less on measuring and more on describing and illuminating teaching and learning events, as well as on identifying the array of meanings that these events have for different people. Evaluation broadly conceived involves *judgment* more than measurement. Judgments of teaching and learning are less fixed, more personal, and are embedded in a particular context or situation (Dewey, 1958). Of interest in judgmental evaluation are *particular* teachers and students; *specific* teaching situations and events, and the *actual* teaching and learning issues, understandings, and meanings emerging from teaching. Although measuring against preexisting standards has its place in the process of supervision and evaluation, the present onerous view of evaluation will be greatly lessened if principals emphasize judgmental aspects.

Using the word *evaluation* in its ordinary, rather than technical, sense will also help dissipate its negative effects among teachers. Commonplace in our ordinary lives, evaluation is an inescapable aspect of most of what we do. Whether we are buying a pair of shoes, selecting a recipe for a dinner party, rearranging the livingroom furniture or enjoying a movie, baseball game, or art show, evaluation is part of the process. In its ordinary sense, evaluation means to discern, understand, and appreciate, on the one hand, and to value, judge, and decide on the other. These very same natural and ordinary processes are at play in evaluating teaching. As in ordinary life, these processes serve to heighten our understanding and appreciation of teaching and to inform our intuition as we make decisions about teaching. Heightened sensitivity and informed intuition are the trademarks of accomplished practice in all the major professions. It is by increasing and informing their sensitivities and intuitions that attorneys, architects, and physicians make better practice decisions and improve their performance. Professional practice in teaching, supervision, and the principalship improve similarly.

Supervision and evaluation of teaching should look for answers to the following questions:

What is actually going on in this classroom?

What is the teacher and what are students actually doing?

What are the actual learning outcomes?

What ought to be going on in this classroom given our overall goals, educational platform, knowledge of how children learn, and understandings of the structure of the subject matter to be taught?

What do these events and activities of teaching and learning mean to teachers, students, and others?

What are the personal meanings that students accumulate regardless of teacher intents?

How do teacher and principal interpretations of teaching reality differ?

What actions should be taken to bring about even greater understanding of teaching and learning and better congruence between our actions and beliefs?

These questions provide a broader and more complex conception of the supervisory process than that implied just in rating teachers or in measuring outcomes for comparison with stated intents. Indeed, for supervision to work the way it should, teachers must share responsibility for its success. This means teachers have to assume roles as supervisors—working with each other to improve their teaching and even to help maintain quality control. Unless teachers accept this responsibility, supervision will remain what it too often is today—principals going into classes with checklists and making quick evaluations that have doubtful validity and little or no meaning to most teachers.

Purposes

The multifaceted nature of teacher supervision and evaluation can be illustrated by providing a framework for describing and bringing together key dimensions of the process. Included in this framework are general purposes of supervision and evaluation, specific perspectives that stem from these purposes, key competency areas that serve as benchmarks for evaluation, and critical knowledge areas that help define and describe teaching competence. This framework is designed to help principals analyze supervisory problems and plan supervisory strategies.

What is supervision for? Who is to be served? Why evaluate? How one answers such questions determines how one approaches the tasks of supervision and evaluation and influences the relationships emerging among teachers and between teachers and the principal. Supervision and evaluation have many purposes. These range from ensuring that minimum standards are being met and that teachers are being faithful to the school's overall purposes and educational platform, to helping teachers grow and develop as persons and professionals.

Purposes can be grouped into three major categories:

1. *Quality control.* The principal is responsible for monitoring teaching and learning in her or his school and does so by visiting classrooms, touring the school, talking with people, and visiting with students.
2. *Professional development.* Helping teachers to grow and to develop in their understanding of teaching and classroom life, in improving basic teaching skills, and in

expanding their knowledge and use of teaching repertoires is the second purpose of supervision.

3. *Teacher motivation.* Often overlooked, but important nonetheless, is a third purpose of supervision—building and nurturing motivation and commitment to teaching, to the school's overall purposes, and to the school's defining educational platform.

One hallmark of a good supervisory system is that it reflects these multiple purposes. No supervisory system based on a single purpose can succeed over time. A system that focuses only on quality control invites difficulties with teachers and lacks needed expansive qualities. By the same token, a supervisory system concerned *solely* with providing support and help to teachers (and thus, by omission, neglects teaching deficiencies and instances where overriding purposes and defining platforms are ignored) is not sufficiently comprehensive. Quality control and teacher improvement are, therefore, basic purposes that should drive any system of supervision and evaluation. A third purpose, often neglected but important in the long run, is that of teacher motivation. Overwhelming evidence exists suggesting that "knowledge of results" is an important ingredient in increasing a person's motivation to work and in building commitment and loyalty to one's job (Hackman and Oldham, 1976; Hackman et al., 1975).

Different Purposes, Different Standards

Different teacher-evaluation purposes require different teacher-evaluation standards and criteria. When the purpose is quality control to ensure that teachers measure up, standards, criteria, expectations, and procedures take one form. When the purpose is professional improvement to help increase teachers' understanding and enhance teaching practice, standards, criteria, expectations, and procedures take on a different form. In evaluation for quality control the process is formal and documented; criteria are explicit and standards are uniform for all teachers; criteria are legally defensible as being central to basic teaching competence; the emphasis is on teachers meeting requirements of minimum acceptability; and responsibility for evaluation is in the hands of administrators and other designated officials. When the purpose of teacher evaluation is professional improvement, the process is informal; criteria are tailored to the needs and capabilities of individual teachers; criteria are considered to be appropriate and useful to teachers before they are included in the evaluation; the emphasis is on helping teachers reach agreed-upon professional development goals; and teachers assume major responsibility for the process by engaging in self-evaluation and collegial evaluation, and by obtaining evaluation information from students.

The outcome of evaluation for quality control is the protection of students and the public from incompetent teaching. Unquestionably this is an important outcome and a highly significant responsibility for principals and other supervisors. The outcome of evaluation for professional improvement is quite different. Rather than ensuring minimum acceptability in teaching, professional improvement guarantees quality teaching and schooling for the students and the public.

The *80/20 quality rule* spells out quite clearly what the balance of emphasis should be as schools engage in teacher evaluation. *When more than 20 percent of the principal's time and money is expended in evaluation for quality control or less than 80 percent of the principal's time and money is spent in professional improvement, quality schooling suffers.* The 80/20 quality rule provides a framework for those responsible for evaluation of teachers to evaluate whether their efforts are indeed directed toward quality schooling. In making this assessment, one should give less attention to the rhetoric that one hears (i.e., to what those responsible for teacher evaluation say their purposes are) and more to the standards and procedures that they use. The standards and procedures associated with each of the two purposes of evaluation are outlined in Exhibit 11–1. If the standards at the left side of the exhibit are emphasized, quality control is the purpose of the evaluation regardless of what is claimed.

Teaching Competency Areas

The typical evaluation program puts the emphasis on the wrong thing. It relies almost exclusively on classroom observations of teaching behaviors and recording the presence

---

EXHIBIT 11–1   Purposes and Standards for Evaluation

Purposes

Quality control (ensuring that teachers meet acceptable levels of performance)	Professional improvement (increasing understanding of teaching and enhancing practice)

Standards

The process is formal and documented.	The process is informal.
Criteria are explicit, standard, and uniform for all teachers.	Criteria are tailored to needs and capabilities of individual teachers.
Criteria are legally defensible as being central to basic teaching competence.	Criteria are considered appropriate and useful to teachers.
Emphasis is on meeting minimum requirements of acceptability.	Emphasis is on helping teachers reach agreed-upon professional development goals.
Evaluation by administrators and other designated officials counts the most.	Self-evaluation, collegial evaluation, and evaluation information for students count the most.

Outcome

Protects students and the public from incompetent teaching.	Guarantees quality teaching and schooling for students and the public.

The 80/20 Quality Rule: When more than 20 percent of supervisory time and money is expended in evaluation for quality control *or* less than 80 percent of supervisory time and money is expended in professional improvement, quality schooling suffers.

From T. J. Sergiovanni and R. J. Starratt (1993). *Supervision: A Redefinition,* 5th ed., p. 222. New York: McGraw-Hill.

or absence of these behaviors on instruments and forms. This results in placing the emphasis on whether the teacher can do the job as required while being observed. Even if it were possible to identify the correct list of teaching behaviors, the approach is still narrow. A good evaluation is not only concerned with "can do," but with other teaching competency areas as well.

What are the major competency areas for which teachers should be accountable? Teachers should *know how* to do their jobs and to keep this knowledge current. The areas of knowledge for professional teaching include purposes, students, subject matter to be taught, and teaching techniques. However, knowing and understanding are not enough; teachers should be able to put this knowledge to work—to demonstrate that they *can do* the job of teaching. Demonstrating knowledge, however, is a fairly low-level competency. Most teachers are competent enough and adept enough to come up with the right teaching performance when they are required to do so. More important is whether they *will do* the job well consistently and on a sustained basis. Finally, all professionals are expected to engage in a lifelong commitment to self-improvement. Self-improvement is the *will-grow* competency area. Self-employed professionals, such as physicians and attorneys, are forced by competition and by more visible performance outputs to give major attention to the will-grow dimension. Teachers are "organizational" professionals whose "products" are difficult to measure and who have not felt as much external pressure for continued professional development. Increasingly, however, school districts are making the will-grow dimension a significant part of their supervision and evaluation program. As teachers strive for further professionalism, they too recognize the importance of this dimension.

A comprehensive system of supervision and evaluation is, therefore, concerned with all four professional development competency areas: knowledge about teaching, ability to demonstrate this knowledge by actual teaching under observation, willingness to sustain this ability continuously, and demonstration of a commitment to continuous professional growth. Although each of the competency areas represents a discrete category that suggests different evaluation strategies, the four remain largely interdependent in practice. When observing classrooms, principals naturally are interested in the knowledge base exhibited by teachers. Most observations, in turn, lead to issues and ideas that form the basis for informing continuing growth plans and more formal staff development programs.

Substantive Aspects of Professional Development

When one speaks of knowledge about teaching, demonstrating this knowledge, and improving one's teaching, what substance areas are of concern? Rubin (1975) has identified four critical areas in good teaching that he believes can he improved through supervision:

- The teacher's sense of purpose
- The teacher's perception of students
- The teacher's knowledge of subject matter
- The teacher's mastery of technique

Sense of purpose and perception of students represent values, beliefs, assumptions, and action theories that teachers hold about the nature of knowledge, how students learn, appropriate relationships between students and teachers, and other factors. Composing the teacher's educational platform, they thus become the basis for decisions made about classroom organization and teaching. For example, a teacher who views teaching as primarily the dissemination of information will likely rely heavily on direct instruction as a teaching methodology and on formally structured classroom arrangements as a method of organizing for teaching. A teacher who views children as being basically trustworthy and interested in learning is likely to share responsibility for decisions about learning, and so forth. A principal who was interested in reducing the amount of teacher talk in a given classroom or in increasing the amount of student responsibility in another would have to contend with the critical considerations of purposes and perceptions as key components of the teachers' educational platforms.

The third factor in good teaching is the teacher's knowledge of subject matter to be taught. Rubin (1975) notes:

> *There is considerable difference between the kind of teaching that goes on when teachers have an intimate acquaintance with the content of the lesson and when the acquaintance is only peripheral. When teachers are genuinely knowledgeable, when they know their subject well enough to discriminate between the seminal ideas and the secondary matter, when they go beyond what is in the textbook, the quality of pedagogy becomes extraordinarily impressive. For it is only when a teacher has a consummate grasp of, say arithmetic, physics, or history, that their meaning can be turned outward and brought to bear upon the learner's personal experience. Relevancy lies less in the inherent nature of a subject than in its relationship to the child's frame of reference. In the hands of a skilled teacher, poetry can be taught with success and profit to ghetto children. (47)*

Although content versus process arguments continue in teaching, both aspects are necessary. The less a teacher knows about a particular subject, the more trivial her or his teaching is likely to be. Content is important. Still, one can have a great appreciation of a particular field of study and not be able to disclose its wonder and excitement effectively. Shulman (1989) believes that teaching what one knows to someone else represents a distinct level of knowledge different from each of the other five levels of Bloom's taxonomy. The substance of this level is the ability to create a bridge between what a teacher knows and the students' experiences. To Shulman, content and pedagogy are inseparable. Mastery of technique, knowing how this technique relates to the subject matter one wants to teach (Stodolsky, 1988), classroom organization and management, and other pedagogical skills make up the fourth critical dimension of effective teaching. A comprehensive system of supervision and evaluation is concerned with all four substance areas: the teacher's conception of purpose, sensitivities to students, intimacy with subject matter, and basic repertoires of teaching techniques.

Figure 11–1 combines professional development competency areas and teaching substance areas to provide an "angle" for appreciating the complexity involved in supervision and evaluation, for analyzing existing supervisory programs, and for planning future strategies. Professional competency areas represent the range that should be in-

Teaching Substance Areas	Professional Development Competency Areas			
	Knows how	Can do	Will do	Will grow
Purpose				
Students				
Subject Matter				
Teaching Techniques				

FIGURE 11–1   Competency and Substance Areas in Supervision and Evaluation

cluded in a comprehensive supervision and evaluation system. Substance areas represent the content concerns to be included.

In summary, supervision and evaluation are concerned with the extent to which teachers demonstrate they know how, can do, will do, and will grow in such teaching knowledge areas as purpose, students, subject matter, and teaching techniques. The following questions provide examples of evaluation concerns raised in Figure 11–1. Within each substance area, *know how, can do, will do,* and *will grow* questions are provided:

1. *Sense of purpose.* To what extent does a teacher know and understand how behavior modification classroom management techniques work, what the philosophical base of this approach is, what the advantages and disadvantages are, and under which circumstances would this approach be more or less effective? Can and will the teacher demonstrate this approach to classroom management when circumstances call for it? Does the teacher know when to avoid this approach? Is there evidence that the teacher is growing in knowledge and skill in using this and other classroom management techniques? Does the teacher, for example, understand and use developmental approaches and morally based approaches to student discipline?

2. *Knowledge of students.* Is the teacher sensitive to, and does the teacher know about, problems of peer identity among students and pressures for conformity that students face at certain ages and grade levels? Does the teacher understand how peer pressure can affect student motivation, classroom attention, voluntary participation in class, and other activities? Does the teacher exhibit knowledge about how to cope with peer pressure? Can and will the teacher demonstrate this knowledge by effective planning and teaching? Does the teacher show a commitment to increasing competence and skill in this area?

✓3. *Knowledge of subject matter.* Does the teacher have a firm grasp of the subject matter in the area she or he is teaching? Is there evidence, for example, that the teacher has an adequate cognitive map of the subject, appreciates the structure of knowledge inherent in the disciplinary base of the subject, and understands the major concepts undergirding this structure? Does the teacher demonstrate this mastery in her or his teaching? Is there evidence that concept attainment and other higher-level cognitive concerns are continuously emphasized? In what ways does the teacher keep up with expanding knowledge in her or his field?

✓4. *Mastery of technique.* Is the teacher knowledgeable about an array of teaching methods and strategies? Does the teacher show sensitivity to the conditions under which each is more or less effective? Can the teacher demonstrate a variety of techniques in teaching? Does this ability to demonstrate variety occur continuously? Is there evidence that the teacher expands her or his repertoire of teaching over time? Is there evidence that the teacher is becoming more effective in matching teaching strategies to circumstances? What is the link between the subject being taught and how it is taught? Do methods change when content changes? How successful is the teaching in building bridges between the teacher's knowledge and student experiences?

When one takes into account different evaluation purposes and perspectives and different teaching competence and substance areas, it becomes clear that limiting one's supervision and evaluation strategy to only classroom observation, rating scales, paper and pencil tests, target setting, clinical supervision, portfolio development, or any other *single* strategy does not account for the complexities involved in providing a comprehensive, meaningful, and useful system of evaluation. In summary, principals are responsible for the school's supervisory program. At the very minimum, this responsibility includes ensuring that a helpful, useful, and comprehensive system of supervision is operating. Teachers should report that they find the system helpful and satisfying. The following are questions that can reasonably be asked in evaluating a school's supervisory program:

- Are teachers involved in shaping, implementing, and evaluating the supervisory program?
- Are multiple purposes provided for? Does the program, for example, address issues of quality control, professional development, and teacher motivation and commitment? Are formative, summative, and diagnostic perspectives all included in the program?
- Is the program sufficiently comprehensive to include *know how, can do, will do,* and *will grow* as basic teaching performance expectations?
- Does the program focus on improving knowledge and skill in such basic teaching essentials as purpose, student needs and characteristics, subject matter, and teaching techniques?

These questions highlight the importance of including teacher development programs as part of the school's overall design for supervision. The major emphasis in supervision should be on teacher growth and development. Both supervision and teacher development should be planned and provided as *interdependent* parts of a school's overall commitment to striving for quality.

References

Blumberg, Art. 1980. *Supervisors and Teachers: A Private Cold War.* 2d ed. Berkeley, CA: McCutchan.

Bolin, Frances S. 1987. "Reassessment and Renewal in Teaching," in F. S. Bolin and J. McConnel Falk, Ed., *Teacher Renewal: Professional Issues, Personal Choices.* New York: Teachers College Press.

Bolin, Francis S., and Judith McConnel Falk, Eds. 1987. *Teacher Renewal: Professional Issues, Personal Choices.* New York: Teachers College Press.

Dewey, John. 1958. *Art as Experience.* New York: Putnam.

Hackman, J. R., G. Oldham, R. Johnson, and K. Purdy. 1975. "A New Strategy for Job Enrichment," *California Management Review* 17(4).

Hackman, J. R., and Greg Oldham. 1976. "Motivation Through the Design of Work: Test of a Theory," *Organizational Behavior and Human Performance* 16(2), 250–279.

Little, Judith Warren. 1993. "Teachers' Professional Development in a Climate of Educational Reform," *Educational Evaluation and Policy Analysis,* (15)2, 129–151.

Rubin, Louis. 1975. "The Case for Staff Development," in Thomas J. Sergiovanni, Ed., *Professional Supervision for Professional Teachers,* 33–49. Washington, DC. Association for Supervision and Curriculum Development.

Shulman, Lee. 1989. "Teaching the Disciplines Liberally." The Third Annual Meeting of The Holmes Group, Atlanta, January 28.

Stodolsky, Susan S. 1988. *The Subject Matters.* Chicago: The University of Chicago Press.

Thelan, Herbert. 1971. "A Cultural Approach to In-Service Education," in Louis Rubin, Ed., *Improving In-Service Education.* 72–73. Boston: Allyn and Bacon.

Zimpher, Nancy Z., and Kenneth R. Howey. 1987. "Adapting Supervisory Practice to Different Orientations of Teaching Competence," *Journal of Curriculum and Supervision* 2(1), 101–127.

Chapter *12*

Options for Supervision

What are the options for a differentiated system of supervision? How does a principal decide which options would be best for a particular teacher? This chapter describes five possible options for supervision: clinical, collegial, individual, informal, and inquiry based. The rationale for a differentiated system of supervision is simple: Teachers are different. They have different needs and temperaments, and these needs should be recognized. When they are, teachers are likely to respond more positively to supervision than when a one-best-way approach is used. Yet for a differentiated system of supervision to work, the roles of principals and teachers will have to change. Teachers will have to assume the responsibility for developing the options. They will also have to play key roles in deciding which of the options makes most sense to them. Most importantly, they will have to accept responsibility for making the options work. They will, in other words, have to become supervisors—not supervisors in the old factory sense of monitoring, inspecting, and evaluating, but in the sense of colleagues working together to help each other understand their own teaching and to improve their practices.

In such a design, principals would not be excluded. They have important roles to play. They need to give leadership to the supervisory program, marshall resources to make sure the program works, help provide the administrative structures and other arrangements that will enable teachers to work effectively together, and participate as supervisors—engaging in dialogue and helping in the improvement of teaching wherever they can.

Clinical Supervision as an Option

In the late 1950s, Robert Goldhammer (1969), Morris Cogan (1973), and their colleagues at Harvard University began to develop the clinical supervision concept as they sought more effective ways to supervise graduate students enrolled in the Master of Arts in Teaching program. Since then, this idea has been further developed to accommodate not only preservice supervision of teachers but also inservice supervision of beginning teachers and of seasoned professional teachers. Cogan (1973) defines clinical supervision as follows:

> *The rationale and practice is designed to improve the teacher's classroom per-*
> *formance. It takes its principal data from the events of the classroom. The*
> *analysis of these data and the relationships between teacher and supervisor form*
> *the basis of the program, procedures, and strategies designed to improve the*
> *students' learning by improving the teacher's classroom behavior. (54)*

Clinical supervision is considered by many experts (Garman, 1982; Goldhammer, Anderson, and Krajewski, 1993) to be a very effective strategy for bringing about improvements in teaching. It requires a more intense relationship between supervisor and teacher than typically is found in supervisory strategies. The perspective for clinical supervision is basically formative. Its focus is on building teacher motivation and commitment on the one hand, and on providing for "on-line" staff development for teachers on the other. Because teachers assume active roles in the process, they often find this a satisfying approach. Furthermore, clinical supervision need not be hierarchical; that is, it lends itself to peer and collegial relations among teachers.

The purpose of clinical supervision is to help teachers to modify existing patterns of teaching in ways that make sense to them. Evaluation is, therefore, responsive to the needs and desires of the teacher. It is the teacher who decides the course of a clinical supervisory cycle, the issues to be discussed, and for what purpose. Obviously, principals who serve as clinical supervisors will bring to this interaction a considerable amount of influence; however, ideally, this should stem from their being in a position to provide the help and clarification needed by teachers. The supervisor's job, therefore, is to help the teacher select goals to be improved and teaching issues to be illuminated, and to understand better her or his practice. This emphasis on understanding provides the avenue by which more technical assistance can be given to the teacher; thus, clinical supervision involves, as well, the systematic analysis of classroom events.

The Cycle of Clinical Supervision

Most authorities (e.g., Goldhammer, 1969) suggest that a sequence of clinical supervision contain five general steps or stages, as follows:

1. Preobservation conference
2. Observation of teaching
3. Analysis and strategy
4. Postobservation conference
5. Postconference analysis

Preobservation Conference

No stage is more important than the preobservation conference. It is here that the framework for observations is developed and an agreement is reached between supervisor and teacher governing the process that subsequently unfolds. After a brief warm-up period, the supervisor needs to become familiar with the class and with the teacher's way of thinking about teaching. How does the teacher view this class? What are the qualities and characteristics of this class? What frames of reference regarding purposes, models of teaching, classroom management, and so forth does the teacher bring to teaching? Getting into the teacher's "corner" and understanding the class from her or his perspective should help the supervisor to understand what the teacher has in mind for the particular teaching sequence that will be observed. How the particular lesson in question fits into the teacher's broader framework of purposes and view of teaching is also essential to provide the supervisor with a perspective beyond the particular lesson at hand.

The supervisor is now ready to engage the teacher in a mental or conceptual *rehearsal* of the lesson. The teacher provides an overview of her or his intents, outcomes not formally anticipated but likely or possible, and problems likely to be encountered. An overview of how teaching will unfold, what the teacher and students will be doing, and anticipated responses from students should also be provided. The supervisor might wish to raise questions for clarification and, depending on the relationship existing between supervisor and teacher, to make suggestions for improving the lesson before it unfolds.

Typically, this conceptual rehearsal by the teacher identifies an array of teaching issues of interest. Clinical supervision is selective in the sense that an intense and detailed study is made of only a handful of issues at a time. Thus, supervisor and teacher must decide what aspects of teaching will be considered, with the teacher assuming major responsibility for setting the supervisory agenda. What would the teacher like to know about this class and the teaching that will take place? On what aspects of teaching would she or he like feedback? Teachers inexperienced with clinical supervision may have initial difficulty in suggesting agenda items, but careful prodding and guiding by the supervisor usually help to elicit meaningful issues that become the basis for a particular cycle of supervision. This phase of the conference concludes with the teacher and supervisor reaching a fairly explicit agreement or "contract" about the reasons for supervision, along with the teaching and learning agendas to be studied. The contract might contain, as well, some indication of the information to be collected, how this information will be collected, what the supervisor will be doing, and what the supervisor should not do. Clinical supervision advocates feel that the teacher should have as complete as possible a picture of events to occur as the process of supervision unfolds.

Observation of Teaching

The second stage in a clinical supervision cycle—and basic to it—is the actual and systematic observation of teaching. Attention is given to the teacher *in action* and to the classroom story unfolding as a result of this action. Clinical supervision purists would argue that "canned" or standardized devices, or scales for ratings of general teaching characteristics, may well be useful but in themselves are not sufficient; and when used, they should stem from, and be related to, the actual observation of teaching and learning at issue. It is what the teacher actually says and does, how students react, and what actually occurs during a specific teaching episode under study that remains the center of evaluation to advocates of clinical supervision. Student interviews, collections of classroom artifacts, development of evaluation portfolios, bulletin board and classroom arrangements, photo essays, inventories of lessons accomplished by children or books read, and other evaluative data collection strategies should supplement and illuminate this actual teaching.

The teacher will know what to expect because of the preobservation conference. The teacher should understand that the supervisor wishes to make an unobtrusive entrance and to remain as unobtrusive as possible. During the observation the clinical supervisor may take copious notes attempting to record all classroom events. Notes should be descriptive—that is, free from inferences; for example, the supervisor would avoid writing "during the questioning of students on the use of microscopes by criminologists, the students were bored" in favor of something such as "John and Mary both did not hear the question when it was asked" and "two students were looking out the window; a third was playing with materials in his desk during the microscope questioning time." Sometimes the information collected is focused on a particular issue such as cognitive level of questions, attention spans of children, time on task, or cooperative relationships among students. Then, instead of attempting to record everything that takes place during the lesson, the supervisor might record and rate each question asked on the Bloom Taxonomy of Educational Objectives or collect similar, more detailed information. Many clinical supervision purists insist on a written transcript or the collection of firsthand data by the supervisor, and many supervisors using clinical methods have been successful by using television and videotaping equipment or by using audiotaping equipment to record actual teaching. At the conclusion of the observation, the supervisor leaves the classroom as unobtrusively as possible.

Analysis and Strategy

The third step in the cycle of clinical supervision is the analysis of teaching and the building of a supervisory strategy. The analysis stage requires that the supervisor convert the raw data or information collected from the observation into a manageable, meaningful, and sensible form. Clinical supervision advocates recommend that the analysis yield significant teaching patterns and that critical incidents be identified for use in the supervisory conference. Of paramount importance is the contract initially struck with the teacher. What was the purpose of the observation? How did the information collected illuminate this purpose? Can the supervisor arrange this information in a fashion that communicates clearly to the teacher the feedback she or he seeks but at the same time does not prejudge the teaching? This process identifies teaching patterns: recurring teacher verbal and nonverbal behaviors discovered in the course of teaching. Critical incidents are those occurrences that have a particularly noticeable positive or negative effect on the teaching and learning.

Having organized the information, the supervisor now gives attention to building a strategy for working with the teacher. The supervisor takes into account the nature of the contract originally struck, the evaluation issues uncovered during the observation and analysis, the quality of interpersonal relationships existing between teacher and supervisor, the authority base from which she or he is operating, and the competency or experience level of the teacher in deciding on this strategy.

The Postobservation Conference

The fourth stage in the cycle of clinical supervision is the supervisory conference. The supervisor uses the specific information gathered to help the teacher analyze the lesson. Typically, this postobservation conference focuses on a handful of issues previously agreed upon by the teacher and supervisor. It is appropriate as well for the supervisor to introduce new issues as circumstances warrant, but these issues should be few and cautiously introduced. The emphasis remains on providing information to the teacher for fulfilling the contract that was the basis for the observation cycle. Furthermore, the emphasis is not on providing evaluative information but on providing *descriptive* information. The process of making sense of this information is a joint one shared by teacher and supervisor.

Let's assume that the most important issue identified and agreed to in the preconference is "level of cognitive questioning" used by the teacher and cognitive level of assignments given to the students. The teacher uses objectives that span all six levels of the Bloom Taxonomy of Educational Objectives but wishes to emphasize the higher-level objectives of analysis and synthesis. Perhaps this teacher is not confident that actual teaching emphasizes these levels; or perhaps the supervisor, suspecting that teaching is not matching teacher intents, suggests that the level of cognitive questionings be examined. In either event, teacher and supervisor agree to use an inventory that enables the sorting of questions asked into the Bloom categories: remembering, understanding, solving, analyzing, creating, and judging. During the observation of teaching, each question asked by the teacher is classified into an appropriate level. A transcript of actual questions asked could be prepared. During the analysis and strategy stage of the supervisory cycle, the supervisor tallies questions and computes percentages.

The supervisor then decides on a strategy whereby the teacher is asked to restate her or his purposes for the lesson as well as for the unit of which the lesson is a part. The cognitive level of questioning information is then presented and compared with the teacher's intents. The supervisor is careful to avoid drawing conclusions or to elaborate on possible discrepancies, considering these conclusions to be the responsibility of the teacher. The teacher and supervisor might decide that it would be helpful to collect homework assignments given for other lessons in this particular teaching unit as well as to examine questions on tests that have been used. These assignments and test questions could also be categorized into the cognitive level of questioning format. Throughout the process, the supervisor's role is not to condemn, cajole, or admonish, but to provide information useful to the teacher and in a supportive atmosphere. Some suggestions for providing helpful feedback to teachers are provided in Exhibit 12–1.

Postconference Analysis

The fifth and final stage in a cycle of clinical supervision is the postconference analysis. The postconference phase is a natural springboard to staff development for both teacher and supervisor. The supervisor evaluates what happened in the supervisory conference and throughout the supervisory cycle for purposes of improving her or his own efforts. Was the integrity of the teacher protected? Did the teacher participate in the process as a cosupervisor? Was feedback given in response to the teacher's needs and desires? Was the emphasis more on teaching and the improvement of teaching than on teacher and evalu-

---

EXHIBIT 12–1   Some Suggestions for Providing Helpful Feedback to Teachers

1. *When giving feedback to teachers, be descriptive rather than judgmental:* Clinical supervision is designed to help teachers improve ongoing teaching and should not be used as a device for summative evaluation designed to determine the value of a person or program. For example, instead of saying to a biology teacher, "You are spending too much time in lecture and not enough time with students engaged in field work and laboratory," try "Your time log shows that you spent 85 percent of class time these past two weeks in lecture. Let's look at your objectives and plans for this unit and see if this is what you intended."

2. *When giving feedback to teachers, be specific rather than general:* General statements tend to be misunderstood more than specific statements. Instead of saying to a teacher, "You interrupt students and tend not to listen to what they are saying," try, "When you asked John a question, you interrupted his response and seemed uninterested in what he had to say." A cassette transcript of the question, response attempt, and interruptions would be helpful.

3. *When giving feedback to teachers, concentrate on things that can be changed:* A teacher may have little control over a nervous twitch or voice quality, but much can be done about arranging seats, grouping students, improving balance between knowledge level and other objectives, and disciplining students.

4. *When giving feedback to teachers, consider your own motives:* Often feedback is given to impress teachers with one's knowledge or for some other reason that builds the supervisor's status. Feedback is intended for only one purpose—to help the teacher know and understand her or his actual behavior as a teacher and consequences of this behavior on teaching and learning.

5. *Give the teacher feedback at a time as close to the actual behavior as possible:* Details of events are likely to be forgotten easily. Furthermore, fairly prompt attention is likely to upgrade and personalize the importance of clinical supervision.

6. *When giving feedback to teachers, rely as much as possible on information whose accuracy can be reasonably documented:* Photographs of bulletin boards, audio- and videotapes of teachers and students at work, a portfolio of classroom tests, a record of books borrowed from the class library, the number of students who return to shop during free periods or after school, and a tally of questions asked by the teacher sorted into the hierarchy of educational objectives are examples of documented feedback. It will not always be possible or desirable to provide this type of highly descriptive feedback, but it is important, nevertheless, as a technique, for clinical supervision cannot be overemphasized.

---

ating the teacher? What can the supervisor do to improve her or his skills in clinical supervision? A typical outcome of the first four phases of clinical supervision is agreement on the kinds of issues to be pursued next as further cycles are undertaken. The postconference analysis is, therefore, both the end of one cycle and the beginning of another.

Is Clinical Supervision for Everyone?

Clinical supervision is demanding in the time it requires from both supervisor and teachers. Principals who have difficulty finding the time to use this approach with all teachers might reserve it for working with two or three teachers at a time. If it is desirable for more teachers to be involved, then using collegial or peer clinical supervision may be the answer. Here teachers take turns assuming the role of clinical supervisor as they help each other. Collegial clinical supervision, however, often results in teachers being burdened with additional time demands. Furthermore, participation requires much more training in conferencing, information collecting, interpreting, and other supervisory techniques than is typically necessary for other forms of supervision. If teachers are to be clinical supervisors, they will need to receive the proper training; this, too, can present problems because training takes time and is expensive.

A further issue is that *clinical supervision may be too much supervision for some teachers.* Although all teachers would profit from clinical supervision from time to time, it does not appear that this strategy should be used all the time for all teachers. Going through this process every second, third, or fourth year may be less burdensome and tiresome for some. Unfortunately, this supervisory process can become too routinized and ritualized if overused. Finally, teacher needs and dispositions as well as work and learning styles vary. Clinical supervision may be suitable for some teachers but not for others when these concerns are taken into consideration.

Collegial Supervision

Allan Glatthorn (1984) uses the phrase *cooperative professional development* to describe a collegial process within which teachers agree to work together for their own professional development. He prefers this term over *peer supervision* or *collegial supervision,* fearing that these labels might suggest that teachers are supervising one another in a management sense. Cooperative professional development is a nonevaluative strategy for teachers to help one another as equals and professional colleagues. Glatthorn (1984:39) defines this approach as a "moderately formalized process by which two or more teachers agreed to work together for their own professional growth, usually by observing each other's classroom, giving each other feedback about the observation, and discussing shared professional concerns."

Cooperative professional development, or in the terms of this book, *collegial supervision,* can take many different forms. In some schools, teachers might be organized into teams of three. In forming such teams, teachers would have an opportunity to indicate with whom they might like to work. Often at least one member of the team is selected by the principal or the supervisor, but there are no rigid rules for selecting teams. Once formed, the teams may choose to work together in a number of ways ranging from clinical supervision to less intensive and more informal processes. They may, for example, simply agree to observe each other's classes, providing help according to the desires of the teacher being observed. The teachers then might confer, giving one another informal feedback and otherwise discussing issues of teaching that they consider to be important. An approach relying on Hunter's teaching steps and elements of lesson design might be used on another occasion. In this case the emphasis on teaching might be narrowly focused on specific issues identified by the teacher. On still another occasion the emphasis might be quite unfocused in order to provide a general feel or rendition of teaching. All that is needed is for team members to meet beforehand to decide "the rules and issues" for the observation and for any subsequent conversations or conferences.

It is a good idea for collegial supervision to extend beyond classroom observation. It should provide a setting in which teachers can informally discuss problems they are facing, share ideas, help one another in preparing lessons, exchange tips, and provide other support to one another. Some suggestions for principals seeking to implement collegial supervision are provided in Exhibit 12–2.

Self-Directed Supervision

Another option suggested by Glatthorn (1984) in establishing a differentiated system is what he calls *self-directed development.* Here teachers working alone assume responsibility for their own professional development, They develop a yearly plan comprising targets or goals derived from an assessment of their own needs. This plan is then shared with the supervisor, principal, or other designated individual. Teachers are allowed a great deal of leeway in developing the plan, but supervisors should ensure that the plan and selected targets are both realistic and attainable, At the end of a specified period, normally a year, the supervisor and teacher meet to discuss the teacher's progress in meeting professional development targets. Teachers are expected to provide some form of documentation (e.g., time logs, reflective practice diaries, schedules, photos, tapes, samples of students' work,

---

EXHIBIT 12–2   Guidelines for Implementing Cooperative or Collegial Supervision

1. Teachers should have a voice in deciding with whom they work.
2. Principals should retain final responsibility for putting together collegial supervisory teams.
3. The structure for collegial supervision should be formal enough for the teams to keep records of how and in what ways time has been used and to provide a general *nonevaluative* description of collegial supervisory activities. This record should be submitted annually to the principal.
4. The principal should provide the necessary resources and administrative support enabling collegial supervisory teams to function during the normal range of the school day. The principal might, for example, volunteer to cover classes as needed, to arrange for substitutes as needed, to provide for innovative schedule adjustments enabling team members to work together readily.
5. If information generated within the team about teaching and learning might be considered even mildly evaluative, it should stay with the team and not be shared with the principal.
6. Under no circumstances should the principal seek evaluation data from one teacher about another.
7. Each teacher should be expected to keep a professional growth log that demonstrates that she or he is reflecting on practice and growing professionally as a result of collegial supervisory activities.
8. The principal should meet with the collegial supervisory team at least once a year for purposes of general assessment and for sharing of impressions and information about the collegial supervisory process.
9. The principal should meet individually at least once a year with each collegial supervisory team member to discuss her or his professional growth log and to provide any encouragement and assistance that may be required.
10. Generally, new teams should be formed every second or third year.

other artifacts) illustrating progress toward goals. This conference then leads to the generation of new targets for subsequent individual professional development cycles.

A number of problems are associated with approaches to supervision that rely heavily on target setting. Supervisors, for example, sometimes rigidly adhere to prespecified targets and sometimes impose targets on teachers. Rigidly applying a target-setting system unduly focuses the evaluation and limits teachers to the events originally anticipated or stated. When this happens, teaching energies and concerns are directed to a prestated target and other areas of importance not targeted can be neglected. Target setting is meant to help and facilitate, not to hinder, the self-improvement process.

Individual approaches to supervision are ideal for teachers who prefer to work alone or who, because of scheduling or other difficulties, are unable to work with other teachers. This supervisory option is efficient in use of time, less costly, and less demanding in its reliance on others than is the case with other options. For these reasons self-directed supervision is a feasible and practical approach. This approach is ideally suited to competent and self-directed teachers. Some guidelines for implementing self-directed supervision are provided in Exhibit 12–3.

Informal Supervision

Included in every differentiated system of supervision should be a provision for *informal supervision.* Informal supervision is a casual encounter by supervisors with teachers at

---

EXHIBIT 12–3   Guidelines for Implementing Individualized Supervision

1. *Target setting.* Based on last year's observations, conferences, summary reports, clinical supervision episodes, or other means of personal assessment, teachers develop targets or goals that they would like to reach in improving their teaching. Targets should be few, rarely exceeding five or six and preferably limited to two or three. Estimated time frames should be provided for each target, which are then shared with the supervisor, along with an informal plan providing suggested activities for teacher engagement.
2. *Target-setting review.* After reviewing each target and estimated time frame, the principal provides the teacher with a written reaction. Furthermore, a conference is scheduled to discuss targets and plans.
3. *Target-setting conference.* Meeting to discuss targets, time frames, and reactions, the teacher and principal revise targets if appropriate. It may be a good idea for the principal to provide a written summary of the conference to the teacher. Teacher and principal might well prepare this written summary together.
4. *Appraisal process.* Appraisal begins at the conclusion of the target-setting conference and continues in accordance with the agreed-upon time frame. The specific nature of the appraisal process depends on each of the targets and could include formal and informal classroom observations, an analysis of classroom artifacts, videotaping, student evaluation, interaction analysis, and other information. The teacher is responsible for collecting appraisal information and arranges this material in a portfolio for subsequent discussion with, and review by, the principal.
5. *Summary appraisal.* The principal visits with the teacher to review the appraisal portfolio. As part of this process, the principal comments on each target, and together the teacher and principal plan for the next cycle of individual, self-directed supervision.

work and is characterized by frequent but brief and informal observations of teachers. Typically no appointments are made and visits are not announced. Successful informal supervision requires that certain expectations be accepted by teachers. This approach, for example, assumes that principals and supervisors are indeed first and foremost lead or principal-teachers and thus have a right and responsibility to be a part of all the teaching that takes place in the school. They are instructional partners to every teacher in every classroom for every teaching and learning situation. When informal supervision is properly in place, principals and supervisors are viewed as relatively common fixtures in classrooms, coming and going as part of the natural flow of the school's daily work.

Informal supervision should not be considered a sole option for teachers. Glatthorn (1984), for example, believes that a differentiated system of supervision should require all teachers to participate in informal supervision. In addition to informal supervision they would be involved in one additional approach such as clinical, collegial, or individual supervision. In selecting additional options, principals and supervisors should try to accommodate teacher preferences, but they should retain final responsibility for deciding the appropriateness of a selected option as well as reserve the right to veto the teacher's choice.

Inquiry-Based Supervision

One lesson that is clear from examining the new research on teaching is that teachers must become problem solvers and researchers of their own practice. Both problem solving and researching are at the heart of inquiry-based supervision. With inquiry-based supervision, teachers either work alone or with others to engage in action research. Mixing the words action and research provides a different image of research than the typical one. In the minds of most, research is something mysterious, remote, abstract, and distant. It has nothing to do with action or practice.

Although action research might take many forms, it typically starts with the identification of a problem. Then hunches are formulated about what the causes of this problem are and how it can be solved. The teacher, either alone or with colleagues, then develops a plan to investigate one or more of these hunches. This plan involves collecting information, data, or other evidence about the situation. Once a problem is understood, tentative solutions to the problem are generated. If I did this rather than that, would things be better? New practices are then evaluated to see whether they have the desired effect. If what happens makes sense, then the practices are vindicated. If not, then other practices might be tried. Consider the different examples offered by Emily Calhoun (1993):

> *Anita Simmons records her 1st graders' responses to questions about simple fractions after using different displays and activities with them. She wants to determine which presentations are more effective than others.*
>
> *Four middle school teachers—Elitrus and Paula from Rogers School, and Angie and Robert from Wilshire School—experiment with mnemonic key words in their science classes. They want to help students better retain and understand key science concepts and terms. They consult frequently with a member of the*

county intermediate agency and a professor from the nearby state university, both of whom are experimenting with the same method.

The faculty at Thomas High School wants to increase student achievement. To obtain this goal, all faculty members add a new instructional strategy, such as the inquiry approach or inductive thinking strategies. They observe and record student responses to the change in instruction and discuss their findings. A leadership team meets bimonthly for technical assistance with the Consortium for Action Research, a regional group sponsored by the state department of education. (62)

The three examples that Calhoun provides illustrate three different approaches to action research: individual, collaborative, and school-wide. In individual action research, teachers work alone on problems of interest to them. The focus is on change in a single classroom. In collaborative action research, several teachers join together either to investigate a shared problem or to help each other solve individual problems. In school-wide action research, the faculty identifies a problem that is of interest to most. They then research the problem, analyzing its findings with implications for school-wide change.

Differentiated Supervision and the Contingency View

A *contingency view of supervision* is based on the premise that teachers are different and that matching supervisory options to these differences is important. In recent years, developmental theorists such as Costa (1982) and Glickman (1981, 1985) have made considerable progress in suggesting how this matching might be done. These experts examine such dimensions as levels of professional maturity and cognitive complexity and suggest that as levels vary among teachers, so should supervisory approaches and styles. Another group of theorists, such as Dunn and Dunn (1979) and Kolb, Rubin, and McIntyre (1984), have been interested in the concept of learning styles and how, as these styles vary, opportunities for learning, problem solving, and personal growth should also vary. Accounting for motives of teachers provides still a third dimension to the matching of individual teachers with supervisory options. Social motives theories such as McClelland and his colleague's (1953) find that as such important work motives as the need for achievement, power, and affiliation vary among workers, the work conditions and setting they find motivating vary as well. Matching supervisory options to individual needs, therefore, has great potential for increasing the motivation and commitment of teachers at work. The following sections explore these important individual dimensions and suggest compatible supervisory options. Readers should not be under the illusion that tight and concise matching is possible. It isn't. However, more informed matching decisions can be made by considering the possibilities discussed.

Cognitive Complexity Levels of Teachers

Important to developmental theorists is the concept of *cognitive complexity,* These theorists are concerned with levels of cognitive growth for teachers as embodied in the cognitive complexity they exhibit in their teaching practice. Lower levels of growth are characterized by simple and concrete thinking and practice, whereas higher levels of growth are characterized by more complex and abstract thinking and practice. An important finding from the research on teaching is that teachers with higher levels of cognitive complexity provide a greater range of teaching environments to students and that their practice is characterized by a wider variety of teaching strategies and methods (Hunt, 1966; Hunt and Joyce, 1967). Furthermore, students of teachers with higher levels of cognitive complexity tend to achieve more than students of teachers with lower levels (Harvey, 1966).

Cognitive complexity is concerned with both the *structure and content* of a teacher's thoughts, with particular emphasis on the structure (Harvey, 1966). Two teachers may share the same beliefs about the value of informal teaching but may differ markedly in the complexity with which they view these beliefs. The content of these beliefs is similar, but the structure is different. The first teacher views informal teaching as universally applicable rather than as one of many strategies. The second teacher, however, views informal teaching as a strategy more appropriate for some teaching and learning settings but less appropriate for others. Although both teachers share common beliefs about informal teaching, they differ in the structure with which these beliefs are held. The second teacher's thinking is characterized by higher levels of cognitive complexity than the first's. Teachers with higher levels of cognitive complexity are able to give attention to a number of different concepts relating to a particular issue and to see interconnections among these concepts. They are able to be more reflective in their practice, to understand better the subtleties of teaching, and to make more complex decisions about teaching.

Supervisory strategies that account for levels of cognitive complexity actually enhance this complexity. As Sprinthall and Thies-Sprinthall (1982) point out, cognitive complexity increases as teachers are exposed to more stimulating teaching environments. Examples would he teachers who have greater opportunities to interact with their supervisors and other teachers about teaching, have greater opportunities for obtaining feedback about their teaching and thus for reflecting on their practice, have greater opportunities for experimenting in a supportive environment, and have greater opportunities for assuming more responsibility for the outcomes of their teaching. The differentiated system of supervision that provides informal supervision combined with other options can provide these benefits. When teachers are provided with an intellectually stimulating, challenging, and supportive supervisory environment, levels of cognitive complexity increase, with subsequent improvements in teaching and learning (Harvey, 1966).

Supervisory Styles and Cognitive Complexity

Within any supervisory option, supervisors may choose to provide leadership and help in a number of different ways. These behavioral choices represent styles of supervision. The developmental theorist Glickman (1985) refers to three major supervisory styles as directive, collaborative, and nondirective.

Styles are different from options in that different styles can be used when working with different teachers even though all the teachers may be involved in supervision using the same option. For example, when working with three different teachers within individualized supervision, it might make sense to use a directive approach with one, a collaborative with the second, and a nondirective approach with the third. The directive approach would emphasize structure and more frequent interaction with the teacher; the collaborative would emphasize shared responsibility, joint decision making, and collegiality; and the nondirective would emphasize facilitating the teacher's plans and efforts and providing necessary support.

The matching of teacher concerns, levels of responsibility, maturity, cognitive complexity, supervisory options, and supervisory styles is illustrated in Figure 12–1. This figure suggests an alignment between concerns of teachers and levels of responsibility and maturity and levels of cognitive complexity. Teachers who are primarily concerned with the problems, needs, and learning characteristics of students; autonomous with respect to accepting responsibility; and growing in levels of maturity are likely to display moderate or medium levels of cognitive complexity. Cognitive complexity is, therefore, an important construct. The intersection line brings together these dimensions of teacher development and indicates the recommended supervisory style and supervisory option.

Teachers located at or near point 1 on the intersection line would probably benefit best from directive supervision regardless of the supervisory option being used. Informal supervision characterized by frequent and direct contact with the supervisor is recommended as the most suitable option. Collegial and individual supervision would be appropriate as supplements. Should collegial be chosen (e.g., teaming the teacher with another teacher who might be located at point 3 on the intersection line), the supervisor will need to be involved to ensure that this teacher is getting the direction and help most needed.

The collaborative supervisory style would be most appropriate for teachers at intersection point 2. In this case, both teacher and supervisor tackle problems together, plan activities and events, and make decisions cooperatively. Individual professional development is highly recommended as an option.

Teachers with more professional concerns that bring together students with broader issues affecting quality schooling and who reflect higher levels of cognitive complexity in their practice will be found at or near point 3 on the intersection line. These mature professionals are more willing and able to assume full responsibility for their own self-evaluation and improvement. When this is the case, supervision is more appropriately nondirective. Cooperative professional development is ideally suited to teachers at point 3. Here, groups of teachers work together as mature colleagues. Individual professional development may be selected by some teachers who might prefer to work alone. Informal supervision would remain an important part of a comprehensive supervisory system in the school and thus should be used as well with teachers at or near point 3. For these highly motivated and competent teachers, the purpose of informal supervision is one of providing needed recognition and support.

Peaks and dips appear periodically on the intersection line of Figure 12–1. Peaks represent occasions when teachers might require more intense and prolonged help in the classroom, perhaps because they face a special problem or challenge. Dips represent trouble spots that might be identified by either the teacher or the supervisor. On these occasions, clinical supervision can be an effective and appropriate option.

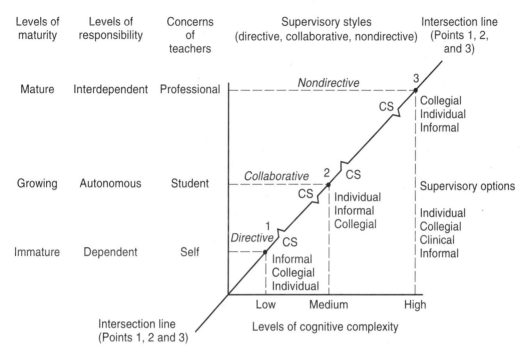

| Levels of maturity | Levels of responsibility | Concerns of teachers | Supervisory styles (directive, collaborative, nondirective) | Intersection line (Points 1, 2, and 3) |

FIGURE 12–1   Matching Teacher Variables and Supervisory Styles

All of this sounds complicated, and it is. Whenever we try to accommodate individual differences in people and settings we have to deal with diverse strategies and tactics. Figure 12–1 can be helpful if it is viewed not as an algorithm or script, but merely as a model, a metaphorical one at that, which portrays ideas that might be helpful in sorting out what to do and when. Ultimately the process of deciding is one of trial and error, much as physicians practice. In medicine, models suggesting treatments are tried but quickly abandoned for others as the physician monitors progress and gets feedback that something is not working.

Learning Styles of Teachers

Two additional situational characteristics that should be considered in a contingency view of supervision are learning styles of teachers and the particular motivational needs that they bring to work. Teachers, like students, are unique in their learning styles and in the ways in which they solve problems. A reflective supervisory program would take note of these differences and seek to accommodate them in assigning teachers to supervisory options and in providing appropriate supervisory styles within options. Kolb, Rubin, and McIntyre (1984) provide a model of learning that conceives of adult learning and problem solving as one process. The model is intended to increase understanding of how adults generate from their experience the concepts, rules, and principles that guide their behavior in new situations and how they modify these concepts to improve their effectiveness in learning at work. Within the model, learning and problem solving are viewed as a four-stage cycle beginning with concrete experiences and progressing in turn through observation and reflection, the formulation of concepts and generalizations, to experimenting with what is learned in a new setting. This model represents an ideal conception of learning.

Kolb and his colleagues identify four different learning modes, each corresponding to one of the stages of this learning cycle: concrete experience (CE), reflective observation (RO), abstract conceptualization (AC), and active experimentation (AE). They believe that learners

> *must be able to involve themselves fully, openly and without bias in new experiences (CE); they must be able to reflect on and observe these experiences from many perspectives (RO); they must be able to create conceptions that integrate their observations into logically sound theories (AC); and they must be able to use these theories to make decisions and solve problems (AE). (Kolb, Rubin, and McIntyre, 1984:32)*

People give different weights to each of these learning styles. Some teachers feel more comfortable with and are more confident with some of the stages of the cycle than with others. Simply put, some teachers learn best when dealing concretely with something and may have difficulty responding to this same thing when presented abstractly. Others are confused by starting with concrete matters, preferring instead to read about something—to become cognitively oriented before experiencing it firsthand. Others might prefer to observe new learning possibilities in action first and then to reflect on what is observed before developing a conceptual map or having concrete experience. Still other teachers are quick to jump in and experiment with new ideas and practices, using a process of muddling through as they then move to more reflective, abstract, or concrete understandings. What is clear is that learning takes place best when all of the four learning modes are tended to. What is not clear is the order in which different individuals progress through the learning cycle. Some learn best starting with a concrete experience, others learn best starting with a more abstract approach, and so forth. Typically one's actual learning style represents a blending of modes. For practical purposes it is more useful to think of a person as being oriented toward a particular learning mode than as being typed or labeled more rigidly. Patterns are intended to reveal relative emphases on one or another learning mode and to suggest strengths and weaknesses.

Teacher Learning Styles and Supervisory Options

Learning styles can be useful in helping to decide which particular supervisory option is most suitable for a given teacher, but the real value is less in deciding the option itself and more in suggesting ways in which supervisors and others can work most effectively with teachers within options. Following are some recommendations for matching supervisory option with teacher learning style. They are based on our interpretation of the literature and on our clinical experience as supervisors.

Collegial supervision is the recommended choice for teachers oriented toward concrete experience for it gives them opportunities to interact with other teachers about their work. Concrete-experience teachers are less interested in "bookish" interpretations of practice and more interested in knowing about and experiencing "what works" in the classroom next door. They often like the opportunity to try out a new idea or teaching practice, much as does an apprentice by working side by side with another teacher. Sometimes their concern for what is immediate prevents them from "seeing the forest because of the trees." Sometimes they adopt practices by mimicking them and thus do not understand them fully. As a result they may have difficulty in extending their practice, in applying newly learned practices to new situations, and in modifying practices as situations change.

Concrete-experience teachers typically like to interact with each other and are not likely to prefer options that require them to work alone. Thus, they are not likely to be comfortable with individual professional development. Should this be the choice anyway, concrete-experience teachers will need a fair amount of close supervision and a reasonable amount of directiveness. In collegial supervision settings it makes sense to team concrete-experience teachers with those who have strengths in abstract conceptualization or reflective observation. Both types of teachers will profit by this combination.

High-reflective–observation teachers are likely to respond favorably to supervisory situations that allow them to be self-directed and to work collegially with other teachers. In each case, however, the teacher is likely to be passive, preferring to observe and make sense of what is going on rather than taking a more active role. If assigned to individual supervision and left alone, the reflective observer will often not make much progress. If this must be the choice it might be a good idea for supervisors to insist on the development of an explicit contract detailing the action outcomes of supervisions. Targets and goals should be action-oriented and should specify the teaching behaviors or classroom changes being sought. Care should be taken to ensure that targets have been met and the supervisory contract has been fulfilled.

A better choice for the reflective observer would be assignment to collegial teams, but care should be taken to provide that other team members are reasonably action-oriented and can provide the teacher with the kinds of practical assistance that will be needed to get on with the work of self-improvement. In exchange the reflective observing teacher can provide others with the kind of reflection that will help them to view their teaching with greater depth and meaning.

Abstract-conceptualization–oriented teachers resemble reflective-observation teachers in many ways but are more action-oriented and better able to focus on problems of practice and the theoretical ideas associated with these problems. They like reading about theoretical ideas, issues of practice, and reports of research regarding teaching and learning and discussing these issues and ideas in depth. They like to "see the data and are frequently good at making sense of these data. Sometimes in their enthusiasm for abstract concerns they have less energy available for getting on with the day-to-day implementation of ideas. They are good planners, however, and when assigned to individual supervision will often prepare elaborate and reasoned sets of target-setting documents. This supervisory option works well for them if time is taken to ensure that action deadlines are set and that teachers follow these deadlines with evidence of practical accomplishments of their objectives and targets.

Teachers oriented toward abstract conceptualization often profit from collegial supervision and can contribute to it, but sometimes they can be distracting to group efforts because of their tendency to emphasize theoretical issues. To abstract conceptualizers the theoretical is a delight in its own right and well worth discussing regardless of implications for practice. In using the collegial option, therefore, care should be taken to form a team that includes more action-oriented teachers to provide the necessary balance.

Individual self-directed supervision is the most likely choice for teachers oriented toward active experimenting. These teachers are doers and as such are interested in getting on with their work. They like to set objectives and enjoy focusing on tasks. They are willing to take risks and are not afraid to modify their practice. Individual supervision provides these teachers with an opportunity to grow and develop at their own rates. They need help, however, in sticking with a course of action, in tempering their experiments, and in reflecting on their practice to ensure that it is reasonably stable and sensible. Active experimenters tend not to prefer collegial supervision, and if assigned to this option can often be a hindrance to other teachers. Other teachers assigned to the same option are likely to view the active experimenter as being a maverick. As with teachers oriented toward each of the other three learning styles, an appropriate supervisory strategy is one that leads with the teacher's strengths and provides the necessary help, and sometimes discipline, to ensure that the less favored learning modes are tended to as well. If Kolb, Rubin, and McIntyre (1984) are right, sustained learning will not take place unless all four dimensions of the learning cycle are experienced.

Accounting for Motives of Teachers

Differences in reactions of teachers to the same supervisory option or style are in part natural reflections of the motives they bring to their work. Motivational theories are often grouped into two major categories—active and internal. Active theories assume that teachers bring to their work certain needs that are translated into goals and desires. According to active theories, teachers are motivated to work in exchange for achieving desired goals. Internal theories, by contrast, assume that teachers are already motivated to work and that this motivation is related more to complex personality characteristics than to desired goals. According to internal theorists, carrot and stick approaches to motivation are likely to be less effective than understanding underlying motives and creating conditions allowing these motives to be expressed. Thus, motives and aroused motivation are considered to be different. Motives are construed as underlying personality characteristics. They resemble energy valves that are related to motivation. When the valves are closed, a teacher's energy remains in a state of potential and behavior is not motivated. Aroused motivation results from opening the motive valve and is reflected in a release of energy in the form of motivated behavior. Key motives differ for different individuals. When teachers find themselves in work settings that correspond to their underlying motives, the motive valve is opened and the potential for motivation is greatly enhanced.

Three motives have been identified as having particular importance to the world of teachers at work: achievement, power influence, and affiliation. McClelland (1961) found that the three motives are present in all people but not to the same degree. Some teachers are influenced greatly by the need for affiliation, only moderately by the need for power influence, and only modestly by the need for achievement. Other teachers might be very high on the need for achievement and comparatively low on the needs for affiliation and power and influence. The first group of teachers are likely to think more about social interaction, friendships, and human relationships at work and in controlling others at work than in job objectives and how well they can accomplish various teaching tasks. In contrast, the second group would probably be much more concerned with work issues and progress in achieving objectives than in interacting with and controlling others.

The achievement motive is associated with teachers wanting to take personal responsibility for their own success or failure, liking working situations where goals are clear and reasonably obtainable though challenging, and preferring frequent and concrete feedback allowing them to gauge their success and failure rates in a continuous fashion. High-achievement–motivated teachers are task-oriented, prefer short-range specific targets to more ambiguous and long-range targets, like to be on top of things, and seek personal responsibility for their actions. They find it difficult to delegate responsibility and to share authority with others. It is often difficult for them to emphasize human relationships and social interaction behaviors for their own sake. High-need-for-achievement teachers are likely to be committed to building achievement-oriented classrooms with visible and detailed standards. They seek and accept responsibility for their own work behaviors and growth, and gladly accept moderate risks in an effort to achieve personal success.

Supervisory options that encourage individual initiative, target-setting, and charting of accomplishments are favored by high-achievement–oriented teachers. Self-directed supervision, for example, is ideally suited to them, but they are likely to respond less favorably to collegial supervision. They respond well to informal supervision if the feedback they desire is provided. Continuing with the valve metaphor, when the supervisory situation is properly matched, the achievement-motive valve is opened and motivation results.

The affiliation motive is associated with people who have a high concern for warm and friendly relationships and for social interaction. Teachers for whom this need is important enjoy working with other teachers in group settings and find teaching and other assignments that require them to work alone, learn alone, or problem solve alone to be less satisfactory. They depend heavily on other teachers for much of their work satisfaction and enjoy interacting with others about work. Affiliation-oriented teachers suffer more from isolation and experience more loneliness than do their achievement and power-influence counterparts. They need and seek opportunities to interact with other adults. Should they find this opportunity within the supervisory situation, their affiliation-motive valve is opened and they respond with motivated behavior.

Individual self-directed supervision and other supervisory options that leave them to their own devices are not likely to be viewed favorably by high-affiliation teachers. However, collegial supervision elicits a very positive response. Affiliation teachers can feel uncomfortable when involved in informal supervision unless the supervisor makes a point of providing *supportive* feedback after every classroom visit.

High-need-for-power-and-influence teachers are interested in influencing other people. They like group contacts and social interaction supervisory settings but view these less as opportunities for satisfying social interaction needs and more as opportunities that will enable them to exercise leadership. When provided with supervisory situations of this type, the power-influence-motive valve is opened and motivative behavior results.

High-power-influence teachers like to assume supervisory roles and will respond very positively to collegial supervision. Because they like to be in charge and enjoy assuming leadership roles, they often resent competition in these areas from other teachers and from supervisors. An important strategy is to harness the motivational potential of high-power-influence teachers by delegating responsibility to them and in other ways sharing leadership roles and functions.

During the early stages of social motives research it was thought that the achievement motive was associated with increased performance at work and successful accomplishment of goals, and that the other two motives actually interfered with the accomplishment of work. More recent research, however, suggests that none of the three emerges as being superior. Teachers with high needs for affiliation and teachers with high needs for power and influence can be every bit as productive and effective as teachers with high needs for achievement. The key to motivation is not the most pressing motive of a particular teacher but whether a person's work circumstances allow for expression of the motive—the opening of the motive-energy valve, so to speak.

Flexibility in Practice

Throughout this discussion of contingency views, supervisory options and styles have been characterized as models and ideal types with fairly fixed features that clearly differentiate one from another. Let's take the case of Bill, a high-need-for-achievement teacher with a learning style emphasizing abstract conceptualization. Bill likes to set targets, plan events in stages, and keep track of his progress. He derives a great deal of satisfaction from his own accomplishments and in this sense makes a game of learning. Individual self-directed supervision is a good choice for Bill.

As the principal thinks about how to work with Bill and to be helpful to him, certain issues come to mind. Bill's targets are typically abstract. He tackles such issues as: "How can I learn more about individual differences of the students I teach?' The principal would like Bill to focus more on developing actual teaching strategies and on experimenting with various classroom organizational patterns that emphasize individual differences in practice. The principal decides to keep close tabs on Bill, who will not mind close supervision if its main purpose is to provide him with feedback as to how well he is doing and with recognition for his success. These feedback sessions will also be used to emphasize other issues that the principal thinks are important—translating abstract ideas into concrete practices. The principal urges Bill to visit the classroom of another teacher working on a similar problem and, after this observation, discusses with Bill what has been observed. This develops links between Bill's theories and abstract understandings of individual differences and what has been observed in practice. Together they develop a plan for reorganizing the structure of the classroom for language arts teaching that illustrates some of the ideas Bill is working on with respect to individual differences. Throughout, the principal is sensitive to Bill's need for achievement and for feedback about his work and uses this need as a means to build bridges between abstract conceptualization and the other learning modes of reflective observation, concrete experience, and active experimentation.

Betty, however, is a high-need-for-affiliation teacher with a concrete-experience learning style. Working with Betty within individual self-directed supervision is possible but will require a different strategy by the principal. To begin with, Betty will need much more contact with the principal than Bill did. High affiliation teachers seek and require social interaction. The issue for the principal in this case is how to give Betty a sound theoretical understanding of her practice that will enable her to teach with more meaning and to increase her practice repertoire. Individual supervision can work for Betty if the principal is willing to take the necessary time. In this case, however, collegial supervision might well be a better choice. Allowing Betty to work with other teachers not only provides her with the necessary interaction but also relieves the time demands of the principal as teachers assume supervisory responsibility. Within collegial supervision, the principal's role will change from direct supervisor to general supervisor as she maintains contact with the group to ensure that the process initially complements Betty's learning style and subsequently extends it.

Helping Teachers to Achieve Goals

The key to the contingency view and at the heart of reflective practice within the principalship is a very simple but deceptive axiom. Teachers have work goals that are important to them. Given the opportunity, they will work very hard at achieving these goals. This chapter has suggested that the nature of these goals is influenced by growth stages, cognitive complexity levels, learning styles, and motives that teachers bring to the school. Supervisory options and styles should respond to these differences among teachers, for such responsiveness makes it easier for work goals to be realized. In this sense, supervision is little more than a system of help for teachers as they achieve goals that they consider important. Principals are needed to provide help as this process unfolds.

Robert J. House (1971) has proposed a "path-goal" theory of leadership that summarizes much of our discussion and provides a handle on key aspects of effective helping. He believes that leaders are responsible for "increasing the number and kinds of personal payoffs to the subordinates for the work-goal attainment and making paths to these payoffs easiest to travel by clarifying the paths, reducing roadblocks and pitfalls, and increasing the opportunities for personal satisfaction en route" (323).

Translated to teacher supervision, principals assume responsibility for "clarifying and clearing the path" toward goals that teachers consider important. Clarifying the path requires that goals be set and reasonably defined and understood. Ambiguous and unstructured situations and unclear expectations can be a source of frustration and dissatisfaction for teachers. Thus, it becomes important to provide the necessary task emphasis to help clarify goals. Clearing the path requires that principals provide the necessary assistance, education, support, and reinforcement to help achieve goals. Key to a path-goal approach is understanding that the richer sources of satisfaction for teachers come not from an emphasis on human relationships and social interaction separate from the accomplishment of work but from having accomplished worthwhile and challenging tasks within a pleasant atmosphere.

Providing a system of differentiated supervision is one way in which principals can provide the necessary paths that enable teachers to accomplish work goals 'they consider to be important.

Appendix 12–1 provides a description of how one principal began the process of changing supervision and evaluation in her school. Beginning with the assumption that a principal and her teachers need to "bend" the existing system of evaluation in order to create one that encourages learning from one another, she invited her teachers to consider alternatives. Not surprisingly they responded enthusiastically. Her story is a fitting place to end our discussion of teacher development and supervision. Neither teacher development nor supervision are things that we can do for teachers, but are things that they must do for themselves. The test of leadership is to be able to extend to teachers an invitation to accept responsibility for themselves, and to have them accept it.

References

Calhoun, Emily F. 1993. "Action Research: Three Approaches," *Educational Leadership* 51(1), 62–65.

Cogan, Morris. 1973. *Clinical Supervision.* Boston: Houghton Mifflin.

Costa, Art L. 1982. *Supervision for Intelligent Teaching: A Course Syllabus.* Orangevale, CA: Search Models Unlimited.

Dunn, Rita S., and K. J. Dunn. 1979. "Learning Styles Teaching Styles: Should They . . . Can They . . . Be Matched?" *Educational Leadership* 36(4).

Garman, Noreen. 1982. "The Clinical Approach to Supervision," in Thomas J. Sergiovanni, Ed., *Supervision of Teaching,* 35–52. Alexandria, VA: Association for Supervision and Curriculum Development.

Glatthorn, Allan A. 1984. *Differentiated Supervision.* Alexandria, VA: Association for Supervision and Curriculum Development.

Glickman, Carl D. 1981. *Developmental Supervision.* Alexandria, VA: Association for Supervision and Curriculum Development.

Glickman, Carl D. 1985. *Supervision and Instruction: A Developmental Approach.* Boston: Allyn and Bacon.

Goldhammer, Robert. 1969. *Clinical Supervision: Special Methods for the Supervision of Teachers.* New York: Holt, Rinehart and Winston.

Goldhammer, Robert, Robert H. Anderson, and Robert A. Krajewski. 1993. *Clinical Supervision: Special Methods for the Supervision of Teaching,* 3rd ed. New York: Holt, Rinehart and Winston.

Harvey, O. J. 1966. "System Structure, Flexibility and Creativity," in O. J. Harvey, Ed., *Experience, Structure, and Adaptability,* 39–65. New York: Springer.

House, Robert J. 1971. "A Path Goal Theory of Leadership Effectiveness," *Administrative Science Quarterly* 16(3), 321–338.

Hunt, David E. 1966. "A Conceptual Systems Change Model and Its Application to Education," in O. J. Harvey, Ed., *Experience, Structure, and Adaptability,* 277–302. New York: Springer.

Hunt, David E., and Bruce R. Joyce. 1967. "Teacher Trainee Personality and Initial Teaching Style," *American Educational Research Journal* 4(3), 253–255.

Kolb, David A., Irwin M. Rubin, and James M. McIntyre. 1984. *Organizational Psychology: An Experiential Approach to Organizational Behavior.* Englewood Cliffs, NJ: Prentice-Hall.

McClelland, David C. 1961. *The Achieving Society.* Princeton, NJ: Van Nostrand.

McClelland, David C., J. W. Atkinson, R. A. Clark, and E. L. Lowell. 1953. *The Achievement Motive.* New York: Appleton-Century-Croft.

Rooney, Joanne. 1993. "Teacher Evaluation: No More "Super"vision," *Educational Leadership,* 51(2), 43–44.

Sprinthall, N. A., and L. Thies-Sprinthall. 1982. "Career Development of Teachers: A Cognitive Perspective," in H. Mitzel, Ed., *Encyclopedia of Educational Research,* 5th ed. New York: Free Press.

Appendix 12–1   Teacher Evaluation

No More "Super"vision

Joanne Rooney, Principal
Pleasant Hill School

Our teacher evaluation system wasn't working. . . . After examining our evaluation system, I realized that it was based on several assumptions:

1. The power to change teacher behavior is inherent in my role as principal.
2. Teachers are all, in some way, "broken" and need "fixing." My job is to repair and improve (somewhat like bringing in a car for a brake job).
3. Clinical supervision is the model for our evaluation system. This, done well, requires multiple observations and a *coaching* relationship—not an evaluative one.
4. Because a small minority of teachers could be considered "incompetent," the system of remediation is used for all.
5. The ranking of teachers as *Excellent, Satisfactory,* and *Unsatisfactory* in some way relates to improved instruction.

Personally, I subscribed to none of these beliefs.

A change was needed; yet, because the evaluation system had been negotiated between the teachers' union and district officials, it was imperative that any modifications of the given procedure stay within the negotiated parameters. Our challenge was to bend, without breaking, the existing teacher evaluation system.

Were teachers ready to try something different? I decided to ask them.

Early in the school year, I met with teachers who were to be evaluated that year. We addressed some basic questions: Did the "yellow tablet" system improve their teaching? Could the many hours expended in our current evaluation system be used more creatively? Was it possible to devise a new and worthwhile system within given parameters?

The teachers were amazingly candid. Their response was unanimous. They, too, felt we could "massage" the process, use our time more advantageously, and learn more about instruction.

A Giant Step Forward

The ball was in their court. The improvement of instruction belonged to them, as, in fact, it always had. By acknowledging this premise, we allowed the power of action to pass to the professional staff. We left that meeting committed to a new system in which the letter of the law had been preserved, and that which had value was salvaged. We all agreed on the following:

Excerpted from Joanne Rooney. 1993. "Teacher Evaluation: No More "Super"vision," *Educational Leadership* (51)2, 43–44.

Appendix 12–1 *(Continued)*

- This initial planning meeting would be called the "pre" conference. Previous policy did not specify that this initial conference had to be done on an individual basis. This decision itself saved time.
- All of my visits were designated as "formal." As there was no definition of "formal" in the Teacher Evaluation Handbook, we defined it to mean any and all visits. I promised to be in classrooms more often, not less.
- In lieu of my formal observation, teachers agreed to visit one another. In some cases, teachers paired up; others decided to work with two others. The speech pathologist and music teacher decided to visit their counterparts in other schools—something they had never had the opportunity to do.
- I volunteered to substitute for the teachers when they were observing. (All thought this was an excellent use of my time!) Being back in the classroom would also give me a fresh insight into their teaching.
- The "visiting" teachers would meet. I would be present, thus fulfilling the requirement for a "post" conference. I would facilitate the conversation between the two teachers, asking thoughtful questions and staying away from any evaluative remarks.
- We would repeat the procedure during the second semester, when teachers could observe the same person or choose another.
- The final conference would be maintained. We felt strongly that principal and teacher needed to talk—one on one—at some point.
- Any teacher who preferred the "old" system was free to stay with it. None did.
- We would evaluate this plan at the end of the year, asking if any changes needed to be made or if we wanted to go back to the old system.

The year went well. Teachers gained many insights into one another's teaching and became thoroughly immersed in discussing instruction. And we took a giant step toward working together.

A Learning Experience
We are in year two of our new procedure, and, as with any change of this sort, we are learning more than we expected:

- Barriers between teachers and classrooms are breaking down. In some instances, teachers had taught next to each other for years, yet this was their first chance to actually see one another in action. Many want to return and see more.
- Peer coaching, long accepted as an effective way for teachers to improve instruction, is becoming the norm.
- Individual differences in teachers are respected. Some, a bit uncertain about teaching in front of someone else, chose their friends as partners. Others reviewed the lesson as though they now had the yellow tablet, making suggestions for improvement.

Appendix 12–1 *(Continued)*

Teachers are more tolerant of one another, and of me, as we sometimes stumble through this learning process.

- The spirited exchange of the post-conference often continues long after the formal time is over. Each visit and conference is very different, but all agree that we are learning. Many plan to visit again—to observe, learn, and discuss.
- When we subsequently planned an inclusion program for special education students, teachers devised a col-teaching model. Not only have classroom doors been unbolted, but teachers' minds have opened more widely, too.

That our system of teacher evaluation is currently in place does not limit contact with teachers. Concerns can be expressed—and are—if they are productive for kids and do not demean those who struggle each day to do their very best for kids. However, I have found that support and encouragement have much more effect than criticism—however thinly veiled under the guise of supervision.

What happens to the teacher who needs help? Who is incompetent? Who truly has much to improve in teaching? The matter should be pursued diligently, but we principals work with few teachers who are so incompetent that they could be terminated. Nevertheless, our evaluation systems are technically based on the process through which incompetent teachers can be dismissed.

What has changed in our system—more than anything else—is the concept of the principal. I am no longer the one responsible for a teacher's behavior. Teachers are now responsible for their own professional growth—both individually and as a group.

Principals are overwhelmed with the job of leading schools. To think that we also have some kind of "super"vision is simply ludicrous. Teachers are, and should be, the instructional leaders in our schools. We must rely on the collective expertise of the staff to bring our schools into the 21st century.

C h a p t e r *13*

Motivation, Commitment, and the Teacher's Workplace

Much is known about how to arrange job dimensions and work conditions within schools so that teachers are more personally satisfied and are inspired to work harder and smarter on behalf of teaching and learning. Few topics are more important. When high motivation and strong commitment are absent, teachers are likely to be connected to their jobs on a "fair day's work for a fair day's pay" basis (Sergiovanni, 1968). Instead of giving their best, teachers emphasize meeting basic work requirements in exchange for material and other extrinsic benefits. Should teachers become dissatisfied, their performance is likely to fall below even this fair day's work level (Brayfield and Crockett, 1955; Vroom, 1964). Should teachers experience loss of meaning and significance with what they are doing, they are likely to become detached, even alienated, from their jobs (Argyris, 1957).

Despite what is known about how to improve teacher motivation and commitment and the links between such improvement and effective schooling, this knowledge base does not inform policy development and administrative practice very much. State and local policy makers, for example, frequently mandate changes in school organizational patterns, curriculum, and teacher evaluation in ways that contradict the motivation research. Although well intended, these policy initiatives can actually inhibit—even lower— teacher motivation and commitment, with predictable effects on effective schooling.

Problems and Contradictions in Policy and Practice

Two examples of policies and practice that contradict what motivation research tells us are examined in this section: mandating and implementing highly structured, prescriptive, and standardized curriculum and teaching formats that result in increasing bureaucracy in the classroom; and school organizational patterns that encourage isolation, privatism, and lack of social interaction among teachers.

249

Bureaucracy in the Classroom

Exhibit 13–1 contains the "Quality of Work Life in Teaching," scale that is adapted from a more general one developed by Marshall Sashkin and Joseph J. Lengerman (Pfeiffer and Goodstein, 1984). The scale is designed to assess perceptions of job conditions in one's work setting. If you are a teacher, please respond to the questions following the directions provided. If you are a principal, respond in the way you think the teachers in your school would respond.

Response patterns indicate the extent to which one perceives her or his job to be growth-oriented on a number of dimensions considered important by job-enrichment theorists and researchers. Later in this chapter the instrument will be scored, and response patterns will be examined as the concept of job enrichment is discussed.

The instrument can also be used to assess the extent to which one's job is bureaucratized. Responses to items 1, 3, 4, 6, 8, 11, and 24 hint at the extent to which the teaching job you describe is bureaucratic. The more prevalent the job characteristics described in the items, the more bureaucratic that job is likely to be.

It is generally assumed that teaching is a profession, although perhaps a fledgling one. Professionals and bureaucrats operate quite differently at work. The work of bureaucrats is programmed for them by their work system. The work of professionals emerges from an interaction between available professional knowledge and individual client needs. Webster, for example, describes a bureaucrat as "a government official following a narrow, rigid, formal routine." In contrast, professionals are assumed to command a body of knowledge enabling them to make informed judgments in response to unique situations and individual client needs. Essential to professionalism is sufficient discretion for professionals to use informed judgment as they practice.

In recent years there has been a trend toward greater centralization in deciding what will be taught in schools: when, with what materials, to whom, and for how long. During the 1970s, approximately two-thirds of the states enacted policies that sought to standardize and regulate teacher behavior (Darling-Hammond, 1984). States were even more active during the 1980s. There are many legitimate and desirable reasons for the state to be involved in matters of education, and many alternatives are open to states as they set standards, provide guidelines, promote equity, and ensure accountability. However, the problem lies in how far the state should go and the consequences of going too far. Providing leadership to local districts is an important responsibility. Legislating learning to the point of installing a system of bureaucratic teaching is quite another matter (Wise, 1979).

When curriculum and teaching decisions are programmed in a way that diminishes the influence of students and teacher in making teaching and learning decisions, then impersonal, standard, and formal learning goals dominate; teaching and learning become "teacher proof" and "student proof"; instructional leadership is discouraged as the teacher spends more time managing the learning process by monitoring, inspecting, regulating, and measuring; and commitment to teaching and learning by both teacher and students is lessened. For students, the consequences can be more emphasis on learnings and meanings defined by the school (Coombs, 1959; MacDonald, 1964) and less emphasis on intrinsic motivation for learning. Student learning is enhanced when teaching is characterized by a balanced emphasis on personally and school-defined meanings and

EXHIBIT 13–1   Quality of Work Life in Teaching

Directions: The following questions ask you to describe the objective characteristics of your job, as well as the activities of your co-workers and supervisor. Try not to use these questions to show how much you like or dislike your job; just be as factually correct as possible—imagine what an outside observer would say in response to these questions. Circle the appropriate letter.

(A)ll of the time, (M)ost of the time, (P)art of the time, (N)ever

1. Teachers in my school are allowed to make some decisions, but most of the decisions about their work have to be referred to their supervisor or are shaped by rules, curriculum requirements, or testing requirements. A   M   P   N

2. Teachers in my job normally move on to better jobs as a direct result of the opportunities my job offers. A   M   P   N

3. Teachers in my school are required to produce or cover a specific amount of work each day or each week. A   M   P   N

4. Teachers in my school perform tasks that are repetitive in nature. A   M   P   N

5. My work requires me to coordinate regularly with other teachers. A   M   P   N

6. Teachers in my school have a great deal of control over their work activities. A   M   P   N

7. Teachers in my job have the opportunity to learn new skills in the course of their work. A   M   P   N

8. Teachers in my school must work according to a fixed schedule; it is not possible to let the work go for a time and then catch up on it later. A   M   P   N

9. Teachers in my job are required to follow certain procedures in doing their work that they wouldn't choose if it were up to them. A   M   P   N

10. Teachers in my position work alone, on their teaching, with little or no contact with other teachers. A   M   P   N

11. When they encounter problems in their teaching, teachers in my school must refer these problems to their supervisor; they cannot take action on their own. A   M   P   N

12. My work requires me to learn new methods in order to keep up with changes and new developments. A   M   P   N

13. Teachers in my position must work very rapidly. A   M   P   N

14. My work involves completing a "whole" task. A   M   P   N

15. Teachers in my position are able to help out one another as they teach. A   M   P   N

16. My principal acts on some of the suggestions of teachers in my school. A   M   P   N

17. Teachers in my position are encouraged to try out methods of their own when teaching. A   M   P   N

18. Teachers in my position have considerable control over the pace or scheduling of work. A   M   P   N

19. Jobs at my level fail to bring out the best abilities of teachers because they are designed too simply. A   M   P   N

Continued

EXHIBIT 13–1   *(Continued)*

20. Teachers in my position must interact with other teachers as they teach.   A   M   P   N

21. Teachers at my level can make their own decisions without checking with anyone else or without consulting approved teaching and curriculum requirements.   A   M   P   N

22. Teachers at my level have the opportunity to learn about the teaching that is occurring at other grade levels and in other departments.   A   M   P   N

23. My work must be completed on a set schedule.   A   M   P   N

24. Teachers in my position perform the same series of tasks all day.   A   M   P   N

25. My work requires a great deal of contact with other teachers.   A   M   P   N

Adapted from J. W. Pfeiffer & L. D. Goodstein, *The 1984 Annual: Developing Human Resources,* San Diego, CA: Pfeiffer & Company, 1984. Used with permission. Modeled after a more general job-enrichment instrument developed by Marshall Sashkin and Joseph J. Longeman entitled "Quality of Work Life Scale."

learning outcomes and on students being intrinsically motivated to learn. These characteristics are not encouraged by bureaucratic teaching.

Teachers as "Origins" and "Pawns"

What are the consequences of legislated learning and bureaucratic teaching on motivation and commitment of teachers? Is there a link between teacher motivation and commitment and school effectiveness In successful schools, teachers are more committed, are harder workers, are more loyal to the school, and are more satisfied with their jobs. The research on motivation to work (Hackman and Oldham, 1980; Herzberg, 1966; Peters and Waterman, 1982) suggests that these highly motivating conditions are present when teachers:

- Find their work lives to be *meaningful,* purposeful, sensible, and significant, and when they view the work itself as being worthwhile and important.
- Have reasonable *control over their work activities* and affairs and are able to exert reasonable influence over work events and circumstances.
- Experience *personal responsibility* for the work and are personally accountable for outcomes.

Meaningfulness, control, and personal responsibility are attributes of teachers functioning as "Origins" rather than as "Pawns." According to De Charms (1968), "An Origin is a person who perceives his behavior as determined by his own choosing: a Pawn is a person who perceives his behavior as determined by external forces beyond his control." He continues:

> An Origin has a strong feeling of personal causation, a feeling that the locus for causation of effects in his environment lies within himself. . . . A Pawn has a

feeling that causal forces beyond his control, or personal forces residing within others, or in the physical environment determine his behavior. This constitutes a strong feeling of powerlessness or ineffectiveness. (274)

Personal causation is an important dimension of motivation. People strive to influence the events and situations of their environment, to be Origins of their own behavior.

Legislated learning and bureaucratic teaching threaten personal causation by creating work conditions more associated with Pawn feelings and behavior. In referring to Pawn feelings and behavior among teachers, the economist and Nobel laureate Theodore Schultz (1982) states:

Most of these attitudes of school teachers should have been anticipated in view of the way schools are organized and administered. The curriculum is not for them to decide; nor is the content of the course to be taught and the plans to be followed. . . . In assessing the performance of teachers, it is a dictum of economics that incentives matter. School teachers are responding to the much circumscribed opportunities open to them. They are not robots but human agents who perceive, interpret, and act in accordance with the worthwhile options available. (43)

There is a paradox at play here. On the one hand, clear mandates, mission statements, goals and purposes, and high achievement expectations for teachers provide them with a needed sense of direction and clear signal of what is important and significant. This realization was an important leadership theme of earlier chapters, which discussed the concepts of purposing and symbolic and cultural aspects of leadership. On the other hand, if such mandates are described and prescribed in such detail that teachers come to feel and behave like Pawns rather than Origins, problems in motivation arise. Mandates that provide direction, define meaning, and promote significance in one's work are motivating and contribute to building commitment. Mandates that reduce the decision-making prerogatives of teachers and make teaching "teacher-proof" discourage motivation and contribute to detachment, even alienation, rather than to commitment.

Principals are responsible for monitoring this delicate balance by ensuring that mandates are sensibly interpreted and articulated into administrative, supervisory, and teaching practices that promote Origin feelings and behaviors among teachers. They must ask whether interpretation and implementing decisions will promote professionalism or bureaucracy in teaching. Responsive to unique situations, professionals take their cues from the problems they face and the students they serve. They draw on the wealth of knowledge and technology available to them as they create professional knowledge in use in response to student needs. Bureaucrats, by contrast, are not driven by student problems but by the technology itself. They are appliers of rules, regulators of formats, direction followers, and managerial implementers. They strive for a one-best-way to treat all cases, and, pursuing standard outcomes, they apply formal procedures in standardized ways. It is in this sense that legislated learning and bureaucratic teaching encourage Pawn feelings and behaviors among teachers and students, contributing to less effective teaching and learning. Legislated learning and bureaucratic teaching are related to teacher job dissatisfaction and to teacher motivation to work. Appendix 13–1 contains excerpts from a Rand Corporation report on the problem of teacher job dissatisfaction. Many of the identified factors contributing to dissatisfaction can be attributed to increased bureaucracy in teaching.

In bureaucratic schools even the best of intentions are often displaced by other intentions. This displacement occurs without people being aware of what is going on. Rules, procedures, and processes, for example, that are originally devised to help the school run better, to help teachers teach better, and to help students learn better become ends in themselves.

Teachers are particularly vulnerable to goal displacement. Faced with a fast-paced and tight schedule, a prescribed curriculum, a list of student behavior rules and consequences that must be implemented, a universal grading policy, and other "rules" to follow, these frameworks become ends in themselves, displacing such ends as caring for students and doing one's best to teach them well. Soon teachers become transformed from skilled and caring teachers to expert deliverers of instruction to detached clients.

Bruce Bimber (1993) believes that the transformation from caring to bureaucratic teacher is a natural response to how schools are organized and operated. He differentiates between "functional" rationality and "substantial" rationality to show how this transformation happens.

> When workers strive to carry out procedures and adhere closely to rules, they are exercising functional rationality: They use their judgment and skills to adhere to the rules to perform a well-defined function. This is rational because it is the behavior for which they are best rewarded. On the other hand, when workers use their judgment and skills to devise solutions to client problems on their own, when they judge for themselves what would be best in a given situation, they are exercising substantial rationality: Rather than follow rules they make substantial decisions about their work. . . . functional and substantial rationality do not arise because of personality traits or individual's temperaments, but from the system of rewards and sanctions that structures the work environment. (29)

If Bimber's analysis is correct, then it appears that much of what we do in schools first victimizes our teachers and then victimizes our students.

Isolation in Teaching

Teaching can be aptly described as a lonely profession. Typically teachers work alone. As a result, no one else in the school knows what they are doing or how well they are doing it (Bidwell, 1975; Lortie, 1975; Waller, 1932). Related to isolation in teaching are tendencies to encourage the value of privatism and the consequences of this value on social interaction. Privatism forces teachers to look inward, discourages sharing, and encourages competition; furthermore, it promotes feelings of inadequacy and insecurity. Lack of social interaction deprives teachers of opportunities to help and seek help from others, to give feedback, and to get feedback from others—both essential ingredients in most motivation to work models. These conditions not only contradict what is known about sound management practices, but also impede professional growth and effective teaching. Despite the debilitating effects of isolation in teaching, schools persist in organizational structures and supervisory and evaluation practices that encourage these conditions. Let's examine further the effects of isolation, privatism, and lack of social interaction in teaching.

Susan Rosenholtz (1984) identifies isolation as one of the major impediments to school improvement. Her recent review of the research on this topic leads to the following conclusions:

> *In isolated settings, teachers come to believe that they alone are responsible for running their classrooms and that to seek advice or assistance from their colleagues constitutes an open admission of incompetence.*
>
> *Teacher isolation is perhaps the greatest impediment to learning to teach, or to improving one's existing skills, because most learning by necessity occurs through trial and error. One alarming consequence of trial and error learning is that teachers' limits for potential growth depend heavily on their own personal ability to detect problems and to discern possible solutions.*
>
> *Another consequence is that teachers in isolated settings have few role models of good teaching to emulate. As a matter of fact, it is more typical of teachers in isolated settings to use role models that they recall from their own student days than to seek models of teaching excellence among their contemporaries.*
>
> *. . . in interpreting and formulating solutions to classroom problems, teachers realize little benefit from the advice, experience, or expertise of colleagues with whom they work. That is, any pre-existing practical knowledge is seldom passed along to new recruits, who must then, of their own accord, sink or swim,*
>
> *For teachers restricted to trial-and-error learning then, there is a limit to their capacity to grow in the absence of others' professional knowledge. . . . Teachers teach their prime after about four or five years and thereafter, perhaps because of little teaching input, their effectiveness with students actually begins to decline. (4–6)*

Lieberman and Miller (1984) point out that being private means not sharing experiences about teaching, classes, students, and learning. By being private, teachers forfeit the opportunity to share their successes with colleagues but gain the security of not having to disclose shortcomings. Having worked in isolation and not having accurate knowledge of the teaching of others, teachers tend to assume that they are not measuring up to colleagues.

Isolation and privatism contribute to fewer social interaction opportunities among teachers. The three conditions combine to force teachers to look inward for sources of feedback and rewards. Indeed, teachers rely almost exclusively on interactions with students as sources of satisfaction in teaching (Lortie, 1975; Waller, 1932). The question, though, is whether the satisfaction derived from student social interaction is enough to provide the kind of motivation and commitment needed for effective schooling. How does social interaction with adults fit into the picture?

Social interaction is a key ingredient in the supervisory process. Contrary to myth, teachers report increases in satisfaction as supervision increases moderately (Dornbush and Scott, 1975). Moderate increases in supervision seem also to be related to increases in teaching effectiveness. From his research, Natriello (1984) concludes: "Teachers who report more frequent evaluation activities also report being markedly more effective in teaching tasks" (592). Social interaction, as a form of feedback about one's teaching, is a contributor to these findings. Social interaction is also the medium by which recognition is given and received. Furthermore, social interaction seems to be a key factor in evoking the achievement, power-influence, and affiliation motives of persons at work and is an integral part of most motivation-to-work and job-enrichment models emerging from the research (Hackman and Oldham, 1980).

Many experts believe that social interaction among teachers, and between teachers and supervisors, is essential for promoting and institutionalizing change in schools and is related as well to successful staff-development efforts. With respect to institutionalizing changes, Clark, Lotto, and Astuto (1984) point out that the focus of staff development must reach beyond the development of new teaching skills to the development of new concepts and behaviors within a supportive school climate. Their review of the research on effective school improvement efforts leads them to conclude that interaction among teachers, and between teachers and administrators, provides the needed opportunities for technical and psychological support that enhances effective implementation. "Teachers report that they learn best from other teachers. Teacher-teacher interactions provide for technical and psychological support as well as personal reinforcement" (Clark, Lotto, and Astuto, 1984:58). Although more than social interaction opportunities may be necessary for school improvement efforts to be successful, success will not be likely without social interaction. Informal professional development efforts are also linked to social interaction among teachers. When provided with opportunity and encouragement, teachers learn a great deal from one another and trust one another as sources of new ideas and as sharers of problems they face (Glatthorn, 1984; Keenan, 1974).

Appendix 13–2, "Studying the Climate of Your School," provides a brief overview of the concept of school climate and how this climate can be assessed. The appendix relies on the work of Rensis Likert, a pioneer in the organizational climate literature.

Legislated learning and bureaucratic teaching, isolation in the work place, the tradition of privatism, and lack of social interaction are urgent problems that principals and their faculties must address as they work to improve the quality of work life in schools, encourage professional development, increase teacher motivation and commitment, and build professional community in our schools. Community, Milbrey McLaughlin and Joan Talbert (Bradley, 1993:7) conclude, is not only good for teachers, but good for students as well. Their research reveals that teachers who belong to learning communities have more positive views of students and are more successful in changing their practice for the better.

Using Motivation Theory and Research to Inform Practice

In Chapter 6 it was pointed out that leadership practice might usefully be understood through use of the metaphor "developmental stages." Four stages were discussed: leadership by bartering, building, bonding, and binding. Virtually all the available research on motivation addresses the first two stages, leadership by bartering and building. Leadership by bartering makes the assumption that the interests of leaders and those being led are different, and, therefore, a bargain needs to be struck whereby the leader gives to the led something they want in return for their compliance with the leader's wishes. For the most part, the trading that takes place in leadership by bartering focuses on extrinsic factors. Tradeoffs occur in leadership by building as well, although they tend to address higher-order need factors and intrinsic motives of the led.

These ideas are captured by the theorizing of the psychologist Abraham Maslow (1943) and by the research of Frederick Herzberg (1966). These experts make the assumption that people have many needs and that the needs stem from at least two human desires—avoidance of pain, hardship, and difficulty; and the desire for growth and development in an effort to realize one's potential (e.g., Herzberg, 1966:56). Perhaps most well known is the need classification scheme proposed by Maslow (1943). He proposed that human needs could be classified into five broad categories: physiological, security-safety, social-belonging, esteem, and self-actualization. Key to Maslow's theory is that the need categories are arranged in a hierarchy of prepotency, with individual behavior motivated to satisfy the need most important at the time. Furthermore, according to theory, the strength of this need depends on its position in the hierarchy and the extent to which lower-order needs are met or satiated. The press from esteem needs, for example, will not be very great for individuals whose security needs are not met. Maslow's ideas form much of the basis for the material and psychological bartering that takes place between leader and led as each seeks an accommodation of their needs. The leader needs to get work done in a certain way. The led need to get certain needs met. One is traded for the other.

Maslow's ideas are helpful, but have limitations. When applied in the management literature, an assumption is often made that some of the needs in his theory are more valued than others. Esteem, autonomy, and self-actualization, for example, are considered to be better than belonging. Indeed, belonging needs are sometimes considered to be a nuisance that must be met to get a person motivated at a higher level. The higher the level, the more motivated a person will be and the more productive that person will be. This is spurious thinking, especially when applied to young people. To most students, belonging is the most important need.

Another problem is that Maslow's needs are typically viewed as being universally applicable, however, needs are culturally determined. Belonging may be less valued in one culture and more valued in another. The same thing is true of achievement and the other needs in Maslow's formulation.

The work of Frederick Herzberg (1966) and his colleagues (Herzberg, Mausner, and Snyderman, 1959) provides a more sophisticated set of ideas for engaging in this kind of bartering. Herzberg's approach, often referred to as *two-factor theory* is based on the premise that job characteristics contributing to work motivation are different from those contributing to work dissatisfaction. He called the first set of factors *motivators* and the second *hygienic.* According to the theory, if hygienic factors are not attended to by principals, poor work hygiene will occur, with corresponding feelings of teacher job dissatisfaction and poor performance. However, tending to these factors and eliminating job dissatisfaction will not result in increased teacher commitment or job performance. The motivation factors that contributed to increased teacher performance when present seemed not to result in job dissatisfaction or work performance that was below par when absent. According to the theory, if principals do not attend to the motivation factors, teachers will not be motivated to work, but they will not be dissatisfied either. They will perform up to a certain level considered satisfactory, but will make little or no effort to exceed this level (Sergiovanni, 1966).

The factors identified by Herzberg and his associates as being related to work hygiene included interpersonal relationships with students, teachers, and supervisors; quality of supervision; policy and administration; working conditions; and personal life. The factors related to work motivation were achievement, recognition, the work itself, responsibility, and advancement.

The two-factor theory suggests that job satisfaction and motivation to work are related to two decision possibilities for teachers: participation and performance (Sergiovanni, 1968). The decision to participate in one's job is associated with the fair day's work concept. When participating, one takes a job and does all that is necessary to meet minimum commitments; in return, one receives "fair pay" in the form of salary, benefits, social acceptance, courteous and thoughtful treatment, and reasonable supervision. Because these dimensions are *expected* as part of fair pay, they tend not to motivate a person to go beyond. The decision to perform, however, results in exceeding the fair day's work for a fair day's pay contract. This decision is voluntary because all that school districts can require from teachers is fair work. Rewards associated with the fair day's work are for the most part extrinsic, focusing on the conditions of work. Rewards associated with the performance investment tend to be more intrinsic (e.g., recognition, achievement, feelings of competence, exciting and challenging work, interesting and meaningful work).

Principals need to be concerned with both extrinsic and intrinsic rewards. Schools cannot function adequately unless the participation investment is made and continued by teachers. However, schools cannot excel unless the majority of teachers make the performance investment as well. The two-factor theory can provide principals with a cognitive map for ensuring that administrative, organizational, curricular, and teaching practices provide for both levels of work investment by teachers. Yet, a map is different than a recipe, not everything will work for everyone. Much trial and error will be necessary as principals practice leadership by bartering.

The Potential of Work Itself as a Motivator

A major problem with leadership by bartering is that it relies heavily on making deals. At the heart of the deals are bureaucratic and psychological authority as the means to obtain compliance. Bureaucratic authority promises sanctions and punishments if compliance is not forthcoming. Psychological authority gives rewards in exchange for compliance. Both forms of authority are limited in two ways. First, they lead to calculated involvement. A person's compliance is contingent on either the avoidance of penalties or the obtaining of rewards. When neither is forthcoming, continued compliance is often risky and sometimes nonexistent.

Both rewards and penalties are based on the economic concept of utility function. Human beings are driven by a desire to maximize their self-interests, and, thus, continually calculate the costs and benefits of all their options, choosing the course of action that either makes them a winner or keeps them from losing. In Chapter 3 it was pointed out that the concept of utility function is now being successfully challenged by a new economics that does not dismiss the importance of self-interest but gives equal weight to emotions and values—to expressive and moral authority as motivators (Etzioni, 1988). Leadership by bartering is based on the principle that "what gets rewarded gets done." Leadership by building, by contrast, is based on the principle "what *is* rewarding gets done." Here the emphasis is on intrinsic returns and expressive reasons for involvement in one's work. To these, Etzioni would add the principle "what is right and good gets done." He has in mind the addition of moral authority as a means to understand why people choose to do something and to do it well.

Flow Theory

Mihaly Csikszentmihalyi (1990) proposes *flow theory* as a way to understand the potential of work itself as a source of motivation. He studied highly accomplished and motivated experts (e.g., rock climbers, composers, surgeons, authors) in a number of different fields. Although the work of these experts differed, each experienced a certain flow that Csikszentmihalyi attributes to intrinsic motivation. Flow is characterized by opportunity for action; the merging of action and awareness; focused attention characterized by concentration, narrowing of consciousness, and being absorbed in what one is doing; loss of self-consciousness as one works; clarity of goals and norms; direct and immediate feedback; and feelings of competence and of being in control of what one does. He concludes that the satisfaction derived from this total absorption in one's work provides a powerful source of motivation.

Csikszentmihalyi is convinced that experiencing flow can be a very common experience under the right conditions. One must first be faced by a *challenge* that is not too great for the *skills* needed to meet it, but great enough for a person to meet the challenge with enjoyment on the one hand and to grow in competence, confidence, and/or skill on the other. Should one's skills be greater than the challenge, then boredom is likely to result. One can speculate, for example, that when teachers are bored with their work their available skills may not be used fully enough. Some experts maintain that this is the likely consequence of teachers who are subjected to curriculum and supervisory mandates that specify unduly what it is they must do and how. Such specification can lead to work simplification and the subsequent "de-skilling" of teachers (McNeil, 1987).

Sometimes teachers are faced with levels of challenge that far exceed their skills, with the result being feelings of anxiety. When neither level of challenge nor level of skill is very high, the response is likely to be one of apathy, another version of the de-skilling hypothesis. It might be useful at this point to inventory one's own personal experience with teachers and with students. Compare occasions when they responded to work with apathy, boredom, anxiety, or total absorption (flow). What are the mixes of challenge and skills levels that seemed to contribute to these states?

The message of flow theory for principals is that maintaining the right balance between level of skill and level of challenge makes good motivational sense. When challenge is up, principals need to provide the necessary support on the skill dimension to avoid frustration and fear of failure. In areas where teacher skill levels are high, challenging opportunities will need to be provided. Successful matching of challenge and skill, according to the theory, is likely to result in flow—total absorption in one's work.

Job-Enrichment Theory

Another window through which one might view the potential of the work itself to motivate is provided by the research of Richard Hackman and Greg Oldham (1980). These scholars have developed a theory of job enrichment—the Job Characteristics model—that has been successfully applied in practice. Key to the model is the presence of three psychological states found to be critical in determining a person's work motivation and job satisfaction:

- *Experience meaningfulness,* which is defined as the extent to which an individual perceives her or his work as being worthwhile or important by some system of self-accepted values
- *Experience responsibility,* which is defined by the extent to which a person believes that she or he is personally accountable for the outcomes of efforts
- *Knowledge of results,* which is defined as the extent to which a person is able to determine, on a fairly regular basis, whether or not performance is satisfactory and efforts lead to outcomes. (Hackman et al., 1975:57)

According to the Job Characteristics model, when these psychological states are experienced, one feels good and performs better—internal work motivation occurs. Internal work motivation means how much an individual experiences positive feelings from effective performance. Hackman and Oldham have found that the content of one's job is an important critical determiner of internal work motivation. Furthermore, when certain characteristics of one's job are improved or enhanced, internal work motivation can be increased. They found, for example, that experiencing meaningfulness is enhanced by jobs characterized by skill variety, task identity, and task significance. Autonomy was the job characteristic related to experiencing responsibility, and feedback was related to knowledge of results.

The Job Characteristics model suggests that in teaching, jobs that require: (1) different activities in carrying out the work and the use of a variety of teacher talents and skills (skill variety); (2) teachers to engage in tasks identified as whole and comprising identifiable pieces of work (task identity); (3) teachers to have substantial and significant impact on the lives or work of other people (task significance); (4) substantial freedom, independence, and direction be provided to teachers in scheduling work and in deciding classroom organizational and instructional procedures (autonomy); and (5) teachers be provided with direct, clear information about the effects of their performance (feedback) are likely to evoke the psychological states of meaningfulness, responsibility, and knowledge of results. Hackman and Oldham's research reveals that these conditions result in high work motivation, high-quality performance, high job satisfaction, and low absenteeism among teachers.

Figure 13–1 illustrates the Job Characteristics model. In addition to job dimensions, psychological states, and personal and work outcomes, an "implementing concepts" panel is included. Implementing concepts are suggestions the researchers offer to principals

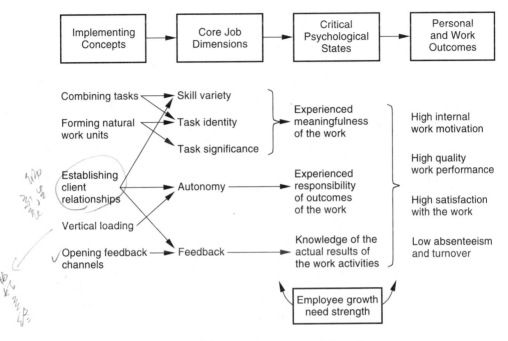

FIGURE 13–1   Job Enrichment Concepts and Practices

From J. R. Hackman, G. Oldham, R. Johnson, and K. Purdy, "A New Strategy for Job Enrichment," © 1975 by The Regents of the University of California. Reprinted from *California Management Review*, Vol. XVII, no. 4, p. 64, by permission of The Regents.

interested in building more of the job dimensions into the work of the school. The principle of combining tasks, for example, suggests that as much as possible, fractionalized aspects of teaching should be put together into larger, more holistic modules. Comprehensive curriculum strategies, interdisciplinary teaching approaches, and team-group teaching modes all contribute to the combining of teaching and curriculum tasks. Combining teaching tasks increases not only skill variety for teachers, but their identification with the work as well.

Although establishing close relationships with students ("clients") is a natural part of teaching and learning, some patterns of school organization and teaching encourage impersonal relationships between teachers and students. Forming "natural work units" points to the importance of thinking in community terms. The intent of such units would be to increase one's sense of ownership and continuing responsibility for identifiable aspects of the work by more closely connecting people to each and by connecting them more closely to their work. The self-contained elementary school classroom comes closer to this concept than does the departmentalized and quick-moving secondary school teaching schedule. But even in the elementary setting, the building of teaching teams that plan and work together and whose members share a common responsibility for students is often lacking. "Vertical loading" suggests strategies that bring together actual teaching and planning to teach. Providing teachers with more control over schedules, work methods, evaluation, and even the training and supervision of less experienced teachers might be examples of vertical loading.

"Opening feedback channels" is another way of saying that the more principals are able to let teachers know how well they are doing, the more highly motivated they will be. Indeed, motivation and satisfaction are neglected benefits of teacher-evaluation supervisory programs designed to provide teachers with helpful feedback. Examples of helpful programs would be those that include clinical supervision, peer supervision, target settings, and similar formats. Principals should strive to create ways in which feedback to teachers occurs naturally from their day-to-day activities and from working closely with colleagues.

The Job Characteristics model suggests that virtually every decision principals make about schooling, classroom organization, curriculum development and implementation, selection of materials, and teaching itself has implications for building motivation and commitment of teachers. Principals need to assess the consequences of a particular decision on promoting job-enrichment opportunities for teachers.

Friendship opportunities and opportunities to work with others are two other dimensions identified in the Job Characteristics model (Sashkin and Morris, 1984). "Friendship opportunities" refers to the extent to which the work setting provides for the development of close contacts among teachers and the development of friendly patterns of interaction. "Working with others" refers to the extent to which the accomplishment of tasks requires that teachers interact with other teachers in order to complete the work successfully. These dimensions seem related to the extent to which workers are involved in their jobs, experience satisfaction, and report improvements in work quality (Sashkin and Morris, 1984).

In summary, the Job Characteristics model provides principals with a conceptual framework allowing them to make informed decisions about the nature and structure of the work of teaching to help teachers feel that their job is meaningful, to enable them to learn the actual outcomes of their efforts, to provide them with feelings of control and responsibility for results, and to help them become part of a social unit. These conditions are related to high intrinsic work motivation, increases in quality performance, high job satisfaction, and lower absence and turnover rates.

Appendix 13–3 contains a key that allows you to score your responses to the Quality of Work Life in Teaching form. Please score by following the directions provided. Note that five subscores are provided, each corresponding to an important dimension of most job-enrichment models. With the exception of work speed and routine, the higher the score, the more enriched is the job, the greater are the possibilities for increased motivation and commitment, and the more likely that connections between and among people will embody community.

Women as a Special Case

Much of the available motivation literature is subject to male bias, thus, the accompanying prescriptions for practice may not apply to women. The problem, according to Shakeshaft (1987), is androcentrism, defined as "the practice of viewing the world and shaping reality from a male perspective. . . . the elevation of the masculine to the level of the universal and the ideal and honoring of men and the male principle above women and female" (94). Maslow's theory, the two-factor theory, and the job enrichment theory, for example, give heavy emphasis to competition, the setting of task goals, individual achievement, the building of self-competence and self-esteem, individual autonomy, and self-actualization. Women, by contrast, give emphasis to such themes as cooperation, intimacy, affiliation, the construction of interpersonal networks, and community building. In using teamwork as an example, Shakeshaft (1987) points out that men tend to view the concept in terms of goals, roles, and responsibilities. A team must first define what needs to be done and then allocate responsibilities to roles making clear not only what is expected, but how one person's niche fits that of others who comprise the team. The metaphor for team, in this context, is sport in the form of baseball, basketball, or football. For women, teamwork is not the parallel play of men, but the meshing of individual identities to create a new configuration and the bonding together of people in a common cause.

Key in applying the concepts from traditional motivation theory is redefining concept indicators. Achievement, for example, can mean the accumulation of a series of individual successes on the one hand or the successful constructing of a learning community on the other. Application of the motivation theory and research, therefore, should be idiosyncratic. If you want to know what motivates people start by asking them.

The Power of Beliefs

In this and other chapters, adding moral authority to bureaucratic and psychological authority was recommended. Doing so depends on schools being able to develop a set of shared values and beliefs that spells out who they are, what they want to accomplish, and how. Centers or covenants provide the basis for bonding people together as members of a learning community that knows why it exists and detail as well what the community owes its members and what its members in turn owe the community. This theme was at the heart of earlier discussions of leadership and school culture and will be returned to in the final chapter, "Administering as a Moral Craft."

Interpreted properly, the theory and research in the area of teacher motivation and commitment can be helpful. Often, policy mandates, administrative directives, and our own complacency in insisting on "business as usual" present conditions and practices at odds with this knowledge base. School practices, for example, too often encourage bureaucratic teaching, promote isolationism among teachers, encourage privatism, and discourage social interaction. These conditions are typically associated with decreases in teacher motivation and commitment. Effective teaching and learning and other school improvement efforts are enhanced as teachers work harder and smarter and as their commitment to the school and its success is increased. This gap between present practice and what we know represents a test of leadership for principals.

Even more challenging is the attempt to broaden present conceptions of the nature of human potential. Without dismissing the importance of self-interest, principals and faculties must give far more attention to expressive and moral reasons for determining courses of action. As expressive and moral authority gain acceptance as legitimate ways of working with teachers, attention will need to be given to applying these same ideas to students as well.

References

Argyris, Chris. 1957. *Personality and Organization.* New York: Harper & Row.

Bidwell, Charles E. 1975. "The School as a Formal Organization," in James O. March, Ed., *Handbook of Organizations,* 972–1022. Chicago: Rand McNally.

Bimber, Bruce. 1993. "School Decentralization: Lessons From the Study of Bureaucracy." Institute on Education and Training, Santa Monica, CA: The Rand Corporation.

Bradley, Ann. 1993. "By Asking Teachers About 'Context' of Work, Center Moves to Cutting Edge of Research," *Education Week,* March 31, p. 7.

Brayfield, A. H., and W. H. Crockett. 1955. "Employee Attitudes and Employee Performance," *Psychological Bulletin* 52(1), 415–422.

Clark, David L., Linda S. Lotto, and Terry A. Astuto. 1984. "Effective Schools and School Improvement: A Comparative Analysis of Two Lines of Inquiry," *Educational Administration Quarterly* 20(3), 41–68.

Coombs, Arthur W. 1959. "Personality Theory and Its Implication for Curriculum Development," in Alexander Frazier, Ed., *Learning More About Learning.* Washington, DC: Association for Supervision and Curriculum Development.

Csikszentmihalyi, Mihaly. 1990. *Flow: The Psychology of Optimal Experience.* New York: Harper & Row.

Darling-Hammond, Linda. 1984. *Beyond the Commission Reports: The Coming Crisis in Teaching.* Santa Monica, CA: The Rand Corporation.

De Charms, Richard. 1968. *Personal Causation.* New York: Academic Press.

Dornbush, S. M., and W. R. Scott. 1975. *Evaluation and the Exercise of Authority.* San Francisco: Jossey-Bass.

Etzioni, Amitai. 1988. *The Moral Dimension: Toward A New Economics.* New York: The Free Press.

Glatthorn, Allan A. 1984. *Differentiated Supervision.* Alexandria, VA: Association for Supervision and Curriculum Development.

Hackman, J. R., and G. R. Oldham. 1980. *Work Redesign.* Reading, MA: Addison-Wesley.

Hackman, J. R., G. Oldham, R. Johnson, and K. Purdy. 1975. "A New Strategy for Job Enrichment," *California Management Review* 17(4).

Herzberg, F. 1966. *Work and the Nature of Man.* New York: World Publishing.

Herzberg, F., B. Mausner, and B. Snyderman. 1959. *The Motivation to Work.* New York: Wiley.

Keenan, Charles. 1974. "Channels for Change: A Survey of Teachers in Chicago Elementary Schools." Doctoral dissertation. Urbana: Department of Educational Administration, University of Illinois.

Lieberman, Ann, and Lynne Miller. 1984. *Teachers, Their World, and Their Work.* Alexandria, VA: Association for Supervision and Curriculum Development.

Lortie, Dan. 1975. *School Teacher.* Chicago: The University of Chicago Press.

MacDonald, James. 1964. "An Image of Man: The Learner Himself," in Ronald R. Doll, Ed., *Individualizing Instruction.* Washington, DC: Association for Supervision and Curriculum Development.

Maslow, A. H. 1943. "A Theory of Human Motivation," *Psychological Review* 50(2), 370–396.

McNeil, Linda M. 1987. "Exit Voice and Community: Magnet Teachers Responses to Standardization," *Educational Policy* 1(1).

Natriello, Gary. 1984. "Teachers' Perceptions of the Frequency of Evaluation and Assessments of Their Effort and Effectiveness." *American Educational Research Journal,* 21(3), 579–595.

Peters, Thomas J., and Robert H. Waterman, Jr. 1982. *In Search of Excellence.* New York: Harper & Row.

Pfeiffer, J. William, and Leonard D. Goodstein. 1984. *The 1984 Annual: Developing Human Resources.* San Diego, CA: University Associates.

Rosenholtz, Susan J. 1984. "Political Myths about Educational Reform: Lessons from Research on Teaching." Paper prepared for the Education Commission of the States, Denver, CO.

Sashkin, Marshall, and William C. Morris, 1984. *Organizational Behavior Concepts and Experiences.* Reston, VA: The Reston Co.

Schultz, Theodore W. 1982. "Human Capital Approaches in Organizing and Paying for Education," in Walter McMahan and Terry G. Geste, Eds., *Financing Education: Overcoming Inefficiency and Inequity,* 36–51. Urbana: University of Illinois Press.

Sergiovanni, Thomas J. 1966. "Factors Which Affect Satisfaction and Dissatisfaction of Teachers," *Journal of Educational Administration* 5(1), 66–82.

Sergiovanni, Thomas J. 1968. "New Evidence on Teacher Morale: A Proposal for Staff Differentiation," *The North Central Association Quarterly* 62(3), 259–266.

Shakeshaft, Charol (1987). *Women in Educational Administration.* Beverly Hills, CA: Sage Publications.

Vroom, V. H. 1964. *Work and Motivation.* New York: Wiley.

Waller, Willard. 1932. *Sociology of Teaching.* New York: Wiley.

Wise, Arthur E. 1979. *Legislated Learning: The Bureaucratization of the American Classroom.* Berkeley: University of California Press.

Appendix 13–1 Factors Contributing to Dissatisfaction in Teaching

This appendix, excerpted from a report issued by the Rand Corporation and prepared by Linda Darling-Hammond,* describes factors contributing to dissatisfaction in teaching. To what extent are these the result of increases in legislated learning and bureaucratic teaching? The Rand report points out that teachers are feeling more like "Pawns" in an impersonal system of schooling that is increasingly beyond their control. The Rand report was published in 1984. How would today's teachers view the excerpt from the report that appears here? Would they say that things are better, about the same, or worse? If Darling-Hammond were writing today, would the problems she describes still be the same? If not, what new ones would be added?

Changes in schooling are needed to restore teachers to "Origin" status. How can two-factor and job-enrichment theory and research help in rethinking ways in which schools are organized and the ways in which work settings and conditions of teachers are arranged? What can school principals do to help improve the quality of work life for teachers? The Rand report excerpt begins below:

> For several decades, the National Education Association has polled several thousand teachers annually about their teaching conditions and views. One question asked in each poll is, if you could go back and start all over again, would you still become a teacher? Chart 1 shows the dramatic change in responses to that question over twenty years. Between 1971 and 1981 the proportion of respondents saying they would not teach again more than tripled, rising from about 10 percent to nearly 40 percent. Less than half of the present teaching force say they plan to continue teaching until retirement.[1]
>
> It is easy to summarize the factors that contribute to teacher dissatisfaction. Teachers feel that they lack support—physical support in terms of adequate facilities and materials; support services such as clerical help for typing, duplicating, and paperwork chores, and administrative support that would provide a school environment in which their work is valued and supported rather than obstructed by interruptions and a proliferation of non-teaching tasks. They see their ability to teach hampered by large class sizes and non-teaching duties. And they feel that they are not treated as professionals. They have limited input to decisions that critically affect their work environment, and they see few opportunities for professional growth.[2]

Let us translate these categories into more concrete terms. Imagine that you are a high-school English teacher. You have at least a master's degree (as do most teachers today) and you would like to impart to your students the joys of great literature and the

---

*Linda Darling-Hammond (1984). *Beyond the Commission Reports: The Coming Crisis in Teaching,* Santa Monica, CA: The Rand Corporation, 11–13.

[1]National Education Association, *Status of the American Public School Teacher,* 1980–81, 1982, 73–76.

[2]Ibid., pp. 76–78; National Education Association, *Nationwide Teacher Opinion Poll,* 1983, p. 9; American Federation of Teachers, *Schools as a Workplace: The Realities of Stress,* Vol. 1, 1983, 15–17.

Appendix 13–1   *(Continued)*

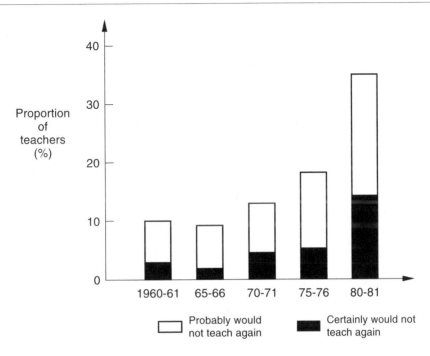

Chart 1

skills of effective communication. You have at your disposal a set of 100 textbooks for your 140 students. You cannot order additional books so you make copies of some plays and short stories, at your own expense, and you jockey with the 50 other teachers in your school for access to one of the two available typewriters so that you can produce other materials for your class. You stand in line after school to use the secretary's telephone to call parents of students who have been absent or are behind in their work.

You spend roughly 12 hours each week correcting papers, because you believe your students should write a theme each week. You feel guilty that this allows you to spend only 5 minutes per paper. You spend another 6 hours each week preparing for your five different sections, mostly writing up the behavioral objectives required by the system curriculum guide, which you find meaningless and even counterproductive to your goals for your students. You do all of this after school hours, because your one preparation period is devoted to preparing attendance forms, doing other administrative paperwork, and meeting with students who need extra help. Between classes, you monitor hallways and restrooms, supervise the lunch room, and track down truants.

You are frustrated that the districts new competency-based curriculum is forcing you to spend more and more of your time teaching students to answer multiple-choice questions about the mechanics of grammar. Meanwhile, your efforts to teach writing and critical thinking are discouraged, as they do not seem to fit with the district mandated curriculum and testing program. You have no input into decisions about curriculum,

Appendix 13–1   *(Continued)*

teaching methods, materials, or resource allocations. You will, of course, never get a promotion; nor will you have an opportunity to take on new responsibilities. You receive frequent feedback about public dissatisfaction with schools and teachers, but little reinforcement from administrators or parents that your work is appreciated. Sometimes you wonder whether your efforts are worth the $15,000 a year you earn for them.

This description is not an overdramatization. It reflects the modal conditions of teaching work in this country today. The importance of professional working conditions to teacher satisfaction and retention has recently been recognized in a number of studies at Rand and elsewhere. Conditions that undermine teacher efficacy, ie., the teacher's ability to do an effective job of teaching, are strongly related to teacher attrition. These conditions include lack of opportunity for professional discourse and decision making input; inadequate preparation and teaching time; and conflict with or lack of support from administrators.[3]

[3]See, for example, Linda Darling-Hammond and Arthur E. Wise, "Teaching Standards or Standardized Teaching?," *Educational Leadership,* October 1983, pp. 66–69; Susan J. Rosenholtz and Mark A. Smylie, *Teacher Compensation and Career Ladders: Policy Implications from Research,* Paper commissioned by the Tennessee General Assembly's Select Committee on Education, December 1983; D. W. Chapman and S. M. Hutcheson, "Attrition from Teaching Careers: A Discriminant Analysis," *American Educational Research Journal,* Vol. 19, 1982, pp. 93–105; M. D. Litt and D. C. Turk, *Stress, Dissatisfaction, and Intention to Leave Teaching in Experienced Public High School Teachers,* Paper presented at the annual meeting of the American Educational Research Association, Montreal, April 1983.

Appendix 13–2 Studying the Climate of Your School

The pioneering work of Rensis Likert and his colleagues at the Institute for Social Research, University of Michigan, from the late 1950s through the 1960s, placed the concept climate in the mainstream of management thought. This research introduced into practice the idea that principals and other school administrators needed to focus not only on "end results" indicators of effectiveness of their policies, actions, and decisions, but on the "mediating" indicators as well (Likert, 1961, 1967).

Mediating Variables

According to Likert's theory, school policies, standard operating procedures, and accompanying administrative actions and decisions do not influence school effectiveness and other end results variables directly. Instead, they influence how teachers, students, and others perceive and feel, the attitudes and values they share, the trust and support binding them together, and the degree to which they are motivated to work and are committed to school goals and purposes. It is these mediating indicators that in turn influence school effectiveness.

Initiating —> mediating —> school effectiveness variables

Likert reached these conclusions by studying the characteristics of more and less effective work groups and organizations. He found that differences in the mediating variables of these group and organization types followed consistent patterns. He was able to identify four distinct patterns of management: Systems 1, 2, 3, and 4. System 1 resembles a rigid bureaucracy and is characterized by little mutual confidence and trust among supervisors and workers, direct supervision, high control, centralized decision making, detailed rules and regulations and work operating procedures, top-down communications, and routine work regulation by inspection. System 4 reflects a commitment to the development and use of human resources and is characterized by trust, supportive relationships, goal clarity and commitment, autonomy with responsibility, group decision making, authority more closely linked with ability, team work, social interaction, and controls linked to agreed-upon goals and purposes. Systems 2 and 3 are at intermediate positions on this continuum. Although they represent a distinct improvement over the rigid bureaucratic management of System 1, they do not recognize human potential as fully as does System 4.

The basic features of Likert's theory are illustrated in Appendix Figure 13–1, "How Management Systems 1 and 4 Influence Mediating and School Effectiveness Variables." The principal's assumptions and resulting behavior with regard to leadership, control, organization, goals and purposes, and the motivation of teachers and students provide a specific pattern of management that can be described on a continuum from System 1 to 4. This management system elicits a predictable response from teachers at work that influences their motivation and performance. Teacher attitudes and behavior, it follows, have predictable consequences on school effectiveness. The effects of management systems 2 and 3 on mediating and school effectiveness variables would fall somewhere between the indicators provided in Appendix Figure 13–1.

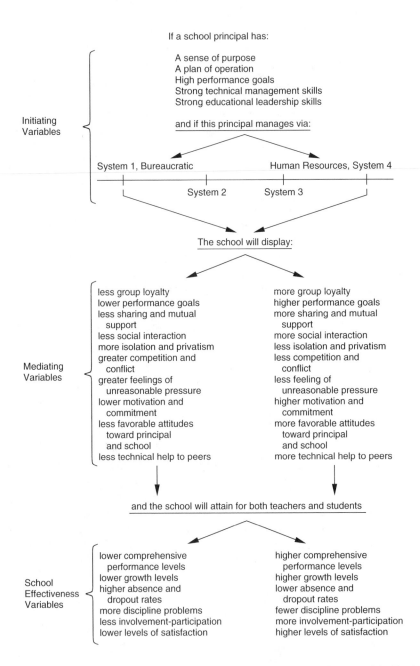

If a school principal has:

A sense of purpose
A plan of operation
High performance goals
Strong technical management skills
Strong educational leadership skills

Initiating Variables

and if this principal manages via:

System 1, Bureaucratic   Human Resources, System 4

System 2   System 3

The school will display:

Mediating Variables

less group loyalty	more group loyalty
lower performance goals	higher performance goals
less sharing and mutual support	more sharing and mutual support
less social interaction	more social interaction
more isolation and privatism	less isolation and privatism
greater competition and conflict	less competition and conflict
greater feelings of unreasonable pressure	less feeling of unreasonable pressure
lower motivation and commitment	higher motivation and commitment
less favorable attitudes toward principal and school	more favorable attitudes toward principal and school
less technical help to peers	more technical help to peers

and the school will attain for both teachers and students

School Effectiveness Variables

lower comprehensive performance levels	higher comprehensive performance levels
lower growth levels	higher growth levels
higher absence and dropout rates	lower absence and dropout rates
more discipline problems	fewer discipline problems
less involvement-participation	more involvement-participation
lower levels of satisfaction	higher levels of satisfaction

FIGURE 13–1   How Management Systems 1 and 4 Influence Mediating and School Effectiveness Variables

Summarized from Rensis Likert. 1961. *New Patterns of Management.* New York: McGraw-Hill, and Rensis Likert. 1967. *The Human Organization: Its Management and Value.* New York: McGraw-Hill.

Appendix 13–2   *(Continued)*

Evaluating the Climate of Your School

Likert (1967) developed the Profile of Organizational Characteristics (POC) as a tool for measuring and charting system characteristics of the organizations he studied. The POC provides an indication not only of which management system characterizes a particular organization, but of that organization's climate as well.

The POC was adopted for school use in the form of The Profile of a School (Likert and Likert, 1977). An abbreviated version of the profile appears in Appendix Figure 13–2. Appendix Figure 13–3 provides a score sheet for the profile. Use the instrument and the score sheet to evaluate your school or another school you know very well. Try to imagine how most of the teachers who work in this school would respond if they had the chance. Following the directions, plot your scores on the score sheet and draw a profile depicting your perceptions of that school's climate.

There are limitations in evaluating school "secondhand"; nonetheless, comparing your responses with those of others who know this school should reveal some similarities. Chances are your profile line reveals that this school can be characterized as System 2 or 3. Consistencies are likely in your ratings as you move from item to item, although your profile line probably has certain peaks toward System 4 and dips toward System 1. Peaks represent unusually strong qualities of the school's climate. Dips, by contrast, suggest areas where improvements are needed. Analyzing peaks and dips on the profile line allows principals and teachers to diagnose their school climate.

Dips can also be used as benchmarks for evaluating school climate improvement efforts. Imagine a school with relatively low climate scores on dimensions describing the extent to which students trust teachers and feel free to consult with them on academic and nonacademic matters. Principals and teachers might agree on a plan to improve this situation. Perhaps they decide to initiate voluntary open forum sessions for students and teachers on a weekly basis. They might agree as well to conduct weekly "that was the week that was" sessions in homerooms, in which students are free to summarize their academic week, pointing out highs and lows. More informally, teachers might resolve to be more sensitive to this issue as they interact with students. After several months, a second reading of the school climate might be taken; new responses could be compared with benchmark responses to detect improvements.

One implicit benefit of the POS and other climate instruments is that they provide handy structures for encouraging conversation and dialogue about events and conditions that ordinarily are difficult to discuss. It is much easier, for example, for teachers and principals to discuss items and item responses and their meanings than to engage in more unstructured conversations about school conditions and school improvements.

Take a moment to reflect on the climate of the school that you just evaluated. Using the POS, in its entirety, or a shortened version comprised of items that you select, evaluate the climate by first indicating how you would like it to be. What discrepancies do you note between your ideal and real responses? Assume that your responses represent average responses for the entire faculty. Based on the scoring profile that you prepare, what improvements need to be made in the climate of this school?

Organizational Variable	System 1		System 2		System 3		System 4	
A. Leadership Processes used:	RARELY		SOMETIMES		OFTEN		VERY OFTEN	
1. How often is your behavior seen by students as friendly and supportive?	①	②	③	④	⑤	⑥	⑦	⑧
How often does the principal seek and use your ideas about: 2. academic matters	①	②	③	④	⑤	⑥	⑦	⑧
3. non-academic school matters	①	②	③	④	⑤	⑥	⑦	⑧
4. How often do you see the principal's behavior as friendly and supportive?	①	②	③	④	⑤	⑥	⑦	⑧
	VERY LITTLE		SOME		QUITE A BIT		A VERY GREAT DEAL	
5. How much confidence and trust does the principal have in you?	①	②	③	④	⑤	⑥	⑦	⑧
6. How much confidence and trust do you have in the principal?	①	②	③	④	⑤	⑥	⑦	⑧
	NOT FREE		SOMEWHAT FREE		QUITE FREE		VERY FREE	
7. How free do you feel to talk to the principal about school matters?	①	②	③	④	⑤	⑥	⑦	⑧
	VERY LITTLE		SOME		QUITE A BIT		A VERY GREAT DEAL	
8. How much confidence and trust do you have in students?	①	②	③	④	⑤	⑥	⑦	⑧
9. How much confidence and trust do students have in you?	①	②	③	④	⑤	⑥	⑦	⑧
	NOT FREE		SOMEWHAT FREE		QUITE FREE		VERY FREE	
10. How free do students feel to talk to you about school matters?	①	②	③	④	⑤	⑥	⑦	⑧
How often are students' ideas sought and used by the principal about:	RARELY		SOMETIMES		OFTEN		VERY OFTEN	
11. academic matters	①	②	③	④	⑤	⑥	⑦	⑧
12. non-academic school matters	①	②	③	④	⑤	⑥	⑦	⑧
How often does the principal use small group meetings to solve school problems?	①	②	③	④	⑤	⑥	⑦	⑧
B. Character of Motivational Forces:	DISLIKE		SOMETIMES DISLIKE IT, SOMETIMES LIKE IT		USUALLY LIKE IT		LIKE IT VERY MUCH	
14. What is the general attitude of students toward your school?	①	②	③	④	⑤	⑥	⑦	⑧
How often do you try to be friendly and supportive to:	RARELY		SOMETIMES		OFTEN		VERY OFTEN	
15. the principal	①	②	③	④	⑤	⑥	⑦	⑧
16. other teachers	①	②	③	④	⑤	⑥	⑦	⑧
	USUALLY A WASTE OF TIME		SOMETIMES A WASTE OF TIME		OFTEN WORTH-WHILE		ALMOST ALWAYS WORTH-WHILE	
17. In your job is it worthwhile or a waste of time to do your best?	①	②	③	④	⑤	⑥	⑦	⑧
	NOT SATISFYING		SOMEWHAT SATISFYING		QUITE SATISFYING		VERY SATISFYING	
18. How satisfying is your work at your school?	①	②	③	④	⑤	⑥	⑦	⑧
To what extent do the following feel responsible for seeing that educational excellence is achieved in your school:	VERY LITTLE		SOME		CONSIDER-ABLE		VERY GREAT	
19. principal	①	②	③	④	⑤	⑥	⑦	⑧
20. department heads	①	②	③	④	⑤	⑥	⑦	⑧
21. teacher	①	②	③	④	⑤	⑥	⑦	⑧
22. To what extent do students help each other when they want to get something done?	①	②	③	④	⑤	⑥	⑦	⑧
23. To what extent do students look forward to coming to school?	①	②	③	④	⑤	⑥	⑦	⑧
24. To what extent do students feel excited about learning?	①	②	③	④	⑤	⑥	⑦	⑧
25. To what extent do you look forward to your teaching day?	①	②	③	④	⑤	⑥	⑦	⑧
26. To what extent are you encouraged to be innovative in developing more effective and efficient educational practices?	①	②	③	④	⑤	⑥	⑦	⑧

FIGURE 13–2   Profile of a School: Teacher Form

Items and scoring formats are from The Profile of a School, Form 3, Teacher Form. Items have been regrouped and renumbered, and system designations have been added. The original questionnaire contains additional items that enable evaluation of high school departments, grade levels, or teaching teams. Used by permission of Rensis Likert Associates, Inc., Ann Arbor, Michigan 48104. Copyright © 1977 by Jane Gibson Likert and Rensis Likert. Distributed by Rensis Likert Associates, Inc. All rights reserved. No further reproduction in any form authorized without written permission of Rensis Likert Associates, Inc., Ann Arbor, Michigan 48104.

Organizational Variable	System 1		System 2		System 3		System 4	

C. Character of Communication Process:

	VERY LITTLE		SOME		QUITE A BIT		A VERY GREAT DEAL	
27. How much do students feel that you are trying to help them with their problems?	①	②	③	④	⑤	⑥	⑦	⑧
28. How much accurate information concerning school affairs is given to you by students?	①	②	③	④	⑤	⑥	⑦	⑧

D. Character of Interaction-Influence:

How much influence do the following *have* on what goes on in your school:

	VERY LITTLE		SOME		QUITE A BIT		A VERY GREAT DEAL	
29. principal	①	②	③	④	⑤	⑥	⑦	⑧
30. teachers	①	②	③	④	⑤	⑥	⑦	⑧
31. central staff of your school system	①	②	③	④	⑤	⑥	⑦	⑧
32. students	①	②	③	④	⑤	⑥	⑦	⑧

How much influence do you think the following *should have* on what goes on in your school:

33. principal	①	②	③	④	⑤	⑥	⑦	⑧
34. teachers	①	②	③	④	⑤	⑥	⑦	⑧
35. central staff of your school system	①	②	③	④	⑤	⑥	⑦	⑧
36. students	①	②	③	④	⑤	⑥	⑦	⑧
37. How much influence do students *have* on what goes on in your school?	①	②	③	④	⑤	⑥	⑦	⑧
38. How much influence do you think students *should have* on what goes on in your school?	①	②	③	④	⑤	⑥	⑦	⑧

	USUALLY IGNORED		APPEALED BUT NOT RESOLVED		RESOLVED BY PRINCIPAL		RESOLVED BY ALL THOSE AFFECTED	
39. In your school, how are conflicts between departments usually resolved?	①	②	③	④	⑤	⑥	⑦	⑧

	VERY LITTLE		SOME		QUITE A BIT		A VERY GREAT DEAL	
40. How much do teachers in your school encourage each other to do their best?	①	②	③	④	⑤	⑥	⑦	⑧

	[EVERY ONE FOR SELF]		LITTLE COOPER- ATIVE TEAMWORK		A MODERATE AMOUNT OF COOPER- ATIVE TEAMWORK		A VERY GREAT AMOUNT OF COOPER- ATIVE TEAMWORK	
41. In your school, is it "every man for himself" or do principals, teachers, and students work as a team?	①	②	③	④	⑤	⑥	⑦	⑧

	VERY LITTLE		SOME		QUITE A BIT		A VERY GREAT DEAL	
42. How much do different departments plan together and coordinate their efforts?	①	②	③	④	⑤	⑥	⑦	⑧

E. Character of Decision-Making Processes:

	RARELY		SOMETIMES		OFTEN		VERY OFTEN	
43. How often do you seek and use students' ideas about academic matters, such as their work, course content, teaching plans and methods?	①	②	③	④	⑤	⑥	⑦	⑧
44. How often do you seek and use students' ideas about non-academic school matters, such as student activities, rules of conduct, and discipline?	①	②	③	④	⑤	⑥	⑦	⑧

	VIEWED WITH GREAT SUSPICION		SOME VIEWED WITH SUSPICION, SOME WITH TRUST		USUALLY VIEWED WITH TRUST		ALMOST ALWAYS VIEWED WITH TRUST	

How do students view communications from

45. you	①	②	③	④	⑤	⑥	⑦	⑧
46. the principal	①	②	③	④	⑤	⑥	⑦	⑧

	NOT WELL		SOMEWHAT WELL		QUITE WELL		VERY WELL	
47. How well do you know the problems faced by students in their school work?	①	②	③	④	⑤	⑥	⑦	⑧

	VERY LITTLE		SOME		CONSIDER- ABLE		VERY GREAT	
48. To what extent is the communication between you and your students open and candid?	①	②	③	④	⑤	⑥	⑦	⑧
49. To what extent does the principal give you useful information and ideas?	①	②	③	④	⑤	⑥	⑦	⑧

	FROM THE TOP DOWN		MOSTLY DOWN		DOWN AND UP		DOWN, UP AND LATERALLY	
50. What is the direction of the flow of information about academic and non-academic school matters?	①	②	③	④	⑤	⑥	⑦	⑧

FIGURE 13–2   *(Continued)*

Organizational Variable	System 1	System 2	System 3	System 4
	VIEWED WITH GREAT SUSPICION	SOME VIEWED WITH SUSPICION, SOME WITH TRUST	USUALLY VIEWED WITH TRUST	ALMOST ALWAYS VIEWED WITH TRUST
51. How do you view communications from the principal?	① ②	③ ④	⑤ ⑥	⑦ ⑧
	USUALLY INACCURATE	OFTEN INACCURATE	FAIRLY ACCURATE	ALMOST ALWAYS ACCURATE
52. How accurate is upward communication to the principal?	① ②	③ ④	⑤ ⑥	⑦ ⑧
	NOT WELL	SOMEWHAT WELL	QUITE WELL	VERY WELL
53. How well does the principal know the problems faced by the teachers?	① ②	③ ④	⑤ ⑥	⑦ ⑧
To what extent is communication open and candid:	VERY LITTLE	SOME	CONSIDERABLE	VERY GREAT
54. between principal and teachers	① ②	③ ④	⑤ ⑥	⑦ ⑧
55. among teachers	① ②	③ ④	⑤ ⑥	⑦ ⑧
	VERY LITTLE	SOME	QUITE A BIT	A VERY GREAT DEAL
56. How much help do you get from the central staff of your school system?	① ②	③ ④	⑤ ⑥	⑦ ⑧
	VERY LITTLE	SOME	QUITE A BIT	A VERY GREAT DEAL
57. How much are students involved in major decisions affecting them?	① ②	③ ④	⑤ ⑥	⑦ ⑧
	AT MUCH TOO HIGH LEVELS	AT SOMEWHAT TOO HIGH LEVELS	A QUITE SATISFACTORY LEVELS	AT THE BEST LEVELS
58. Are decisions made at the best levels for effective performance?	① ②	③ ④	⑤ ⑥	⑦ ⑧
	VERY LITTLE	SOME	CONSIDERABLE	VERY GREAT
59. To what extent are you involved in major decisions related to your work?	① ②	③ ④	⑤ ⑥	⑦ ⑧
60. To what extent are decision makers aware of problems, particularly at lower levels?	① ②	③ ④	⑤ ⑥	⑦ ⑧
F. Character of goal setting:				
61. To what extent does the principal make sure that planning and setting priorities are done well?	① ②	③ ④	⑤ ⑥	⑦ ⑧
G. Character of control processess:	HIGHLY AUTHORITARIAN	SOMEWHAT AUTHORITARIAN	CONSULTATIVE	PARTICIPATIVE GROUP
What is the administrative style of:				
62. the principal	① ②	③ ④	⑤ ⑥	⑦ ⑧
63. the superintendent of schools	① ②	③ ④	⑤ ⑥	⑦ ⑧
How competent is the principal:	NOT COMPETENT	SOMEWHAT COMPETENT	QUITE COMPETENT	VERY COMPETENT
64. as an administrator	① ②	③ ④	⑤ ⑥	⑦ ⑧
65. as an educator	① ②	③ ④	⑤ ⑥	⑦ ⑧
H. Performance goals:	VERY LITTLE	SOME	CONSIDERABLE	VERY GREAT
66. To what extent does the principal try to provide you with the materials, equipment and space you need to do your job well?	① ②	③ ④	⑤ ⑥	⑦ ⑧
	VERY LITTLE	SOME	QUITE A BIT	A VERY GREAT DEAL
67. How much do you feel that the principal is interested in your success as a teacher?	① ②	③ ④	⑤ ⑥	⑦ ⑧
68. How much interest do students feel you have in their success as students?	① ②	③ ④	⑤ ⑥	⑦ ⑧
69. How much does the principal try to help you with your problems?	① ②	③ ④	⑤ ⑥	⑦ ⑧
70. To what extent do students accept high performance goals in your school?	① ②	③ ④	⑤ ⑥	⑦ ⑧
	INADEQUATE	SOMEWHAT INADEQUATE	QUITE ADEQUATE	VERY ADEQUATE
71. How adequate are the supplies and equipment the school has?	① ②	③ ④	⑤ ⑥	⑦ ⑧
	LOW	ABOUT AVERAGE	QUITE HIGH	VERY HIGH
72. How high are the principal's goals for educational performance?	① ②	③ ④	⑤ ⑥	⑦ ⑧

FIGURE 13–2   *(Continued)*

Item	System 1		System 2		System 3		System 4	
1	1	2	3	4	5	6	7	8
2	1	2	3	4	5	6	7	8
3	1	2	3	4	5	6	7	8
4	1	2	3	4	5	6	7	8
5	1	2	3	4	5	6	7	8
6	1	2	3	4	5	6	7	8
7	1	2	3	4	5	6	7	8
8	1	2	3	4	5	6	7	8
9	1	2	3	4	5	6	7	8
10	1	2	3	4	5	6	7	8
11	1	2	3	4	5	6	7	8
12	1	2	3	4	5	6	7	8
13	1	2	3	4	5	6	7	8
14	1	2	3	4	5	6	7	8
15	1	2	3	4	5	6	7	8
16	1	2	3	4	5	6	7	8
17	1	2	3	4	5	6	7	8
18	1	2	3	4	5	6	7	8
19	1	2	3	4	5	6	7	8
20	1	2	3	4	5	6	7	8
21	1	2	3	4	5	6	7	8
22	1	2	3	4	5	6	7	8
23	1	2	3	4	5	6	7	8
24	1	2	3	4	5	6	7	8
25	1	2	3	4	5	6	7	8
26	1	2	3	4	5	6	7	8
27	1	2	3	4	5	6	7	8
28	1	2	3	4	5	6	7	8
29	1	2	3	4	5	6	7	8
30	1	2	3	4	5	6	7	8
31	1	2	3	4	5	6	7	8
32	1	2	3	4	5	6	7	8
33	1	2	3	4	5	6	7	8
34	1	2	3	4	5	6	7	8
35	1	2	3	4	5	6	7	8
36	1	2	3	4	5	6	7	8
37	1	2	3	4	5	6	7	8
38	1	2	3	4	5	6	7	8
39	1	2	3	4	5	6	7	8
40	1	2	3	4	5	6	7	8
41	1	2	3	4	5	6	7	8
42	1	2	3	4	5	6	7	8
43	1	2	3	4	5	6	7	8
44	1	2	3	4	5	6	7	8
45	1	2	3	4	5	6	7	8
46	1	2	3	4	5	6	7	8
47	1	2	3	4	5	6	7	8
48	1	2	3	4	5	6	7	8
49	1	2	3	4	5	6	7	8

FIGURE 13–3   Profile of a School Scoring Sheet

Item	System 1		System 2		System 3		System 4	
50	1	2	3	4	5	6	7	8
51	1	2	3	4	5	6	7	8
52	1	2	3	4	5	6	7	8
53	1	2	3	4	5	6	7	8
54	1	2	3	4	5	6	7	8
55	1	2	3	4	5	6	7	8
56	1	2	3	4	5	6	7	8
57	1	2	3	4	5	6	7	8
58	1	2	3	4	5	6	7	8
59	1	2	3	4	5	6	7	8
60	1	2	3	4	5	6	7	8
61	1	2	3	4	5	6	7	8
62	1	2	3	4	5	6	7	8
63	1	2	3	4	5	6	7	8
64	1	2	3	4	5	6	7	8
65	1	2	3	4	5	6	7	8
66	1	2	3	4	5	6	7	8
67	1	2	3	4	5	6	7	8
68	1	2	3	4	5	6	7	8
69	1	2	3	4	5	6	7	8
70	1	2	3	4	5	6	7	8
71	1	2	3	4	5	6	7	8
72	1	2	3	4	5	6	7	8

FIGURE 13–3   *(Continued)*

An important strength of the POS is that climate is not conceived as the product of only the principal's behavior or of any other single source. As one reads the items, it becomes clear that climates are based on a mix of attitudes, beliefs, and behaviors of everyone who lives and works in the school. They are manifestations of the school's culture. This being the case, school improvement efforts require that teachers and principals work together. Striving toward a System 4 climate, for example, requires a shared commitment. As you review the climate profile of the school you evaluated, what ideas come to mind as to how you as principal (and the faculty whose responses are represented by your responses) can plan to work together to improve the school?

Appendix 13–3 Quality of Work Life in Teaching Scoring Form

Instructions: Transfer your answers to the questions on the QWLinT instrument (Exhibit 13–1) to the scoring grid below, circling the number below the letter of the answer you selected. When you have transferred all answers and circled the appropriate numbers, add up all the numbers circled in each of the columns and enter the total in the empty box at the bottom of the column. Each of these totals refers to one of the scales of the QWLinT. Note that high scores for autonomy, personal growth, work complexity, and task-related interaction indicate a strong presence of these characteristics and suggest high job-enrichment opportunities in one's job. High scores for work speed and routine indicate a weak presence of this characteristic and low job enrichment.

Q.1				Q.2				Q.3				Q.4				Q.5			
A	M	P	N	A	M	P	N	A	M	P	N	A	M	P	N	A	M	P	N
1	2	3	4	4	3	2	1	1	2	3	4	1	2	3	4	4	3	2	1

Q.6				Q.7				Q.8				Q.9				Q.10			
A	M	P	N	A	M	P	N	A	M	P	N	A	M	P	N	A	M	P	N
4	3	2	1	4	3	2	1	1	2	3	4	1	2	3	4	1	2	3	4

Q.11				Q.12				Q.13				Q.14				Q.15			
A	M	P	N	A	M	P	N	A	M	P	N	A	M	P	N	A	M	P	N
1	2	3	4	4	3	2	1	1	2	3	4	4	3	2	1	4	3	2	1

Q.16				Q.17				Q.18				Q.19				Q.20			
A	M	P	N	A	M	P	N	A	M	P	N	A	M	P	N	A	M	P	N
4	3	2	1	4	3	2	1	4	3	2	1	1	2	3	4	4	3	2	1

Q.21				Q.22				Q.23				Q.24				Q.25			
A	M	P	N	A	M	P	N	A	M	P	N	A	M	P	N	A	M	P	N
4	3	2	1	4	3	2	1	1	2	3	4	1	2	3	4	4	3	2	1

Autonomy	Personal Growth Opportunity	Work* Speed and Routine	Work Complexity	Task-Related Interaction

Scale Score Interpretation:
5 to 9, low job enrichment
10 to 15, moderate job enrichment
16 to 20, high job enrichment

*High scores for work speed and routine indicate low job enrichment

C h a p t e r **14**

The Change Process

The more things change, the more things stay the same. This all too familiar saying still haunts us in education. Real change comes hard. Sure, we can all point to new programs and other innovations that have been adopted in our schools, but most just don't seem to matter very much. Some changes quickly fade away, some changes stay, but few changes touch teachers and students and few changes affect teaching and learning in the long run.

More than Adoption, More than Implementation

Much of the literature on change in schools assumes that adoption is the same as implementation. The two, however, are different (Gaynor, 1975). Schools frequently adopt innovations that are not implemented or, if implemented, innovations are shaped to the way things were to the point that the "change is hardly noticeable. The open-space concept, popular during the late 1960s and early 1970s, is an example. "Implementation" of open space was characterized by carving schools into traditional classrooms through the use of bookcases, room dividers, lockers, and other partitions. Goodlad and Klein (1970) make a similar observation with respect to the adoption of team teaching and the ungraded classroom concept. Frequently, implementation was characterized by "turn" teaching and the creation of grades within grades. From your own experiences you probably know of a junior high school that has adopted, but not really implemented, the middle school concept.

Sometimes changes have unanticipated consequences that when forced on the system make things worse than they were. Site-based management, for example, has been widely adopted, but instead of becoming a means to help us get somewhere it often is an end in itself. Site-based management can not only become a non-event in the teaching and learning life of the school, but it can create problems as well. Lichtenstein, McLaughlin, and Knudsen (1992) explain:

> We observed and read about instances in which site-based authority resulted in little of consequence in the classroom. Rather than feeling empowered to exercise

*greater authority in their teaching, many teachers found their time bound up with
committees wrestling with decisions about what color to make the curtain on the
auditorium stage, or whether to spend $500.00 on a slide projector or bookcases.
In some cases, we discovered that "restructuring" mandates provided weak
school administrators an excuse to delegate significant responsibilities to teachers who then floundered because of insufficient orientation, resources, support,
and expertise. Further, we saw instances where efforts to expand teacher's
authority without also attending to their capacity resulted in the ironic outcome
of diminished performance of school, classroom, or system. (39)*

Too often changes are introduced that contradict each other. As a result, they raise
havoc and cause confusion. Espousing Deming's (1993) philosophy and touting "Total
Quality Management" (TQM) or using TQM to create "The Quality School" are good
examples. Deming rarely uses the word quality in his writing and lectures, and does not
recommend its use. Furthermore, the notion of totally managing something is alien to him.
To Deming, the secret is not to manage for control (the word management, for example,
is derived from the Latin word *manus* and its Italian cousin *maneggio,* which means the
training or handling of a horse), but to honor variation. He takes exception to the use of
the word "customer" in educational settings. Unlike most appliers of TQM to practice, he
believes you can't view his 14 principles as a buffet of ideas from which one picks and
chooses only the ideas that are liked. Deming's ideas comprise a whole and must be
applied as a whole. That means the slogan TQM has to be dropped because slogans are
out. It means that grading and testing students, evaluating teachers, honor rolls, and other
student rankings cannot be used because they violate two of his principles (eliminating
work standards on the one hand and extrinsic rewards on the other).

Sometimes Deming's ideas are packaged together with other movements, such as
Outcomes-Based Education (OBE), but like oil and water, Deming's philosophy and OBE
cannot be mixed. In OBE, process is not important, one must focus on outcomes and let
process take care of itself. People are free to do whatever they want as long as the job gets
done. The only requirement is to "design down" what you do from the outcomes. To
Deming, outcomes are part of the problem, his answer is to focus on process. It is the
activity of teaching and learning, the curriculum, the classroom climate, and the numerous
social contracts that are struck between teachers and students, among teachers, and among
students that count the most. Tend to these and the outcomes that will take care of
themselves. No wonder change comes so hard—new ideas are accompanied by mixed
signals. Too often new ideas come in prepackaged forms and are marketed as if they were
a new breakfast food.

Even successful implementation of a change in schooling is not enough. School
improvement requires that such implementation be sustained over time; this, in turn,
requires that the change be institutionalized. Institutionalization means that the change is
"built in" to the life of the school (Miles, 1983). As Huberman and Crandall point out:
"New practices that get built into the training, regulatory, staffing, and budgetary cycles
survive, others don't. Innovations are highly perishable goods" (cited in Miles, 1983:14).
Institutionalization is a process of making a change routine; it becomes part of the
ordinary life of the school. Changes requiring new dollars, for example, become institu-

tionalized when these new dollars become regularly budgeted dollars. Changes requiring new structural arrangements become institutionalized when regular school policies are revised to reflect these arrangements. Changes requiring new patterns of behavior become institutionalized when the regular reward system (salary, promotions, psychological rewards) is adjusted to reflect these patterns. Institutionalization cannot be taken for granted. School improvement, therefore, requires that adoption, implementation, *and* institutionalization become the principal's goals.

The "One-Best-Way" Problem

For every successful school improvement effort, one hears horror stories about unsuccessful efforts. The major reason for failure, beyond lack of management and leadership effort by the principal, is a limited view of what the process of change involves. Unsuccessful school improvement efforts tend to put "all their eggs in one basket" by using a one-best-way to approach the problem.

Some experts advocate engineering the social and political context within which the school exists in an effort to provide the necessary support and momentum for change (see, for example, Baldridge, 1971; Gaynor, 1975). Other experts emphasize the development of favorable school climates that provide the necessary interpersonal support for change. In recent years, scholars from this group have focused on the concept of school culture and have emphasized the importance of developing values and norms that include the proposed changes (Likert, 1967; Sergiovanni and Corbally, 1984). Still other experts concentrate almost exclusively on the individual and her or his needs, dispositions, stages of concern for the proposed change, and the driving and restraining forces that pull and tug, causing resistance to the change (Bennis, Benne, and Chin, 1969; Reddin, 1970). Finally, some experts give primary attention to engineering the work context as a means to program and structure teacher behavior to ensure that the school improvement effort is implemented properly (Hunter, 1984). All these concerns are important, but none alone is an adequate model for school improvement.

A Systems View of Change

When one brings together each of these concerns, a systems view begins to emerge—one that provides a dynamic, integrative, and powerful view of change. Within this view the unit of change is not limited to the individual teacher, the school, the workflow of teaching and schooling, or the broader political and administrative context. Instead, the four are viewed as interacting units of change, all requiring attention. When attended to properly, these units of change are the roads to successful school improvement.

The systems view is depicted in Figure 14–1. Note that the direct road to changes relating to teaching and learning is through structuring the workflow of schooling. However, teaching is human-intensive, which means that regardless of how hard one might try to introduce change, teachers cannot be ignored. They count whether one wants them to or not. They make the day-to-day and minute-to-minute decisions influencing what

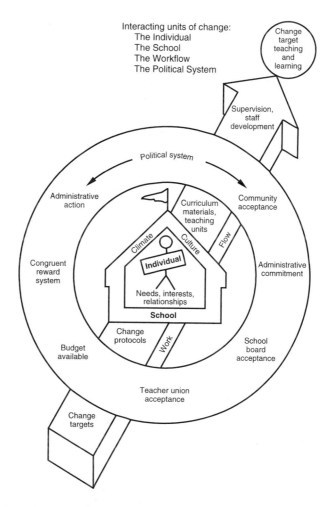

FIGURE 14–1   Interacting Units: A Systems View of Change

happens to students. For changes in the workflow of teaching to count they must be directly linked to changes in teaching behavior, and this inevitably means changes in the attitudes and beliefs of individual teachers and the faculty as a whole.

Teachers typically work alone. This isolation has telling negative consequences on teaching effectiveness and school improvement (Lieberman and Miller, 1984; Rosenholtz, 1989). Still, teachers are members of social groups that make up the larger school faculty. Social groups create norms, customs, and traditions that define ways of living. *School culture* is the term often used to refer to the sense of order and being that emerges. School culture defines what is of worth for teachers, specifies acceptable limits of behavior and beliefs, and is a powerful factor in promoting or resisting school improvement efforts (Saranson, 1971).

Schools do not exist in isolation; thus, another dimension of importance in the school improvement process is the broader administrative, social, and political environment. School climates, for example, are influenced by actions and attitudes of the teachers' union, the school board, and central office school district administrators (Kirst, 1984). Influences from this political system trickle down from the school level to the individual teacher and finally to the workflow. All four levels—individual, school, workflow, and political context—are, therefore, interacting units of change needing attention as principals promote school improvement. In the following sections, each of the four units of change is examined more closely.

The Individual as the Unit of Change

When considering the individual teacher as the unit of change, needs, values, beliefs, and levels of readiness are important. Change is often frightening. So much is at stake as present circumstances, norms, and ways of operation are threatened. Before most teachers are able to examine the worth of a proposed new idea for improving teaching and learning, they are apt to view this idea selfishly. The first reaction is likely to be, "How will this proposed change affect me?" For example, the prospect of family grouping, team teaching, or a new pattern of organization (e.g., school within the school or middle school) raises such questions in teachers' minds as: How will my relationship with other teachers change? How will my view of myself change? How will my authority over students and influence in the school change? How will the amount of work I do change? How will my relationship with parents and administrators change? Will I be more or less successful as a teacher? Who will be the team leader or master teacher? What will other teachers think of me as a person? What will other teachers think of me as a teacher?

These questions reflect concerns that are normal and deserve answering. Unless these human concerns are adequately resolved, continued emphasis on educational and other job-related aspects of the change will likely increase anxiety and promote skepticism. Principals react similarly when faced with the prospects of change; so do professors and superintendents. Healthy individuals are naturally concerned with how changes will affect them, their work, their relationships with others; all these concerns require attention.

For some time, researchers have been interested in the concerns of teachers and how these concerns focus their attention on a limited range of issues relating to change (Fuller, 1969; Hall and Loucks, 1978; Hord et al., 1987). This work has led to the development of the "concern-based adoption model," which describes the changing feelings of people as they learn about a proposed change, prepare to use it, use it, and modify it as a result. The model proposes seven stages of concern as follows (Hall and Loucks, 1978).

1.	Awareness	I am not concerned about it.
2.	Informational	I would like to know more about it.
3.	Personal	How will using it affect me?
4.	Management	I seem to be spending all my time getting material ready.
5.	Consequence	How is my use affecting kids?
6.	Collaboration	I am concerned about relating what I am doing with what other teachers are doing.
7.	Refocusing	I have some ideas about something that would work even better.

The developers of the model do not maintain that every teacher marches through all the stages beginning with awareness and ending with refocusing or that the stages are mutually exclusive with only one being tended to at a time. The stages do, however, represent the general kind of development that takes place as changes are adopted and used on a continuous basis. They are therefore developmental *in nature* rather than being strictly developmental.

The progression of concerns seems to follow this pattern. In the early stages of a change effort, teachers are likely to have self concerns that center on learning more about the proposed change and how the change will affect them personally. Once these concerns are taken care of, they tend next to focus on the management problems they are likely to face as they begin to implement the change. Next their attention shifts to the impact the change is likely to have on their students and, as this change is remediated, to issues of collaboration with other teachers in an effort to implement the change and to improve its effects. Finally, because teachers are different and their situations are varied, adaptions are made in the change in an effort to improve its fit.

Principals and others who are interested in promoting change can use the concern-based model as a general framework for evaluating where various individuals are with respect to change concerns and for matching their own strategies to these levels. It makes little sense, for example, to spend an inordinate amount of time worrying about management concerns or consequences that a particular change is likely to have for students when teachers are still pretty much focused on such personal concerns as whether they will indeed be able to successfully adopt the change, how it will affect their relationships with other teachers, and so forth.

Resistance to change occurs when one's basic work needs are threatened. Although individual differences among teachers exist in the relative importance of specific work needs, four fairly universal needs can be identified (Mealiea, 1978):

1. *The need for clear expectations.* Most of us require fairly specific information about our jobs to function effectively. We need to know what is expected of us, how we fit into the total scheme of things, what our responsibilities are, how we will be evaluated, and what our relationships with others will be. Without such information our performance is likely to decline and our job satisfaction will be lessened (Katz and Kahn, 1978). Change upsets this "equilibrium" of role definition and expectations.

2. *The need for future certainty.* Closely related to knowing how we fit into the job system is being able to predict the future. We need to have some reliability and certainty built into our work lives to provide us with security and allow us to plan ahead (Coffer and Appley, 1964). Change introduces ambiguity and uncertainty, which threaten our need for a relatively stable, balanced, and predictable work environment.

3. *The need for social interaction.* Most of us value and need opportunities to interact with others. This interaction helps us to define and build our own self-concepts and to reduce anxiety and fear we experience in the work environment. We seek support and acceptance from others at work. Change is often perceived as threatening to these important social interaction patterns, and the prospects of establishing new patterns can present us with security problems.

4. *The need for control over our work environment and work events.* Most of us want and seek a reasonable degree of control over our work environment (Argyris, 1957).

We do not wish to be at the mercy of this system. We want to be Origins and not Pawns (De Charms, 1968) when it comes to making decisions that affect our work lives.

When control is threatened or reduced, the net effect for teachers is not only less job satisfaction but also a loss of meaning in work that can result in job indifference and even alienation. Change efforts that do not involve teachers and changes that threaten to lessen their control over teaching, learning, and other aspects of schooling can have serious consequences for school effectiveness.

Teachers vary in the intensity with which the four universal needs are held. The greater the intensity, the more likely change threats will be felt. Still, for all teachers, change will likely create some disturbance in their present situation. Principals can help get teachers back onto a more comfortable and stable course by providing as much relevant information as possible about the change and how it affects the work of teaching. Teachers need to know what will be expected of them as the change is put into operation. This theme will be discussed further, when the workflow as the unit of change is considered. Allowing—indeed, welcoming—teacher participation in planning the proposed change will help to provide for these needs and will very likely result in ideas about how to improve the proposal. Keeping the proposed change simple and implementing aspects of the change gradually will increase teachers' confidence in themselves as successful implementers.

Mealiea (1978) suggests that changes be accompanied by a nonevaluation period during which the teacher's performance cannot have a negative effect on income, career ladder promotion, or other school benefits. During this period, the emphasis would be solely on providing feedback to teachers to help them learn more about the change and to increase proficiency in implementing the change. Directing change efforts first to teachers who might be considered as role models and who optimally would become early adopters of the change can be helpful to successful school improvement. If teachers who are widely respected by others are moving ahead with the change, a certain confidence and calm are likely to occur and resistance is likely to be lessened.

The School as the Unit of Change

Concentrating on individual teachers as units of change is important, but many experts maintain that too much emphasis has been given to this level. The well-known social psychologists Daniel Katz and Robert Kahn (1978) state: "Attempts to change organizations by changing individuals have a long history of theoretical inadequacy and practical failure. Both stem from a disregard of the systematic properties of organizations and from the confusion of individual changes with modifications in organizational variables" (658).

Katz and Kahn believe that individuals and individual behavior remain important in change considerations but take on different qualities and meanings when viewed within the context of the group. Consider, for example, recent interactions you had with your supervisor one to one and in a group context. In many respects you were two different persons. Many individuals, for example, feel more an equal with supervisors when interacting within a group context rather than interacting on a one-to-one basis.

The school as a community needs to be considered as an important unit of change. Schools have cultures and these cultures are governed by the webs of meaning and the customs, rituals, and other patterns of life that teachers create. A culture is manifested in norm systems that determine what it is that people think, believe, and do.

The distinguished sociologist Willard Waller (1932) pointed out many years ago that

Schools have a culture that is definitely their own. There are, in the school, complex rituals of personal relationships, a set of folk ways, mores, and irrational sanctions, a moral code based on them. There are games, which are sublimated wars, teams, and an elaborate set of ceremonies concerning them. There are traditions, and traditionalists waging their world-old battle against innovators. (103)

Lieberman and Miller (1984) identified four themes within the school culture—rhythms, rules, interactions, and feelings—that are played out in the daily lives of teachers. The elementary school teaching day, for example, has morning activities, lunch hour, afternoon activities, recess, and so forth. Bells ring in the high school to signal the passing of classes. The school day is divided into periods or hours with collections of hours comprising courses. Within each class period, a universal routine is followed. Attendance is taken, new material is introduced, and then homework is assigned for the next day. This routine is repeated five times a day, five days a week, four weeks a month for nine months. Soon teachers become such a part of this daily rhythm that a proposed change in any part of it upsets the whole, and this is often too much to take. In many respects, teachers become victims of the rhythm of the day, the week, the month, and the school year. Although they may want to escape the rhythm, they simply are not able to.

Lieberman and Miller point out that teaching has its rules, both codified and informal. Codified rules are stated up front and informal ones are held tacitly. Teachers, for example, must keep their distance from students to maintain a certain objectivity that enables them to deliver expert services fairly and equitably. Prime among the rules is for teachers to be practical and to be private.

Practical knowledge in schools is defined in terms of its opposites. Being practical is the opposite of being theoretical; being practical is the opposite of being idealistic. . . . new teachers in search of practical knowledge, then, must reject the university professors who train them as well as their own tendencies to seek ideal solutions to difficult problems. Practical knowledge is lodged in the experiences and practices of teachers at work in their classrooms. (Lieberman and Miller, 1984:7)

Ideas are practical when they have immediate application, when they are offered by practical people, and when they address such practical problems as discipline, attendance, order, and achievement.

The norm of privatism runs deep within the school culture. Lieberman and Miller point out that new teachers learn their place in the school quickly and learn to keep their practice to themselves. "What does private mean? It means not sharing experiences about teaching, about classes, about students, about perceptions" (Lieberman and Miller, 1984:8).

The norms of practicality and privatism limit the depth and scope of interactions that teachers have. There is little opportunity for teachers to visit among themselves. All that is left are the interactions that they have with their students, and from these they must derive any rewards that they experience.

The accumulated effects of the rhythms, rules, and interactions that characterize the daily life of teachers takes its toll on feelings. There is conflict, frustration, satisfaction, joy, self-doubt, vulnerability, and uncertainty.

Terence Deal (1987) points out that there is a basic contradiction between culture and change. Culture, he argues, is something people invent in order to find meaning. Its purpose is to provide stability, certainty, and predictability. Meaning is derived through symbols that create a sense of control. Change challenges all of this, it threatens to eat away at the very essence of what culture is supposed to do for people. In a sense, change requires the creation of a new culture, and that is difficult to accomplish. Deal points out that in order to create a new culture we have to struggle with the loss of the old. This involves re-creating the history of the school and articulating new shared values and conceptions, while at the same time celebrating the old in ceremonies that enable them to be let go. Little will be accomplished in dealing with culture without addressing the school itself as the unit of change.

The Workflow as the Unit of Change

Change experts who focus their efforts almost entirely on the individual and school as units of change are often successful in promoting adoption of a school improvement idea but not in implementing it. Adoption goals create the necessary readiness and enthusiasm for change and result from a bit of salespersonship on the one hand and psychological reassurance on the other. Too often, however, enthusiasm wanes, teachers experience frustration with implementation attempts, and the proposed change is modified to resemble the familiar "business as usual" or abandoned entirely. Focusing almost exclusively on the individual or the school or the two in combination results in "up-front" commitment (Crandall, 1983:7), but this commitment may not be expanded or sustained as teachers begin to put the change into practice. Up-front commitment, of course, is important because it gets us into the water. Now we need help learning how to swim differently, and this requires that we focus on the workflow as the unit of change.

Workflow focus builds commitment during and after teachers are actually engaged in new practices (Crandall, 1983). No secrets are involved in focusing on the workflow. The process is simple and direct. It involves making known specifically what is to be accomplished; defining carefully how this will be accomplished; giving specific attention to what teachers will actually be doing that is different; providing the necessary teaching apparatus, equipment, and curriculum materials; and providing the necessary ongoing training, assistance, supervision, and evaluation for ensuring that teachers' attempts to implement the change will be successful. Sometimes changes have unanticipated consequences that when forced on the system make things worse than they were.

The dimensions of the workflow requiring attention from principals can be summarized as follows:

1. *The Change Goal*—This is what the school wants to accomplish.
2. *The Change Targets*—These are practical and operational definitions, descriptions, and examples of the goal.
3. *The Change Protocols*—These are practical and operational definitions, descriptions, and examples of arrangements and behaviors that need to be provided or articulated to reach targets.
4. *The Curriculum and Teaching Requirements*—These are the curriculum and teaching materials and units that teachers will need for them to work differently and successfully.
5. *The Supervisory and Staff Development Support*—This is the help teachers will need before they begin the process of change and while the process of change continues.

Expectancy theory of motivation can help us understand the importance of the dimensions of the workflow described above. According to expectancy theory, before motivation to change occurs, teachers need answers to the following questions:

1. Do I know what it is that needs to be accomplished?
2. Are the benefits of accomplishment important to me and desired by me?
3. Do I have a clear idea of exactly what it is that I need to do to accomplish this?
4. Should I attempt accomplishment; will I be successful?

A "no" answer to any of these questions means that teachers will not be motivated to participate in the school improvement effort. "Yes" answers that result in motivation depend on the attention principals give to the workflow as the unit of change. Particularly key is the supervisory support available to teachers to ensure successful implementation.

The Political System as the Unit of Change

Adoption and implementation are not the same as institutionalization of a change. Institutionalization occurs when the change is no longer viewed as an innovation; instead, it is considered part of the regular pattern of operation within the school and school district. Institutionalization requires changes in school district policies, rules, and procedures; actual budget allocations; school structural and administrative arrangements; and the official reward system that is made available to teachers. In school settings very few change attempts ever reach the institutional level; this explains, in part, why changes tend not to stick.

Principals are the main characters in bringing about adoption and implementation goals. They play key roles in planning and providing leadership for changes addressed to individuals, the school, and the workflow as units of change. Yet, when it comes to institutionalizing changes, they do not have much power. The reality is that principals will need the help of the superintendent and central office staff and, at the very least, the acquiescence of the school board and teachers' union. There is no way around this reality. The best of ideas and the most enthusiastic of responses to these ideas at the school level are not enough to make an adopted and implemented school improvement attempt a permanent fixture of the school.

It is common practice among the best school districts in the country for the superintendent and the central office staff to meet regularly with school principals. These meetings are typically held monthly, but often more frequently. They can last for a full day and often well into the evening. The purpose of the meetings is to exchange information and ideas about what is occurring in each of the schools. Principals are given an opportunity to update the superintendent and other administrators, including peers, on the last month's happenings in each school and to share plans for the next month. Superintendents and principals do not view these sessions as evaluation and review but as communication and assistance. Good ideas from schools become better ones as other principals and central office staff consider them. More importantly, these sessions allow the superintendent to "buy in" to local school improvement initiatives, and this buying in is the first step to ensure that the necessary support for institutionalization will be forthcoming.

Michael Fullan (1982) points out that adoption of a change does not occur without an advocate, and one of the most powerful advocates is the superintendent of schools with her or his staff in combination with the school board. This conclusion is supported by many other studies (e.g., Berman and McLaughlin, 1977, 1979).

Leadership for School Improvement

The systems view of change depicted in Figure 14–1 emphasizes interactions among individual teachers, the school, the workflow of teaching and learning, and the broader political context as units of change. This view represents a strategy map for planning school improvement efforts and for increasing the possibility that such efforts will be not only adopted, but also implemented and institutionalized. Yet, the question remains: What should the principal do to help things along as each of the units of change is addressed? What are the *specific* principal behaviors associated with successful school improvement efforts?

Change Facilitator Styles

Let's begin our inquiry into this topic by describing the behavior of a principal whose school is, or has recently been, involved in a change effort. It is hard to separate all the aspects of a principal's change facilitator style from her or his general style or orientation; thus, you will want to focus on both the general style and the change style as we begin our analysis. What kind of leadership does the principal bring to the school? What does the leader stand for and how effective is she or he in communicating these standards to teachers? What kind of interpersonal leader is the principal? How does the principal work to facilitate change that will result in school improvement? Before continuing further, turn to the Change Facilitator Styles Inventory (CFSI), which appears as Appendix 14–1; following the directions, describe the principal you have been thinking about.

The CFSI is based on an extensive research program investigating links between principal behaviors and successful school improvements (Hall et al., 1983). This research was conducted at the Research and Development Center for Teacher Education at the University of Texas at Austin. The investigators were able to group principal leadership behaviors into three general change facilitator styles: Responder, Manager, and Initiator. These three styles correspond to the R, M, and I response categories on the CFSI and are described in the following extract (Hall and Rutherford, 1983):

Responders *place heavy emphasis on allowing teachers and others the opportunity to take the lead. They believe their primary role is to maintain a smooth-running school by focusing on traditional administrative tasks, keeping teachers content, and treating students well. Teachers are viewed as strong professionals who are able to carry out their instructional role with little guidance. Responders emphasize the personal side of their relationships with teachers and others. Before they make decisions they often give everyone an opportunity to have input so as to weigh their feelings or to allow others to make the decision. A related characteristic is the tendency toward making decisions in terms of immediate circumstances rather than in terms of longer-range instructional or school goals. This seems to be due in part to their desire to please others and in part to their limited vision of how their school and staff should change in the future.*

Managers *represent a broader range of behaviors. They demonstrate both responsive behaviors in answer to situations or people and they also initiate actions in support of the change effort. The variations in their behavior seem to be linked to their rapport with teachers and central office staff as well as how well they understand and buy into a particular change effort. Managers work without fanfare to provide basic support to facilitate teachers' use of the innovation. They keep teachers informed about decisions and are sensitive to teacher needs. They will defend their teachers from what are perceived as excessive demands. When they learn that the central office wants something to happen in their school, they then become very involved with their teachers in making it happen. Yet, they do not typically initiate attempts to move beyond the basics of what is imposed.*

Initiators *have clear, decisive long-range policies and goals that transcend but include implementation of the current innovation. They tend to have very strong beliefs about what good schools and teaching should be like and work intensely to attain this vision. Decisions are made in relation to their goals for the school and in terms of what they believe to be best for students, which is based on current knowledge of classroom practice. Initiators have strong expectations for students, teachers, and themselves. They convey and monitor these expectations through frequent contacts with teachers and clear explication of how the school is to operate and how teachers are to teach. When they feel it is in the best interest of their school, particularly the students, Initiators will seek changes in district programs or policies or they will reinterpret them to suit the needs of the school. Initiators will be adamant but not unkind, they solicit input from staff and then decisions are made in terms of the goal of the school even if some are ruffled by their directness and high expectations. (84)*

Which of these general change facilitator styles best corresponds with your response patterns on the CFSI? Can you estimate which of these styles were most and least associated with successful school improvement efforts? Hall and Rutherford (1983) found that Initiator principals were more likely to be successful than were Manager and Responder principals. Responders were least likely to be successful. As you review the principal behavior descriptions on the CFSI associated with each of these styles, note that Initiators have a clear sense of what needs to be accomplished and take more active roles in planning, prodding, encouraging, advising, participating, checking, stimulating, monitoring, and evaluating change efforts. Furthermore, they assume more direct roles in obtaining and providing the necessary material and psychological support for successful change efforts.

Levels of Leadership Behavior

As a result of their research on principals at work, Leithwood and Montgomery (1986) identified four levels of leadership behavior, each with a different focus and style and each with different consequences for principal effectiveness. They found that the "higher" the level of principal behavior, the more effective the school. Effectiveness was defined as gains in student achievement in the "basics" and increases in student self-direction and problem solving.

Each of the levels represents increasingly complex and effective principalship behaviors. Principals functioning at level one, the *Administrator*, believe that it is the teacher's job to teach and the principal's job to run the school. Principals functioning at level two, the *Humanitarian*, believe that the basis of a sound education is a good interpersonal climate. Principals functioning at level three, the *Program Manager*, believe that their job is to provide the best possible programs for students. Principals functioning at level four, the *Systematic Problem Solver*, are committed to doing whatever is necessary by way of invention and delivery in order to give students the best possible chance to learn. Program Managers and Systematic Problem Solvers both bring to their practice a focus on students, but Program Managers are largely committed to proper implementation of officially sanctioned goals and programs. They are more dependent on established guidelines, resources, and procedures than are Systematic Problem Solvers.

> *Systematic Problem Solvers are 'bottom liners' virtually all the time; bottom line is the goals for students by their school. Their focus is largely unconstrained by established practice and their client orientation leads them to the invention and delivery of whatever legitimate services are likely to realize the goals held by their school for students. (Leithwood and Montgomery, 1986:83)*

Important to Liethwood and Montgomery's formulation is the concept of level. What administrators do at level one is not necessarily ineffective, only less effective than the other three levels if this behavior pattern is dominant. Humanitarians at level two carry with them some ,of the Administrator's style but focus primarily on more complex behaviors that emphasize human relationships. Although more effective than Administrators, Humanitarians are not as effective as Program Managers. Program Managers bring aspects of the Administrator and Humanitarian style to their practice but focus primarily on more complex matters of educational program development and implementation.

Finally, the strategic Problem Solvers focus primarily on students' success. This entrepreneurial stance is supported, nonetheless, by competent administrative, human relations, and program management skills.

Leithwood and Montgomery's research suggests that as principals come to view their jobs in more complex ways they become more effective operating at higher levels of practice. They recognize, of course, the important management demands in their job and the need to provide an environment that supports and enhances human relationships. Yet, neither management nor human relations processes are viewed as ends in themselves. They believe that process always serves substance. The substance of the school is defined by its educational programs and levels of commitment to teaching and learning. Yet, neither process nor substance can be viewed as something static, they are, instead, pursued in a context characterized by an array of demands, constraints, and choices. Realizing that expanding choices results in better schooling, principals at level four work for this expansion by taking a problem-solving, even entrepreneurial, approach to their leadership practice.

Some Ethical Questions

Principals often feel uncomfortable when they are asked to assume fairly direct roles in bringing about change. Change is, after all, a form of "social engineering"; and, as one becomes more skilled at bringing about change, ethical issues are naturally raised. Are we talking about leadership or are we really talking about manipulation? No easy answer exists to this question, but one thing is certain—principals have an obligation to provide leadership to the school, and this involves following a course of action leading to school improvement. The change agent role is therefore unavoidable.

Kenneth Benne (1949) proposes a set of guidelines for principals to ensure that their change behavior is ethical. He believes that the engineering of change and the providing of pressure on groups and organizations to change must be collaborative. Collaboration suggests that principals and teachers form a change partnership, with each being aware of the intentions of others. Change intents are honest and straightforward. Teachers, for example, do not have to endure being "buttered up" today for the announced change of tomorrow.

The engineering of change should be educational to those involved in the process. "Educational" suggests that principals will try to help teachers to become more familiar with the process of problem solving and changing so that they are less dependent on her or him. Giving a teacher a solution is not as educational as helping the teacher muddle through a problem.

The engineering of change should be experimental. "Experimental" implier, that changes will not be implemented for keeps but will be adopted tentatively until they have proven their worth or until a better solution comes along.

The engineering of change should be task-oriented; that is, controlled by the requirements of the problem and its effective solution rather than oriented to the maintenance or extension of prestige or power of the principal and others who are encouraging changes. Task orientation refers to one's primary motive for change. The principal should have job-related objectives in mind first—objectives that are concerned with improving teaching and learning for students. If such school improvement efforts are successful, the principal and others responsible for the change enjoy personal success and a certain amount of fame as well. These are the rewards for hard work, but they are not the reasons for bringing about the change in the first place. Principals who emphasize change to get attention from their supervisors or to improve their standing or influence in the school district may well be violating this ethical principle.

The Change Facilitating Team

This is a book for principals; therefore, it is natural to emphasize the principal's role and its significance in school improvement efforts. Yet, the principal cannot do it alone. In highlighting this issue, Hord, Hall, and Stiegelbauer (1983:1) point out: "This rhetoric, abundant in literature, quite obviously hangs like a heavy mantle on the principal. However, what is becoming equally certain and abundantly clear is that the principal does not bear the weight of leadership responsibility alone." Their research reveals that often one or two other key people in the school emerge as key change facilitators. As a result of their research on school improvement and analysis of the change literature, Loucks-Horsley and Hergert (1985:ix) conclude: "The principal is not *the* key to school improvement. Although the principal is important so are many other people." Teachers and supervisors have important roles to play, as do superintendents and specialists at the central office.

The research suggests that it may be more useful to view the principal as the leader of the change facilitating team (Hall, 1988), with as many as four change facilitators serving on the team. The principal, for example, might be viewed as the primary change facilitator. Very often a second change facilitator (assistant principal, department chairperson, resource teacher, or teacher on a special assignment) was identified by the researcher. Frequently a third level of change facilitator existed. Typically, facilitators at this level were teachers whose roles were less formalized but whose help was substantial and sought by their peers (Hord et al., 1987). This group of facilitators served the process of change primarily by modeling the use of the new practices, disseminating information to other teachers, cheerleading, and providing support. The principals who were most effective in implementing change were team-oriented, working closely with these other levels of change facilitators. Often, structures were built that allowed them to work together as a change facilitator team.

In some schools, they may meet each week to review data about the school improvement process, generate ideas, and plan who will do what during the ensuing week. When they meet again, they debrief to ascertain what went well and what needs more attention. In other schools we observe a more hierarchical organization of facilitators: the first CF (the principal) appeared to interact only with the second CF, who in turn related to the third CF. All communications flowed through this "chain of command." Whether the team of CFs has a "flat"

*or horizontal collegial structure or a more hierarchical one, however, the impor-
tant aspects to remember are what they need to do as group. (Hord et al.,
1987:85)*

These researchers identified even a fourth category, the *external facilitator.* Frequently
this role was filled by someone from the central office who served as a facilitative link
between the office resources and the school.

The Meaning of Educational Change

One theme emerges from this discussion of the process of change. Although principals are
important and their visions key in focusing attention on change and in successfully
implementing the process of change, what counts in the end is bringing together the ideas
and commitments of a variety of people who have a stake in the success of the school. As
this process unfolds, principals can often find themselves on thin ice. They need to be
clear about what it is that they want but cannot be so clear that they are providing people
with road maps. They need to allow people to have an important say in shaping the
direction of the school and deciding on the changes needed to get there, but they cannot
be so detached that these individual aspirations remain more rhetorical than real. Michael
Fullan (1982), after reviewing Lighthall's (1973) work, points out that there is strong
support for the assertion that

> *leadership commitment to a particular version of a change is negatively related
> to ability to implement it . . . educational change is a process of coming to grips
> with the multiple realities of people who are the main participants in implement-
> ing change. The leader who presupposes what the change should be and acts in
> ways which preclude others' realities is bound to fail. (82)*

Key, of course, are the visions of teachers. If change is not responsive to the world of
teaching as teachers experience it, it is likely to be viewed as irrelevant if not frivolous
(Lortie, 1975). Fullan (1991) believes that the assumptions that principals and others
make about change are key because they represent powerful, although frequently uncon-
scious, sources of one's actions. His analysis of the process of change leads him to identify
certain do's and don'ts assumptions as being basic to the successful implementation of
educational change:

> *1. Do not assume that your vision of what the change should be is the one that
>   should or could be implemented. On the contrary, assume that one of the
>   main purposes of the process of implementation is to exchange your reality
>   of what should be through interaction with implementers and others con-
>   cerned. Stated another way, assume that successful implementation con-
>   sists of some transformation or continual development of initial ideas.
>   (Particularly good discussions of the need for this assumption and the folly*

of ignoring it are contained in Lighthall, 1973; Marris, 1975, Ch. XVIII; Schön, 1971, Ch. 5; Louis & Miles, 1990).

2. *Assume that any significant innovation, if it is to result in change, requires individual implementers to work out their own meaning. Significant change involves a certain amount of ambiguity, ambivalence, and uncertainty for the individual about the meaning of the change. Thus, effective implementation is a* process of clarification. *It is also important not to spend too much time in the early stages on needs assessment, program development, and problem definition activities—school staff have limited time. Clarification is likely to come in large part through* practice *(see Cohen, 1987; Loucks-Horsley & Hergert, 1985).*

3. *Assume that conflict and disagreement are not only inevitable but fundamental to successful change. Since any group of people possess multiple realities, any collective change attempt will necessarily involve conflict. Assumptions 2 and 3 combine to suggest that all successful efforts of significance, no matter how well planned, will experience an implementation dip in the early stages. Smooth implementation is often a sign that not much is really changing (Huberman & Miles, 1984).*

4. *Assume that people need pressure to change (even in directions that they desire), but it will be effective only under conditions that allow them to react, to form their own position, to interact with other implementers, to obtain technical assistance, etc. Unless people are going to be replaced with others who have different desired characteristics, relearning is at the heart of change.*

5. *Assume that effective change takes time. It is a process of "development in use." Unrealistic or undefined time lines fail to recognize that implementation occurs developmentally. Significant change in the form of implementing specific innovations can be expected to take a minimum of two or three years; bringing about institutional reforms can take five or more years. Persistence is a critical attribute of successful change.*

6. *Do not assume that the reason for lack of implementation is outright rejection of the values embodied in the change, or hard-core resistance to all change. Assume that there are a number of possible reasons: value rejection, inadequate resources to support implementation, insufficient time elapsed.*

7. *Do not expect all or even most people or groups to change. The complexity of change is such that it is impossible to bring about widespread reform in any large social system. Progress occurs when we take steps (e.g., by following the assumptions listed here) that* increase *the number of people affected. Our reach should exceed our grasp, but not by such a margin that we fall flat on our face. Instead of being discouraged by all that remains to be done, be encouraged by what has been accomplished by way of improvement resulting from your actions.*

8. *Assume that you will need a* plan *that is based on the above assumptions and that addresses the factors known to affect implementation . . . Evolutionary*

planning and problem-coping models based on knowledge of the change process are essential (Louis & Miles, 1990).

9. *Assume that no amount of knowledge will ever make it totally clear what action should be taken. Action decisions are a combination of valid knowledge, political considerations, on-the-spot decisions, and intuition. Better knowledge of the change process will improve the mix of resources on which we draw, but it will never and should never represent the sole basis for decision.*

10. *Assume that changing the culture of institutions is the real agenda, not implementing single innovations. Put another way, when implementing particular innovations, we should always pay attention to whether the institution is developing or not.* *

School improvement may not be easy, but it is well within reach of most schools. Successful efforts depend on the principals taking a comprehensive view of the problem. This view acknowledges the importance of leadership density and emphasizes implementation and institutionalization of change as well as adoption. Furthermore, successful change efforts are directed to the four levels of the school's interacting system: individual, school, workflow, and administrative-political context.

References

Argyris, Chris. 1957. *Personality and Organizations.* New York: Harper & Row.

Baldridge, Victor A. 1971. "The Analysis of Organizational Change: A Human Relations Strategy Versus a Political Systems Strategy." Stanford, CA: R & D Memo #75, Stanford Center for R & D in Teaching, Stanford University.

Benne, Kenneth D. 1949. "Democratic Ethics and Social Engineering," *Progressive Education* 27(4).

Bennis, Warren, Kenneth D. Benne, and Robert Chin. 1969. *The Planning of Change,* 2d ed. New York: Holt, Rinehart and Winston.

Berman, Paul, and Milbrey Wallin McLaughlin. 1977. *Federal Programs Supporting Educational Change.* Vol. VII *Factors Affecting Implementation and Continuation.* Santa Monica, CA: Rand Corporation.

Berman, Paul, and Milbrey Wallin McLaughlin. 1979. *An Explanatory Study of School District Adaptations.* Santa Monica, CA: Rand Corporation.

Coffer, C. N., and M. H. Appley. 1964. *Motivation: Theory and Research.* New York: Wiley.

Cohen, M 1987. "Designing State Assessment Systems." *Phi Delta Kappan.* 70(8), 583–588.

Crandall, David P. 1983. "The Teacher's Role in School Improvement," *Educational Leadership* 41(3), 6–9.

Deal, Terence E. 1987. "The Culture of Schools," in Linda T. Sheive and Marian B. Schoenheit, *Leadership Examining the Illusive,* 1987 Yearbook of the Association for Supervision and

Curriculum Development. Alexandria, VA: Association for Supervision and Curriculum Development.

De Charms, Richard. 1968. *Personal Causation: The Internal Affective Determinants of Behavior.* New York: Academic Press.

Deming, W. Edwards. 1993. *The New Economics for Industry, Government, and Education,* Cambridge, MA: M.I.T. Press.

Fullan, Michael. 1991. *The New Meaning of Change,* 2nd ed. New York: Teachers College Press.

Fuller, Frances F. 1969. "Concerns of Teachers: A Developmental Conceptualization," *American Educational Research Association Journal* 6(2).

Gaynor, Alan K. 1975. "The Study of Change in Educational Organizations: A Review of the Literature." Paper presented at the University Council for Educational Administration, Ohio State University Career Development Seminar, Columbus, March 27–30.

Goodlad, John I., and Frances M. Klein. 1970. *Behind the Classroom Door.* Worthington, OH: Charles A. Jones.

Hall, Gene E. 1988. "The Principal as Leader of the Change Facilitating Team," *Journal of Research and Development in Education* 22(1).

Hall, Gene E., and Susan F. Loucks. 1978. "Teacher Concerns as a Basis for Facilitating Staff Development," *Teachers College Record* 80(1).

Hall, Gene E., and William L. Rutherford. 1983. "Three Change Facilitator Styles: How Principals Affect Improvement Efforts." Paper presented at the Annual Meeting of the American Educational Research Association, Montreal, Canada, April.

Hall, Gene E., Shirley M. Hord, Leslie L. Huling, William L. Rutherford, and Suzanne M. Stiegelbauer. 1983. "Leadership Variables Associated with Successful School Improvement." Papers presented at the Annual Meeting of the American Educational Research Association, Montreal, Canada, April.

Hord, Shirley M., Gene E. Hall, and Suzanne Stiegelbauer. 1983. "Principals Don't Do It Alone: The Role of the Consigliere." Paper presented at the Annual Meeting of the American Educational Research Association, Montreal, Canada, April.

Hord, Shirley M., William L. Rutherford, Leslie Huling-Austin, and Gene E. Hall. 1987. *Taking Charge of Change.* Alexandria, VA: Association for Supervision and Curriculum Development.

Huberman, A. M., and D. P. Crandall. 1982. *People, Policies and Practices: Examining the Chain of School Improvement. Vol. IX: Implications for Action.* Andover, MA: The Network.

Huberman, M. and M. Miles. 1984. *Innovation up Close.* New York: Plenum.

Hunter, Madeline. 1984. "Knowing, Teaching and Supervising," in Philip L. Hosford, Ed., *Using What We Know about Teaching.* Alexandria, VA: Yearbook of the Association for Supervision and Curriculum Development.

Katz, Daniel, and Robert L. Kahn. 1978. *The Social Psychology of Organization,* 2d ed. New York: Wiley.

Kirst, Michael W. 1984. *Who Controls Our Schools?* New York: Freeman.

Leithwood, Kenneth A., and Deborah J. Montgomery. 1986. *Improving Principal Effectiveness: The Principal Profile.* Toronto: Ontario Institute for Studies in Education Press.

Lichtenstein, Gary, Milbrey W. McLaughlin, and Jennifer Knudsen. 1992. "Teacher Empowerment and Professional Knowledge" in Ann Lieberman, Ed., *The Changing Context of Teaching,* Ninety-first Yearbook of the National Society for the Study of Education, Part I. Chicago: The University of Chicago Press.

Lieberman, Ann, and Lynne Miller. 1984. "Teachers, Their World and Their Work: Implications for School Improvement," Alexandria, VA: Association for Supervision and Curriculum Development.

Lighthall, F. 1973. "Multiple Realities and Organizational Nonsolutions: An Essay on Anatomy of Educational Innovation," *School Review,* February.

Likert, Rensis. 1967. *The Human Organization: Its Management and Value.* New York: McGraw-Hill.

Lortie, Dan. 1975. *Schoolteacher: A Sociological Study.* Chicago: The University of Chicago Press.

Loucks-Horsley, Susan, and Leslie F. Hergert. 1985. *An Action Guide to School Improvement.* Arlington, VA: Association for Supervision and Curriculum Development and The Network.

Louis, K., and M. B. Miles. 1990. *Improving the Urban High School: What Works and Why.* New York: Teachers College Press.

Marris, P. 1975. *Loss and Change.* New York: Anchor Press/Doubleday.

Mealiea, Laird W. 1978. "Learned Behavior: The Key to Understanding and Preventing Employee Resistance to Change," *Group and Organizational Studies* 3(2), 211–223.

Miles, Matthew B. 1983. "Unraveling the Mystery of Institutionalization," *Educational Leadership* 41(3), 14–19.

Reddin, W. J. 1970. *Managerial Effectiveness.* New York: McGraw-Hill.

Rosenholtz, Susan J. 1989. *Teachers Workplace: A Social-Organizational Analysis.* New York: Longman.

Saranson, Seymour B. 1971. *The Culture of the School and the Problem of Change.* Boston: Allyn and Bacon.

Schön, D. 1971. *Beyond the Stable State.* New York: Norton.

Sergiovanni, T. J., and John E. Corbally, Eds. 1984. *Leadership and Organizational Culture.* Urbana-Champaign: University of Illinois Press.

Waller, Willard. 1932. *The Sociology of Teaching.* New York: Wiley.

Appendix 14–1 Change Facilitator Styles Inventory

This inventory contains descriptions of principal behavior grouped by style. The items are drawn from actual research comparing more and less effective principals involved in school improvement. The inventory provides an opportunity for you to describe a principal you know (or perhaps yourself) and to compare your responses with the change facilitator styles of these principals.

Each item comprises three different descriptors of principal behavior. Using a total of 10 points, distribute points among the three to indicate the extent to which each describes your principal's behavior. Record your responses on the score sheet provided.

Score Sheet

Principal Behaviors		*R*	*M*	*I*	*Totals*
A. Vision	1.	——	——	——	10
	2.	——	——	——	10
	3.	——	——	——	10
B. Structuring the school	4.	——	——	——	10
as a work place	5.	——	——	——	10
	6.	——	——	——	10
	7.	——	——	——	10
	8.	——	——	——	10
C. Structuring	9.	——	——	——	10
involvement	10.	——	——	——	10
with change	11.	——	——	——	10
	12.	——	——	——	10
	13.	——	——	——	10
	14.	——	——	——	10
D. Sharing of	15.	——	——	——	10
responsibility	16	——	——	——	10
	17.	——	——	——	10
E. Decision making	18.	——	——	——	10
	19.	——	——	——	10
	20.	——	——	——	10
F. Guiding and	21.	——	——	——	10
supporting	22.	——	——	——	10
	23.	——	——	——	10
	24.	——	——	——	10
	25.	——	——	——	10
	26.	——	——	——	10
G. Structuring his/her	27.	——	——	——	10
professional role	28.	——	——	——	10
	29.	——	——	——	10
	30.	——	——	——	10
	31.	——	——	——	10

Appendix 14–1 *(Continued)*

Principal Behaviors		R	M	I	Totals
	32.	——	——	——	10
	33.	——	——	——	10
	34.	——	——	——	10
	35.	——	——	——	10
	36.	——	——	——	10
	37.	——	——	——	10
	TOTALS				370

Score	Style Emphasis
0–39	Very Low
40–136	Low
137–233	Medium
234–330	High
331–370	Very High

Change Facilitator Styles Inventory (CFSI)

Principal Behaviors		R	M	I
A. Vision	1.	Accepts district goals as school goals	Accepts district goals but makes adjustments at school level to accommodate particular needs of the school	Respects district goals but insists on goals for school that give priority to this school's student need
	2.	Future goals/direction of school are determined in response to district level goals/ priorities	Anticipates the instructional and management needs of school and plans for them	Takes initiative in identifying future goals and priorities for school and in preparing to meet them
	3.	Responds to teachers', students' and parents' interest in the goals of the school and the district	Collaborates with others in reviewing and identifying school goals	Establishes framework of expectations for the school and involves others in setting goals within that framework
B. Structuring the school as a work place	4.	Maintains low profile relative to day-by-day operation of school	Very actively involved in day-by-day management	Directs the ongoing operation of the school with emphasis on instruction through personal actions and clear designation of responsibility

Appendix 14–1 *(Continued)*

Principal Behaviors	R	M	I
	5. Grants teachers autonomy and independence, provides guidelines for students	Provides guidelines and expectations for teachers and students	Sets standards and expects high performance levels for teachers, students, and self
	6. Ensures that district and school policies are followed and strives to see that disruptions in the school day are minimal	Works with teachers, students, and parents to maintain effective operation of the school	First priority is the instructional program; personnel and collaborative efforts are directed at supporting that priority
	7. Responds to requests and needs as they arise in an effort to keep all persons involved with the school comfortable and satisfied	Expects all involved with the school to contribute to effective instruction and management in the school	Insists that all persons involved with the school give priority to teaching and learning
	8. Allows school norms to evolve over time	Helps establish and clarify norms for the school	Establishes, clarifies, and models norms for the school
C. Structuring involvement with change	9. Relies on information provided by other change facilitators, usually from outside the school, for knowledge of the innovation	Uses information from a variety of sources to gain knowledge of the innovation	Seeks out information from teachers, district personnel, and others to gain an understanding of the innovation and the changes required
	10. Supports district expectations for change	Meets district expectations for change	Accommodates district expectations for change and pushes adjustments and additions that will benefit his/her school
	11. Sanctions the change process and strives to resolve conflicts when they arise	Involved regularly in the change process, sometimes with a focus on management and at other times with a focus on the impact of the change	Directs the change process in ways that lead to effective use by all teachers
	12. Expectations for teachers, relative to change, are given in general terms	Tells teachers that they are expected to use the innovation	Gives teachers specific expectations and steps regarding application of the change

Appendix 14–1 *(Continued)*

Principal Behaviors		R	M	I
	13.	Monitors the change effort principally through brief, spontaneous conversations and unsolicited reports	Monitors the change effort through planned conversations with individuals and groups and from informal observations of instruction	Monitors the change effort through class-room observation, review of lesson plans, reports that reveal specific teacher involvement, and specific attention to the work of individual teachers
	14.	May discuss with the teacher information gained through monitoring	Discusses information gained through monitoring with teacher in relation to teacher's expected behavior	Gives direct feedback to teacher concerning information gained through monitoring, which includes a comparison with expected behaviors and a plan for next steps, possibly including improvements
D. Sharing of responsibility	15.	Allows others to assume the responsibility for the change effort	Tends to do most of the intervening on the change effort but will share some responsibility	Will delegate to carefully chosen others some of the responsibility for the change effort
	16.	Others who assume responsibility are more likely to be outside the school, e.g., district facilitators	Others who assume responsibility may come from within or from outside the school	Others who assume responsibility are likely to be from within the school
	17.	Others who assume responsibility have considerable autonomy and independence in which responsibilities they assume and how they carry them out	Coordinates responsibilities and stays informed about how others are handling these responsibilities	First establishes which responsibilities will be delegated and how they are to be accomplished, then works with others and closely monitors the carrying out of tasks
E. Decision making	18.	Makes decisions required for ongoing operation of the school as deadlines for those decisions approach	Actively involved in routine decision making relative to instructional and administrative affairs	Handles routine decisions through established procedures and assigned responsibilities, thereby requiring minimal time
	19.	Makes decisions influenced by the immediate circumstances of the situation and formal policies	Makes decisions based on the norms and expectations that guide the school and the management needs of the school	Makes decisions based on the standard of high expectations and what is best for the school as a whole, particularly learning outcomes and the longer-term goals

Appendix 14–1 *(Continued)*

Principal Behaviors	R	M	I
	20. Willingly allows others to participate in decision making or to make decisions independently	Allows others to participate in decision making but maintains control of the process through personal involvement	Allows others to participate in decision making and delegates decision making to others within carefully established parameters of established goals and expectations
F. Guiding and supporting	21. Believes teachers are professionals and leaves them alone to do their work unless they request assistance or support	Believes teachers are a part of the total faculty and establishes guidelines for all teachers to be involved with the change effort	Believes teachers are responsible for developing the best possible instruction, so expectations for their involvement with innovation is clearly established
	22. Responds quickly to requests for assistance and support in a way that is satisfying to the requester	Monitors the progress of the change effort and attempts to anticipate needed assistance and resources	Anticipates the need for assistance and resources and provides support as needed as well as sometimes in advance of potential blockages
	23. Checks with teachers to see how things are going and to maintain awareness of any major problems	Maintains close contact with teachers involved in the change effort in an attempt to identify things that might be done to assist teachers with the change	Collects and uses information from a variety of sources to be aware of how the change effort is progressing and to plan interventions that will increase the probability of a successful, quality implementation
	24. Relies on whatever training is available with the innovation in order to aid in the development of teacher's knowledge and skill relative to the innovation	In addition to the regularly provided assistance, seeks out and uses sources within and outside the school to develop teacher knowledge and skills	Provides increased knowledge or skill needed by the teachers through possible utilization of personnel and resources within the building
	25. Provides general support for teachers as persons and as professionals	Provides support to individuals and to subgroups for specific purposes related to the change as well as to provide for their personal welfare	Provides direct programmatic support through interventions targeted to individuals and to the staff as a whole

Appendix 14–1 *(Continued)*

Principal Behaviors	R	M	I
	26. Tries to minimize the demands of the change effort on teachers	Moderates demands of the change effort to protect teachers perceived overload	Keeps ever-present demands on teachers for effective implementation
G. Structuring her/his professional role	27. Sees role as administrator	Sees role as avoiding or minimizing problems so instruction may occur	Sees role as one of ensuring the school has a strong instructional program with teachers teaching students so they are able to learn
	28. Believes others will generate the initiative for any school improvement that is needed	Engages others in regular review of school situation to avoid any reduction in school effectiveness	Identifies areas in need of improvement and initiates action for change
	29. Relies primarily on others for introduction of new ideas into the school	Is alert to new ideas and introduces them to faculty or allows others in school to do so	Sorts through new ideas presented from within and from outside the school and implements those deemed to have high promise for school improvement
	30. Is concerned with how others view him	Is concerned with how others view the school	Is concerned with how others view the impact of the school on students
	31. Accepts the rules of the district	Lives by the rules of the district but goes beyond minimum expectations	Respects the rules of the district but determines behavior by what is required for maximum school effectiveness
	32. Opinions and concerns of others determine what will be accomplished and how.	Is consistent in setting and accomplishing tasks and does much of it herself/himself	Tasks determined and accomplished are consistent with school priorities but responsibility can be delegated to others
	33. Maintains a general sense of "where the school is" and of how teachers are feeling about things	Is well informed about what is happening in the school and who is doing what	Maintains specific knowledge of all that is going on in the school through direct contact with the classroom, with individual teachers, and with students

Appendix 14–1 *(Continued)*

Principal Behaviors	R	M	I
34.	Responds to others in a manner intended to please them	Responds to others in a way that will be supportive of the operation of the school	Responds to others with concern but places student priorities above all else
35.	Develops minimal knowledge of what use of the innovation entails	Becomes knowledgeable about general use of the innovation and what is needed to support its use	Develops sufficient knowledge about use to be able to make specific teaching suggestions and to troubleshoot any problems that may emerge
36.	Indefinitely delays having staff do tasks if perceiving that staff are overloaded	Contends that staff are already very busy and paces requests and task loads accordingly	Will knowingly sacrifice short-term feelings of staff if doing a task now is necessary for the longer-term goals of the school
37.	Ideas are offered by each staff member, but one or two have dominant influence	Some ideas are offered by staff and some by the principal; then consensus is gradually developed	Seeks teachers' ideas as well as their reactions to her/his ideas; then priorities are set

The items on this inventory were identified as a result of an extensive research program investigating the relationship between principal behavior and successful school improvement. This program was conducted at the Research and Development Center for Teacher Education, University of Texas, Austin. The items are from Gene E. Hail and William, L. Rutherford (1983), "Three Change Facilitator Styles: How Principals Affect Improvement Efforts," paper presented at the Annual Meeting of the American Educational Research, Association, Montreal, April. Available from the RDCTE, Austin, TX, document number 3155. See also "Leadership Variables Associated with Successful School Improvement" (Austin, TX: RDCTE, 1983).

Part V

The Moral Dimension

C h a p t e r **15**

Administering as a Moral Craft

In this book a number of conceptions of the principal have been discussed: Strategic problem solver, cultural leader, barterer, and initiator are examples. It's fair to ask whether these are the roles and images of leadership that one should follow in order to be an effective principal. The answer is yes—well, no—actually maybe. Similarly, what about the motivational concepts and ideas presented in Chapter 11, the new principles of management and leadership presented in Chapter 3, the characteristics of successful schools, the forces of leadership, strategies for bringing about change, and the dimensions of school culture discussed in other chapters? Will these ideas, if routinely applied, help one to be an effective principal? The answer is the same. Yes—well, no—actually maybe. Unfortunately there is no guarantee that the concepts presented in this book will fit all readers or the contexts and problems they face in the same way. Leadership is a personal thing. It comprises three important dimensions—one's heart, head, and hand.

The Heart, Head, and Hand of Leadership

The *heart* of leadership has to do with what a person believes, values, dreams about, and is committed to—that person's *personal vision,* to use a popular term. To be sure, sharing personal conceptions of what is a good school will reveal many common qualities, but what often makes them personal statements is that they will differ as well. The *head* of leadership has to do with the theories of practice each of us has developed over time and our ability to reflect on the situations we face in light of these theories. This process of reflection combined with our personal vision becomes the basis for our strategies and actions. Finally, the *hand* of leadership has to do with the actions we take, the decisions we make, the leadership and management behaviors we use as our strategies become institutionalized in the form of school programs, policies, and procedures. As with heart and head, how we choose to manage and lead are personal reflections not only of our vision and practical theories but of our personalities and our responses to the unique situations we face as well. In this idiosyncratic world, one-best-way approaches and cookie cutter strategies do not work very well. Instead, diversity will likely be the norm as principals practice. Each principal must find her or his way, develop her or his approach if the heart, head, and hand of leadership are to come together in the form of successful principalship practice.

Does that mean that the concepts presented in this book are not true? If they are not truths to be emulated and imitated, what are they? They comprise a different kind of truth. They represent a concept boutique on one hand and a metaphor repository on another. The idea is to visit the boutique trying on one idea after another seeking a fit here or there and to visit the repository seeking to create new understandings of situations one faces and new alternatives to one's practice. As boutique and repository the role of knowledge about schooling changes from being something that principals apply uniformly to being something useful that informs the decisions they make as they practice. This is the nature of reflective practice.

The Moral Imperative

Although many may prefer the work of administration to be some sort of an applied science that is directly connected to a firm knowledge base of theory and research, the reality we face is that it is much more craftlike. The message from this reality is equally clear. Successful practice requires the development of craft know-how. Craft know-how according to Blumberg (1989) includes the following:

- Being able to develop and refine "a nose for things."
- Having a sense of what constitutes an acceptable result in any particular problematic situation.
- Understanding the nature of the "materials" with which one is working. This includes oneself as a "material" that needs to be understood, as well as others. It also includes understanding the way other parts of the environment may affect the materials and the acceptableness of the solution at a particular point in time.
- Knowing administrative techniques and having the skill to employ them in the most efficacious way possible.
- Knowing what to do and when to do it. This involves not only pragmatic decisions— what behavior or procedure is called for at a particular time—but also implies issues of right and wrong. Much as Tom's (1984) description of teaching is that of a "moral" craft, so too is the practice of administration one in which there are moral dimensions to every action taken, with the possible exception of those that are simply mundane. This is not to suggest that administrators are aware of these moral dimensions at all times; it is simply to suggest that they are present.
- Having a sense of "process," that is, being able to diagnose and interpret the meaning of what is occurring as people interact in any problematic situation. (47)

Yet, administering schools, as Blumberg suggests, is no ordinary craft. Bringing together head, heart, and hand in practice; the unique nature of the school's mission; and the typically loosely structured, nonlinear, and messy context of schooling combine to make administering a *moral* craft, a fate shared with teaching (Tom, 1984) and supervision (Sergiovanni and Starratt, 1988). The reasons for this moral imperative are as follows.

1. The job of the principal is to transform the school from being an organization of technical functions in pursuit of objective outcomes into an *institution*. Organizations are little more than technical instruments for achieving objectives. As instruments they celebrate the value of effectiveness and efficiency by being more concerned with "doing things right" than with "doing right things." Institutions, however, are effective and efficient and more. They are responsive, adaptive enterprises that exist not only to get a particular job done but as entities in and of themselves. As Selznick (1957) points out, organizations become institutions when they transcend the technical requirements needed for the task at hand. In his words, "Institutionalization is a *process*. It is something that happens to an organization over time, reflecting the organization's own distinctive history, the people who have been in it, the groups it embodies and the vested interests they have created, and the way it has adopted to its environment. . . ." (Selznick, 1957:16). He continues:

> *Organizations become institutions as they are* infused with value, *that is, prized not as tools alone but as sources of direct personal gratification and vehicles of group integrity. This infusion produces a distinct identity for the organization. Where institutionalization is well advanced, distinctive outlooks, habits, and other commitments are unified, coloring all aspects of organizational life and lending it a* social integration *that goes well beyond formal coordination and command. (Selznick, 1954:40)*

Selznick's conception of institution is similar to the more familiar conception of school as *learning community*. To become either, the school must move beyond concerns for goals and roles to the task of building purposes into its structure and embodying these purposes in everything that it does with the effect of transforming school members from neutral participants to committed followers. The embodiment of purpose and the development of followership are inescapably moral.

2. The job of the school is to transform its students not only by providing them with knowledge and skills but by building *character* and instilling *virtue*. As Cuban (1988) points out, both technical and moral images are present in teaching and administering. "The technical image contains values that prize accumulated knowledge, efficiency, orderliness, productivity, and social usefulness; the moral image, while not disregarding such values, prizes values directed at molding character, shaping attitudes, and producing a virtuous, thoughtful person" (xvii). Technical and moral images of administration cannot be separated in practice. Every technical decision has moral implications. Emphasizing orderliness, for example, might serve as a lesson in diligence for students and might be a reminder to teachers that professional goals cannot be pursued to the extent that bureaucratic values are compromised.

3. Whether concern is for virtue or efficiency, some *standard* has to be adopted. What is efficient in this circumstance? How will virtue be determined? Determining criteria for effective teaching, deciding on what is a good discipline policy, or coming to grips with promotion criteria standards, for example, all require value judgments. Answers to questions of how and what cannot be resolved objectively as if they were factual assertions, but must be treated as normative assertions. Normative assertions are true only because we decide that they are. As pointed out in Chapter 9, "we must decide what ought to be the case. We cannot *discover* what ought to be the case by investigating what is the case" (Taylor, 1961:248). Normative assertions are moral statements.

4. Despite commitments to empowerment and shared decision making, relationships between principals and others are inherently unequal. Although often downplayed, and whether they want it or not, principals typically have more *power* than teachers, students, parents, and others. This power is in part derived legally from their hierarchical position, but for the most part it is obtained de facto by virtue of the greater access to information and people that their position affords them. They are not chained to a tight schedule. They do a lot of walking around. They are the ones who get the phone calls, who are out in the streets, who visit the central office, who have access to the files, and so forth. As a result they function more frequently in the roles of figurehead and liaison with outside agencies. They have greater access to information than do other people in the school. This allows them to decide what information will be shared with others, what information will be withheld, and frequently what information will be forgotten. Often teachers and others in the school rely on the principal to serve as the "coordinating mechanism" that links together what they are doing with what others are doing. In teaching, where much of the work is invisible, the coordinating function is a powerful one. Furthermore, much of the information that principals accumulate is confidential. When teachers have problems they frequently confide in the principal. Information is a source of power, and the accumulation of power has moral consequences.

Whenever there is an unequal distribution of power between two people, the relationship becomes a moral one. Whether intended or not, leadership involves an offer to control. The follower accepts this offer on the assumption that control will not be exploited. In this sense, leadership is not a right but a responsibility. Morally speaking, its purpose is not to enhance the leader's position or make it easier for the leader to get what she or he wants but to benefit the school. The test of moral leadership under these conditions is whether the competence, well-being, and independence of the follower are enhanced as a result of accepting control and whether the school benefits. Tom (1980) makes a similar argument in pointing out that "the teacher–student relationship is inherently moral because of its inequality" (317).

5. The context for administration is surprisingly loose, chaotic, and ambiguous. Thus, despite demands and constraints that circumscribe the principal's world, in actuality, *discretion* is built into the job, and this discretion has moral implication.

For example, frequently how things look is different than how things work. In their research on the reality of managing schools, Morris and colleagues (1984) discovered numerous instances in which principals and schools were able to develop implicit policies and pursue courses of action that only remotely resembled officially sanctioned policies and actions. They noted that not only maintaining student enrollment levels but increasing them was often viewed as a managerial necessity by principals. However, they were not motivated for official "educational" or "societal" reasons, but to protect or enhance the resource allocation base of their schools. Staffing patterns and budget allocations were often linked to a principal's standing among peers and were related as well to morale and productivity levels among teachers. Furthermore, principals of larger schools had more clout with the central office. Simply put, more staff and bigger budgets were viewed as being better. Schools losing resources, however, "usually suffer a decline in purposefulness, security, and confidence that goes beyond the loss of operating funds" (128).

As a result, principals tended to view monitoring, protecting, and increasing school enrollments and attendance as one of their key, albeit implicit, tasks. This led them to engage in courses of action that were at variance with the officially sanctioned definition of their tasks and roles. There was, for example, a concerted effort to change existing programs and revise the existing curriculum so they were more attractive to students and thus better able to hold their enrollment. One of the principals reported, "We may have to cut physics, for instance, and add environmental science. It's in. . . . I've got to get my faculty to see that they have to reshape the traditional curriculum of the school. Their jobs are at stake" (Morris et al., 1984:128–129). Another principal in their study worked to change his school's kindergarten program so that it was more structured and "rigorous," not for educational reasons or philosophical commitments but so that the school would be better able to compete with the neighborhood Catholic school.

Despite clear guidelines governing attendance procedures (e.g., fixed attendance boundaries and age requirements), principals became flexible by bending the rules for student admissions and taking liberties with reporting enrollment information to the central office. In the words of one principal, "In general, I'm not picky about where the students in the school live," noting further that if a child subsequently became a behavioral problem or was suspected of being a behavioral problem she always checked the home address (Morris et al., 1984:30). Some principals were inclined to look the other way even when they knew that students came from other school districts if they thought the students were "extremely bright." Some principals used leniency in enforcing attendance boundaries as the lever to extract better behavior and more achievement from students. Principals stressed that they were doing the parents and students a favor and expected good behavior in return. Not all students were treated equally. While bright students were encouraged to attend, "troublemakers" were not. In the words of one principal, "Let him go, that guy's been nothing but trouble for us" (Morris et al., 1984:131).

Although discretion can provide principals with a license for abuse, it is also a necessary prerequisite for leadership. "From choice comes autonomy. Autonomy is the necessary condition for leadership to arise. Without choice, there is no autonomy. Without autonomy, there is no leadership" (Cuban, 1988:xxii). Discretion, therefore, is necessary if principals are to function effectively. Yet, how principals handle discretion raises moral issues and has moral consequences for the school.

Normative Rationality

Key to understanding the moral dimension in leadership is understanding the difference between *normative rationality* (rationality based on what we believe and what we consider to be good) and *technical rationality* (rationality based on what is effective and efficient). Happily, the two are not mutually exclusive. Principals want what is good and what is effective for their schools, but when the two are in conflict, the moral choice is to prize the former over the latter. Starratt makes the point poignantly as follows: " 'Organizational effectiveness' employs technical rationality, functional rationality, linear logic. Efficiency is the highest value, not loyalty, harmony, honor, beauty, truth. One can run an efficient extermination camp or an efficient monastery. The principles of efficiency are basically the same in either context" (Sergiovanni and Starratt, 1988:218).

Normative rationality provides the basis for moral leadership. Instead of just relying on bureaucratic authority to force a person to do something or a psychological authority to manipulate a person into doing something, the leader—principal or teacher as the case may be—provides reasons for selecting one alternative over another. The reasons are open to discussion and evaluation by everyone. To pass the test of normative rationality, the reasons must embody the purposes and values that the group shares—the sacred covenant that bonds everyone in the school together as members of a learning community.

One might properly ask: What is the place of scientific authority in the form of expertness established by educational research in getting a person to do something? Isn't it enough that research says we ought to do this or that? Scientifically speaking, teaching, management, and leadership are underdeveloped fields. As a result, research findings are often so general as to comprise common understandings widely known to the general public (e.g., a positive school climate provides a better setting for learning than a negative one; students who spend more time learning learn more; relating school content to personal experiences helps students understand better; teachers are more likely to accept a decision they help shape and make) or so idiosyncratic (e.g., discovering that making Billy a blackboard monitor has helped his behavior in class; or noting that teacher Barbara does not respond well to one-on-one supervision but seems to get a lot out of collegial supervision) that they are difficult to apply beyond the setting from which they come.

Nonetheless, research and reflecting on personal experience can often provide us with patterns of characteristics to which many students or teachers are likely to respond in the same way. These insights can help, and this form of knowledge is often invaluable to principals. But this knowledge cannot represent a source of authority for action that replaces moral authority. As Smith and Blase (1987) explain,

> *A leader in moral terms is one who fully realizes the . . . serious limitations on our ability to make accurate predictions and master the instructional process. Moreover, such a leader must encourage others to fully realize these limitations. Based on this awareness, a moral leader refuses to allow discussions of major pedagogical issues to be dominated by what the research supposedly demonstrates. . . . To do so would be to perpetuate the fiction that we have the kind of knowledge that we do not in fact possess. Rather, disagreements over how and*

what to teach must be played out in terms of reasoned discourse. The generalizations of educational inquiry can of course be part of these reasons, but they are not epistemologically privileged—they must share the stage with personal experience, a recounting of the experience of others, with philosophical and sociological considerations, and so on. (39)

The key is the phrase "epistemologically privileged." It is not that research findings are unimportant but that they are *no more important than other sources of authority.* One "so on" that might be added to Smith and Blase's list is conceptions of what is valued by the school that define it as a unique learning community.

Normative rationality influences the practice of leadership in schools in two ways. Principals bring to their job normative baggage in the form of biases and prejudices, ways of thinking, personality quirks, notions of what works and what doesn't, and other factors that function as personal theories of practice governing what they are likely to do and not do, and school cultures are defined by a similar set of biases that represent the center of shared values and commitments that define the school as an institution. Both are sources of norms that function as standards and guidelines for what goes on in the school. As a school's culture is strengthened and its center of values becomes more public and pervasive, normative rationality becomes more legitimate. Everyone knows what the school stands for and why and can articulate these purposes and use them as guidelines for action. This in-building of purpose "involves transforming [persons] in groups from neutral, technical units into participants who have a peculiar stamp, sensitivity, and commitment" (Selznick, 1957:150).

Followership Is the Goal

The importance of purposing to leadership changes how it is understood and practiced. With purposing in place in a school, one cannot become a leader without first becoming a follower. The concept of followership was discussed in Chapters 6 and 7. It was pointed out that what it means to be a follower and what it means to be a subordinate are very different. Subordinates respond to bureaucratic authority and sometimes to personal authority. Followers, by contrast, respond to ideas. You can't be a follower unless you have something to follow. Furthermore, as Zaleznik (1989) suggests, subordinates may cooperate with the management system but are rarely committed to it. By contrast, one of the hallmarks of being a follower is commitment. As Kelly (1988) points out, followers "are committed to the organization and to a purpose, principle, or person outside themselves. . . . [And as a result] [t]hey build their competence and focus their efforts for maximum impact" (144). Followers, by definition, are never constrained by minimums but are carried by their commitment to performance that typically exceeds expectations. Subordinates, by contrast, do what they are supposed to; they tend not to do more.

When subordinateness is transcended by followership, a different kind of hierarchy emerges in the school. Principals, teachers, students, parents, and others find themselves equally "subordinate" to a set of ideas and shared conceptions to which they are committed. As a result, teachers respond and comply not because of the principal's directives but out of a sense of obligation and commitment to these shared values. That's what it means to be a follower.

The principal's job is to provide the kind of purposing to the school that helps followership to emerge. She or he then provides the conditions and support that allow people to function in ways that are consistent with agreed-upon values. At the same time, the principal has a special responsibility to continually highlight the values, to protect them, and to see that they are enforced. The true test of leadership under these conditions is the principal's ability to get others in the school to share in the responsibility for guarding these values. This litany of roles was discussed in the text as leadership by purposing, empowerment and enablement, outrage, and finally kindling outrage in others.

One of the persistent problems of administration is obtaining compliance, which is at the heart of the principal's role. Invariably, compliance occurs in response to some sort of authority, but not all sources of authority are equally powerful or palatable. In this book, four sources of authority have been described: bureaucratic, personal, professional, and moral. All four have a role to play if schools are to function effectively, however, the four compete with each other. When principals use bureaucratic authority, they rely on rules, mandates, and regulations in efforts to direct thought and action. When principals use personal authority, they rely on their own interpersonal style, cleverness, guile, political know-how, and other forms of managerial and psychological skill in order to direct thought and action. When principals rely on professional authority, they appeal to expertness, expecting everyone to be subordinate to a form of technical rationality that is presumably validated by craft notions of what constitutes best educational practice or scientific findings from educational research. When principals rely on moral authority, they bring to the forefront a form of normative rationality as discussed above that places everyone subordinate to a set of ideas, ideals, and shared values and asks them to respond morally by doing their duty, meeting their obligations, and accepting their responsibilities. All are important, but the art of administration is balancing the four competing sources of authority in such a way that moral and professional authority flourish without neglecting bureaucratic and personal authority.

The Challenge of Leadership

In the principalship, the challenge of leadership is to make peace with two competing imperatives, the managerial and the moral. The two imperatives are unavoidable and the neglect of either creates problems. Schools must be run effectively and efficiently if they are to survive. Policies must be in place. Budgets must be set. Teachers must be assigned. Classes must be scheduled. Reports must be completed. Standardized tests must be given. Supplies must be purchased. The school must be kept clean. Students must be protected from violence. Classrooms must be orderly. These are essential tasks that guarantee the survival of the school as an organization. Yet, for the school to transform itself into an institution, a learning community must emerge. Institutionalization is the moral imperative that principals face.

Discussing the moral imperative in administration; proposing such leadership values as purposing, empowerment, outrage, and kindling outrage in others; and arguing for the kind of balance among bureaucratic, psychological, professional, and moral sources of authority in schools that noticeably tilts toward professional and moral challenge the "professional manager" conception of the principalship by placing concerns for substance firmly over concerns for process.

On the upside, the development of school administration as a form of management technology brought with it much needed attention to the development of better management know-how and of organizational skills badly needed to deal with an educational system that continues to grow in technical, legal, and bureaucratic complexity. On the downside, professionalism has too often resulted in principals thinking of themselves less as statespersons, educators, and philosophers, and more as organizational experts who have become absorbed in what Abraham Zaleznik (1989) refers to as the *managerial mystique.* "As it evolved in practice, the mystique required managers to dedicate themselves to process, structures, roles, and indirect forms of communication and to ignore ideas, people, emotions, and direct talk. It deflected attention from the realities [of education] while it reassured and rewarded those who believed in the mystique" (2). The managerial mystique holds so strongly to the belief that "the right methods" will produce good results that the methods themselves too often become surrogates for results, and to the belief that management and bureaucratic controls will overcome human shortcomings and enhance human productivity that controls become ends in themselves. School improvement plans, for example, become substitutes for school, improvements; scores on teacher appraisal forms become substitutes for good teaching; accumulating credits earned in courses and required inservice workshops become substitutes for changes in school practice; discipline plans become substitutes for student control; leadership styles become substitutes for purpose and substance; congeniality becomes a substitute for collegiality; cooperation becomes a substitute for commitment; and compliance becomes a substitute for results,

Zaleznik (1989) maintains that the managerial mystique is the antithesis of leadership. The epitome of the managerial mystique is the belief that anyone who can manage one kind of enterprise can also manage any other kind. It is the generic management techniques and generic interpersonal skills that count rather than issues of purpose and substance. Without purpose and substance, Zaleznik argues, there can be no leadership. "Leadership is based on a compact that binds those who lead and those who follow into the same moral, intellectual and emotional commitment" (15).

Building the Character of Your School

One of the major themes of this book is the importance of the school's culture. For better or for worse, culture influences much of what is thought, said, and done in a school. Character is a concept similar to culture but much less neutral. A school's character is known by how the school is viewed by members and outsiders in ethical and moral terms. Building and enhancing the school's character is the key to establishing its credibility among students, teachers, parents, and administrators and externally in the broader community. Wilkins (1989) notes that the components of an organization's character are its common understandings of *purpose* and identity that provide a sense of "who we are";

faith of members in the fairness of the leadership and in the ability of the organization to meet its commitments and to get the job done; and the distinctive cultural attributes that define the tacit customs, networks of individuals, and accepted ways of working together and of working with others outside of the organization. How reliable are the actions of the school? How firm is the school in its convictions? How just is its disposition? Wilkins points out that purpose, faith, and cultural attributes "add up to the collective organizational competence" (1989:27). To him, faith is a particularly important component of an organization's character, and loss of faith in either the organization or its leadership results in loss of character. Building faith restores character. Enhancing faith increases character. Without faith and character the organization and its members are not able to move beyond the ordinary to extraordinary performance. With faith such a transformation is possible. No matter how relentlessly principals pursue their managerial imperative, reliability in action, firmness in conviction, and just disposition are the consequences of the moral imperative. Without tending to the moral imperative there can be no organizational character, and without character a school can be neither good nor effective.

A Commitment to Democratic Values

The inescapable moral nature of administrative work and in particular seeking to establish moral authority embodied in the form of purposing and shared values and expressed as "cultural leadership" raises important questions of manipulation and control. Cultural leadership can provide principals with levers to manipulate others that are more powerful than the levers associated with bureaucratic and psychological authority. Lakomski (1985) raises the question squarely:

> To put the objection more strongly, it may be argued that if all cultural analysis does is to help those in power, such as principals and teachers, to oppress some students more effectively by learning about their views, opinions, and 'student cultures', then this method is just another and more sophisticated way to prevent students (and other oppressed groups) from democratic participation in educational affairs. (15).

Her comments apply as well to teachers and others. Furthermore, cultural leadership can become a powerful weapon for masking the many problems of diversity, justice, and equality that confront schools. There is nothing inherently democratic about cultural leadership, and, indeed, depending on its substance this kind of leadership can compromise democratic values. Consensus building and commitment to shared values can often be little more than devices for maintaining an unsatisfactory status quo and for discouraging dissent. Finally, not all covenants are equal. The values that define the "center" of different school communities are not interchangeable.

Cultural leadership can be understood and practiced as a technology available to achieve any goal and to embody any vision or as a means to celebrate a particular set of basic values that emerge from the American democratic tradition. It makes a difference, for example, whether the basic values that define a school community revolve around themes of efficiency, effectiveness, and excellence or whether these are considered to be mere means values in service to such ends values as justice, diversity, equality, and goodness. In the spirit of the latter point of view, Clark and Meloy (1984) propose the Declaration of Independence as a metaphor for managing schools to replace bureaucracy. This metaphor guarantees to all persons that school management decisions will support such values as equality, life, liberty, and the pursuit of happiness based on the consent of the governed.

Discussion of democracy in schools typically wins nods from readers. However, as Quantz, Cambron-McCabe, and Dantley (1991) point out, democracy is not always understood as both process and substance.

> *There is often a confusion of democracy with pure process—the belief that as long as there is some form of participatory decision-making that democracy has been achieved. We argue, however, that democracy implies both a process and a goal, that the two, while often contradictory, cannot be separated. We believe that democratic processes cannot justify undemocratic ends. For example, we cannot justify racial and gender inequity on the basis that the majority voted for it. While this dual-reference test for democracy is not simple or clean, while it often requires us to choose between two incompatible choices, both in the name of democracy, we can conceive of no other way to approach it. In other words, even though an appeal to democratic authority cannot provide a clear and unequivocable blueprint for action in every particular instance, it can provide a general and viable direction for intelligent and moral decision-making by school administrators.*

One of the challenges of moral leadership in schools is to engage oneself and others in the process of decision making without thought to self-interest. Can we discuss and decide our grading policies, discipline procedures, student grouping practices, supervisory strategies, and so forth without regard to whether we will be winners or losers? Sending children routinely to the principal's office for discipline, for example, or favoring homogeneous grouping of students may be in the interest of teachers but not students. Requiring all teachers to teach the same way may make it easier for the principal to hold teachers accountable, but not for teachers who want to teach in ways that make sense to them. Discouraging parental involvement in school governance makes for fewer headaches for school people but disenfranchises the parents. What is just under these circumstances? John Rawls (1971) has suggested that decisions such as these should be made by people choosing in a hypothetical position of fairness under what he called "a veil of ignorance." The idea is to pretend that we don't know anything about ourselves—our sex, our race, our position in the school, our talents, and so forth. We don't know, in other words, whether we are black or white, principal or teacher, student or custodian, parent or teacher aide. Our identities are only revealed when the veil of ignorance is lifted. Rawls maintains that in this way we are likely to fashion our principles and make decisions regardless of who we turn out to be. With bias diminished, chances are that the principles would be fairer and the decisions more just.

A Personal Note

How committed are you to becoming a successful school principal? Generally speaking, commitment to your present job provides a good idea of one's overall commitment to work. For an indication of your present job commitment, respond on the Job Commitment Scale Exhibit 15–1. This scale contains 16 items about how people feel about their jobs. Indicate the extent to which you agree or disagree with each item. As you count your score, reverse-score items 6, 8, and 16. Your score will range from a low of 16 to a high of 64, with 64 representing the highest level of commitment. Keep in mind that there is always the chance that a person's commitment to work may be high, but that her or his present job presents such unusual difficulties that low commitment and a low score result.

Anyone aspiring to the principalship had better have a strong commitment to work. This assertion should perhaps be modified as follows: Anyone who is aspiring to be a *successful* principal had better have a strong commitment to work. Success has its price. Consider, for example, the following statement:

> *A passion for excellence means thinking big and starting small: excellence happens when high purpose and intense pragmatism meet. This is almost but not quite, the whole truth. We believe a passion for excellence also carries a price, and we state it simply: the adventure of excellence is not for the faint of heart.*
>
> *Adventure? You bet. It's not just a job. It's a personal commitment. Whether we're looking at a billion dollar corporation or a three-person accounting department, we see that excellence is achieved by people who muster up the nerve (and the passion) to step out—in spite of doubt, or fear, or job description (to maintain face-to-face contact with other people, namely customers and colleagues). They won't retreat behind office doors, committees, memos or layers of staff, knowing this is the fair bargain they make for extraordinary results. They may step out for love, because of a burning desire to be the best, to make a difference, or perhaps, as a colleague recently explained, "because the thought of being average scares the hell out of me." (Peters and Austin, 1985:414)*

In his studies of high-performing leaders, Peter Vaill (1984) found that "(1) Leaders of high-performing systems put in extraordinary amounts of time; (2) Leaders of high-performing systems have very strong feelings about the attachment of the system's purposes; and (3) Leaders of high-performing systems focus on key issues and variables" (94). Vaill notes that "there are of course many nuances, subtleties, and local specialists connected with the leadership of many high-performing systems, but over and over again, Time, Feeling, and Focus appear no matter what else appears" (94). The three go hand in hand. Vaill states, for example, that administrators who put in large amounts of time without feeling or focus are exhibiting "workaholism." Time and feeling without focus, however, often lead to dissipated energy and disappointment. Finally, time and focus without feeling seem to lack the necessary passion and excitement for providing symbolic and cultural leadership. Successful leaders—principals among them—are not afraid of hard work. By putting in large amounts of time, they demonstrate that they are not afraid of

EXHIBIT 15–1   Job Commitment Index

Responses: 4—Strongly Agree, 3—Agree, 2—Disagree, 1—Strongly Disagree

	1	2	3	4
1. Most of the important things that happen to me involve my work.	—	—	—	—
2. I spend a great deal of time on matters related to my job, both during and after hours.	—	—	—	—
3. I feel badly if I don't perform well on my job.	—	—	—	—
4. I think about my job even when I'm not working.	—	—	—	—
5. I would probably keep working even if I didn't have to.	—	—	—	—
6. I have a perspective on my job that does not let it interfere with other aspects of my life.	—	—	—	—
7. Performing well on my job is extremely important to me.	—	—	—	—
8. Most things in my life are more important to me than my job.	—	—	—	—
9. I avoid taking on extra duties and responsibilities in my work.	—	—	—	—
10. I enjoy my work more than anything else I do.	—	—	—	—
11. I stay overtime to finish a job even if I don't have to.	—	—	—	—
12. Sometimes I lie awake thinking about the next day's work.	—	—	—	—
13. I am able to use abilities I value in doing my job.	—	—	—	—
14. I feel depressed when my job does not go well.	—	—	—	—
15. I feel good when I perform my job well.	—	—	—	—
16. I would not work at my job if I didn't have to.	—	—	—	—

The Job Commitment Index is generally adapted from the Occupational Commitment Scale developed by Becky Heath Ladewig and Priscilla N. White, The Department of Human Development and Family Life, University of Alabama, University, AL.

hard work; however, they don't dissipate this time by taking on everything, Instead, they concentrate their efforts on those characteristics and values that are clearly more important to the success of their organization than are others. Furthermore, unlike cold, calculated, objective, and uninvolved managers, they bring to their enterprises a certain passion that affects others deeply.

As a result of his extensive studies of the principalship and school leadership, William Greenfield (1985) concludes that principals need to be more passionate about their work, clearer about what they seek to accomplish, and more aggressive in searching for understandings that lead to improved schooling. Greenfield speaks of passion as "believing in the worth of what one seeks to accomplish and exhibiting in one's daily action a commitment to the realization of those goals and purposes" (17). He maintains that clarity about goals and outcomes should be accompanied by a commitment to flexibility regarding processes, procedures, and other means to attain ends.

Finally, anyone who is aspiring to be a good principal needs to have some sense of what she or he values, something to be committed to, a compass to help navigate the way—a personal vision. As Roland Barth (1990) points out,

> *Observers in schools have concluded that the lives of teachers, principals, and students are characterized by brevity, fragmentation, and variety. During an average day, for instance, a teacher or principal engages in several hundred interactions. So do many parents. A personal vision provides a framework with which to respond and to make use of the many prescriptions and conceptions of others. But more important, these ideas centered around schools as communities of learners and leaders have provided me with a road map which has enabled me to respond to the hundreds of daily situations in schools . . . in a less random and more thoughtful way. Without a vision, I think our behavior becomes reflexive, inconsistent, and shortsighted as we seek the action that will most quickly put out the fire so we can get on with putting out the next one. In five years, if we're lucky, our school might be fire free—but it won't have changed much. Anxiety will remain high, humor low, and leadership muddled. Or as one teacher put it in a powerful piece of writing, "Without a clear sense of purpose we get lost, and our activities in school become but empty vessels of our discontent." Seafaring folk put it differently: "For the sailor without a destination, there is no favorable wind." (211)*

One of the great secrets of leadership is that before one can command the respect and followership of others, she or he must demonstrate devotion to the organization's purposes and commitment to those in the organization who work day by day on the ordinary tasks that are necessary for those purposes to be realized. As Greenleaf (1977) points out, people "will freely respond only to individuals who are chosen as leaders because they are proven and trusted as servants" (10). This perspective has come to be known as *servant leadership* (Greenleaf, 1977), with its basic tenets found in the biblical verse: "Ye know that the rulers of the Gentiles lorded over them, and that their great ones exercised authority over them. Not so shall it be among you: but whosoever would become great among you shall be your minister and whosoever would be first among you shall be your servant" (Matthew 20:25).

Servant leadership describes well what it means to be a principal. Principals are responsible for "ministering" to the needs of the schools they serve. The needs are defined by the shared values and purposes of the school's covenant. They minister by furnishing help and being of service to parents, teachers, and students. They minister by providing leadership in a way that encourages others to be leaders in their own right. They minister by highlighting and protecting the values of the school. The principal as minister is one who is devoted to a cause, mission, or set of ideas and accepts the duty and obligation to serve this cause. Ultimately her or his success is known by the quality of the followership that emerges. Quality of followership is a barometer that indicates the extent to which moral authority has replaced bureaucratic and psychological authority. When moral authority drives leadership practice, the principal is at the same time a leader of leaders, follower of ideas, minister of values, and servant to the followership.

References

Barth, Roland S. 1990. *Improving Schools from Within.* San Francisco: Jossey-Bass.

Blumberg, Arthur. 1989. *School Administration as a Craft.* Boston: Allyn and Bacon.

Clark, David L., and Judith M. Meloy. 1984. "Renouncing Bureaucracy: A Democratic Structure for Leadership in Schools," in T. J. Sergiovanni and J. H. Moore, Eds., *Schooling for Tomorrow: Directing Reforms to Issues that Count.* Boston: Allyn and Bacon.

Cuban, Larry. 1988. *The Managerial Imperative and the Practice of Leadership in Schools.* Albany: State University of New York Press.

Greenfield, William D. 1985. "Instructional Leadership: Muddles, Puzzles, and Promises." Athens: The Doyne M. Smith Lecture, University of Georgia, June 29.

Greenleaf, Robert K. 1977. *Teacher as Servant.* New York: Paulist Press.

Kelly, Robert E. 1988. "In Praise of Followers," *Harvard Business Review* (Nov.–Dec.).

Lakomski, Gabriele. 1985. "The Cultural Perspective in Educational Administration." in R. J. S. Macpherson and Helen M. Sungaila, Eds., *Ways and Means of Research in Educational Administration.* Armidale, New South Wales: University of New England.

Morris, Van Cleave, Robert L. Crowson, Cynthia Porter-Gehrie, and Emanual Hurwitz, Jr. 1984. *Principals in Action.* Columbus, OH: Merrill.

Peters, Tom, and Nancy Austin. 1985. *A Passion for Excellence.* New York: Random House.

Quantz, Richard A., Nelda Cambron-McCabe, and Michael Dantley. 1991. "Preparing School Administrators for Democratic Authority: A Critical Approach to Graduate Education," *The Urban Review,* 23(1), 3–19.

Rawls, John. 1971. *A Theory of Justice.* Cambridge, MA: Harvard University Press.

Selznick, Philip. 1957. *Leadership in Administration: A Sociological Interpretation.* New York: Harper & Row. California Paperback Edition 1984. Berkeley: University of California Press.

Sergiovanni, Thomas J., and Robert J. Starratt. 1988. *Supervision: Human Perspectives.* New York: McGraw-Hill.

Smith, John K., and Joseph Blase. 1987. "Educational Leadership as a Moral Concept." Washington, DC: American Educational Research Association.

Taylor, Paul W. 1961. *Normative Discourse.* Englewood Cliffs, NJ: Prentice-Hall.

Tom, Alan. 1980. "Teaching as a Moral Craft: A Metaphor for Teaching and Teacher Education," *Curriculum Inquiry* 10(3).

Tom, Alan. 1984. *Teaching as a Moral Craft.* New York: Longman.

Vaill, Peter B. 1984. "The Purposing of High-Performing Systems," in Thomas J. Sergiovanni and John E. Corbally, Eds., *Leadership and Organizational Culture.* Urbana-Champaign:University of Illinois Press.

Wilkins, Alan L. 1989. *Developing Corporate Character.* San Francisco: Jossey-Bass.

Zaleznik, Abraham. 1989. *The Managerial Mystique Restoring Leadership in Business.* New York: Harper & Row.

Index